The
Autobiography of
MADAME GUYON

The
Autobiography of
MADAME GUYON

Translated by THOMAS TAYLOR ALLEN

Edited and Selected by WARNER A. HUTCHINSON

Introduction by RUTH BELL GRAHAM

Illustrations by RON McCARTY

KEATS PUBLISHING, INC.   NEW CANAAN, CONNECTICUT

THE AUTOBIOGRAPHY OF MADAME GUYON

Shepherd Illustrated Classic edition published in 1980

Selection and special contents of this edition copyright © 1980 by
Keats Publishing, Inc.

All Rights Reserved

Library of Congress Catalog Card Number: 80-82328
ISBN: 0-87983-234-7

Printed in the United States of America

SHEPHERD ILLUSTRATED CLASSICS are published by
Keats Publishing, Inc. 36 Grove Street, New Canaan, Connecticut 06840

CONTENTS

ILLUSTRATIONS

INTRODUCTION

This is a strange autobiography, deeply inspiring, at times disturbing, always intensely personal.

I had read another translation years ago which left me with an impression of Madame Guyon's extraordinarily difficult life, her apparent lack of humor, yet her remarkable piety. The more I read, the better I understood.

It was while reading Nancy Mitford's *The Sun King* that I came to marvel that any Christian mystic could survive in such an affluent, morally decadent society as that which surrounded the court of Louis XIV at Versailles in the seventeenth century.

Yet the God who preserved a Joseph in Egypt, a Daniel in Babylon and saints in Caesar's household preserved for himself and for us such remarkable servants as Archbishop François de Salignac de la Moth Fénelon and the writer of this remarkable autobiography, Madame Jeanne Marie Bouviere de la Mothe Guyon.

I suggest as you read you keep this background in mind and you will realize that there is nothing too hard for God.

Ruth Bell Graham
October 1980

EDITOR'S PREFACE

The name of Madame Guyon (Jeanne-Marie Bouvier de la Mothe Guion) is well-known to readers of spiritual classics. A Roman Catholic who lived during the late 17th and early 18th centuries—she died in 1717—she writes of her experience of God in Jesus Christ in a way which has transcended denominational boundaries. In fact, her reputation as a mystic shines brighter in Protestant circles than in Catholic ones, probably because of her difficulties with the French hierarchy during her life.

Most renditions of her work in English are highly edited excerpts which tell only of her spiritual insights and conclusions. These accounts seldom describe the traumatic events of her life which led her to reach these insights. This edition of Madame Guyon's *Autobiography* provides far more of the account of her life—as she saw it and recorded it—than any other edition in print today.

In accordance with Roman Catholic practice at the time, Madame Guyon as a devout aristocratic woman had a priest who served as her spiritual director. She took matters of conscience and spiritual concern to him for advice and guidance.

Her *Autobiography* was originally written only for her spiritual director as part of his program of guidance. It was written before and during her first imprisonment in 1688, but added to later, and finally revised in 1709. Madame Guyon sensed it would later be published. It was in fact published first in Cologne in 1720, less than three years after her death. She had entrusted her papers to some English and German noblemen during the last years of her life, and they asked a man named Poiret to edit them and prepare them for publication.

Thomas Taylor Allen, an Englishman who served in the Bengal Civil Service, became acquainted with the literature of the French Catholic mystics during the period just before the French Revolution, especially with the work of Madame Guyon and Archbishop Fénelon, while he was in India. After his retirement, Allen found a copy of the Cologne *Autobiography* and compared it with English-language versions available. He believed that the English translators had omitted many events and interpretations of those events from their work because they might not be palatable to English Protestant sensibilities. So he published his translation of the complete Cologne edition in 1898 in London.

In this edition, I have retained most of the events which Madame Guyon recorded, as well as the main body of her reflections of the meaning of those events to her personally. I have omitted some extensive interpretations of biblical passages which were highly individualistic and which do not serve to carry the narrative forward. I also omitted passages in which she repeated earlier events or reflections. Allen's work is two volumes, and has long been unavailable except in specialist libraries. I wish to give special thanks to Dr. Anne-Marie Salgat of the General Theological Seminary Library for her kind permission to work from a very fragile set of books. The set literally fell apart and the paper disintegrated as I turned the pages.

In his introduction, Allen focuses on the value of reading the *Autobiography*: "Madame Guyon belongs to no Church, or sect, or nationality. Stripped of the purely accidental, due to her education and surroundings, her life illustrates the catholic, universal doctrine proclaimed by Christ . . . that 'God is a Spirit, and they who worship him must worship him in spirit and in truth'—further defined by St. Paul, 'I live, yet not I, Christ lives in me'—the creature, NOTHING: Christ, ALL."

Warner Hutchinson

The
Autobiography of
MADAME GUYON

PART I

CHAPTER I

GOD ALONE.—SINCE you wish me to write a life so worthless and so extraordinary as mine, I wish to do what you desire of me; although the labor appears to me a little severe in the state I am in, which does not allow me to reflect much. I should extremely wish to make you understand the goodness of God to me, and the excess of my ingratitude; but it would be impossible for me to do it, as well because you do not wish me to write my sins in detail, as because I have lost the memory of many things. I will endeavor to acquit myself as well as I can. But I assure you at the same time, that you will not attain this save by much trouble and labor, and by a road which will appear to you quite contrary to your expectation. You will not, however, be surprised at it if you are convinced that God does not establish his great works except upon "the nothing." It seems that he destroys in order to build.

Oh, if you could understand this mystery—so profound it is!—and conceive the secrets of God's conducting, revealed to the little ones, but concealed from the great and wise of the earth, who imagine themselves to be the councillors of the Lord, and to penetrate the depth of his ways; who persuade themselves that they attain this divine wisdom, unknown to those who still live to themselves and in their "own" operations, "concealed even from the birds of the heaven"—that is to say, from those who by the vivacity of their lights and by the strength of their elevation, approach the heaven, and think to penetrate the height, the depth, the breadth, and the length of God! This divine wisdom is unknown even to those who pass in the world for persons extraordinary in light and in learning. To whom, then, will it be known and who will be able to tell us news of it? "Destruction and death." It is they

3

who "declare to have heard with their ears the sound of its reputation." It is, then, in dying to all things and in truly losing one's self as regards them; to pass into God, and to subsist only in him, that one has some intelligence of the true wisdom. Oh, how little one understands her ways, and the course she leads her most chosen servants! Hardly does one discover something of it, than, surprised at the difference of the truth one discovers from the ideas one had formed of the true perfection, one exclaims with St. Paul, "O depth of knowledge and of wisdom of God, how incomprehensible are your judgments, and your ways difficult to know!" You do not judge things as men judge of them, who call good, evil, and evil, good, and who regard as great righteousness things abominable before God, and which according to his prophet he values no more than if they were dirty rags; who will even examine with rigor those selfhood-begotten righteousnesses, which will be matters for his indignation and his anger, and not the object of his love and the subject of his recompenses. Jesus Christ has had only severity for self-righteous persons, and seemed to dishonor them before men. The picture he made of them was strange, while he regards the sinners with mercy, compassion, and love, and protests he is only come for them, that it is these sick ones who have need of a physician; that while the Savior of Israel, he is yet come to save only the lost sheep of the House of Israel. O Love! it appears you are so jealous of the salvation you yourself give, that you prefer the sinner to the righteous. It is true, a poor sinner, seeing in himself only wretchedness, is, as it were, constrained to hate himself; finding himself an object of horror, he casts himself headlong into the arms of his Savior. He plunges with love and confidence into the sacred bath of his blood, whence he comes forth white as wool. It is then that, all confused at his disorders, and all full of love for him who, having alone been able to remedy his evils, has had the charity to do it, he loves him so much the more as his crimes have been more enormous, and his gratitude is so much the greater as the debts which have been forgiven him are more abundant; while the righteous, supported by the great number of works of righteousness he presumes to have done, seems to hold his salvation in his own hands, and regards heaven as the recompense due to his merits. He damns all sinners in the bitterness of his zeal. He makes them see the entrance of heaven shut for them. He persuades them they ought not to regard it but as a place to which they have no right, while he believes its opening so much the more assured to him as he flatters himself to deserve it more. His Savior is for him almost useless. He goes away so loaded with merits that he is overwhelmed with their weight. Oh, but he will remain a long time weighed down under that vain-glorious burden, while sinners, stripped of everything, are carried swiftly by the wings of love and confidence into the arms of their Savior, who gives them gratuitously what he has infinitely merited for them.

This granted, you will have no trouble to conceive the design of God in the graces he has bestowed on the most worthless of creatures. You will even believe them without difficulty. They are all graces—that is to say, gifts—which I have never merited; on the contrary, of which I have made myself very unworthy. But God, through an extreme love of his power, and a righteous jealousy of the way in which men attribute to other men the good that God puts in them, has willed to take the most unworthy subject that ever was, to show that his bounties are effects of his will, and not fruits of our merits; that it is the peculiarity of his wisdom to destroy what is proudly built, and to build what is destroyed, to make "use of weak things to confound the strong." But if he makes use of things vile and contemptible, he does it in a manner so astonishing that he renders them the object of contempt to all creatures. It is not in procuring for them the approbation of men that he makes use of them for the salvation of those same men, but in rendering them the mark for their insults and an object of execration. This is what you will see in the life you ordered me to write.

CHAPTER II

I WAS born, according to some accounts, on Easter Even, 18th April—although my baptism was not till 24th May—in the year 1648, of a father and mother who made profession of very great piety, particularly my father, who had inherited it from his ancestors; for one might count, from a very long time, almost as many saints in his family as there were persons who composed it. I was born, then, not at the full time, for my mother had such a terrible fright that she brought me into the world in the eighth month, when it is said to be almost impossible to live. I no sooner received life than I was on the point of losing it, and dying without baptism. They carried me to a nurse, and I was no sooner there than they came to tell my father I was dead. He was very distressed at it. Some time after they came to inform him I had given some sign of life. My father immediately took a priest, and brought him to me himself. But as soon as he came to the room where I was they told him that mark of life I had given was a last sigh, and that I was absolutely dead. It is true they could not observe in me any sign of life. The priest went away, and my father also, in extreme desolation.

O my God, it seems to me that you have permitted so strange a course in my case only to make me better comprehend the greatness of your bounties to me, and how you willed I should be indebted to you alone for my salvation and not to the industry of any creature. If I had died then I should never perhaps have either known or loved you, and this heart, created for you alone, would have been separated from you without having been one instant united to you.

These alternations of life and death at the commencement of my life were fateful auguries of what was to happen to me one day; now dying by sin, now living by grace. Death and life had a struggle. Death was on the point of vanquishing and overcoming life, but life remained victorious. Oh, if it was permitted me to have that confidence, and I could believe at last that life will be for ever victorious over death! Doubtless it will be so if you alone live in me, O my God, who seem to be at present my only life, and my only love. At last they found a moment when the grace of baptism was conferred upon me. As soon as I was baptized they sought the cause of these continual faintings. They saw I had at the bottom of the back a tumor of prodigious size. Incisions were made in it, and the wound was so great the surgeon could introduce his entire hand. So surprising an ailment at such a tender age ought to have deprived me of life; but, O my God, as you willed to make of me a subject of your greatest mercies, you did not permit it. Hardly was this strange ailment cured, than, as they have told me, gangrene attacked one thigh, afterwards the other. My life was only a tissue of ills. At two and a half years, I was placed at the Ursulines, where I remained some time. Afterwards they took me away. My mother, who did not much love girls, neglected me a little, and abandoned me too much to the care of women who neglected me also; yet you, O my God, protected me, for accidents were incessantly happening to me, occasioned by my extreme vivacity, without any serious consequence. I even fell several times through a ventilator into a very deep cellar filled with wood. I was then four years old, when Madame the Duchess of Montbason came to the Benedictines. As she had much friendship for my father, she asked him to place me in that house when she would be there, because I was a great diversion to her. I was always with her, for she much loved the exterior God had given me. I was continually dangerously ill. I do not remember to have committed any considerable faults in that house. I saw there only good examples, and as my natural disposition was towards good, I followed it when I found nobody to turn me aside from it. I loved to hear talk about God, to be at church, and to be dressed as a nun.

In this house I was much loved, but you, O my God, who were unwilling to leave me a moment without some crosses proportioned to my age, permitted that as soon as I recovered from the illness, grown girls who were in this house, one in particular, played numerous tricks upon me through jealousy. They once accused me of a serious fault that I had not committed. I was very severely punished for it, which gave me a dislike to this house, whence I was withdrawn owing to my great and constant illnesses. As soon as I returned to my father's, my mother left me, as before, to the charge of servants, because there was a maid there in whom she trusted. I cannot help here noting the fault mothers commit who, under pretext of devotion or occupation, neglect to keep their daughters with them; for it is not credible that my mother, so virtuous as she was, would have thus left me, if she had thought there was any harm in it. I must also condemn those unjust preferences that they show for one child over another, which produces division and the ruin of families, while equality unites the hearts and entertains charity. Why cannot I make fathers and mothers understand, and all persons who wish to guide youth, the evil they do, when they neglect the guidance of the children, when they lose sight of them for a long time and do not employ them?

This negligence is the ruin of almost all young girls. How many of them are there who would be angels, whom liberty and idleness turns into demons! What is more deplorable is that mothers otherwise devout ruin themselves by what ought to save them. They fall into two extremes; the one wishing to keep young children in church as long as themselves, which gives them a strong disgust for devotion. This arises from their being surfeited with a food they could not relish, because their stomach was not suited for that nourishment, and for want of power of digestion they conceived such aversion to it that, where it would be suitable for them, they will no longer even try it.

The other extreme is still more dangerous. It is that these devout mothers (for I do not speak of those who are addicted to their own pleasures, the luxuries and the vain amusements of the age, whose presence is more hurtful for their daughters than their absence; I speak of those devotees who wish to serve God in their mode, not in his and who, to pursue their style of devotion, disregard the will of God)—these mothers, I say, will be the whole day at church, while their daughters' one thought is to offend God. The greatest glory they could render God would be to prevent his being offended. Of what kind is this sacrifice, which is an occasion of iniquity? Let them perform their devotions, and never separate their daughters from them. Let them treat them as sisters, and not as slaves. This conduct will make them love the presence of their mothers, instead of avoiding it, and, finding much sweetness with them, they will not think of seeking it elsewhere.

My mother failed in these two points, for she left me all day at a distance from her, with servants who could only teach me evil and render it familiar to me. For I was so constituted that good examples attracted me in such a way that where I saw people doing good, I did it and never thought at all of ill; but I no sooner saw people doing ill than I forgot the good. O God, what danger would I not then have run if my infancy had not been an obstacle to it! With an invisible hand, O my God, you put aside all the dangers. As my mother gave no sign of having any love except for my brother, and never showed any tenderness to me, I willingly kept away from her. It is true my brother was more amiable than I; but also the extreme love she had for him shut her eyes to my exterior qualities, so that she saw only my defects, which would have been of no consequence if care had been taken for me. I was often ill, and always exposed to a thousand dangers without, however, doing at that time, it appeared to me, anything worse than saying many pretty things, as I thought, to divert. As my liberty increased each day, it went so far that one day I left the house and went into the street to play with other children at games which were not suited to my rank. You, O my God, who continually watched over a child who incessantly forgot you, permitted that my father came home and saw me. As he loved me very tenderly, he was so vexed that, without saying a word to any one, he took me straight away to the Ursulines.

CHAPTER III

I WAS then nearly seven years of age. Two of my sisters were there as nuns—one the daughter of my father, the other of my mother; for both my father and my mother had been married before having married each other. My father made me over to the charge of his daughter, and I can say she was one of the most capable and the most spiritual persons of her time, and most fit to form young girls. It was for me, O my God, an effect of your providence and your love, and the first means of my salvation. For as she loved me much, her affection made her discover in me a number of qualities you had placed there, O my God, by your goodness alone. She endeavored to cultivate them. I believe that if I had always been in such wise hands, I should have had as much of virtue as I have subsequently contracted of evil habits. This worthy woman employed all her time to instruct me in piety and in learning suited to my capacity. She had natural talents, which had been well cultivated, and moreover was a person of great prayer, and her faith was very great and very pure. She deprived herself of all gratification to be with me and to talk to me, and her love for me was such that it made her find, she told me, more pleasure with me than anywhere else. If I made her some pleasant reply more by chance than wit, she thought herself only too well paid for all her pains. In short, she instructed me so well that, after a short time, there were hardly any things of those suited for me which I was ignorant of. There were even many persons of full age who could not have answered the questions I used to answer.

My father used often to send for me to see him, and it happened that the Queen of England came to the house when I was there. I was then nearly eight years of age. My father told the queen's confessor, if he wished for some pleasure, he should converse with me and put questions to me. He asked me even very difficult ones. I answered them so *à propos* that he took me to the Queen, and said to her, "Your Majesty must have the diversion of this child." She did so, and seemed so pleased with my lively answers and my manners, that she urgently asked me from my father, assuring him she would take particular care of me, intending me to be maid of honor to Madame. My father resisted and vexed her. O my God, it was you who permitted the resistance of my father, and thereby turned aside the stroke on which, perhaps, depended my salvation. For being as weak as I was, what could I have done at Court but destroy myself?

They sent me back to the Ursulines, where my sister continued her charity towards me; but as she was not mistress of the boarders, and I had sometimes to go with them, I contracted evil habits. I became a liar, passionate, undevout. I passed days without thinking of you, O my God, who watched continually over me, as what I shall tell in the sequel will prove. I did not long continue in this evil state, for the care of my sister brought me back. I loved much to hear talk of you, O my God, and I never wearied of it. I was not tired at church, and I loved to pray to you, and I had tenderness for the poor. I was naturally greatly opposed to persons whose doctrine was doubtful, having sucked in the purity of the faith with my milk, and you have always preserved this grace to me, O my God, in the midst of my greatest infidelities.

There was, at the end of the garden, a chapel dedicated to the Child Jesus. I conceived a devotion for it, and or some time every morning I carried my breakfast there and concealed it all behind his image; for I was so childish I thought I was making a considerable sacrifice in depriving myself of it. I was, however, greedy. I wished, indeed, to mortify myself, but I did not wish to be mortified, which proves how much self-love I already had. One day, when they were thoroughly cleaning out this chapel, they found behind the picture what I had carried there. They knew it was I, because I was seen going there every day. You, O my God, who leave nothing without recompense, you soon repaid me with interest this petty childish devotion. One day, when my companions, who were big girls, were amusing themselves, they went to dance over a well which, the water not being good, had been used as a cesspool for the kitchen. This cesspool was deep, and it had been covered with boards for fear of accident. When they had gone away, I wished to do as they, but the boards broke under me. I found myself in that frightful sink, supported by a little morsel of wood, so that I was only soiled and not stifled. O my Love, was there not here a figure of the state I should hereafter bear? How often have you left me with your prophet in a deep pit of mud, whence I could not get out! Have I not been fouled in this pit where I was all covered with mud? But you have preserved me there by your goodness alone. I have been soiled, but not stifled. I have been even to the gates of death, but death has had no power over me. I may say, O my God, that it was your adorable hand which sustained me in that frightful place, rather than this stick by which I was stopped; for it was very small, and the long time I was in the air with the weight of my body ought doubtless to have broken it. I cried with all my strength. The boarders, who saw me fall, instead of getting me out, went to look for the servants. Those Sisters, in place of coming to me, not doubting I was dead, went to the church to inform my sister, who was there in prayer. She at once prayed for me, and, after having invoked the Holy Virgin, she came to me half dead. She was not a little astonished when she saw me in the midst of that sink, seated in the mud as if upon a chair. She admired your goodness, O my God, who had supported me in a miraculous manner; but, alas! how happy would I have been if this had been the only filth into which I should fall! I escaped from that, only to fall into another a thousand times more dangerous. I repaid so remarkable a protection with the blackest ingratitude. O Love, I have never wearied your patience, because it was infinite. I have wearied myself of displeasing you sooner than you of supporting me!

I remained still some time with my sister, where I retained the love and fear of God. My life was very tranquil. I grew up pleasantly with her. I even profited much during the time I had my health; for I was continually ill with diseases, as sudden as they were extraordinary. In the evening I would be quite well; the morning I was found swollen and full of violet marks. Another time it was fever. At nine years of age I was seized with a vomiting of blood so violent they thought I was about to die.

A little before this time the enemy, jealous of my happiness, caused another sister I had in this house to become jealous and wish to have me in her turn. Although she was good, she had no talent for the education of children. I can say that was the end of the happiness I enjoyed in this house. She caressed me much at first, but all her caresses made no impression on my heart. My other sister did more with one look than she with her caresses or her threats. As she saw I loved her less than her who had reared me, she changed her caresses to ill treatment. She would not even let me speak to my other sister, and when she knew I had spoken to her, she caused me to be whipped or beat me herself. I could not hold out against this rigorous conduct, and I paid with the blackest ingratitude all the kindness of my paternal sister, seeing her no more. My father, informed of all that passed between my sisters and me, withdrew me to his own house. I was then nearly ten years of age.

While with my father I became still more wicked. My former habits grew stronger day by day, and I incessantly contracted new ones. Yet you guarded me, O my God, in all these things, and I cannot without astonishment consider that, with the liberty I had of being all day away from my mother, you have so preserved me that I have never done anything unworthy of your protection. I was only a short time with my father, for a nun of the order of St. Dominic, of very high birth, and an intimate friend of my father, urgently begged him to place me at her convent, of which she was Superior; that she would herself take care of me, and she would allow me to sleep in her room, for this lady conceived much friendship for me. As people saw only my exterior, and knew not how wicked I was, I used to please those who saw me. As soon as the opportunity was wanting, I forgot the evil which I committed, not so much from inclination, as because I allowed myself to be led away. I did not appear wicked to this lady, because I loved the church, and used to remain there a long time; but she was so occupied with her community, where there was then much quarrelling, that she could not give her attention to me.

You sent me, O my God, small-pox which kept me in bed for three weeks. I no longer thought at all of offending you. I remained much neglected and without help, though my father and my mother believed I was perfectly well cared for. Those worthy ladies feared so much the small-pox that they dared not approach me. I passed almost all this time without seeing any one except at the hours when it was necessary to take nourishment, which a lay sister brought me and immediately retired. I providentially found a Bible in the room where I lay. As I much loved reading, I attached myself to it. I read from morning till evening. I had a very good memory, so I learned everything in the nature of history. After I was recovered, another lady, seeing me so neglected owing to the great occupation of the prioress, took me into her room. Since when I had a reasonable person with whom I could converse I again became more devout, I was very well disposed to pray to the Holy Virgin: I do not understand how I was made. In my greatest infidelities I used to pray, and I was careful to confess often. In another way I was very unhappy in this house, for as I was the only one of my age, and the other boarders were very grown, they severely persecuted me. As to eating and drinking, I was so neglected that I grew very thin.

CHAPTER IV

AFTER having been about eight months in this house, my father withdrew me. My mother kept me with her. She was for some time very well pleased with me, and loved me a little more as she found me to her taste. She nevertheless still preferred my brother to me, which was so visible, every one disapproved of it; for when I was ill and found something to my taste, my brother used to ask for it, and, although he was quite well, it was taken from me to give him. From time to time he caused me divers vexations. At other times he used to beat me. My mother never said anything to him for it. This conduct embittering my natural disposition, which would otherwise have been gentle, I neglected to do good, saying I was none the better for it. O God, it was then not for you alone I used to behave well, since I ceased to do so because they no longer had any consideration for me. I was jealous of my brother, for on every occasion I remarked the difference my mother made between him and me. However he behaved, he always did right, and I always wrong. My mother's servant-maids paid their court by caressing my brother and ill-treating me. It is true I was bad, for I had fallen back into my former defects of telling lies and getting in a passion. With all these faults I nevertheless willingly gave alms, and I much loved the poor. I assiduously prayed to you, O my God, and I took pleasure in hearing you spoken of, and in good reading. I do not doubt you will be astonished, Sir, by such resistance, and by so long a course of inconstancy; so many graces, so much ingratitude; but the sequel will astonish you still more, when you shall see this manner of acting grow stronger with my age, and that reason, far from correcting so irrational a procedure, has served only to give more force and more scope to my sins. It seemed, O my God, that you doubled your graces as my ingratitudes increased. There went on in me what goes on in the siege of towns. You were besieging my heart, and I thought only of defending it against your attacks. I put up fortifications to that miserable place, redoubling each day my iniquities to hinder you from taking it. When it seemed you were about to be victorious over this ungrateful heart, I made a cross-battery, I put up barriers to arrest your bounties and to hinder the course of your graces. It required nothing less than you to break them down, O my divine Love, who by your sacred fire were more powerful than even death, to which my sin has so oftentimes reduced me.

You maintained over me, my God, a crucifying conduct to make me return to you, of which I knew not how to make proper use; for I have been in troubles from my tender youth, either through illnesses or through persecutions. The maid who had care of me used to strike me when settling my hair, and never made me turn round except with a slap. Everything was in concert to make me suffer. But in place of turning to you, O my God, I fretted and my spirit became embittered. My father knew nothing of all this; for his love for me was so great, he would not have allowed it. I loved him much, but, at the same time, I was so much afraid of him I did not speak to him of anything. My mother often complained of me to him, but he had only one answer, "There are twelve hours in the day; she will be converted." This harsh treatment was not the worst for my soul, although it much embittered my temper, which was very mild. But what caused my ruin was that, being unable to endure persons who ill-treated me, I took refuge with those who caressed me to my destruction.

My father, seeing I was grown, placed me for Lent with the Ursulines, in order that I should have my first Communion at Easter, when I should complete eleven years of age. He placed me in the hands of his daughter, my very dear sister, who redoubled her cares that I might perform this action with all possible preparation. I thought only, O my God, of giving myself to you once for all. I often felt the combat between my good inclinations and my evil habits. I even performed some penances. As I was almost always with my sister, and the boarders of the grown class with whom I was, although I was very far from their age, were very reasonable, I became very reasonable with them. I let myself be easily won by gentleness, and my sister, without using harshness, made me unresistingly do all she wished. At last, on Easter Day I made my first Communion (after a general confession) with much joy and devotion. Until Pentecost I remained in that house, but as my other sister was mistress of the second class, she required that in her week I should be in her class. The utterly different manners of my two sisters cooled my first fervor. I no longer felt this new ardor, O my God, that you had made me taste in my first Communion. Alas! it lasted but a short time, for my troubles returned. I was withdrawn from the convent.

My mother, seeing I was very tall for my age and more to her taste than usual, only thought of bringing me out, making me see company, and dressing me well. She took a regrettable delight in that beauty you had given me, O my God, only that you might be praised and blessed for it, and which has yet been for me a source of pride and vanity. Numbers of proposals were made, but as I was only twelve years old, my father would not listen to them.

I greatly loved reading, and I shut myself up alone almost every day in order to read in quiet. I shut myself up all day to read and pray; I gave all I had to the poor, taking even the house linen to make up for them. I taught them the Catechism, and, when my father and my mother were absent, I made them eat with me, and helped them with great respect. At this time I read the works of St. Francis de Sales and the Life of Madame de Chantal. It was there that I learned that people prayed. I begged my confessor to teach me to do it, and, as he did not do so, I endeavored to do it by myself the best I could.

I could not succeed in it, as it then appeared to me, because I could not imagine anything, and I was persuaded that without forming to one's self distinctions and much reasoning one could not pray. This difficulty for a long time caused me much trouble. I was, however, very assiduous at it, and I earnestly begged God to give me the gift of prayer. All that I saw written in the Life of Madame de Chantal delighted me, and I was so childish I thought I ought to do all that I saw there. All the vows she had made I made also; as that of aiming always at the most perfect, and doing the will of God in all things. I was not yet twelve years of age; nevertheless I took the discipline according to my strength. One day, when I read she had placed the name of Jesus on her heart, in order to follow the counsel of the Bridegroom, "Place me as a seal upon thy heart," and that she had taken a red-hot iron on which was engraved that holy name, I remained very afflicted at not being able to do the same. I bethought me of writing this sacred and adorable name in large characters on a morsel of paper; with ribbons and a big needle I fixed it to my skin in four places, and it continued for a long time fixed in this manner.

My only thought was to become a nun, and I went very often to the Visitation, to beg them to be willing to receive me;

for the love I had for St. Francis de Sales did not allow me to
think of other communities. I used then to slip away from the
house to go to these nuns, and I urged them very strongly to
receive me; but although they were extremely desirous of
having me, and regarded it even as a temporal advantage, they
never dared give me admittance into their house, as well
because they much feared my father, who was known to love
me specially, as because of my extreme youth—I was then
hardly twelve years old. There was then at our house a niece
of my father, to whom I am under very great obligations. She
was very virtuous, and fortune, which had not been favour-
able to her father, placed her in some sort of dependence on
mine. She discovered my intention and the extreme desire I
had to become a nun. As my father had been absent for some
time, and my mother was ill, and I was under her care, she
feared being accused of having encouraged this idea, or at
least of having entertained it; for my father so greatly feared it
that, although he would not for anything in the world hinder
a true vocation, he could not without shedding tears hear it
said I should be a nun. My mother would have been more
indifferent. My cousin went to my confessor to tell him to
forbid me going to the Visitation. He dared not do this out
and out, for fear of setting that community against him; for
they believed me already one of theirs. When I went to
confession he would not absolve me, on the ground that I
went to the Visitation by myself and by roundabout streets.
In my innocence I thought I had committed a frightful crime,
for absolution had never been refused me. I returned so
afflicted my cousin could not comfort me. I did not cease
weeping till the next day, when at early morning I went to my
confessor. I told him I could not live without absolution; I
begged him to grant it to me. There was no penance I would
not have performed to obtain it. He gave it to me at once. I
still, however, wished to be a nun, and I urgently begged my
mother to take me there, but she would not for fear of vexing
my father, who was absent, and she always put it off till his
return. As I saw I could gain nothing, I counterfeited the
writing of my mother, and I forged a letter in which she
begged those ladies to receive me, making excuse, on the
ground of illness, for not bringing me herself. But the prioress,

who was a relative of my mother and well knew her writing, discovered at once my innocent deceit.

CHAPTER V

MY father had no sooner returned than he fell seriously ill. I constituted myself his nurse. He was in a wing of the house separated from that of my mother, who seldom came to see him, as well because she was still weak as because she feared, perhaps, a relapse. Being alone with him, I had every opportunity of rendering him all the services I was capable of, and I gave him all the marks of affection he could desire of me. I have no doubt my attention was very agreeable to him, for as he loved me extremely, all I did was very pleasant to him. When he was not looking I used to go and empty his basins, seizing the time there were no valets there, as well to mortify myself as to honor what Jesus Christ says, that he had come to serve and not to be served. When he made me read to him, I read with so much devotion he was surprised. I still continued my prayer and the Office of the Virgin, which I had not missed saying since my first Communion. I remembered the instructions my sister had given me, and prayers she had taught me. She had taught me to praise you, O my God, in all your works. All that I saw instructed me to love you. If it rained, I wished all the drops of water were changed into love and into praise. My heart insensibly nourished itself with your love, and my mind was occupied with remembering you. I united myself to all the good that was done upon the earth, and I would have wished to have the heart of all mankind to love you. This habit rooted itself so strongly in me that I preserved it even in the midst of my greatest inconstancy.

My cousin was not a little useful in keeping me in these

good sentiments; for, as I was often with her and I loved her, and she took great care of me and treated me with much gentleness, my spirit became again gentle and reasonable. Perhaps I fell into an extreme, for I so strongly attached myself to her that I used to follow her through the house wherever she went, for I greatly liked to be treated with gentleness and reason. I thought myself in another world. It is true children should never have near them any but reasonable persons, who are in no way passionate. This attachment appeared to me very right for a person who had been given me for my guidance; for her fortune not being equal either to her birth or her virtue, she did with charity and affection that which her present condition imposed upon her. I did not think I was committing an excess, yet my mother thought, in loving my cousin so strongly, I should love her less. The Devil so well managed with his artifices that my mother, who previously trusted me much to myself, and even, when I passed days without entering her room except at bedtime, made no inquiries as to where I was, being satisfied I was in the house, wished me to remain always with her, and would hardly ever leave me with my cousin. My cousin fell ill, and my mother took the opportunity to send her back to her own house, which was for me a very serious blow. God permitted this to try me, for my mother was one of the most charitable women of her age. If there was an excess in this virtue, one might say hers was excessive. She used to give not only what was to spare, but even the necessaries of the house. No poor person was ever sent away by her, nor any destitute one ever applied to her without receiving help. She furnished poor artisans with the means of carrying on their work, and poor traders with the means of supplying their shops. I think it is from her I have inherited charity and love of the poor, for God gave me the grace to succeed her in this holy exercise. There was not in the town or its neighborhood any one who did not benefit by her charity. She has sometimes even given the last pistole that was in the house, without losing or failing in confidence, in spite of the great establishment she had to maintain. Her faith was living, and she had a very great devotion to the Holy Virgin. She meditated every day during the time of a Mass. She never missed repeating the

Office of the Virgin, and all she wanted was a director who would introduce her to the inner life, without which all virtues are weak and languishing. What caused me to have so much liberty as I have mentioned is that, when I was little, my mother relied too much on the care of the maids, and, when I was grown, she trusted too much to my own conduct, and, being assured I loved to be alone to read, she was satisfied at knowing I was in the house, without troubling herself further; for as to going out, she almost never gave me liberty, which is a great thing for a girl. The habit I had acquired of remaining at home was very useful to me after my marriage, as I shall tell in its proper place. My mother was not, then, so much at fault in leaving me to myself; the fault she committed was in not keeping me in her room with an honorable liberty, and not finding out more often the part of the house in which I was.

After the departure of my cousin I remained still for some time in the sentiments of piety of which I have spoken. One grace that God gave me was a great facility in pardoning injuries, which surprised my confessor; for, knowing some young ladies spoke of me unfavorably out of mere envy, I used to speak good of them when I had an opportunity. I fell ill of a fever, which lasted four months, when I suffered considerably, as well from vomiting as from other troubles caused by the fever. I had sufficient moderation and piety during this fever, suffering with much patience. I continued the manner of life of which I have spoken above as long as I continued to pray. About a year or eleven months after, we went to spend some days in the country. My father took with us one of his relatives who was a very accomplished young gentleman. He had a great wish to marry me, but my father, who had resolved not to marry me to any of my relatives, owing to the difficulty of obtaining dispensation, unless false or frivolous reasons were alleged, opposed it. As this young gentleman was very devoted to the Holy Virgin, and used to say her Office every day, I said it with him, and, in order to have time, I gave up prayer, and this was the source of my troubles. I still for a time preserved the spirit of piety, for I used to go and look for the little shepherd-girls to instruct them and teach them to pray to you, O my God; but this remnant of piety was not nourished by prayer. I insensibly relaxed. I became cold to you. All my former faults came back, and I added a frightful vanity. The love I commenced to have for myself extinguished what remained in me of your love. I did not entirely give up prayer without asking my confessor. I told him I thought it better to say every day the Office of the Virgin than to pray; that, having time only for one and not for both, it appeared to me I ought to prefer the Office to prayer; and I did not see, O my God, it was a trick of your enemy and mine to withdraw me from you, and a means of involving me insensibly in the snares he was laying for me; for I could have had enough time for both, having no other occupation than what I chose for myself. My confessor, who was very easy and not a man of prayer, consented to it, to my ruin. O my God, if one knew the value of prayer, and the advantage the soul reaps from conversing with you, and its importance for salvation, every one would be assiduous in it. It is a strong place, into which the enemy can never enter. He may, indeed, attack this place, besiege it, make much noise around its walls, but, provided one is faithful not to leave it, he cannot do us any ill. Prayer is nothing else than the pathway to Paradise, and the pathway to Paradise is prayer— but prayer of the heart, which everybody is capable of, and not of those reasonings which are a play of the intellect, a result of study, an exercise of the imagination, which, while filling the mind with vague things, rarely and only for moments fix it, and do not warm the heart, which remains still cold and languishing.

You love because your heart is made to love what it finds lovable. Is there anything more lovable than God? You know well enough that he is lovable; do not tell me, then, that you do not know him. You know he created you and died for you; but if these reasons are not enough, which of you has not some want, some ill, or some disgrace? Which of you cannot tell his ill and ask a remedy for it? Come, then, to this source of all good, and without amusing yourselves, complaining to feeble and powerless creatures who cannot comfort you, come to prayer, to open out to God your troubles, to ask from him his graces; and above all, come to love him. No one can escape from loving; for none can live without a heart, nor the heart

without love. Why amuse yourselves w̲...̲ s for
loving Love itself? Let us love without ...̲ ̲ove,
and we shall find ourselves filled with ...̲ est
have found the reasons that lead to love. ...̲ all
see; taste love, and you will be more w ...̲ he
cleverest philosophers. In love, as in eve ...̲ ri-
ence teaches better than reasoning.

When I gave up prayer, I left God. I ...̲ e
exposed to pillage, whose broken-down h ...̲ e
passers-by to ravage it. I commenced to s ...̲ e
what I had found in God. You abandon ...̲
because I had first abandoned you, and, wh ...̲
to be plunged in the abyss, you wished to ...̲
stand the need I had of drawing near to you ...̲

I fell into the greatest of all misfortunes; for ...̲ wandered
from you, O my God, who are my light and my life, and you
removed further from me. You withdrew yourself gradually
from a heart which left you, and you are so good that it seems
that you abandoned it only with regret; but when this heart
consents to be converted, ah! you return to it with giant
steps. It is an experience I have made, O my God, which will
be for me an eternal witness of your goodness and my ingratitude. I became then yet more hasty than I had ever been,
because my age gave more strength to my passions. I often lied.
I felt my heart corrupted and vain. There was no longer any
piety in my soul, but a state of lukewarmness and real
undevoutness, although I still preserved the external with
much care, and the habit I had acquired of behaving in
church with modesty, made me appear other than I was. Vanity, which hitherto had left me at peace, seized upon my spirit.
I began to spend a long time before the looking-glass. I found
so much pleasure in seeing myself, that it seemed to me others
were justified in finding it. This love of myself became so
strong, that in my heart I had only scorn for all others of my
sex. In place of making use, O my God, of that exterior you
had given me as a means of loving you more, it was to me the
source of vain complaisance. What ought to win my gratitude,
furnished my ingratitude.

The esteem I entertained for myself made me discover faults
in all the rest of my sex. I had eyes only to see my exterior

good qualities, and to discern the weak points of others. I concealed my defects from myself, and, if I remarked any, they appeared to me very trifling in comparison with those I saw in others, and I even excused them in my mind, picturing them to myself as perfections. The whole idea I had of myself and of others was false. I loved reading madly: I employed day and night at it. Sometimes the next day dawned and I was still reading, so that for several months I had completely lost the habit of sleeping. The books I ordinarily read were Romances. I loved them to folly. I was eager to find out their conclusion, thinking there to discover something, but I found there nothing but a hunger for reading. These books are strange inventions to ruin youth, for though one should commit no other evil but to lose time, is not that too much?

Yet, O my God, your extreme goodness led you to seek me from time to time. You were knocking at the door of my heart. I was often seized with sharp sorrow and abundance of tears. I was afflicted at a state so different from that I had found with you, O my God. But my tears were without effect, and my sorrow vain. I could not of myself withdraw from such a disastrous state. I would have wished that a hand as charitable as powerful had drawn me out of it; but for myself, I had not the strength to do it. Alas! if I had had a confessor who examined the cause of my ill, he would doubtless have applied the remedy, which was merely to make me betake myself again to prayer; but he was content to rebuke me severely, to give me some vocal prayer to repeat, and he did not remove the cause of the ill—he did not give me the true remedy. "I was," said the prophet, "in a deep pit of mud, from which I could not get out." They reprimanded me because I was in this pit, but no one stretched to me a hand to withdraw me from it, and when I tried to make vain efforts to get out, I sunk myself the deeper, and the trouble I had taken served only to make me see my powerlessness, and render me more miserable and more afflicted. Alas! how this sad experience has made me compassionate for sinners! and how it has shown me whence it comes there are so few who correct themselves and who emerge from that miserable state to which they are reduced, because people are content with crying out against their vices and terrifying them with menaces of future punishment! These cries and these menaces at the commencement make some impression on their minds, but a hand is not given them to come out from where they are. They make feeble efforts, but after having many times experienced their powerlessness and the inutility of their attempts, they gradually lose the will to make new efforts, which appear to them as fruitless as the first. Hence it comes that, in consequence of this, all one can say to them is without effect, though one should preach incessantly. We hear nothing else but outcry against sinners, yet no one is converted. If, when a sinner goes to confession, he was given the true remedy, which is prayer; if he was obliged every day to place himself before God in the condition of a criminal, to ask from him the strength to emerge from this condition,—he would soon be changed: that is the way to stretch forth a hand to a man, to drag him from the mud.

Pitiable, then, as was the state to which I was reduced by my infidelities, and the little help I had from my confessor, I did not fail to say every day my vocal prayers, to make confession pretty often, and to communicate almost every fortnight. I was sometimes in church weeping and praying to the Holy Virgin to obtain my conversion. I loved to hear speak of you, O my God, and if I had found persons to speak to me, I should never have wearied of listening to them. When my father spoke thereof I was transported with joy, and when he went with my mother on some pilgrimage, and started very early, either I did not go to bed to avoid being surprised by sleep, or I gave all I had to the maids in order they should wake me up. My father always at that time spoke of you, my God, which gave me extreme pleasure. All other pleasures were then tasteless to me. I would have preferred this to everything. I was very charitable; I loved the poor; and yet I had all the defects of which I have spoken. O God, how reconcile things so opposed?

CHAPTER VI

We subsequently came to Paris, where my vanity increased. Nothing was spared to bring me out. I paraded a vain beauty; I thirsted to exhibit myself and to flaunt my pride. I wished to make myself loved without loving anybody. I was sought for by many persons who seemed good matches for me; but you, O my God, who would not consent to my ruin, did not permit things to succeed. My father discovered difficulties that you yourself made spring up for my salvation. For if I had married those persons, I should have been extremely exposed, and my vanity would have had opportunity for displaying itself. There was a person who had sought me in marriage for some years, whom my father for family reasons had always refused. His manners were a little distasteful to my vanity, yet the fear they had I should leave the country, and the great wealth of this gentleman, led my father, in spite of all his own objections and those of my mother, to accept him for me. It was done without my being told, on the vigil of St. Francis de Sales, 28th January, 1664, and they even made me sign the articles of marriage without telling me what they were. Although I was well pleased to be married, because I imagined thereby I should have full liberty, and that I should be delivered from the ill-treatment of my mother, which doubtless I brought on myself by want of docility, you, however, O my God, had quite other views, and the state in which I found myself afterwards frustrated my hopes, as I shall hereafter tell. Although I was well pleased to be married, I nevertheless continued all the time of my engagement, and even long after my marriage, in extreme confusion. It came from two causes. The first was that natural modesty I never lost. I was very reserved with men. The other was my vanity; for though the

husband provided for me was above what I merited, I did not
believe him such, and the style of those who had previously
sought me appeared to me very different. Their rank dazzled
me, and, as in all things I consulted only my vanity, all that
did not flatter this was insupportable to me. This vanity,
however, was useful to me, for it prevented me falling into
those irregularities which cause the ruin of families. I would
not have been willing to do any external act that would have
exposed me to blame, and I always guarded so well the exteri-
or, that they could not blame my conduct; for as I was modest
at church, and I never went out without my mother, and the
reputation of the house was great, I passed for good. I did
not see my betrothed till two or three days before the marriage. I caused Masses to be said all the time I was engaged,
to know your will, O my God; for I desired to do it at least in
that. Oh, goodness of my God, to suffer me at that time, and
to permit me to pray with as much boldness as if I had been
one of your friends!—I who treated you as if your greatest
enemy!

The joy at this marriage was universal in our town, and in
this rejoicing I was the only person sad. I could neither laugh
like the others, nor even eat, so oppressed was my heart. I
knew not the cause of my sadness; but, my God, it was as if a
presentiment you were giving me of what should befall me.
Hardly was I married when the recollection of my desire to be
a nun came to overwhelm me. All those who came to compliment
me the day after my marriage could not help rallying me because
I wept bitterly, and I said to them, "Alas! I had once so
desired to be a nun; why am I then now married? and by what
fatality is this happened to me?" I was no sooner at home with
my new husband than I clearly saw it would be for me a house
of sorrow. I was obliged to change my conduct, for their
manner of living was very different from that in my father's
house. My mother-in-law, who had been long time a widow,
thought only of saving, while in my father's house we lived in
an exceedingly noble manner. Everything was showy and
everything on a liberal scale, and all my husband and my
mother-in-law called extravagance, and I called respectability,
was observed there. I was very much surprised at this change,
and the more so as my vanity would rather have increased

than cut down expenditure. I was more than fifteen years—in my sixteenth year—when I was married. My astonishment greatly increased when I saw I must give up what I had with so much trouble acquired. At my father's house we had to live with much refinement, learn to speak correctly. All I said was there applauded and made much of. Here I was not listened to, except to be contradicted and to be blamed. If I spoke well, they said it was to read them a lesson. If any one came and a subject was under discussion, while my father used to make me speak, here, if I wished to express my opinion, they said it was to dispute, and they ignominiously silenced me, and from morning to night they chided me. They led my husband to do the same, and he was only too well disposed for it. One thing I ask you, before going further, which is, not to regard things from the side of the creature, for this would make persons appear more faulty than they were; for my mother-in-law was virtuous, and my husband was religious and had no vice. But we must regard all things in God, who permitted these things for my salvation, and because he would not destroy me. I had, besides, so much pride that if a different conduct had been observed with me, I would have been upheld in that, and I should not, perhaps, have turned to God, as I did eventually, through the wretchedness to which I was reduced by crosses.

To return to my subject, I will say that my mother-in-law conceived such a hostility to me, that in order to annoy me she made me do the most humiliating things; for her temper was so extraordinary, from not having conquered it in her youth, that she could not live with any one. There was another cause also that, from not praying, and only repeating vocal prayers, she did not see these sorts of defects, or else, while seeing them, from not gathering strength by prayer, she was unable to rid herself of them; and it was a pity, for she had merit and cleverness. I was thus made the victim of her tempers. Her whole occupation was to continually thwart me, and she inspired her son with the same sentiments. They insisted that persons far below me should take precedence, in order to annoy me. My mother, who was very sensitive on the point of honor, could not endure this, and when she learned it from others—for I never said anything of it—she found

"The joy of this marriage was universal in our town, and in this rejoicing I was the only person sad."

fault with me, thinking I did it from not knowing how to maintain my rank, that I had no spirit, and a thousand other things of this kind. I dared not tell her how I was situated, but I was dying of vexation, and what increased it still more was the recollection of the persons who had sought me in marriage, the difference of their temper and their manner of acting, the love and esteem they had for me, and their gentleness and politeness: this was very hard for me to bear. My mother-in-law incessantly spoke to me disparagingly of my father and my mother, and I never went to see them but I had to endure this disagreeable talk on my return. On the other hand, my mother complained of me that I did not see her often enough. She said I did not love her, that I attached myself too much to my husband; thus I had much to suffer from all sides. What increased still more my crosses was that my mother related to my mother-in-law the troubles I had given her in my childhood, so that the moment I spoke, they reproached me with this, and told me I was a wicked character. My husband wished me to remain all day in the room of my mother-in-law, without being allowed to go to my apartment: I had not therefore a moment for seclusion or breathing a little. She spoke disparagingly of me to every one, hoping thereby to diminish the esteem and affection each had for me, so that she put insults upon me in the presence of the best society. That did not produce the effect she hoped, for those in whose presence it took place preserved for me the greater esteem as they saw me suffer patiently. It is true she discovered the secret of extinguishing the vivacity of my mind and making me become quite dull, so that I could no more be recognized. Those who had not seen me before used to say, "What! is that the person who passed for being clever? She does not say two words. It is a pretty picture." I was not then sixteen years old. I was so timid I dared not go out without my mother-in-law, and in her presence I could not speak. I did not know what I said, so apprehensive was I of vexing her and drawing upon myself some harsh words. For crown of affliction I had a maid they had given me, who was quite in their interest. She kept me in sight like a duenna, and strangely ill-treated me. Ordinarily I suffered in patience an evil that I could not hinder, but at other times I lost my control so as to make some answer; which was for a long time a source of real crosses to me and of bitter reproaches. When I went out, the valets had orders to give an account of all I did. It was then I commenced to eat the bread of tears. If I was at table they did things to me that covered me with confusion. I betook myself to my tears and had a double shame—one, at what was said to me, the other, at not being able to restrain my tears. I had no one with whom to share my grief, who might aid me to bear it. I wished to tell something of it to my mother, and that caused me so many new crosses that I resolved to have no other confidante of my vexations than myself. It was not through harshness that my husband treated me so, but from his hasty and violent temper; for he loved me even passionately. What my mother-in-law was continually telling him irritated him.

It was in a state so every way deplorable, O my God, that I commenced to conceive the need I had of your assistance; for this state was the more perilous for me in that outside my own house, finding only admirers and persons who flattered me for my ruin, it was to be feared, at such a tender age and amidst such strange domestic crosses, that I might turn altogether to the outside world and choose the path of irregularity. You, O my God, by your goodness and the love you bore me, made a quite contrary use of it. You drew me to you by those redoubled blows, and you effected by your crosses what your caresses could not do. You even made use, at the commencement of my marriage, of my natural pride to keep me in my duty. I knew that a woman of honor ought never give umbrage to her husband, and for this reason I was so extremely circumspect I often pushed matters to excess, even to refusing the hand to those who offered it to me.

I endeavored, then, to improve my life by penitence and a general confession, the most particular I had yet made. I gave up at once all Romances, although they were at one time my passion; it had been weakened some time before my marriage by the reading of the Gospel. I found it so beautiful, and I discovered in it a character of truth that disgusted me with all other books, which appeared to me full of lies. I even gave up indifferent books, in order to read none but what were profitable. I resumed prayer, and I endeavored not to offend you, O my God. I felt that, little by little, your love was regaining the supremacy in my heart and banishing from it all other love. I had, however, a frightful vanity and a very great complaisance for myself, which has been my most troublesome and most obstinate sin.

My crosses redoubled each day, and what rendered them more painful was that my mother-in-law was not content with the sharp words she said to me in public and private, but for the smallest things she would continue in a temper for a fortnight at a time. I passed a part of my life in lamentations when I could be alone, and my grief became each day more bitter. I sometimes was carried away when I saw maids who were my servants, and who owed me submission, treating me so ill. Nevertheless, I did what I could to conquer my temper—a thing that has cost me not a little. Such deadly blows diminished my natural vivacity to that degree that I became gentle. The greater part of the time I was like a lamb that is being shorn. I prayed our Lord to help me, and he was my resource. As my age was so different from theirs—for my husband was twenty-two years my senior—I saw there was no chance of changing their temper; it was strengthened with their age.

One day, beside myself with grief—I had only been six months married—I took a knife when I was alone to cut off my tongue, in order to be no longer obliged to speak to persons who made me speak only to have matter for getting into a passion. I would have performed this mad operation, if you had not suddenly stopped me, O my God, and if you had not made me see my folly.

Such was my married life rather that of a slave than of a free person. To increase my disgrace, it was discovered, four months after my marriage, that my husband was gouty. This disease, which doubtless has sanctified him, caused me many real crosses both without and within. That year he twice had the gout six weeks at a time, and it again seized him shortly after, much more severely. At last he became so indisposed that he did not leave his room, nor often even his bed, which he ordinarily kept many months. I watched him with great care, and, though I was very young, I did not fail in my duty. I even did it to excess. But, alas! all that did not win me their friendship. I had not even the consolation of knowing if they were pleased with what I did; never did they exhibit the least sign of it. I deprived myself of all even the most innocent diversions to remain near my husband, and I did what I thought might please him. Sometimes he tolerated me, and I thought myself very happy. At other times I was insupportable. My own friends used to say that I was indeed of a nice age to be nurse to a sick man; that it was a disgraceful thing not to make use of my talents. I answered them that, as I had a husband, I ought to share his troubles as well as his wealth. I did not let any one know I was suffering, and, as my face appeared content, they would have thought me very happy with my husband, if he had not sometimes, in the presence of people, let bitter words to me escape him. Besides, my mother could hardly suffer the assiduity I exhibited to my husband, assuring me I was thereby securing unhappiness for myself, and in the end he would exact as a duty what I was doing as virtue; instead of pitying me, she often found fault with me. It is true that, to look at things humanly, it was a folly to make a slave of myself in this way for persons who had no gratitude for it; but, O my God, how different were my thoughts from those of all these persons! and how different was that which appeared to them on the outside from that which was within! My husband had this foible, that when any one said anything against me, he was at once angered, and his natural violence at once took fire. It was God's mode of leading me; for my husband was reasonable and loved me. When I was ill he was inconsolable, even to a degree I cannot tell; and yet he did not cease to get into passions with me. I believe that, but for his mother and that maid of whom I have spoken, I should have been very happy with him; for as to hastiness, there is hardly a man who has not plenty of it, and it is the duty of a reasonable woman to put up with it quietly without increasing it by sharp answers. You made use of all these things, O my God, for my salvation. Through your goodness you have so managed things that I have afterwards seen this course was absolutely necessary for me, in order to make me die to my vain and haughty natural character. I should not have had the strength to destroy it myself, if you had not worked for it by an altogether wise dispensation of your providence. I urgently asked patience from you, O my God. Nevertheless, I often had outbursts, and my quick and hasty

natural character often betrayed the resolutions I had taken
to hold my tongue. You permitted it, doubtless, O my God, in
order that my self-love should not nourish itself on my patience;
for an outburst of a moment caused me many months of humiliation, reproach, and sorrow. It was a matter for new crosses.

CHAPTER VII

THIS first year I did not make use of my crosses. I was still
vain. I lied to conceal or to excuse some things, because I was
strangely afraid. I gave way to anger, being unable to approve in my mind what appeared to me such unreasonable
conduct, especially in what concerned the ill-treatment from
that maid who attended me. It appeared to me an unheard-of
thing that they should take her side against me when she
offended me; for as for my mother-in-law, her great age and
position rendered things more tolerable. O my God, how you
made me in the end see things with very different eyes! I
found in you reasons for suffering, which I had never found
in the creature, and I saw with complaisance that this unreasonable and crucifying conduct was all necessary for me. I
had still another fault which was common to me and almost all
other women, and arose from the love I bore myself. It was
that I could not hear any beautiful woman praised in my
presence without finding some fault with her, and cleverly
bringing it to notice, to diminish the good they were saying of
her; as if I was esteemed less when any one else was esteemed
with me. This fault lasted for a long time. It is the fruit of a
stupid and coarse pride, which I had in a supreme degree.
What a debt I owe to you, O my God, for having observed
with me the conduct that you have! for if my mother-in-law
and my husband had applauded me, as was done in my father's
house, I should have become insupportable from my pride. I

was careful to go to see the poor. I did what I could to conquer my temper, and especially in things which made my pride ready to burst. I gave much alms. I was exact in my prayer.

I became pregnant with my first child. During this time I was greatly petted as far as the body went, and my crosses were in some degree less severe thereby. I was so indisposed that I would have excited the compassion of the most indifferent. Moreover, they had such a great wish to have children, that they were very apprehensive lest I should miscarry. Yet towards the end they were less considerate to me, and once, when my mother-in-law had treated me in a very shocking manner, I was so malicious as to feign a colic in order to alarm them in my turn; because if I had miscarried they would have been inconsolable, so anxious were they to have children, for my husband was the only son, and my mother-in-law, who was very rich, could have heirs through him alone. Nevertheless, when I saw that this gave them too much trouble, I said that I was better. One could not be more miserable than I was during this pregnancy; for besides a continual sickness, I had such an extraordinary disgust that, with the exception of some fruit, I could not look at food. I was very long ill from this confinement, for besides the fever, I was so weak that after several weeks they could scarcely stir me to make my bed. All these ills, though violent, seemed to me but the shadows of ill in comparison with the troubles I suffered in my family, which, far from diminishing, increased each day. I was also subject to a very violent headache. During this time you increased, O my God, both my love for you and my patience. It is true that, owing to my afflictions, I was so indifferent to life that all the ills, apparently mortal, did not frighten me.

This first confinement improved my appearance, and in consequence made me more vain, for although I would not have been willing to add art to nature, yet I was very complaisant to myself. I was glad to be looked at, and, far from avoiding occasions for it, I went to promenades; rarely however, and when I was in the streets, I took off my mask from vanity, and my gloves, to show my hands. Could there be greater silliness?

In our family there happened an affair of great importance

as to worldly means. The loss was very considerable. This cost me strange crosses for more than a year; not that I cared anything for the losses, but it seemed to me I was the mark for all the bad tempers of the family. It is incredible that my father, who loved me so tenderly, and whom I honored more than I can say, never knew anything of what I suffered. God so permitted it that I should have him also opposed to me for some time; for my mother used constantly to tell him I was ungrateful, that I cared nothing for them, that I was entirely devoted to the family of my husband. All appearances in truth condemned me, for I used not to see my father and my mother a quarter of what I ought; but they were ignorant of the captivity I was in, and what I had to bear to defend them. This talk of my mother, and a disagreeable circumstance that happened, altered a little my father's friendship for me. This, however, did not continue long. My mother-in-law used to reproach me, that no afflictions had ever befallen them till I had entered their house; that all their misfortunes had come with me. On the other hand, my mother wanted to speak to me against my husband, which I could not allow.

I declare it is not without extreme repugnance I tell these things of my mother-in-law, and especially of my husband (for my husband is in heaven, and I am certain of it); I have even some scruples. I do not doubt that by indiscretions, by my provoking temper, by certain outbursts of hastiness which sometimes escaped me, I gave plenty of occasion for all my crosses, so they have not the value and merit they would have had had I been more perfect. Besides, though I then had what is called patience in the world, I had not yet either the taste for or love of the cross, and for this reason I committed many faults.

We continued losing in every way, the King cutting off several sources of income. Meditation in which state I then was did not give me a true peace in the midst of such great troubles. It, indeed, procures resignation, but not peace and joy. I, however, practised it twice a day very exactly, and as I had not that rooted presence of God which I have since had, I was subject to many wanderings. My pride nevertheless subsisted, and sustained itself in spite of so many things which were calculated to crush it. I had no one either to console me or to counsel me, for the sister who had brought me up was then dead—she died two months after my marriage. I had no confidence in the other. Life was very tiresome to me, and the more so because my passions were very quick; for however I tried to conquer myself, I could not avoid giving way to anger, no more than to wishing to please.

I did not curl my hair, or very little; I did not even put anything on my face, yet I was not the less vain of it. I even very seldom looked in the looking-glass, in order not to encourage my vanity, and I made a practice of reading books of devotion, such as the "Imitation of Jesus Christ" and the works of St. Francis de Sales while my hair was being combed, so that as I read aloud the servants profited by it. Moreover, I let myself be dressed as they wished, remaining as they had arranged me—a thing which saves trouble and material for vanity. I do not know how things were, but people always admired me, and the feelings of my vanity reawakened in everything. If on certain days I wished to look to better advantage, I failed, and the more I neglected myself the better I looked. It was a great stone of stumbling for me. How many times, O my God, have I gone to churches less to pray to you than to be seen there! Other women, who were jealous of me, maintained that I painted, and said so to my confessor, who reproved me for it, although I assured him to the contrary. I often spoke to my own advantage, and I exalted myself with pride while lowering others. I sometimes still told lies, though I used all my efforts to free myself from this vice. These faults diminished slightly, for I pardoned nothing to myself, and I was very much afflicted at committing them. I wrote them all down, and I made very careful examinations to see from one week to another, from one month to another, how far I had corrected myself; but, alas! how little use was my labor, although fatiguing, because I placed almost all my confidence in my carefulness! It is not, O my God, that I did not ask you with great urgency to deliver me from all these evils. I even prayed you to guard me, seeing the uselessness of my care, and I protested to you, if you did not do it, I should fall back into all my sins, and even into greater. My great crosses did not detach me from myself. They rendered me very indifferent to temporal wealth; they even made me hate life; but they did not take away those sentiments of vanity, that woke up with strength on all the occasions that I had of appearing. They were few, owing to the assiduity with which I attended on my husband. The church, O my God, was the place where I was most seen, and where I was most beset with sentiments of vanity. It appeared to me I would have wished to be otherwise, but it was a feeble and languishing will.

The long absence of my husband made me resolve to go and see him where he was. My mother-in-law opposed it strongly, but my father having wished it, I was let go. On my arrival, I found he had been near dying. He was greatly changed by the worry, for he was unable to finish his affairs, from not being at liberty to attend to them. He was even concealed in the Hôtel de Longueville, where Madame de Longueville showed me great kindness, but as I was much remarked, he feared I would cause him to be discovered. That greatly troubled him, and he wished me to return home, playing the part of the aggrieved; but love and the long time since he had seen me overcoming all other reasons, he made me remain with him. He kept me eight days without letting me leave his room, through this fear of discovery. This was a panic terror, for it had nothing to do with his business. But as he feared I would get ill in consequence, he begged me to go and walk in the garden, where I met Madame de Longueville, who remained a long time examining me thoroughly. I was surprised a person whose piety made so much noise should dwell so upon the exterior, and appear to make so much of it. She expressed great joy at seeing me. My husband was very pleased, for at bottom he loved me much, and I should have been very happy with him, but for the continual talk my mother-in-law entertained him with.

I cannot tell the kindness that was shown me in this house. All the officials eagerly served me. Everywhere I found only persons who applauded me, owing to this miserable exterior. I was so scrupulous in not listening to any one on this point, I made myself ridiculous. I never spoke to a man alone, and never took one into my carriage unless my husband was there, although they might be my relatives. I never gave my hand without precaution, I never went into the carriages of men. In short, there was no possible measure I did not observe to avoid giving any umbrage to my husband, or any ground for my being talked of. So much precaution had I, O my God, for a vain point of honor, and I had so little for the true honor, which is, not to displease you. I went so far in this, and my self-love was so great, that if I had failed in any rule of politeness, I could not sleep at night. Every one wished to contribute to my diversion, and the outside life was only too agreeable for me; but as to indoors, vexation had so depressed my husband, that each day I had to put up with something new, and that very often. Sometimes he threatened to throw the supper out of the window, and I told him it would be very unfair to me; I had a good appetite. I laughed with him to win him, and oftentimes he quieted down at once, and the manner in which I spoke to him touched him. At other times melancholy got the upper hand, in spite of all I could do, and the love he had for me. He wished me to return home, but I could not desire it, owing to what I had suffered in his absence.

I became quite languishing, for I loved you, O my God, and I would not have wished to displease you. This vanity which I felt, and I could not destroy, caused me much trouble. That, joined to a long succession of vexations, made me fall ill. As I did not wish to cause trouble in the Hôtel de Longueville, I had myself carried elsewhere, and I was so ill and reduced to such extremity that, after they had in seven days taken from me forty-eight pallets of blood, and they could get no more, the doctors despaired of my life, and this state was protracted. There was no probability I could recover. The priest who confessed me, and who had much piety and discernment, for he had been an intimate friend of St. Francis de Sales, appeared so satisfied with me that he said I would die like a saint. It was only I, O my God, who was not satisfied with myself. My sins were too present to my mind, and too painful to my heart, to allow this presumption.

My husband was inconsolable, and was so afflicted he was near dying. When he saw there was no hope; that the disease increased as well as my weakness; that the remedies irritated it; that they found no more blood in my veins, which were drained by the profuse bleedings they had subjected me to,—on the Festival of St. Francis de Sales he vowed me to this saint, and caused many Masses to be said. It was no sooner done than I began to improve. But what is strange is, that in spite of all his love, hardly was I out of danger when he commenced to be vexed with me. Scarcely could I move about when I had to endure new assaults. This illness was very useful to me, for besides a very great patience in the midst of severe pain, it threw a great light for me on the worthlessness of the things of the world. It detached me much from myself. It gave me a new courage to suffer better than I had done in the past. I even felt that your love, O my God, was strengthening itself in my heart, with the desire to please you and to be faithful to you in my condition.

CHAPTER VIII

AT last, after long debility, I recovered my former health, and I lost my mother, who died like an angel. For God, who willed to commence even in this life to recompense her great almsgiving, gave her such a grace of detachment, that, although she was only twenty-four hours ill, she left all that was most dear to her without grief.

I was much indisposed in a second pregnancy, and even sometime ill of a double-tertian fever. I was still weak, and I did not serve you, O my God, with that vigor that you soon afterwards gave me. I would have liked to reconcile your love with the love of myself and of creatures; for I was so unfortunate that I still found persons who loved me and whom I could not hinder myself from wishing to please—not that I loved them, but from the love I bore myself.

You permitted, O my God, that Madame de Ch——, who was exiled, came to my father, and he offered her a portion of the house, which she accepted, and she lived there some time. This lady was of singular piety and very spiritual. As I often used to see her, and she had a friendship for me, because she saw I wished to love God, and that I employed myself in external works of charity, she remarked that I had the virtues of the active and complex life, but that it was not in the simplicity of prayer in which she was. She sometimes dropped a word to me on this subject, but as *the* hour was not yet come, I did not understand her. She was more useful to me from her example than from her words. I saw on her face something that showed a very great presence of God, and I remarked in her what I had never yet seen in any one. I endeavored, through my head and thoughts, to give myself a continual presence of God. I gave myself much trouble, and made no advance. I wished to have by an effort what I could not acquire save in ceasing all effort. This worthy lady charmed me by her virtue, which I saw to be far above the ordinary. Seeing me so complex, she often said something to me; but it was not time—I did not understand her. I spoke of it to my confessor, who told me the exact opposite, and as I discovered to her what my confessor had said thereon, she did not venture to open herself to me.

My father's nephew, of whom I have spoken, who had gone to Cochin China with M. de Heliopolis, arrived. He came to Europe to fetch priests. I was delighted to see him, for I remembered the good his former visit had brought me. Madame de Ch—— was no less pleased than I to see him, for they quickly understood each other, and they had one and the same spiritual language, which was also known to the prioress of a convent of Benedictines, named Genevieve Granger, one of the holiest women of her time. The virtue of this excellent relative charmed me, and I admired his continual prayer, without being able to understand it. I forced myself to meditate continually, to think unceasingly of you, O my God, to repeat prayers and utter ejaculations; but I could not by all these various things give myself what you yourself give, and which is experienced only in simplicity. I was surprised at his telling me that he thought of nothing in prayer, and I wondered at what I could not comprehend. He did all he could to attach me more strongly to you, O my God.

He had an incredible affection for me. The alienation from the corruption of the century which he saw in me, the horror of sin at an age when others only commence to taste its pleasures (for I was not eighteen years old), gave him tenderness for me. I complained of my faults with much ingenuousness, for I have always been clear enough thereon; but as the difficulty I found in entirely correcting them made me lose courage, he supported me, and exhorted me to support myself, and he would have liked to give me another method of prayer, which would have been more efficacious to rid me of myself; but I gave no opening for that. I believe his prayers were more efficacious than his words, for he was no sooner out of my father's house than you had compassion on me, O my Divine Love. The desire I had to please you, the tears I shed, my great labor and the little fruit I reaped from it, moved your compassion. You gave me in a moment, through your grace and through your goodness alone, what I had been unable to give myself through all my efforts. In this state was my soul, when by a goodness the greater in proportion as I had rendered myself unworthy of it, without paying regard either to your graces rejected, or to my sins, any more than to my extreme ingratitude, seeing me rowing with so much toil, helpless, you sent, O my Divine Savior, the favorable wind of your divine working to make me proceed at full sail upon that sea of afflictions. The thing happened as I am about to tell.

I often spoke to my confessor of the trouble I had at not being able to meditate or imagine anything to myself. Subjects of prayer too extended were useless to me, and I did not comprehend anything in them. Those that were very short and full of unction suited me better. This worthy Father did not understand me. At last God permitted that a monk, very spiritual, of the Order of St. Francis, travelled by where we were. He wanted to go by another way, as well to shorten the journey as to avail himself of the ease of water-carriage, but a secret force made him change his plan, and obliged him to pass through the place where I dwelt. He at once saw there was there something for him to do. He fancied that God called him for the conversion of a man of consideration in this neighborhood, but his efforts were useless. It was the conquest of my soul that you wished to effect through him. O my God, it seems that you forgot all the rest to think only of this ungrateful and faithless heart. As soon as this worthy monk had arrived in the country, he went to see my father, who was very glad of it, and who about that time being ill, was near dying. I was then laid up with my second son. For some time they concealed from me my father's illness, through fear for my health, yet an indiscreet person having informed me, ill as I was, I got up and went to see him. The haste with which I had gone about after my confinement caused me a dangerous illness. My father recovered, not perfectly, but enough to give me new marks of his affection. I told him my desire to love you, O my God, and the grief I was in at not being able to do it according to my desire. My father, who singularly loved me, thought he could not give me a more solid proof of it than in procuring for me the acquaintance of this monk. He told me what he knew of this holy man, and that he wished me to see him. I at first made much difficulty, because I never used to go to see monks. I believed I was bound so to act in order to observe the rules of the most scrupulous prudence; yet my father's urgency took with me the place of an absolute command. I thought no harm could come to me from a thing I did only to obey him.

I took with me one of my relatives and went there. When he saw me at a distance he was quite confused; for he was very particular in never seeing women, and a solitude of five years, which he had just left, had made them not a little strangers to him. He was then very much surprised that I was the first who addressed herself to him, and what I told him increased his surprise, as he has since acknowledged to me, assuring me that my appearance and manner of saying things had confused him, so that he did not know if he was dreaming. He hardly advanced, and was a long time without being able to speak to me. I knew not to what to attribute his silence. I continued to speak to him, and to tell him in a few words my difficulties about prayer. He answered me at once: "It is, Madame, because you seek outside what you have within. Accustom yourself to seek God in your heart, and you will find him there." On finishing these words, he left me.

The next morning he was very greatly astonished when I went to see him, and when I told him the effect his words had produced in my soul; for it is true they were for me like an arrow that pierced my heart through and through. I felt in that moment a very deep wound, as delicious, as full of love, a wound so sweet, I desired never to be healed of it. Those words put into my heart what I was seeking so many years, or rather they made me discover what was there, and which I did not enjoy for want of knowing it. O my Lord, you were in my heart, and you asked from me only a simple turning inward to make me feel your presence. O Infinite Goodness, you were so near, and I went running here and there to look for you, and I did not find you. My life was miserable, and my happiness was within me. I was in poverty in the midst of riches, and I was dying of hunger near a table spread and a continual feast. O Beauty ancient and new, why have I known you so late? Alas! I was seeking you where you were not, and I did not seek you where you were. It was for want of understanding those words of your Gospel when you say, "The kingdom of God is not here or there, but the kingdom of God is within you."

I told this worthy Father that I did not know what he had done to me; that my heart was quite changed; that God was there, and I had no longer any trouble to find him; for from that moment I was given an experience of his presence in my central depth, not through thought or application of the mind, but as a thing one possesses really in a very sweet manner. I experienced those words of the spouse of the Canticles, "Your name is like oil poured out; therefore the young girls have loved you." For I experienced in my soul an unction which, like a soothing balm, healed all my wounds, and which even spread itself so powerfully over my senses, that I could hardly open my mouth or my eyes. I did not sleep at all the whole of that night, because your love, O my God, was not only for me like a delightful oil, but also like a devoring fire, which kindled in my soul such a flame that it seemed bound to devour everything in an instant. I was all of a sudden so changed that I was no longer recognizable either by myself or by others. I no longer found either those faults or those dislikes. All appeared to me consumed like straw in a great fire.

This worthy Father, however, could not make up his mind to undertake my direction, although he had seen so surprising a change effected by God. Many reasons led him to decline it: my appearance, which gave him much apprehension; my extreme youth, for I was only nineteen years old; and a promise he had made to God, through distrust of himself, never to undertake the direction of any female unless our Lord imposed it upon him by a special providence. On my urging him, then, to take me under his direction, he told me to pray to God about it; that he would do so on his side. When he was in prayer, it was said to him, "Do not fear to take charge of her: she is my spouse." O my God, permit me to say to you, that you did not mean it. What? your spouse! this frightful monster of filth and iniquity, who had done nothing but offend you, abuse your graces, and pay your goodness with ingratitude? This worthy Father then told me that he was willing to direct me.

Nothing was now more easy for me than to pray. Hours were to me no more than moments, and I was unable not to do it. Love left me not a moment of respite. I said to him, "O my Love, it is enough: leave me." My prayer was, from the moment of which I have spoken, void of all forms, species, and images. Nothing of my prayer passed into my head, but it was a prayer of enjoyment and possession in the will, where the delight of God was so great, so pure, and so simple, that it attracted and absorbed the other two powers of the soul in profound concentration, without act or speech. I had, however, sometimes freedom to say some words of love to my Beloved, but then everything was taken from me. It was a prayer of faith, which excluded all distinction; for I had not any view of Jesus Christ or the divine attributes. Everything was absorbed in a delicious faith, where all distinctions were lost to give love room for loving with more expansion, without motives or reasons for loving. That sovereign of the powers—the will—swallowed up the two others, and took from them every distinct object to unite them the better in it, in order that the distinct should not arrest them, and thus take from them the uniting force and hinder them from losing themselves in love. It is not that they did not subsist in their unconscious and passive operations, but it is that the light of faith, like a general light, similar to that of the sun, absorbs all distinct lights, and throws them into obscurity to our eyes, because the excess of his light surpasses them all.

CHAPTER IX

TRUE ravishment and perfect ecstasy are operated by total annihilation, where the soul, losing all self-hood, passes into God without effort and without violence, as into the place which is proper and natural to her. For God is the center of the soul, and when once the soul is disengaged from the self-hood which arrested her in herself or in other creatures, she infallibly passes into God, where she dwells hidden with Jesus Christ. But this ecstasy is operated only by simple faith, death to all things created, even to the gifts of God, which, being creatures, hinder the soul from falling into the One uncreated. It is for this reason, I say, it is of great importance to make her pass beyond all his gifts, howsoever sublime they may appear, because, as long as the soul dwells in them, she does not veritably renounce herself, and so never passes into God himself, although she may be in those gifts in a very sublime manner. But resting thus in the gifts, she loses the real enjoyment of the Giver, which is an inestimable loss.

Through an inconceivable goodness, O my God, you introduced me into a state very pure, very firm, and very solid. You took possession of my will, and you there established your throne, and in order that I should not let myself aim at those gifts and withdraw myself from your love, you put me at once into a union of the powers and into a continual adherence to you. I was unable to do anything else but to love you with a love as profound as it was tranquil, which absorbed everything else. Souls that are taken this way are the most favored, and they have a shorter road to travel. It is true when you advance them so quickly, O my God, they must expect violent crosses and cruel deaths, especially if they are from the first touched with much faith, abandonment, pure love, disinterestedness, and love of the sole interest of God alone, without any self-regard. These were the dispositions you from the first placed in me, with so vehement a desire of suffering for you, that I was quite languishing from it. I was on a sudden disgusted with all creatures; all that was not my Love was insupportable to me; the cross I had till then borne through resignation became my delight and the object of my complaisance.

CHAPTER X

I WROTE all this to that worthy Father, who was filled with joy and astonishment. O God, what penances did not the love of suffering make me practice! I practiced all the austerities I could imagine, but all was too feeble to satisfy the desire I had of suffering. Although my body was very delicate, the instruments of penance tore me without causing me pain, as it appeared to me. Every day I took long scourgings, which were with iron points. They drew much blood from me, and bruised me, but they did not satisfy me, and I regarded them with scorn and indignation, for they could not content me; and as I had little strength, and my chest was extremely delicate, I wearied my arms and lost my voice without hurting myself. I wore girdles of hair and iron points. The former appeared to me a play of self-love, and the latter caused me extreme pain, putting on and taking off, and yet, when I had them on, they did not cause me pain. I tore myself with brambles, thorns, and nettles, which I kept on me. The pain of these latter caused my heart to fail, and entirely deprived me of sleep, without my being able to remain sitting or lying, in consequence of the points remaining in my flesh. It was these last I used when I could get them, for they satisfied me more than any. I very often kept absinthe in my mouth, colocynth in my food; although I ate so little that I am astonished how I could live; besides, I was always ill or languishing. If I walked, I placed stones in my shoes. It was, O my God, what you inspired me from the first to do, as well as to deprive myself of all the most innocent gratifications. All that could flatter my taste was refused to it. All that was most disagreeable to it was given to it.

When the worthy Father, whom I have mentioned, asked me how I loved God, I told him that I loved him more than the most passionate lover loved his mistress; that this comparison was yet improper, since the love of creatures can never attain to that either in force or depth. This love was so continual, and always occupied me, and so powerful, I could not think of anything else. This profound stroke, this delicious and amorous wound, was inflicted on me on the Magdalen's Day, 1668; and that Father, who was a very good preacher, had been asked to preach in my parish, which was under the invocation of the Magdalen. He made three admirable sermons on this subject. I then perceived an effect which his sermons produced on me, namely, that I could hardly hear the words and what was said; they at once made impression on my heart, and so powerfully absorbed me in God, that I could neither open my eyes nor hear what was said. To hear your name mentioned, O my God, or your love, was enough to throw me into profound prayer, and I experienced that your word made an impression directly on my heart, and that it produced all its effect without the intervention of reflection and intellect; and I have ever since experienced this, although in a different manner, according to the different degrees and states through which I have passed. It was, then, more perceptible to me. I could hardly any more pronounce vocal prayers.

I gave up all society. I renounced for ever games and amusements, the dance, and all useless promenades. Nearly two years before I had given up curling my hair. I was, however, very well dressed, for my husband wished it so. My only diversion was to snatch moments to be alone with you, O my only Love. All other pleasure was for me a pain, not a pleasure. I did not lose your presence, which was given me by a divine and continual influx, not, as I had imagined, through an effort of the head, nor through thinking of you, my divine Love, but in the depths of the will, where I tasted with ineffable sweetness the real enjoyment of the object loved—not, however, as afterwards, through an essential union, but through a true union in the will, which made me taste by happy experience that the soul is created to enjoy you, O my God. This union is the most perfect of all those which are operated in the powers. Its effect is also much greater, for the unions of the other powers enlighten the intellect and absorb the memory, but if they are not accompanied with this, they are of little use, because they produce only temporary effects. The union of the will carries with it, in essence and in reality, what the others have only in distinction. Moreover, it submits the soul to her God, conforms her to all his wills, gradually kills in her all "*own*" will, and at last, drawing with it the other powers by means of charity, of which it is full, gradually makes them unite in that centre, and there lose themselves so far as their operation is "*own*" and natural.

This loss is called "Annihilation of the powers," which must not be understood of a physical annihilation—that would be ridiculous, but they appear annihilated as regards us, although they still remain subsisting. This annihilation or loss of the powers takes place in this way: In proportion as Charity fills and inflames the Will in the manner we have said, this Charity becomes so powerful that it gradually overcomes all the activity of this Will to subject it to that of God, so that when the soul is docile in allowing herself to be perfected and purified by it, and to be emptied of all that she has of the "*own*" and *opposed* to the will of God, she finds herself gradually void of all "*own*" will, and placed in a holy indifference, to will only that which God does and wills. This never can be consummated through the activity of our Will, even though it should be employed in continual resignations, because they are so many "*own*" acts, which, although very virtuous, make the Will still subsist in itself, and consequently hold it in multiplicity, in distinction, in unlikeness with that of God. But when the soul remains submissive, and only suffers freely

and voluntarily, bringing her concurrence, which is her submission, to allow herself to be conquered and destroyed by
the activity of Charity,—this, while absorbing the Will in
itself, perfects it in that of God, first purifying it from all
restriction, unlikeness, and "*ownness.*"

It is the same with the two other powers, where, by means
of Charity, the two other theological virtues are introduced.
Faith seizes so powerfully on the Understanding that it makes
it die away to all reasoning, to all distinct light, to all particular
illuminations, be they the most sublime; which shows how
much visions, revelations, ecstasies, etc., are contrary to this,
and hinder the loss of the soul in God, although in this way
she may appear lost for moments; but it is not a true loss, since
the soul which is truly lost in God never recovers herself. It
is rather a simple absorption, if the thing is in the will, or a
dazzling if it is in the intellect, than a loss. I say, then, that
Faith makes the soul lose all distinct light, and absorbs her
while conquering, to place her in its light, which is above all
light—a light general and indistinct, which appears darkness
to the self-hood on which it shines, because its excessive
clearness prevents one from discerning or recognizing it; as
we are unable to discern the sun and his light, although by
means of this light we so perfectly discern objects that it even
hinders us from making mistakes. As we see that the sun
absorbs in his general light all the little distinct lights of the
stars, but that these little lights in themselves are very easily
discerned, without, however, being able to give light to us;
in the same way, these visions, ecstasies, etc., are very well
discerned, owing to their smallness of extent. But yet, while
making themselves distinct, they cannot, however, place us in
the truth, nor make us see objects such as they are; on the
contrary, they would rather mislead us by their false light. It
is similar with all lights which are not those of passive Faith—
infused light—Faith the gift of the Holy Spirit, which has
the power to undeceive the intellect, and, while obscuring
the "*own*" lights of the Understanding, to place it in the light
of truth; which, although less satisfying for it, is, however, a
thousand times more sure than any other, and is properly the
true light of this life, until Jesus Christ, the eternal Light,
arises in the soul and enlightens her with himself—"He who

enlightens every man coming into the world" with the new life in God. This is abstruse, but I allow myself to be carried away by the spirit who makes me write.

In the same way, the Memory finds itself conquered and absorbed by Hope, and at last everything loses itself in pure Charity, which absorbs the whole soul, through means of the Will that, as sovereign of the powers, has the ability to destroy the others in itself, like as Charity, queen of the virtues, reunites in itself all the other virtues. This reunion which then takes place is called Unity, central union, because everything finds itself united through the will and charity in the center of the soul and in God our ultimate end, according to those words of St. John, "He who dwells in charity, dwells in God; for God is charity." This union of my will to yours. O my God, and this ineffable presence, was so powerful and so sweet at the same time, that I could not wish to resist it, nor to defend myself from it. This dear Possessor of my heart made me see even my smallest faults.

CHAPTER XI

THE more you increased my love and my patience, O my God, the stronger and more continual became my crosses: but love made them light to me. Oh, poor souls who consume yourselves with superfluous worries, if you sought God in yourselves, you would soon find an end of your ills, since their excess would constitute your delight. Love, at this commencement, insatiable of mortifications and penances, made me invent all kinds. But what was admirable is that, without my paying any attention to it, as soon as mortification no longer produced any effect upon me, love made me discontinue it, to practice another to which it directed me itself; for that love was so subtle and enlightened, it saw even the smallest defects. If I was about to speak, it made me see a fault therein, and made me keep silence. If I kept silence, it found a defect there. In all my actions it found defects—my manner of acting, my mortifications, my penances, my alms, my solitude, in short, it found defect in all. If I walked, I noticed a defect in my manner of walking. If I said anything to my advantage—"pride." If I said, "Well, I will say nothing of myself, good or bad"—"selfhood." If I was too concentrated and reserved—"self-love." If I was gay and open, people condemned me. This pure Love always found something to censure, and was extremely careful to let nothing pass with my soul. It is not that I paid attention to myself, for I could regard myself very little, owing to the fact that my attention to him through the adherence of the will was continual. I was unceasingly awake to him, and he kept his eye continually on me, and conducted me in such a way by the hand of his providence, that he made me forget everything, and, although I experienced these things, I was unable to declare them to any one. He so completely took away all regard towards myself, that I could not in any way make an examination. As soon as I set myself to do so, I was removed from all thought of myself, and turned to my one Object, who had no distinct object for me, but an utter generality and vastness. I was, as it were, plunged in a river of peace. I knew by faith it was God who thus possessed all my soul, but I did not think on it, as a wife seated near her husband knows it is he who embraces her, without saying to herself, "It is he," and without occupying her thought with it.

O God, with what rigor do you punish your most faithful and most cherished lovers! I do not speak here of external penances, which are too weak to punish the least fault in a soul that God wills to purify radically, and which, on the contrary, serve rather as a consolation and refreshment; but the manner God uses to punish the least faults in the chosen souls is so terrible, it must be experienced to be understood. All that I could tell of it would be understood only by experienced souls. It is an interior conflagration and a secret fire, which, emanating from God himself, comes to purify the fault, and does not cease to cause an extreme pain until the fault is entirely purified. It is like a bone dislocated, which continues to cause extreme pain until it is entirely replaced.

This pain is so painful to the soul, that she throws herself into a hundred postures to satisfy God for her fault. She would tear herself in pieces rather than suffer such a torment. Oftentimes she goes quickly to confession, to get rid of this great torment, and thus multiplies her confessions without matter, and withdraws herself from the designs of God.

It is, at that time, of great importance to know how to make use of this pain, and on this depends almost the whole advancement of retardation of souls. We must, then, in this painful, obscure, and troubled time, second the designs of God, and suffer this devouring and crucifying pain in all its extent as long as it shall endure, without adding anything to it or diminishing, bearing it passively, without desiring to satisfy God by penances or confession, until this pain be past. To bear it passively is more painful, and that which it is hardest to adjust one's self to, and it would not be believed that an inconceivable courage is needed. Those who have not experienced it will hardly believe me, yet nothing is more true, and I have heard tell of a very great soul (which, however, never attained entirely to God in this life, for want of courage to allow himself to be entirely purified by the devouring fire of justice), that he had never been able to bear this pain more than half an hour without going to free himself of it by confession. You instructed me, O my God, in another way, and you taught me that I must not practice penance nor confession, until you yourself were satisfied. O amiable cruel One! Pitiless and sweet Exactor, you made me bear this pain, not only many hours, but many days, according to the nature of my fault. A useless attention, a hasty word, was punished with rigor. I had, then, to suffer without stirring the least in the world. I have had much trouble to let God perform this operation in all its extent.

I understand, at the moment that I write, that this fire of exact justice is the same as that of purgatory; for it is not a material fire which there burns souls, as some persuade themselves, saying that God for that purpose enhances its activity and natural capacity. It is this exacting divine justice which burns in this way those poor souls, in order, by purifying, to make them fit to enjoy God. All other fire would be refreshment for them. This fire is so penetrating, it goes even into the substance of the soul, and can alone purify her radically. Those who pretend that souls desire to get out of that fire do not know their situation. They remain in peace quite passive in their sufferings, without wishing to shorten them; for they are so powerfully absorbed in God, that, though they suffer extremely, they cannot return upon themselves to contemplate their sufferings, this return being an imperfection of which they are incapable. God applies to them according to his will the prayers that are made for them, and he grants to his saints and to his Church to shorten their torments and diminish the activity of that fire. O God, how very true it is, you are a "devouring fire"!

It was, then, in this purgatory, amorous yet at the same time rigorous, that you purified me from all that was in me contrary to your divine will, and I let you do it, although I sometimes suffered for several days pains that I cannot tell. I would have much wished that I had been permitted to practice some extraordinary penances, but I had to continue practicing only the daily ones, such as love made me practice. This pain ordinarily deprived me of the power of eating. I, however, did violence to myself to let nothing appear, except that there was remarked upon my face a continual occupation by God; for, as the attraction was powerful, it spread itself even over the senses, so that this gave me such a gentleness, modesty, and majesty that people of the world perceived it.

CHAPTER XII

IN whatever way my mother-in-law and my husband treated me, I answered only by my silence, which was not then difficult for me. I rendered my mother-in-law and my husband the lowest services, in order to humiliate myself; anticipating those who were accustomed to do so at such hours. All this did not win them. As soon as they got vexed, either of them, although I was not aware of having given them any cause, nevertheless I asked their pardon.

The violence that I practiced on my natural character, which was hasty and proud, was so great, that it was all I could bear. It sometimes seemed that my entrails were being torn, and I often fell ill from it. When any one came into my room, specially a man, I had given my maid an order to remain there. She sometimes spoke louder than I, in order to annoy me, and this made my friends hate her. If any unusual visitors came to see me, she hurled a thousand reproaches at me in their presence. If I held my tongue, she was still more offended, saying I despised her. My gentleness embittered her, and she made complaints of me to everybody. She defamed me, but my reputation was so well established in the mind of everybody, and in the country, as well owing to my external modesty and my devotion, as the great charities I bestowed, that nothing could then hurt me. Sometimes she ran into the street, crying, "Am I not indeed unfortunate to have such a mistress?" People crowded round her to know what I had done to her, and, being without an answer, she used to say I had not spoken to her for the whole day. They used to go away with a laugh, saying, "She has not, then, done you much harm!" I am surprised at the blindness of confessors, and the little truth there is in the accusations their penitents make to them of themselves, unless God puts them into his truth; for the confessor of this maid passed her off for a saint, and that, because being of the lower class, she assisted at his conference. He made her often communicate, yet she had all those faults and others I suppress, since they are nothing to my subject. That confessor told me also she was a saint, and I made no answer, for Love would not have me speak of my troubles, but that I should consecrate all to him by a profound silence.

My husband was vexed at my devotion, and it was insupportable to him. He said that loving you, O my God, so strongly, I could not more love him; for he did not understand the true conjugal love is that which you yourself form in the heart that loves you. It is true, O God, pure and holy, that you impressed on me from the commencement such a love for chastity that there was nothing in the world I would not have done to have it. I preached nothing else to him, although I endeavored not to make myself disagreeable, and to gratify him in all he could require of me. You gave me then, O my God, a gift of chastity, so that I had not even an evil thought, and marriage was very burdensome to me. He sometimes said to me, "One clearly sees you never lose the presence of God."

The world, which saw I had quitted it, tormented me and turned me into ridicule. I was its topic and the subject of its fables. It could not consent to a woman of hardly twenty years making so vigorous a war upon it. My mother-in-law took the side of the world, and blamed me because I did not do certain things that, at heart, she would have been very vexed had I done. I concealed myself to withdraw from the sight of men, who could by no means understand the operations that took place in my soul. I was as if distracted, for I lived in such separation from all created things, that it seemed to me there were no longer creatures on the earth. My eyes closed in spite of me, and I remained as if without motion, because Love kept me shut up within, as in a strong place, without my being able (whatever pains I took) to distract myself from his presence. I was your captive, O my Divine Love, and you were my jailer. I breathed and lived only through you and for you. I seemed to experience literally those words of St. Paul, "I live, yet not I, but Jesus Christ lives in me." You were, O my God and my Love, the soul of my soul, and the life of my life. Your operations were so powerful, so sweet, and so concealed at the same time, that I could not explain them to myself. I felt myself burning within, with a continual fire, but a fire so peaceful, so tranquil, so divine, that it is inexplicable. This fire consumed gradually my imperfections, and that which was displeasing to my God. It seems to me it consumed, at the same time, all partitions, and placed me in a union of enjoyment which calmed all desires in me. I found in myself no desire except a secret inclination and a more intimate union.

We went into the country for some business. I concealed myself in a corner of a dry river-bed. Who could tell what you then did in my soul, O my God? You alone, who did it, knew it. I got up at four o'clock to pray, and I was insatiable therein. I went very far to the Mass, and the church was so situated the carriage could not get up to it. There was a

mountain to descend and another to climb. All that cost me
nothing. Such a desire I had to receive you, O my only God!
How eager were you on your part to give yourself to your
petty creature, even to working visible miracles for the purpose!
Those who saw me lead so different a life from worldly
women, said that I was not prudent. When I wished to read,
I was so taken with your love, O my God, that at the first
word I found myself absorbed in you—the book fell from my
hands. If I tried to force myself, I did not understand what I
read, and my eyes closed of themselves. I could neither open
them, nor open my mouth to speak. If people talked near me, I
took in nothing of what was said. If I went into society, often
I could not speak, I was so seized by the inner life; I always
went with somebody, in order that it might not appear. It was
attributed to stupidity, and sometimes they said, "But what is
the meaning of this? People believe this lady has cleverness.
None of it appears." When I forced myself to speak, I could
not, and I knew not what I said. I took work in order to
conceal, under occupation, the inner state. When I was alone,
the work used to fall from my hands, and I could do nothing
but allow myself to be consumed by love. I tried to persuade a
connection of my husband's to use prayer. She thought me
mad for depriving myself of all the diversions of the age, but
our Lord has since opened her eyes to make her despise them.
I would have liked to teach all the world to love God, and I
thought it only depended on them to feel what I felt. God
made use of this to gain him many souls.

When I was in society, you possessed me more powerfully.
There took place in my heart a conversation very different
from that which was going on outside. I could not hinder the
presence of so great a Master appearing on my countenance.
It was this which annoyed my husband, as he sometimes told
me. I did what I could to prevent it appearing, but I could
not succeed. I was so occupied within, that I knew not what
I ate. I made a pretense of eating certain food that I did not
take, and I did things so cleverly, it was not perceived. I had
almost always absinthe and colocynth in my mouth. I learned
to eat what I most hated. Love did not let me see anything or
hear anything. Almost every day I took a scourging, and I

often wore the iron girdle without its lessening the freshness of my face.

I had often serious illness. I had no consolation in life except in praying and in seeing Mother Genevieve Granger of the Benedictines; but how dear those two consolations have cost me, especially the former, since it has been the source of all my crosses! But what am I saying, O my Love, estimating the cross as I do? Ought I not to say you have recompensed prayer by the cross, and the cross by prayer? O gifts inseparable in my heart! Since you have been given me, I have never been a moment without cross, nor, methinks, without prayer, although the loss I thought afterwards I had suffered of prayer has augmented my crosses to excess. However, when your eternal light arose in my soul, O Love, I have known the contrary, and that she had never been without prayer, as she had never been without cross.

My confessor at first labored to prevent me from praying and seeing Mother Granger, and, as he had an understanding with my mother-in-law and my husband, the means they used was to watch me from morning to evening. I dared not leave the room of my mother-in-law or the bed of my husband. Sometimes I carried my work to the window, under pretence of seeing better, in order to console myself a little by some moments of quiet; but they came to watch me, to see if I was not praying instead of working. When my mother-in-law and husband were playing cards together, I kept myself turned towards the fire. They used to turn round to see if I was working or if I shut my eyes, and, if they perceived I shut them, they were in a temper for several hours. What was most strange is that when my husband went out, and that he had some days of health, he was not willing I should take the time of his absence for praying. He remarked my work, sometimes returned, and, if he knew I was in my closet, got into a temper. I used to say to him, "But, Sir, when you are absent, what matters it to you what I do, so long as I am attentive to you when you are present?" This did not content him. He wished that in his absence I should not pray either. I do not think there is any torment equal to that of being strongly attracted, and unable to be alone. O my God, the contest they kept up with me, to hinder me from loving you, increased my love, and you yourself carried me away in an ineffable silence, when they hindered me from speaking to you. You united me so much the more powerfully to you, the more they tried to separate me.

I often played picquet with my husband, to please him, and I was then inwardly more attracted than if I had been in church. I could hardly contain the fire that devoured me, and if it had been less peaceable, I would have been unable to support it. I had all the warmth of love, but nothing of its impetuosity. The more ardent it was, the more peaceable it was. It could tell nothing of my prayer, owing to its simplicity. All I could tell of it is that it was continual as my love, and nothing interrupted it. On the contrary, the fire kindled itself with all that was done to extinguish it, and prayer nourished itself and increased from the fact that they deprived me of the time for using it. I loved without motive or reason for loving, for nothing passed through my head, but much in the inmost of myself. If I were asked why I loved God, whether it was owing to his mercy or his goodness, I knew not what was said to me. I knew that he was good, full of mercy. His perfections caused my pleasure, but I had no thought of myself for loving him. I loved him, and I burned with his fire because I loved him, and I loved him in such a way that I could love only him, but in loving him I had no motive save himself. All that was called interest, recompense, was painful to my heart. O my God, why cannot I make men comprehend the love with which you have possessed me from the commencement; and how remote it was from all interest! I thought neither of recompense, gift, nor favor, nor anything which concerned the lover; but the Beloved was the sole object that drew the heart in his complete totality. That love could not contemplate any perfection in detail. It was not drawn to contemplate its love, but it was as if swallowed up and absorbed in this love. All that they told it of way, of degree, of contemplation, of attributes, it ignored all that; it knew only to love and to suffer; all the rest was outside its province—it did not even comprehend it. O ignorance, more learned than all the learning of the doctors! since you taught me so well a Jesus Christ crucified, that I madly loved the cross, and that all that did not bear the character of cross and suffering failed to please me!

At the beginning, I was attracted with such force, that it seemed my head would come off to unite with my heart, and I found that insensibly my body bent itself without my being able to prevent it. I did not understand the cause, but I have since understood, that as everything passed into the Will which is the sovereign of the powers, it drew them after it and reunited them in God, their divine center and sovereign good, and as at the commencement these powers were not accustomed to be united, there was needed more violence to effect this reunion. For this reason it was more perceived. In the end, the coherence is so strong, it becomes quite natural. At that time, it was so strong that I would have wished to die, in order to be united inseparably and immediately to him, who attracted me with so much force. As everything passed into the Will, and my imagination, even the mind and intelligence, were absorbed in this union of enjoyment, I knew not what to say, having never read or heard anything of what I felt. I feared to lose my mind, for I must observe I knew nothing of the operation of God in souls. I said to you, O my God, if you made the most sensual people feel what I feel, they would soon give up their false pleasures to enjoy so true a blessing.

Then all pleasures, the most valued, appeared to me so tasteless, that I could not understand how I had been able to amuse myself with them; so that since this time I have never been able to find any save with God, although I have been faithless enough to use all my efforts to find it elsewhere. I was not at all surprised that the martyrs gave their life for Jesus Christ. I deemed them so happy, I envied their good fortune, and it was martyrdom for me that I could not suffer martyrdom. For it is not possible to love the cross more than I loved it since then; at least, so it appeared to me, and my greatest suffering would have been to have had no suffering.

The esteem and love of crosses have continually increased; although afterwards I lost the sensible or perceived taste for the cross, I have never lost the esteem and love of the cross, any more than the cross has never left me. It has always been my faithful companion, changing and increasing according as my interior dispositions changed and increased. O good cross,

delight of my heart, thou art that which has never left me
since I gave myself up to my divine Master! I hope that
thou wilt never abandon me. I declare I am in love with
thee. I have lost inclination and appetite for all the rest; but
as for thee, I perceive that the more profusely thou givest
thyself to me, the more does my heart desire thee and love
thee. I was then so greedy for the cross that I adopted every
means to make myself feel affliction. But although I cause
myself genuine pains, they appeared to me so trifling that it
only served to reawaken my appetite for suffering, and to
make me see that God alone can produce crosses suitable for
satiating souls that are hungering for them. The more I used
prayer in the way I have said, the more the love of the cross
increased, and at the same time the reality of the cross, for
they came pouring upon me from all quarters. The characteristic of this prayer is further to give a great faith. Mine was
without bounds, as well as my confidence and abandonment to
God, love of his will and of the orders of his providence over
me. I was previously very timorous: afterwards I no longer
feared anything. It is then one feels the effects of those words
of the Gospel, "My yoke is easy, and my burden is light."

CHAPTER XIII

I sometimes went to see Mother Granger, and she helped me;
but my confessor and my husband forbade me to go. I dared
not even write to her, and, if I had written, she could not
have answered me, owing to the weakness of her sight, so that
I did not get much help from her. When they knew I had been
to her, there were never-ending quarrels. Yet I condemned
myself to rigorous silence. My consolation was to communicate
as often as I could; but, when this was known, which often
enough happened, it cost me genuine crosses. My diversion

was to go and see some poor sick people, and to dress the wounds of those who came to the house. That was the only consolation I had. I was like those drunkards or those lovers who think only of their passion.

I was some time in this way, after which prayer became more painful to me. When I was not engaged in it, I burned to be so. When I was in it, I could not continue so. I did violence to myself in order to remain more in prayer when painful than when consolatory. I sometimes suffered inexplicable torments. To relieve myself and cause diversion, I covered all my body with nettles, but, although this gave much pain, what I suffered within was such that I hardly felt the pain of the nettles. As the pain and the dryness still increased, and I no longer found that gentle vigor which made me practice good with pleasure, my passions, which were not dead, were not slow in waking up again, and in giving me new exercise. It seemed to me I was like those young wives, who have trouble to get rid of the love of themselves, and to follow their friend into the battle. I fell back into a vain complaisance for myself. This inclination, which appeared to me dead when I was so smitten with my Love, revived, and it made me groan and pray God incessantly to take away from me this obstacle, and make me become ugly. I would have wished to be deaf, blind, and mute, in order that nothing might be able to divert me from my Love.

I went on a journey, where I shone more than ever, like those lamps which blaze up afresh when they are on the point of going out. Alas! how many snares were spread for me! I met them at every step. I committed infidelities; but, O my God, with what rigor did you punish them! The least look stirred you to anger against me, and your anger was more insupportable to me than death. Those unforeseen faults, where I let myself slip through weakness, and as it were in spite of myself, how many tears did they cost me! O my Love, you know the rigor you exercised on me, after my weaknesses, was not their cause. My God, with what pleasure would I have suffered all your rigors to escape being unfaithful to you! and to what severe chastisement did I not condemn myself! You know, O my God, you treated me sometimes like a father who pities the weakness of his child, and caresses it after its little slips. How many times did you make me feel that you loved me, although I had stains that appeared to me almost voluntary! It was the sweetness of this Love after my falls that made my truest torment. The more amiable and good towards me you appeared, the more inconsolable was I at turning aside from you, though it should be but for moments, and when I had inadvertently done anything, I found you ready to receive me.

When I was at Paris, and the confessors saw me so young, they were astonished. After I had confessed, they said to me that I could not sufficiently thank God for the graces he had bestowed on me; that if I knew them, I would be astonished; and that if I was not faithful, I would be the most ungrateful of all creatures. Some declared they did not know a woman whom God kept so close and in so great purity of conscience. What made it such was that continual care you had over me, O my God, making me experience your intimate presence, as you have promised us in your Gospel, "If any one does my will, we will come unto him, and make our dwelling in him." This continual experience of your presence in me was what guarded me. I experienced what your prophet said, "It is in vain one watches to guard the city, if the Lord does not guard it." You were, O my Love, that faithful Guardian, who continually defended it against all sorts of enemies, preventing the smallest faults, or correcting them, when vivacity had led me to commit them. But, alas! my dear Love, when you ceased yourself to watch, how weak was I! and how my enemies prevailed over me! Let others attribute their victories to their fidelity; for me I will only attribute them to your paternal care. I have too well proved my weakness, and I have made too fatal an experience of what I should be without you, to presume anything on my care. It is to you I owe everything, O my Deliverer, and I have infinite pleasure in owing it to you.

While at Paris I relaxed my exercises, owing to the little time I had, and, besides, trouble and dryness had seized upon my heart. The hand that sustained me was hidden, and my Beloved had withdrawn himself. I committed many infidelities, for I knew the violent passion certain persons had for me, and I suffered them to show it; I was not, however, alone. I also committed faults in leaving my neck a little uncovered, although it was not nearly so much so as others had it. I wept because I saw I was growing slack, and it was a very great torment for me. I sought everywhere for him who was consuming my soul in secret. I asked news of him, but, alas! he was hardly known to any one. I said to him, "O Beloved of my soul, if you had been with me, these disasters would not have happened to me! Alas! 'show me where you feed your flock at midday, and where you rest yourself' in the full day of eternity, which is not like the day of time, subject to nights and to eclipses." When I say I said this to him, it is only to explain and to make myself understood; for, in truth, everything passed almost in silence, and I could not speak. My heart had a language which went on without the sound of speech, and it was understood by its Beloved, as he understands the profound silence of the Word, ever eloquent, who speaks incessantly in the depths of the soul. O language that experience alone can make conceivable! Let no one fancy it was a barren language, an effect of the imagination. Far other is the mute language of the Word in the soul; as he never ceases to speak, so he never ceases to operate. "He spoke, and they were made." He operates in the soul that which he speaks there. Neither let any one think that this language of the Word is carried on in distinct speech. It would be a mistake.

This ineffable speech communicates to the soul in which it is the facility of speaking without words. The speaking of the Word in the soul, the speaking of the soul through the Word, the speaking of the Blessed Ones in heaven—oh, how happy the soul to whom this ineffable speaking is communicated!—a speaking which is understood by souls of the same kind, so that they mutually express themselves without speaking, and this expression causes an unction of grace, peace, and sweetness, and carries with it effects which experience alone can make conceivable. Oh, if souls were sufficiently pure to learn to speak in this way, they would participate beforehand in the language of glory.

I labored to finish the business that kept me at Paris, in order to return to the country; for it seemed to me, O my God, you gave me sufficient strength to avoid the occasions, but when the occasion offered, I could not guarantee myself from complaisance and numerous other weaknesses. The pain I felt after my faults was so great I cannot explain myself. It was not a pain caused by a distinct view, motives, or affections; but it was a devouring fire, which did not cease till the fault was purified. It was a banishment from my central-depth, whence I clearly felt the Spouse in anger rejected me. I could not have access to it; and, as I could not find repose elsewhere, I knew not what to do. I was like Noah's dove, that found no rest for its feet, which was constrained to return to the ark, but on finding the window closed, it only flew round about, unable to enter. Through an unfaithfulness which will render me for ever condemnable, I have sometimes wished, in spite of myself, to find means of satisfaction without, but I could not. This attempt served, O my God, to convince me of my folly, and to make me understand the weakness of the pleasures that are called innocent. When I forced myself to taste them, I felt an extreme repugnance, which, joined to the reproach of my infidelity, made me suffer much, and changed for me diversions into punishments. I said, "O my God, it is not you; there is none but you who can give solid pleasures." Never has creature experienced more the bounties of God, in spite of my ingratitudes. You pursued me, O my God, incessantly, as if the conquest of my heart must have constituted your happiness. In my astonishment I used sometimes to say to myself, "It seems that God has no other care and no other business than to think of my soul."

One day, through infidelity as much as through complaisance, I went to take a turn at the promenade, more in order to have myself looked at through excessive vanity, than to enjoy the exercise. O my God, in what a way did you make me feel this fault! Some carriages separated to come to us; but far from punishing me by letting me enjoy the pleasure, you did it by preserving me, and pressing me so closely, that I could pay attention only to my fault, and the dissatisfaction you exhibited to me at it. Some people wished to give me an entertainment at St. Cloud, and had invited other ladies, and, though ordinarily I took no part in any of these pleasures, I allowed myself to go there through weakness, and also through vanity; but, O my God, how tinged with bitterness was this simple diversion, which the other ladies present, though discreet, enjoyed! I could not eat anything whatsoever; yet the feast was most magnificent. My disquietude appeared upon my countenance, though they were ignorant of the cause. What tears it cost me! and how rigorously you punished me for it! You separated yourself from me for more than three months, but in a manner so harsh, that there was no longer for me anything but an irritated God.

During all this time I endeavored to stifle the martyrdom that I felt within, but it was useless. I lamented my weakness. I made verses to express my trouble, but they served only to augment it. It was such that it must be experienced to be understood. I prayed you, O my God, with tears, to take away this beauty, which had been so disastrous to me. I desired to lose it or to cease to love it. As you pressed me so closely, O my God, I could not resist. In spite of myself, I was obliged to leave everything, and to return in the greatest haste. Yet, notwithstanding my infidelities, you had, O my Love, a care for me that cannot be understood, as the instance I am about to tell will prove.

One day that I had resolved to go to Notre Dame on foot, I told the lackey in attendance to take me the shortest way. Providence allowed him to lead me astray. When I was on a bridge, there came to me a man very badly dressed. I thought he was a poor man, and was about to give him alms. He thanked me, and said he did not ask it, and drawing near me he commenced his conversation on the infinite greatness of God, of which he told me admirable things. He then spoke to me of the Holy Trinity, in a manner so grand and so exalted, that all I had ever heard said on it up to this time, appeared to me shadows compared to what he told me. Continuing, he spoke to me of the Holy Sacrifice of the Mass, of its excellence, of the care one should have in hearing it and assisting at it with respect. This man, who did not know me, and did not even see my face, for it was covered, said to me then, "I know, Madame, you love God, that you are very charitable and give much alms," and many other things of the qualities God had given me, "but yet you are very much astray. God desires something else from you. You love your beauty." Then, giving me a simple but true picture of my defects, my heart could not deny what he said. I listened to him in silence and with respect, while those who followed me said I was conversing with a mad man. I well felt he was enlightened with the true wisdom. He told me, moreover, that God did not wish me to be content to work, like others, to secure my salvation by merely avoiding the pains of hell; but that he further wished me to arrive at such a perfection in this life, that I should avoid even those of purgatory. During this conversation the road, though long, appeared to me short. I did not notice it till my arrival at Notre Dame, where my extreme fatigue made me fall into a faint. What surprised me is that when I arrived at the double bridge, and looked on all sides, I no more perceived this man, and I have never seen him since. On hearing him speak in this way, I asked him who he was; he told me he had once been a porter, but he was so no longer. The thing did not then make upon me anything like the impression it has since done. I at first related it as a story, without telling what he had last said to me; but having conceived there was something divine in it, I spoke of it no more.

CHAPTER XIV

IT was after this, my husband, having had some relief from his continual illness, wished to go to Orleans, and thence into Touraine. On this journey, my vanity triumphed, to disappear for ever. I received many visits and much applause. My God, how clearly I see the folly of men, who let themselves be caught by a vain beauty! I hated passion, but, according to the external man, I could not hate that in me which called it into life, although according to the interior man, I ardently desired to be delivered from it. O my God, you know what this continued combat of nature and grace made me suffer.

Nature was pleased at public approbation, and grace made it feared. I felt myself torn asunder, and as if separated from myself; for I very well felt the injury this universal esteem did me. What augmented it was the virtue they believed united with my youth and my appearance. I went to confessors, to accuse myself of my unfaithfulness, and to complain of the revolts I endured; but they understood not my trouble. They esteemed, O God, what you condemned. They regarded as virtue what appeared to me detestable in your eyes, and what made me die of grief is that, far from measuring my faults by your graces, they regarded what I was in relation to what I might be; so that, far from blaming me, they flattered my pride. They justified me from that of which I accused myself, and they hardly regarded, even as a trifling fault, what in me— whom you had foreguarded with very great mercy—was infinitely displeasing to you, O my God. We must not measure the gravity of faults by the nature of the sins, but by the state of the person who commits them. The least infidelity of a wife is more grievous to her husband than the great errors of his servants. I told them my trouble, because I had not my neck entirely covered, although I was much better than other women of my age. They assured me I was dressed very modestly, and that, as my husband wished it, there was no harm. Besides the vanity I had furnished me with pretexts which appeared to me the justest possible. Oh, if confessors knew the injury they cause women by these soft complaisances, and the evil it produces, they would show a great severity; for if I had found a single confessor who had told me there was harm in being as I was, I would not have continued in it a single moment; but my vanity taking the part of the confessors, and the maids who served me, made me think they were right and my troubles were fanciful.

On this journey we met with accidents and perils which would have frightened any other than me. It was not in my power to fear dangers that appeared inevitable, and which frightened everybody. Without thinking of it, we got entangled in a place the river Loire had undermined, and the road which appeared sound from above was without support. We only perceived the danger when it was impossible to turn to the right or left, and it was necessary to keep on, or to be precipitated into the river. One side of the carriage rolled in the air, and was only supported by the servants, who held the other side. Nothing could exceed the terror. As for me, I felt none of it, and I found myself so abandoned to God for all the events his providence might permit, that I felt even a distinct joy at perishing by a stroke of his hand. However, I had a certain secret confidence no accident would happen, and this proved true.

I went to confession to a man who caused me much trouble. He wanted to know the intention I had had in getting married: and as I answered him that I had had only that of obeying, he told me it was worthless, that I was not properly married—I must be remarried. He would have caused a breach between my husband and me, that we would never see each other again, if I had been credulous, and if God had not assisted me; for he condemned as mortal sin what was absolute duty, so that what with his proclaiming that all was mortal sin, he would have caused us much trouble if God had not assisted us. Under pretext of instructing me, he informed me of sins that up to then I had been ignorant of, and because in marrying my intention had not been to have children, but to obey, he gave me excessive penances. But a Father of the Company of Jesus, whom I went to see at Orleans on my return, released me from them, assuring me I had not committed even a venial sin, which much consoled me; for as that other had made mortal sins of all that to which my duty obliged me, he would have placed me under the necessity either of failing in my duty, or of doing things which he assured me were mortal sins. I further committed faults on this journey in looking at what was curious when I was taken sight-seeing, although I had the idea of turning away my eyes; this, however, rarely happened. On my return I went to see Mother Granger, to whom I related all my frailties and my slips. She restored me, and encouraged me to resume my former course. She told me to cover up entirely my neck with a handkerchief, which I have ever since done, although I am the only person in this style.

I prayed you, O my God, to take away the liberty I had of displeasing you, and I said to you, "Are you not strong enough to hinder this unjust division?" For as soon as I had the opportunity of exhibiting my vanity, I did it; and as soon as I had done it, I returned to you; and you, far from rejecting me, received me often with open arms, and gave me new proofs of love. That was my bitterest pain, for although I had this miserable vanity, my love was such that, after my falls, I loved better your rigors than your caresses. Your interests were more dear to me than my own, and I could not suffer that you should not do justice to yourself. My heart was penetrated with love and grief, and what rendered it very keen was that I could not bear to displease you, O my God, after the graces I had received from you. That those who do not know you should offend you, I am not surprised; but that this heart, which loves you more than itself, and which has felt the strongest proofs of your love, should let itself be carried away by tendencies it detests, oh, it is that which makes its cruellest martyrdom; and a martyrdom so much the more afflicting, as it lasts the longer.

I say to return to my subject, that your caresses after my infidelities were much more difficult for me to bear than your repulses. Oh, if one knew the confusion in which they place the soul! It is not conceivable. That soul would wish with all her strength to satisfy the divine justice, and if one allowed her, she would tear herself to pieces. The martyrdom of suffering nothing is then the most cruel of all martyrdoms. O Love, sweet and painful at the same time, agreeable and cruel, how difficult thou art to bear! I made verses and hymns to express my plaint. I practiced penances, but they were too light for so great a wound; they were like those drops of water which serve only to render the fire more fierce. One would wish to be consumed and punished. Oh, conduct of love to an ingrate! Oh, frightful ingratitude towards such goodness! A great part of my life is only a tissue of similar things, which ought to make me die of grief and love.

CHAPTER XV

ON returning home, I found my little daughter very ill, from her nurse having taken her out while in small-pox, and she was near dying. The gout again attacked my husband, and my eldest son took the small-pox so severely that it broke out three times, and at last rendered him as disfigured as he had been beautiful. As soon as I saw small-pox in the house, I was certain I must take it. Mother Granger told me to go away if I could. My father wished to take me and my second son, whom I very tenderly loved, to his house, but my mother-in-law would not consent. She persuaded my husband it was useless. The doctor she sent for said the same thing, that I would take it as well at a distance as near at hand. I can say she was then a second Jephtha, and she innocently sacrificed us both. Had she foreseen what happened, I am sure she would have acted otherwise, but aged persons have often certain maxims, which they are unwilling to give up. All the town interested itself. Every one begged her to make me leave the house; that it was cruelty to expose me thus; but you, O my God, who had other designs for me, did not permit her to consent. Everyone attacked me, thinking I was unwilling to leave; for I did not tell any one it was owing to their unwillingness, and I had no other instinct then but to immolate myself to you, O my God, and to your divine providence. I made a sacrifice to you of that beauty, which without you would have been so fatal to me; and although I might have withdrawn, in spite of the resistance of my mother-in-law, had I wished it. I was not willing to do so without their consent, because it seemed to me this resistance was an order of heaven. O divine will of my God, in spite of all my worthlessness, you then constituted my life.

"On returning home, I found my little daughter very ill."

I continued, then, in this abandonment, and in this spirit of sacrifice to God, awaiting from moment to moment in entire resignation all that it might please him to ordain. I was not less troubled for my younger son than for myself. My mother-in-law had such excessive love for the one who was ill, she cared nothing for the others; yet I am sure, if she had believed the small-pox would have killed him, she would have been very far from acting as she did. It was a result of your providence, O my God, rather than of her temper. You make use of creatures and their natural inclination to bring things to pass according to your designs; therefore, though I see in creatures conduct which appears at once so unreasonable and crucifying, I ascend higher, and I regard them as the instruments of your justice, and at the same time of your mercy, O my God, for your justice is quite full of your mercy.

When I told my husband that I was sick and the small-pox was about to seize me, he said it was my imagination. I informed Mother Granger of the situation I was in, and, as she had a tender heart, she was troubled at this harshness, and encouraged me to immolate myself to our Lord. At last, nature, seeing that there was no escape, consented to the sacrifice the spirit had already made. On the day of St. Francis D'Assisi, 4th October, 1670, when aged twenty-two years and some months, I found myself so ill at the Mass, that all I could do was to communicate. I was near fainting in the church. When at home, a great shivering seized me, together with a very severe headache and sickness. They would not believe I was ill, and our Lord permitted them to treat me thus harshly; yet in a few hours I was so ill I was at once judged in danger. I was seized with inflammation of the chest, and the remedies for one ailment were very unsuited to the other. The doctor, my mother-in-law's friend, was not in town; nor was the ordinary surgeon. They sent to fetch a surgeon, a skilful man, who said I should be bled. My mother-in-law would not permit it. I remained utterly neglected, so that I was on the point of dying for want of help. My husband, not being able to see me, and relying entirely upon my mother-in-law, let her act. She had resolved that no doctor but her own should treat me, and yet she did not send to fetch him, though he was but a day's journey off. I believe she opposed the bleeding because she, perhaps, feared it might be hurtful to me. She was only wrong in not sending to fetch the doctor in whom she had confidence. It was you, O my God, who ordained this conduct for the good of my soul. I saw all those things, and the extremity in which I was, but you kept me in such a spirit of sacrifice, that I did not open my mouth to ask for help. I awaited life or death from your hand, without manifesting the least trouble at a course so extraordinary. The peace I possessed within, owing to the perfect resignation in which you kept me, O my God, through your grace, was so great, that it made me forgetful of myself in the midst of the most violent illness and the most pressing dangers. But if the resignation you gave me on this occasion was so perfect that I may call it uniformity, since I did not find in myself any repugnance to your will, and I was active in nothing, but bore with love in silence your crucifying operation, without adding anything to what you operated in me and upon me—if, I say, my submission was entire, your protection was miraculous. How many times have you reduced me to extremity! but you have never failed to succor me when things appeared most desperate.

You brought it about that a skilful surgeon passing by the place of my residence made inquiries about me. He was told I was extremely ill. He immediately got off his horse and came to see me. Never was man more surprised when he saw the frightful state I was in. The small-pox, which could not break out, had attacked my nose with such violence it was already quite black. He thought there was gangrene, and the nose was about to fall off. He was so shocked at it he could not conceal his surprise from me. My eyes were like two coals. The strange news did not alarm me. It was far short of what I sacrificed myself to at that moment, and I was very pleased that God should avenge himself of the infidelities this face had made me commit. This surgeon went down to the room of my mother-in-law, and told her that it was a scandalous thing to let me die in this way, for want of a blood-letting. She opposed herself violently to it; she told him she would not suffer it, and that nothing should be done for me until the doctor, her friend, returned from the country. He got so angry at their leaving me in this way, without sending to fetch the doctor, that he said some strong things even to my mother-in-law. He immediately came up to my room, and said to me, "If you consent, I will save your life: I will bleed you." I at once stretched out my arm to him, and although the arm was extremely swollen, he instantly bled me. My mother-in-law was very angry. The small-pox at once broke out, and he ordered I should be bled in the evening; but they would not have it, and I dared not keep him, however great my need, through fear of displeasing my mother-in-law, and from a total surrender into the hands of God.

I give all this in detail, in order to show how advantageous it is to abandon one's self to God without reserve; although he may leave us apparently some moment to prove and exercise our submission, he yet never fails us when the need is most pressing. My nose became its natural size and lost its blackness, and the small-pox appeared in it at once after the bleeding, and, if they had continued to bleed me, I should have got on well; but as the surgeon went away, I fell back into the former state of neglect. All the disease settled on my eyes, which became so inflamed and painful it was thought I should lose them. I was three weeks with these severe pains, without sleeping a quarter of an hour during all that time. I could not close the eyes, because they were full of small-pox, nor open them owing to the pain. I quite expected to be blind, for there was every appearance of it. My neck, my palate, and my gums were so filled, that I could not swallow broth nor take any nourishment without suffering extremely. All my body was like that of a leper, and those who came to see me said they had never seen any one have it in greater quantity or more malignant; but as for my soul, she was in a contentment I cannot express. The hope of her liberty through the loss I endured, rendered her so satisfied and so united to God, that she would not have changed her condition for that of the happiest prince in the world.

Everyone thought I should be inconsolable, and they endeavoured to sympathize in my grief. My confessor came to see me, although he was not satisfied with me. He asked me if I was not very grieved at having the small-pox. I answered him frankly, without much reflection, that if the confusion in which the disease kept me had not made me forget the Te

Deum, I would have said it in thankfulness to God. This worthy man was annoyed with me for my answer, deeming me proud. I made no reply, and I saw clearly I was wrong in speaking to him with so much freedom, because he did not understand my disposition. They watched all my words, and, when they heard me say I should be free, they took that as a complaint I made to you, O my God, of my external captivity, which they attributed to my husband's jealousy, although it was not so. I meant, O my God, a liberty you alone could give me, in removing that snare for my pride, as well as for the passion of men. Oh, if I could describe the ineffable pleasure I tasted at the spoliation you made of the thing which was then most sensible to me! My heart praised you for it in its profound silence and the pain I suffered redoubled my love. They never heard me complain of my ills, nor the loss I experienced. The tranquility of my heart expressed itself outwardly by patience and silence. I kept silent alike as to what you made me suffer through yourself, O my God, and through the hand of creatures. All was welcome from your hand. The only word I said was to rejoice at the interior liberty I received thereby, and they made a crime of it. What I most felt was that my younger son took the small-pox the same day as I, and died of it for want of care. This blow was painful to my heart, which, however, drawing strength from my weakness, sacrificed him, and said to God, like Job, "You had given him to me; you have taken him from me; your holy name be praised." The spirit of sacrifice possessed me so strongly, that, although I loved him tenderly, I never shed a tear on learning his death. The day he was buried, the doctor sent to tell them not to put the tombstone on the grave, because my daughter could not live two days. My eldest son was not yet out of danger when this happened, so that I saw myself almost on the same day despoiled of all my children, my husband ill, and I still very ill. You were not willing, O my God, to take my daughter at this time, and you prolonged her life for some years, only to render her loss more painful to me. My mother-in-law's doctor arrived at last, at a time when he was no longer any use for me. When he saw the strange inflammation of my eyes, he caused me to be bled several times, but the time for it was gone, and these bleedings, which would have been so necessary at the commencement, only served to weaken me. My state was such, it was with great difficulty they could bleed me, for the arm was so swollen they had to bury the lancet up to the handle. Moreover, bleeding at such an unsuitable time was near causing my death; but you were not willing, O my Lord, to withdraw me yet from the world, in order to make me suffer more. I declare that death would have been very agreeable to me, and I looked upon it as the greatest of all blessings; but I saw well there was nothing to hope for in this direction, and, in place of tasting this blessing, I had to endure life.

As soon as my eldest son was a little better, he got up to come into my room. I was surprised at the extraordinary change I saw in him. His face, which before was of extreme delicacy, had become like a ploughed field. This made me curious to see myself in a mirror. The change made me afraid of myself. It was then I saw that God had wished the sacrifice in all its reality. There were some circumstances which, owing to the perversity of my mother-in-law, caused me many crosses, and which finished spoiling my son. My heart was yet firm in my God, and strengthened itself by the greatness and multitude of the ills.

Pomades were sent to me to restore my complexion and fill up the hollows of the small-pox. I had seen wonderful effects from them with others. I at first wished to try their effect with me, but Love, jealous of his work, did not wish it. There was in my heart a voice which said, "If I had wished thee beautiful, I would have left thee as thou wert." I had to give up every remedy, and hand myself over a prey to the rigors of Love, who compelled me to go into the open air, which increased the pitting, and to expose myself to the eyes of everybody in the streets without concealment, when the redness from the small-pox was most marked, in order to make my humiliation triumph where my pride had triumphed. My husband was then almost constantly in bed. He made such good use of his illness, that I could not regret what God sent him, although it involved more captivity for me, and more crosses of all kinds. I was very pleased that God saved him by this way. As he no longer found in me the charms which softened his harshness and calmed his anger, he became more susceptible to the impressions that were made upon him against me. On the other hand, the persons who spoke to him to my disadvantage, seeing themselves better listened to, spoke more strongly and more often. There was only you, O my God, who did not change to me. You redoubled your interior graces in proportion as you increased my exterior crosses.

CHAPTER XVI

THAT maid of whom I spoke became every day more arrogant, and when she saw that her outcries did not annoy me, she thought if she could hinder me from communicating, she would cause me the greatest of all annoyance. She was quite right, O Divine Spouse of pure souls, since the only satisfaction of my life was to receive you and to honor you. I suffered a species of languor when I was some days without receiving you. When I was unable, I contented myself with keeping some hours near you, and, in order to have liberty for it, I applied myself to perpetual adoration. I procured, as far as I was able, that the churches should be well adorned. I gave the most beautiful things I had to make the ornaments. I contributed the most I could to provide silver ciboires and chalices. I founded a perpetual lamp, in order that its immortal flame should be a sign that I did not wish the fire of my love ever to become extinct. I said to you, O my Love, "Let me be your victim, consume me utterly, reduce me to ashes, and spare nothing to annihilate me." I felt an inclination that I cannot express, to be nothing. This maid then knew my affection for the Holy Sacrament, before which, when I could freely, I passed many hours on my knees. She took care to watch every day she thought I communicated. She came to tell my mother-in-law and my husband, who wanted nothing more to get into a rage against me. There were reprimands which continued the whole day. If any word of justification escaped me, or any vexation at what they said to me, it was ground enough for their saying that I committed sacrilege, and crying out against devotion. If I answered nothing, that increased their bitterness. They said the most stinging things possible to me. If I fell ill, which happened often enough, they took the opportunity to come and wrangle with me in my bed, saying it was my communions and my prayers made me ill; as if to receive you, O true Source of all good, could cause any ill!

This maid told me one day, in her passion, that she was going to write to the person she thought to be my director, in order that he should hinder me from communicating, and that he did not know me. When she saw I did not answer her, she cried with all her might that I ill-treated her, and that I despised her. When I went out to go to the Mass, although I had previously given orders about household things, she went and told my husband I had gone out, and that I had not arranged anything. When I returned, I had to put up with much. They would not listen to any of my reasons, and declared them to be lies. On the other hand, my mother-in-law persuaded my sick husband that I let everything be destroyed, and that, if she did not take care of them, he would be ruined. He believed her, and I patiently bore everything, endeavoring to do my duty to my best. What was most painful to me was, not to know what measure to adopt; for when I ordered anything without her, she complained I had no consideration for her, that I did everything in my own way, and that things were very bad; then she ordered them differently. If I asked her what should be done, she said that she had to bear the burden of all.

I had hardly any rest but that I found, O my God, in love of your will, and in submission to its orders, although they were full of rigor for me. My words and my actions were ceaselessly watched, in order to find ground for chiding me. As soon as there was the least ambiguity in them, they were converted into crimes. I was ridiculed the whole day, the same things being incessantly repeated, and that, in the presence of servants. What made me greatly suffer was, that for some time I had a weakness that I could not conquer, which God left me for my humiliation; this was weeping, so that it made me the talk of the house. With all my heart I willed all that was done to me, and yet I could not keep back my tears, which overwhelmed me with confusion, and doubled my crosses; for it increased their anger. How many times have I made my meal of my tears, which appeared the most criminal in the world! They said I should be damned; as if tears had dug hell! they would be more suited to extinguish it. If I repeated anything I had heard, they tried to make me responsible for the truth of those things. If I kept silence; it was through scorn and ill-temper. If I knew anything and did not tell; it was a crime. If I told it; I had invented it. Sometimes I was tormented several days in succession without being given any respite. The maids said I ought to play the invalid in order to be left in quiet. I answered nothing; for Love pressed me so closely that he would not I should relieve myself by a single word, nor even by a look.

Although I extremely loved my father, and he also loved me very tenderly, I never spoke of my crosses to him. A relative, who loved me much, perceived the want of kindness with which I was treated. Even in his presence very hurtful things were said to me. He went, very indignant, to tell my father, adding that I made them no answer, and I would pass for a stupid. I afterwards went to see my father, and he reproved me, contrary to his usual practice, rather sharply, because I allowed them to treat me as they did, without saying anything— that everyone ridiculed me for it; that it seemed I had not the spirit to answer. I replied to my father, that if people observed what my husband said to me, it was confusion enough for me, without bringing more upon myself by my answers; that if it was not remarked, I ought not to bring it into prominence, nor make everybody see the weak point of my husband; that by not saying a word, I stopped all dispute, whereas I should keep it up by my replies. My father, who was very good, told me I did well; that I should continue to act as God would inspire me. He never afterwards spoke to me of it.

What made me most suffer, was that they continually spoke to me against my father, for whom I had as much respect as tenderness, and against my relatives and those I thought highly of. I was much more pained by this than by all that was said against me. I could not keep myself from defending them, and in that I did ill; for what I said only served to embitter them more. If any one complained of my father or my relatives, he was always right, and those who previously to their mind were most unreasonable persons, were approved, as soon as they spoke against my connections. When any one declared himself my friend, he was no longer welcome. I had a relation whom I much loved, because of her piety. When she came to see me, she was either openly told to go back again, or she was treated in such a way she was obliged to do it. That pained me extremely. If there was anything true or false against me, or against my relatives, it was used to reproach me with. When any person out of the common came, they spoke against me, to people who had never seen me, which greatly astonished them; but when they had seen me, they did nothing but pity me.

The crosses would have appeared to me a trifling matter if, drawn to it as I felt myself, I had had freedom to pray and to be alone; but I was compelled to remain in their presence, under a subjection that was not conceivable. My husband looked at his watch if I was more than half an hour at prayer, and, when I exceeded it, he was vexed. I said to him sometimes, "Give me an hour to divert myself; I will employ it as I please;" but he would not give it to me for praying, although he would have given it to me for diversion, had I wished. I confess my lack of experience has caused me much trouble, and that I have thereby often given occasion for their making me suffer; for, in short, was I not bound to see my captivity as an effect of your will, O my God, to be content with it, and to make of it my sole prayer; but I often fell back into the paltriness of wishing to take time for praying, which was not agreeable to my husband. It is true these faults were more frequent at the commencement; afterwards I prayed God at his bedside, and did not go out any more.

CHAPTER XVII

◆—◆

WE went to the country, where I committed many faults, allowing myself to be too much carried away by my interior attraction. I thought I could do so, because my husband was amusing himself in building. He was, nevertheless, dissatisfied with it, for I left him too long without going to see him where he was, because he was constantly speaking to the workmen. I used to place myself in a corner, where I worked. I could hardly do anything from the strength of the attraction, which made the work fall from my hands. I passed hours in this way, without being able either to open my eyes or know what was going on in me, which was so simple, so peaceful, so sweet, that I sometimes said to myself, "Is heaven more peaceful than I?" I told nobody my dispositions, for they had nothing by which they could be distinguished. I could not tell anything of them; all passed in the inmost of the soul, and the will enjoyed what I cannot express.

As it was with difficulty I ordinarily had any time for praying, in order not to disobey my husband, who was unwilling I should rise from bed before seven o'clock, I bethought me I had only to kneel upon my bed, which, because he was ill, was in his room, as I endeavored to show him my attention in everything. I rose at four o'clock, and remained on my bed. He thought I slept, and did not perceive it; but this affected my health and did me harm, for as my eyes were heavy from the small-pox I had had only eight months before, and which had left a serious affection of the eyes, this want of sleep made me unable to pray without falling asleep, and I did not sleep a moment in quiet, as I was apprehensive of not waking up. After dinner I went to pray my half-hour, and, though I was in no way sleepy, I fell asleep at once. I disciplined myself with nettles to keep awake, without being able to succeed.

If I could tell in detail the providences you had for me, which were continual, and threw me into astonishment, there would be material to fill volumes. You made me find providences quite ready for writing to Mother Granger when I was most pressed with troubles, and I felt strong instincts to go out sometimes to the gate, where I found a messenger from her, who brought me a letter that could not otherwise have reached my hands.

I had great confidence in Mother Granger. I concealed from her none of my sins nor of my troubles. I would not have done the least thing without telling it to her. I practiced no austerities but those she permitted me. It was only my interior dispositions I could not tell, because I knew not how to explain them, being very ignorant of these things from never having read or heard of them. My confessor and my husband forbade me anew to see her. It was almost impossible for me to obey, because I had very great crosses, and sometimes some little expression escaped me through infidelity, when nature was so sorely oppressed. This little word brought upon me so many crosses, I thought I had committed great faults; in such confusion was I. I carried within me a continual condemnation of myself, so that I regarded my crosses as defects, and believed I brought them on myself. I knew not how to unravel all this, nor how to remedy it; for oftentimes an involuntary forgetful-ness gave rise to dissatisfaction of several weeks. I made a pretext of going to see my father, and I ran to Mother Granger; but as soon as this was discovered there were crosses that I cannot express, for it would be difficult to tell the excess to which their anger against me proceeded. The difficulty of writing to her was not less, for, as I had an extreme horror of lies, I forbade the lackeys lying; and when they were met they were asked where they went, whether they did not carry letters. My mother-in-law took up her position in a little porch, so that none could go out of the house without her seeing them, and their passing near her. She used to ask them where they went, and what they were carrying. It had to be told her, and when she knew I had written to Mother Granger, there was a terrible commotion.

Sometimes when going on foot to the Benedictines, I had shoes brought, that it might not be seen where I had been, for it was far; but all my precautions were useless, for I dared not go alone, and those who followed me had orders to tell wherever I went. If they failed in it, they were punished or sent away.

They constantly spoke evil to me of this holy woman, whom in their hearts they esteemed; but God willed I should be in continual trouble and contradiction, for as I loved her much, I could not hinder myself from defending and speaking well of her; and this threw them into such anger, they watched still more closely to hinder me from going to see her. I, however, did all I could to please them. It was my constant study, without being able to succeed in it, and as I believed devotion consisted in pleasing them, I was in despair and angry with myself for all the torment they caused me, thinking it was my fault. One of the greatest troubles is to believe a thing to be a matter of duty, and to labor incessantly to do it, without, however, being able to succeed. It is the course of guidance you have observed with me, O my God, so long as I was keeping house. I sometimes complained of it to Mother Granger, who said to me, "How should you content them, since for more than twenty years I am doing what I can for that purpose without being able to succeed?" for as my mother-in-law had two daughters in her convent, she found fault with everything.

The cross I felt most was to see my son revolt against me, whom they inspired with such a scorn for me, I could not see him without dying of grief. When I was in my room with any of my friends, he was sent to listen to what I said; and as the child saw it pleased them, he invented a hundred things to go and tell them. What caused me the most pain was the loss of this child, with whom I had taken extreme trouble. If I surprised him in a lie, which often happened, I dared not reprove him. He told me, "My grandmother says you have been a greater liar than I." I answered him, "It is because I have been so I better know the odiousness of this vice and the difficulty of freeing one's self from it; and it is for this very reason that I will not suffer it in you." He used to say very offensive things to me, and, because he observed the deference I had for his grandmother and his father, when in their absence I wished to reprove him for anything, he reproached me that I wanted to play the mistress because they were not there. They approved all this in the child, so that it strengthened him in his evil dispositions. One day this child went to see my father, and indiscreetly wished to speak of me to my father, as he used to his grandmother. My father was moved to tears, and came to the house to beg they would punish him; but nothing was done, though they promised my father. I had not the strength to chastise him. Similar scenes often happened, and as the child grew bigger, and there was every probability his father would not live, I feared the consequences of so bad an education. I told it to Mother Granger, and she consoled me, and said that, as I could not remedy it, I must suffer it and surrender all to God; that this child would be my cross.

Another of my troubles was that I could not see my attention to my husband was pleasing to him. I knew well I displeased him when I was not there; but when I was he never showed any sign that he was pleased at it, nor at what I did. On the contrary, he had nothing but repugnance for everything that came from me. I sometimes trembled when I approached him, for I well knew I should do nothing to his taste; and if I did not come near him, he complained of it. He was so disgusted with broths, he could not look at them, and those who brought them to him were ill received. Neither my mother-in-law nor any of the servants was willing to bring them, for fear of suffering from his vexation. I was the only one who did not refuse. I used to go and carry them to him, and let his anger exhaust itself; then I endeavored pleasantly to induce him to take them, and when he got more angry, I patiently waited; then I said to him, "I prefer being scolded many times in the day to doing you harm by not bringing you what is necessary for you." Sometimes he took them; at other times he pushed them away; but, as he saw my perseverance, he was often constrained to take them. When he was in good humor, and I brought him something that would have been agreeable, my mother-in-law took it out of my hands in order to carry it to him; and as he thought I did not attend to these things, he was annoyed with me, and gave his mother great thanks. Love hindered me from saying anything, and I suffered all in silence. I used all my efforts to win my mother-in-law, through my attentions, my presence, my services; yet I was not clever enough to succeed. O my God, how wearisome without you would be a life like that! This conduct I have just mentioned has always continued, with the exception of some very short intervals, which served only to make things harder and more felt by me.

CHAPTER XVIII

——— ◆●▶ ———

IT was eight or nine months after I had the small-pox that Father La Combe passed by the place of my residence. He came to the house, bringing me a letter from Father La Mothe, who asked me to see him, as he was a friend of his. I had much hesitation whether I should see him, because I greatly feared new acquaintances. However, the fear of offending Father La Mothe led me to do it. This conversation, which was short, made him desire to see me once more. I felt the same wish on my side; for I believed he either loved God or was quite prepared to love him, and I wished everybody to love him. God had already made use of me to win three monks of his order. The eagerness he had to see me again led him to come to our country house, which was only half a league from the town. Providence made use of a little accident that happened, to give me the means of speaking to him; for as my husband, who greatly enjoyed his cleverness, was conversing with him, he felt ill, and having gone into the garden, my husband told me to go and look for him, lest anything might have occurred. I went there. This Father said that he had remarked a concentration and such an extraordinary presence of God on my countenance, that he said to himself, "I have never seen a woman like that;" and this was what made him desire to see me again. We conversed a little, and you permitted, O my God, that I said to him things which opened to him the way of the interior. God bestowed upon him so much grace, through this miserable channel, that he has since declared to me he went away changed into another man. I preserved a root of esteem for him, for it appeared to me he would be God's; but I was very far from foreseeing that I should ever go to a place where he would be.

Although the love of the cross was so great in me it made me languish when the cross was absent, no sooner did it return to me, that lovable cross, object of my desires and of my hopes, than it concealed from me its beauties to show me only its rigors, so that the cross was keenly felt by me; and, as soon as I committed any fault, God deprived me of it anew, and then it appeared to me in all its beauty, and I could not console myself for not having given it the reception it merited. I then felt myself burning with love for it. It returned, that amiable cross, with so much the more force, as my desire was the more vehement. I could not reconcile two things that appeared to me so much opposed—to desire the cross with so much ardor, and to support it with so much difficulty. These alternations render it a thousand times more felt, for the spirit adapts itself gradually to the cross, and when it commences to bear it strongly, it is taken away for a little time, in order that its return may surprise and overwhelm it. Moreover, when one bears the cross uniformly, one rests upon it, and one even becomes so accustomed to it that it does not occasion so much pain, for the cross has something noble and delicate, which furnishes a great support to the soul.

What caused me most trouble in this time of confusion and crucifixion without and within, was an inconceivable tendency to hastiness, and when any answer a trifle too sharp escaped me, which served not a little to humiliate me, I was told I was in mortal sin. Nothing less than this rigorous guidance, O my God, was needed with me, for I was so proud, so hasty, and naturally so contradictory in temper, wishing always to prevail, and thinking my reasons better than those of others, that if you had spared me those hammer-blows, you would never have polished me to your taste; for I was so vain I was ridiculous. All these crosses were needed to reduce me. Applause made me insupportable. I had the defect of praising my friends to excess, and blaming others without reason.

I bestowed a great deal in charity. You had given me, O my God, so much love for the poor, that I would have liked to supply all their wants. I could not see them in their wretchedness without reproaching myself for my wealth. I deprived myself of what I could in order to succor them. The best that was served me at table was at once removed, owing to the orders I had given, and carried to them. There were hardly any poor in the place where I resided who did not feel the effects of the charity you had given me for them. It seemed, O my God, that you scarcely wanted alms except from me. I was applied to for everything that others refused, and I said to you, "O my Love, it is your wealth; I am only the steward of it; I must distribute it according to your will." I found means of assisting them without letting myself be known, because I had a person who distributed my alms in secret. When there were families ashamed of receiving charity, I sent it to them as if I had owed it to them. I clothed those who were naked, and I had girls taught to earn their livelihood, especially those who were good-looking, in order that, being occupied and having the means of living, they might be saved from the occasion of ruining themselves. I furnished milk for the little children, and particularly at Christmas I redoubled my charities for the little children, in honor of the Child Jesus, who was the center of my love. I went to see the sick—to relieve them, to make their beds. I compounded ointments, and dressed their wounds. I buried the dead. I secretly supplied artisans and shopkeepers with the means of keeping up their shops. It would be hardly possible to carry charity further than our Lord made me carry it, according to my state, both as wife and widow.

Our Lord, in order to purify me more thoroughly from the mixture I might make of his gifts with my "*own*" love, placed me under very severe interior trials. I began to experience that the virtue, which had been so sweet and so easy for me, became an insupportable weight, not that I did not extremely love it, but I found myself powerless to practice it as I had learned it. The more I loved it, the more I struggled to acquire some virtue I saw lacking to me, I fell, it seemed to me, into the very opposite of it. There was only one thing in which you had always afforded me a visible protection—it was chastity. You gave me a very great love for it, and you placed its effects in my soul, putting away, even during my marriage, by providences, sicknesses, and other means, that which might weaken it even innocently; so that, from the second year of my marriage, God so alienated my heart from all sensual pleasures, that marriage has been for me in every way a very severe trial. For many years, it seems to me that my heart and spirit are so separated from my body, that it does things as if it did not do them. If it eats or refreshes itself, it is done with such an aloofness that I am astonished at it, and with an entire mortification of vivacity of sentiment for all natural functions. I believe I say enough to make myself understood.

CHAPTER XIX

To resume the thread of my narrative, I will say that the small-pox had so injured one eye that I feared losing it. A gland at the corner of the eye was relaxed, and from time to time abscesses formed between the nose and the eye, which caused me very great pain until they were lanced. I could not endure the pillow, owing to the excessive swelling of my whole head. The least noise was torture to me, and providence permitted that during this time a very great noise was made in my room. Although this caused me much pain, the time was nevertheless for me a delightful one for two reasons—first, because I was left alone in my bed, where I kept a very sweet retreat; the second, because it gratified the hunger I had for suffering, which was so great that all bodily austerities would have been like a drop of water to extinguish a great fire. I often had my teeth pulled out, although they did not pain me.

It was a refreshment for me, and when my teeth pained me I did not think of having them pulled out; on the contrary, they became my good friends, and I was regretful of losing them without pain. I once poured molten lead on my naked flesh, but it did not cause any pain, because it flowed off and did not stick. In sealing letters I let Spanish wax fall on me, and this causes more pain, because it sticks. When I held a candle, I let it come to an end and burn me for a long time. These are not crosses, nor pains. Our own choice can cause us only light crosses. It is for you. O my Crucified Love, to cut them after your model in order to render them heavy. I do not wonder you are painted in the shop of St. Joseph making crosses. Oh, how skilful you are at this work!

I asked leave to go to Paris to have my eye treated, much less, however, for that reason than to see M. Bertot, whom Mother Granger had a little before given me as director, and who was a man of profound illumination. It was then decided I should go to Paris. I went to say farewell to my father, and he embraced me with very great tenderness. He did not think, any more than I, it was for the last time. Paris was no longer for me a place to be dreaded. The world served only to make me concentrated, and the noise of the streets increased my prayer. I saw M. Bertot, who was not as useful to me as he would have been if at that time I had had the gift of explaining myself; but God so conducted me that, whatever desire I had to conceal nothing, I could not tell him anything. As soon as I spoke to him, everything was taken away from my mind, and I could only remember some defects I told him. My inner disposition was too simple to be able to tell anything of it, and as I saw him very seldom, and nothing dwelt in my mind, and I read nothing similar to what I experienced, I knew not how to explain myself; besides, I desired to let him know only the evil that was in me, for which reason M. Bertot has never known me until after his death. This has been very useful for me, in depriving me of all support, and making me die to myself.

I resolved, after having seen M. Bertot, and finished my cure, to go and pass the ten days from Ascension to Pentecost in an abbey four leagues from Paris, the Abbess of which had much friendship for me. I thought I should there conveniently keep a retreat of ten days. I had at that time an extremely strong interior attraction, and it seemed to me, O my God, that my union with you was continual. I experienced that it constantly grew deeper and withdrew from the sensible, becoming more simple, but at the same time closer and more intimate.

On the Day of St. Erasmus, the patron of that convent, at four in the morning, I awoke with a start, having a vivid impression my father was dead. I had no rest till I had prayed for him as for one dead, and, having done it, I was no more troubled; but there remained with me a strong conviction of his death, together with an extreme prostration and a pleasing grief, which so overwhelmed my body that it was reduced to very great weakness. I went to the church, where I no sooner was than a faint seized me, and, after I recovered, there remained a loss of voice, and I could not speak. I could not eat the smallest thing—the concentration and the grief were too powerful. My soul was in a divine contentment and strength, and my exterior was overwhelmed with grief and weakness. I should not have perceived any grief, so great was the contentment of my soul, if it had not made this powerful impression on my body.

After dinner, while I was with the Abbess, whom I told I had very strong presentiments my father was very ill, if not dead—we were conversing together a little about you, O my God, although I could hardly speak, so powerfully was I seized within and prostrated without—they came to tell her she was wanted in the parlor. It was a man who had come in haste, sent by my husband, because my father had fallen ill, and as he was so only twelve hours, he was dead when the man arrived. The Abbess came and told me, "Here is a letter from your husband, who sends you word your father is seriously ill." I said to her, "He is dead, Madame; I cannot doubt it." I sent at once to Paris to hire a carriage, in order to travel more quickly. Mine was waiting for me half-way. I started at nine o'clock in the evening. They said that I would be lost, for I had with me no one I knew. I had sent my maid to Paris to put everything in order, and, as I was in a religious house, I had not kept lackeys with me. The Abbess told me that, since I believed my father dead, it was rashness for me to expose myself in this way; that carriages with difficulty passed, even the road I must follow not being

marked out. I replied that it was for me an indispensable duty
to go and succor my father; that I ought not, for a simple
presentiment, to excuse myself from this duty. I set out then
alone, abandoned to providence, with persons strangers to
me. My weakness was so great that I could not support myself
at the back of the carriage, and I had often to get out, in spite
of my weakness, in consequence of the dangerous state of the
road. In this way I had to pass by night through a forest
which is a cut-throat place. I was still in it as midnight struck.
That forest is celebrated for the murders and robberies which
have been there committed. The boldest persons feared it. As
for me, O my God, I could not fear anything. The abandonment I was in to your care made me so utterly forget myself,
that I could not reflect upon all this. Oh, what fears and
vexations does a soul that is abandoned spare herself!

I travelled, then, within five leagues of our residence by
myself, with my grief and my Love as companions; but at this
place I found my confessor and a female relative, who were
waiting for me. I could not tell the trouble I suffered when I
say my confessor; for besides that, while quite alone, I tasted
an inexplicable contentment, he, having no knowledge of my
state, opposed it, and gave me no freedom. My grief was of a
nature that I could not shed a tear, and I was ashamed at
learning a thing I knew only too well, without giving any
external sign of grief and shedding tears. The peace I possessed
within was so profound that it spread over my countenance.
Moreover, the state I was in did not permit me to speak, nor
perform those external acts which are ordinarily expected from
persons of piety. I could only love and keep silent.

I arrived at home, and found they had already buried my
father, owing to the great heat. It was ten o'clock at night.
Every one was already dressed in mourning. I had traveled
thirty leagues in one day and one night. As I was very weak,
as well because my state undermined me, as because I had not
taken food, I was at once put to bed. About two hours after
midnight my husband got up, and having left my room, he
suddenly returned, crying, with all his strength, "My daughter is dead!" It was my only daughter, a child as much loved as
she was amiable. You had provided her, O my God, with so
many graces, spiritual and corporal, that one must have been

insensible not to love her. There was noticeable in her a quite extraordinary love for God. She was constantly found in corners in prayer. As soon as she perceived that I prayed to God, she came near me to pray, and when she knew I had done it without her, she wept bitterly, and said, "You pray to God, and I do not pray to him." As my concentration was great, as soon as I was at liberty I used to close my eyes, and she used to say to me, "You sleep?" then suddenly, "Oh, it is you are praying to my good Jesus!" and place herself near me to pray. She oftentimes suffered the whip of her grandmother, because she said she would never have any other Spouse than our Lord, without their being able to make her say otherwise. She was pure and modest as a little angel, very sweet and obedient. Her father, to test her obedience, gave her very nasty things to eat, and she ate them, in spite of her dislike, without saying anything. She was very beautiful, and had a very good figure. Her father loved her with passion, and she was very dear to me, much more for the qualities of her soul than for those of her body. I regarded her as my sole consolation on earth, for she had as much attachment for me as her brother had alienation.

She died of an unseasonable blood-letting. But what am I saying? She died by the hand of Love, who wished to despoil me of all. There remained to me only the son of my sorrow. He fell mortally ill. God gave him back to the prayers of Mother Granger, my only consolation after God. The news of the death of my daughter surprised me very much. My heart was, nevertheless, not shaken, although I saw myself deprived at the same time, without my having known it, of my father and my daughter, who were how dear to me, you know, O my God. My interior state was such that I could not be either more afflicted for all imaginable losses, nor more content for all possible blessings. It is necessary to have experienced these delicious griefs to comprehend them. I no more wept the daughter than the father. All I could say was, "You had given her to me, Lord. It pleases you to take her back. She was yours." My father and my daughter died in the month of July, 1672.

The eve of the Magdalen's Day of the same year, Mother Granger sent me—I know not by what inspiration—a little

contract already drawn up. She told me to fast that day and
to bestow some extraordinary alms, and next morning, the
Magdalen's Day, to go and communicate with a ring on my
finger, and when I had returned home to go into my closet,
where there was an image of the Holy Child Jesus in the arms
of his holy mother, and to read my contract at his feet, sign it,
and put my ring to it. The contract was this: "I, N——,
promise to take for my Spouse Our Lord, the Child, and to
give myself to him for spouse, though unworthy." I asked of
him, as dowry of my spiritual marriage, crosses, scorn, confusion, disgrace, and ignominy; and I prayed him to give me the
grace to enter into his dispositions of littleness and annihilation, with something else. This I signed; after which I no
longer regarded him but as my Divine Husband. Oh, how
that day has been since for me a day of grace and of crosses!

Since that time crosses have not been spared me, and although I had had many previously, I may say they were only
the shadow of those that I have had to suffer in the sequel.
As soon as crosses gave me any moment of respite, I said to
you, "O my dear Spouse, I must enjoy my dowry; give me back
my cross." You oftentimes granted my request. At other times
you made me wait for it, and ask more than once, and I then
saw I had rendered myself unworthy of it through some
infidelity towards this same cross. When the overwhelming
and abandonment were more severe, you sometimes consoled
me, but ordinarily my nourishment was a desolation without
consolation.

The Day of the Assumption of the Virgin, the same year
1672, I was in a strange desolation, whether owing to the
redoubling of the exterior or the overwhelming of the interior
crosses, and I had gone to hide myself in my closet to give
some outlet to my grief. I said to you, "My God and my
Spouse, you alone know the greatness of my trouble." There
occurred to me a certain wish, "Oh, if M. Bertot knew what I
suffer!" M. Bertot, who rarely wrote, and even with considerable trouble, wrote me a letter of this very date on the
cross—the most beautiful and the most consoling he has written on that subject. It must be noted he was more than a
hundred leagues from where I was. Sometimes I was so
overwhelmed, and nature so distracted by the continual crosses,

which gave me no respite, or, if they seemed to give me an instant of repose, it was only to return with more fury, and nature was sometimes at such a point from them that, when alone, I perceived without paying attention to it, that my eyes turned from side to side as if distracted, seeking if they could not find some relief. A word, a sigh, a trifle, or to know that some one sympathized in my grief, would have relieved me; but this was not granted to me; not even to look towards the heaven, or make a complaint. Love held me then so close, that he willed that this miserable nature should be allowed to perish without giving it any food. It would have sometimes wished relief, and wished it with so much violence, that I suffered infinitely more in restraining it than from all the rest.

You gave my soul, O my dear Love, a victorious support, which made her triumph over the weaknesses of nature, and you even put the knife into her hand to destroy it without giving it a moment's respite; yet this nature is so malignant, so full of artifices to preserve its life, that at last it took on the rôle of nourishing itself from its despair. It found succor in the absence of all succor. This faithfulness during so continual an overwhelming served it for secret food—a fact which it concealed with an extreme care, in order not to be discovered; but your divine eyes were too penetrating not to discover its malignity. It is for this reason, O my Divine Shepherd, you changed your conduct towards it. You consoled it for a time with your crook and your staff; that is to say, by your conduct, as loving as it was crucifying; but it was only to reduce it to the last extremities, as I shall tell.

CHAPTER XX

A LADY that I sometimes used to see, as she was wife of the governor of our town, had taken a liking to me, because, she said, my person and my manners did not displease her. She sometimes told me that she therein noticed something extraordinary. I believe this great attraction I had within shone out upon my exterior; for there was one day a man of the world, who said to an aunt of my husband, "I have seen your niece, but one clearly perceives she never loses the presence of God," which, having been reported to me, greatly surprised me, for I did not think he understood what it was to have God present in this way. This lady, I say, began to be touched by God, because once, when she wished to take me to the comedy, I was not willing to go; for I never used to go to it, and I made use of the continued illness of my husband for an excuse. She strongly pressed me, and said a continued illness like that ought not to hinder me from diverting myself; that my age was not such that I should confine myself to being a nurse. I explained to her the reasons I had for behaving so, but she concluded it was rather through a principle of piety I did not go, than because of my husband's illness, and, having strongly urged me to tell her my opinion on the subject of comedy, I told her I did not approve of this diversion, especially for women truly Christian. As she was much older than I, what I said to her made so strong an impression on her mind that she never afterwards went to the comedy.

Once, being with her and with another lady, who spoke much and had even studied the Fathers, they engaged in a conversation where there was much talk of God. The lady spoke of him learnedly. I said hardly anything, for I was drawn to keep silence, being even grieved at this manner of speaking of God. The lady, my friend, came to see me next day, and told me God had so powerfully touched her, she could no longer resist. I ascribed it to the conversation of the other lady, but she said to me, "Your silence had something that spoke to me, even to the depth of the soul, and I could not enjoy what she was saying to me." On this we spoke with open hearts. It was then, O my God, that you so entered into the depth of her heart, that you never after withdrew up to her death. She continued so a-hungered for you, O my God, that she could not bear to hear anything else spoken of. As you wished her to be entirely yours, at the end of three months you took from her her husband, whom she loved extraordinarily, and by whom she was greatly loved. You sent her crosses so terrible and at the same time graces so strong, that you made yourself absolute master of her heart. After the death of her husband, and the loss of almost all her wealth, she came to within four leagues of us, to an estate she still had. She obtained my husband's consent for me to go and spend eight days with her, to console her for her losses. God gave her, through my means, all that was necessary for her. She had much cleverness. She was astonished that I said to her things so far above my grasp. I should have been myself surprised at it if I had reflected, for my natural intellect was not capable of those things. It was you, O my God, who gave them to me for her sake, making the waters of your grace flow into her soul without considering the unworthiness of the channel which you willed to use. Since that time her soul has been the temple of the Holy Spirit, and our hearts have been united by an indissoluble bond.

As my husband's ailments became every day severer and more obstinate, he resolved to go to Ste. Reine, for which he had a great devotion. He appeared to me to have a great desire of being alone with me, so that he could not help saying, "If people never spoke to me against you, I should be more pleased and you more happy." I committed many faults from self-love and self-consciousness of this journey, and as I was in a very great interior abandonment, I had the means of experiencing what I should be without you, O my God. For some time already you had withdrawn from me that sweet interior correspondence, which previously I had only to follow; I had become like one astray, who no longer found either way, path, or route, but as I reserve for another place a description of the terrible darkness through which I have passed, I will continue the course of the narrative. My husband, on his return from Ste. Reine, wished to pass by St. Edme, for, as he had no children but my eldest son, who was often at the gates of death, and he wished extremely to have heirs, he urgently asked for them through the intercession of that saint. As for me, I could ask for nothing; but he was heard, and God gave me a second son. The time when I was near my confinement was for me one of great consolation; for, although I was very ill at my confinement, the love I had for the cross made me face it with pleasure. I rejoiced that nature must suffer so much; besides, as I was some weeks after my confinement without their venturing to make me speak, owing to my great weakness, it was a time of retreat and silence for me, when I endeavored to compensate myself for the little leisure I had at other seasons for praying to you, O my God, and remaining alone with you.

During my pregnancy, God took a new possession of me. He did not leave me an instant, and those nine months passed in continued uninterrupted enjoyment. As I had already experienced interior trouble, weakness, and desertions, this appeared to me a new life. It seemed to me I already enjoyed blessedness; but how dearly this happy time cost me! since this enjoyment, which appeared to me entire and perfect, and so much the more perfect as it was more inward, more remote from the sensible, more constant, more free from vicissitudes, was yet only preparatory to a total privation for many years, without any support or hope of return.

This terrible state commenced with the death of a person who was my sole consolation, after God. I had, before my return from Ste. Reine, learned that Mother Granger was dead. I declare that this blow was the most severely felt of any I yet had.

As I felt myself utterly deserted inwardly and outwardly, I thought only of the loss I sustained as a person who would have conducted me on a road where I no longer found track nor path. O my God, how well you know how to inflict your blow! You had left me this Mother at a time when she was but little useful to me, since from the care you had of me and your continual guidance of me, except at certain times, I had nothing to do but to follow you step by step, while at the time that you deprived me as to the interior of all perceived guidance, that you overturned my paths, that you blocked my ways with squared stones—it is at this time you took from me her who could guide me in this road, all devious, covered with precipices and sowed with thorns.

O adorable conducting of my God! There must be no guide for him whom you wish to lead astray, no conductor for him whom you wish to destroy. After having saved me with so much mercy, O my Love, after having conducted me by the hand in your paths, it seems that you have been eager for my destruction. Shall not one say of you that you save only to destroy; that you no longer go to seek the lost sheep? You take pleasure in building that which is destroyed and destroying what is built. Therein, then, is the play of your magnificence, and it is in this way you overthrow the temple so carefully and almost miraculously built by the hand of men, to rebuild one that shall not be made by the hand of men!

To increase my exterior crosses, my brother changed towards me, for his hatred was noticed by everybody. His marriage took place at this time, and my husband had the amiability to go to it, although he was ill, and the road so bad and so covered with snow that we were on the point of upsetting more than fifteen times; but my brother, far from being grateful, quarreled more than ever with my husband. I had to suffer from two persons who made me the mark for their vexation. On this occasion all the right was with my husband, and the wrong with my brother. The whole time I was at Orleans, where this wedding took place, I had a remnant of affection so strong that it devoured me. I committed many faults, for I gave way to it too much, remaining too long at church, at the expense of the attention I owed my husband; but I was then so intoxicated with love that I only perceived the fault when the remedy was past. I committed also another, which was in being too expansive in speaking to a Jesuit Father of what I then felt, which was very strong. He was one of those who admire these sorts of things, and as it appeared to do him good, and I felt a great gratification in speaking to him, I gave way to it. It was a notable fault which happened to me sometimes at that period, but never since. Oh, how often one mistakes nature for grace! and how dead to self one must be for these outpourings to be from God!

While returning from Orleans, I had the same preoccupation as in going there, so that, though there was much greater danger on the return, I had no attention for myself, but only for my husband, and on seeing the carriage upsetting, I said to him, "Have no fear; it is on my side it is turning over: you will not be injured." I believe everything might have perished, and I should not have been disturbed, and my peace was so profound nothing could shake it. If these times lasted, one would be too strong, but, as I said, they began to come only very rarely, and for a short period, and to be followed by longer and trying privations. On the return from the wedding, my brother treated me with extreme contempt. As I had had much attachment for him, these blows were keenly felt by me. Since that time he has greatly changed, and has turned towards God, although he has never altered as regards me. I am, however, glad he is reformed. The loss of my brother has been the more felt by me, as he cost me many crosses, both on the part of my husband and of others. I can say the crosses he has caused me and has procured for me since that time have been some of my greatest. It is not that he is not virtuous, but it is an altogether special permission of God and his providence in conducting my soul, which has brought to pass that he and all the other persons of piety who have persecuted me have thought to render glory to God by doing it, and to acquire merits; and they were right; for what greater justice than this, that all creatures should be unfaithful to me, and declare themselves against her who had been so many times unfaithful to her God, and had taken the opposite side?

We had, further, after this, an affair that cost me great crosses, and which seemed to have been brought about simply for that. There was a person who conceived such an ill feeling towards my husband, that he determined to ruin him if he could. The only means he found was to make friends with my brother, in order to induce him to do readily what he wished. He agreed with him to demand from us in the name of Monsieur, the brother of the King, two hundred thousand livres, which he made out my brother and I owed him. My brother signed the documents under an assurance that he should not pay anything of it for his part. I believe his extreme youth engaged him in a business he, perhaps, did not understand. This affair gave so much annoyance to my husband, and justly, that I have reason to believe it greatly hastened his end. He was so indignant with me at this, for which I was no way responsible, that he could not speak to me without anger. He would not instruct me in the matter, and I know not its nature. He said he was not willing to mix himself up in this business, that he was going to hand over my property and leave me to live as I could, and a hundred things still more harsh.

The day it was to be decided, there was one portion of the judges who were both judges and parties. After Mass I felt myself strongly urged to go and see the judges. I was extremely surprised to find that I knew all the twists and niceties of this business, without knowing how I had been able to learn it. The first judge was so surprised to see a thing so different from what he thought, that he himself urged me to go and see the other judges, and especially the Intendant, who was acting uprightly, but who was misinformed. You gave, O my God, so much power to my words for making known the truth, that the Intendant could not sufficiently thank me for having made it known to him. He assured me that if I had not been to speak to him, the affair was lost; and when they saw the falsity of the whole business, they would have condemned the party to the costs, if we had not had to do with so great a Prince, who had only lent his name to officers that had misled him. To save the honor of Monsieur, judgment was given against us for fifty crowns, so that two hundred thousand livres were reduced to one hundred and fifty. My husband was very pleased at what I had done, but my brother appeared to me so angry at it, that if I had caused him a very great loss he could not have been more so.

CHAPTER XXI

ABOUT this time I fell into a state of total privation, very great and very long; in a state of weakness and entire desertion, which lasted near seven years. O grief the most violent of griefs! This heart, which was occupied only with its God, found itself no longer occupied but with the creature. It seemed to be cast down from the throne of God to live, like Nebuchadnezzar, for seven years with the beasts. But before describing this deplorable state, which, through the altogether admirable use Divine Wisdom made of it, was advantageous to me, I must tell the infidelities I committed in it.

As I commenced to lose you, O my God, and to lose you utterly, it appeared to me that I fell each day into the purely natural, and that I no longer loved you at all—a thing which I had only experienced by alternations. For although, before entering into this state, I had experienced long privations, almost continual towards the close, I had however, from time to time, inflowings of your Divinity, so profound and so inward, so quick and so penetrating, that it was easy for me to judge that you were only concealed for me, but not lost. All the times that you returned with greater goodness and power, you returned also with greater magnificence, so that you re-established in a few hours the ruins of my infidelities, and you profusely compensated for my losses; but it was not the same during the whole time of which I am about to speak.

During the other privations my soul continually sought him whom she had lost. But here it is quite the contrary; not only does it appear one no longer loves, but this heart so loving and so beloved finds itself filled only with the love of creatures and of itself. At all the other times one was not deprived of every facility for doing good; though one did it in a languishing and tasteless manner, often even with repugnance, one nevertheless did it; but here it is no longer repugnance, but impotence—an impotence of such a nature that the soul does not know her impotence; it appears only as an unwillingness to do it.

The time of great festivals, of those even for which I had a singular affection, was that when interiorly I was most forsaken. What will appear surprising is that when I communicated, however penetrated by God I might previously be, dryness took the place of abundance, and emptiness that of plenitude. At present I know very well its cause, which was that, as my road was a road of death and of faith, the great festivals and the reception of the Sacrament operated in me according to the designs of God, death, faith, cross, spoliation, annihilation; for our God operates through his mysteries and through his

Sacraments that which he operates through himself, so that if the state is entirely in the sentiments, the Sacraments and the mysteries celebrated at the festivals operate quick and tender sentiments of God. If the state is in light, they operate admirable lights, either active or passive, according to the degree of the soul. If it is faith, they will operate dryness, obscurity, more or less, according to the degree of faith, and so with the rest. They operate crosses, spoliation, annihilation, according to the designs of God for the souls and the degree of each one. It is the same with prayer—it is dry, obscure, crucifying, despoiling, annihilating, etc. Those who complain of prayer (supposing fidelity), and what they experience at the reception of the Sacraments, do it only for want of light; for there is always given to them what is needful for them, although not what they wish and desire. If one was thoroughly convinced of these truths, far from passing all his life in complaining of God and of himself, one would employ it only in making use in death and dying fidelity of all these different dispositions in which God places us, so that by causing death to us they would procure for us life.

I fell then into the purely natural; yet my infidelities were of a kind that would have appeared a good and virtue to any other but to my God, who does not judge virtue by the name people give it, but by the purity and uprightness of the heart that practices it. I felt my inclination grow each day, and that my heart, which previously was occupied and filled with its God alone, was full and occupied only with creatures. I used all sorts of penances, prayers, pilgrimages, and vows. It seemed, O my God, I found an increase of my ill in all that I took as a remedy for it, so that I entered upon an inconceivable desolation. I can say tears became my drink, and grief my nourishment. Whereas your love, O my God, had put in my heart a peace as profound as it seemed unalterable, this inclination brought trouble and confusion into my heart with so much force that I could not resist the violence.

I had two enemies equally powerful, who never gained the victory one over the other, so that they mutually combated with the more obstinacy as the advantage never turned to either side. It was the desire of pleasing you, O my God, and the fear of displeasing you—a leaning of my whole center

towards you, O my supreme Felicity, and an impulse of my
whole self towards the creature; but as this latter was strongly
felt, the other appeared to me only as a thing that was not. I
had within me an executioner, who tormented me without
relaxation. I felt within me a pain that I could never make
understood save by those who have experienced it.

I lost all prayer, being utterly unable to use any. The time
I took for it was filled only with creatures, and quite void of
God. It served only to make me better feel my loss and my
misfortune, because then there was no diversion. I could no
longer mortify myself, and my appetite woke up again for a
thousand things, and when I used them I found therein no
taste; so there remained to me only disgust at having been
unfaithful, without having the satisfaction I had promised
myself. I could not express what I suffered, and the infidelities I committed during this time. I believed myself lost: for all I
had for exterior and interior was taken from me.

What could I do in this state? The heaven was shut for me,
and it seemed to me it was with justice. I could neither console
myself nor complain of it. I had not any creature on earth to
whom I could address myself, and if I wished to address myself
to some saint, besides that I had not any facility, since for
many years I found them only in God, I then found them only
full of the fury of God.

There was no longer for me a God, Husband, Father,
Lover—if I dared to call him so. There was only a rigorous
Judge, whose anger appeared to kindle every day. Oh, if I
had been able to find in the abyss a place to conceal me from
his fury, without withdrawing me from his justice, I would
have availed myself of it. I could no more go to see the poor;
either I forgot them entirely, or I no longer found the time for
it, or I had a disgust for it that amounted to opposition. If I
would do violence to myself, to go to them in spite of my
repugnance, I found myself most part of the time in veritable
impotence. If, in short, I sometimes made an effort to go to
them, I could not remain there a moment, and if I wished to
speak to them, it was impossible for me. When I would force
myself, I said absurdities that had not common sense. I could
no longer remain a moment at church, and whereas formerly it
was torture to me not to have time to pray, my torture then

was to have time and to be obliged to be at church. I neither took in, nor heard anything. The Mass went on without my being able to pay any attention. I sometimes heard several in succession, in order to make up by the one the defect of that which had preceded, but it was still worse. My eyes, which formerly of themselves closed in spite of me, then continued open, without it being possible for me to close them or to concentrate myself a moment.

I sometimes gave way to exterior hastiness, without any power to control myself. I could no longer restrain my tongue. I was like those children who cannot help themselves from falling. I made some verses which were subjects of infidelity for me. I resolved to make no more, but my resolutions were barren. It was enough for me to have formed a resolution, to immediately do the contrary. You deprived me of all facility for carrying it out. I could no longer speak of you, O my God; I envied all those who loved you. Oh, is it possible this heart, all fire, should have become ice; that this heart, so loving, should have fallen into the most utter indifference? It seemed to me at every moment as if hell were about to open to swallow me up, and that which then caused me so much terror would have afterwards been the object of my wishes; for it must be understood I believed myself guilty of all the sins of which I had the sentiments, and as I had the sentiment of all sins. I believed myself to have the reality. I could not believe, O my God, that you should ever pardon me. Everything was so effaced from my mind that I no longer regarded myself but as a victim destined to hell. The illness I previously endured with pleasure became insupportable to me. A slight headache made me shudder; I felt in myself only movements of impatience. In place of that peace of paradise there was a trouble of hell. Formerly I rejoiced before my lying-in because I must suffer in it, and then I feared the shadow of pain.

CHAPTER XXII

———◆●◆———

BUT before speaking further of a state which was only commencing, and the course of which has been so long and
trying, I must resume where I stopped; and understand, that
all I shall hereafter tell was accompanied by the state of which
I have just spoken. As my husband approached his end, his
ailments were without relaxation. He no sooner escaped from
one illness than he fell into another: gout, fever, gravel,
succeeded each other incessantly. He suffered great pain
with considerable patience. He offered it to you, my God,
and made a good use of it. The anger he had against me
increased, because they multiplied reports, and did nothing
but embitter him. He was the more susceptible of these impressions as his ailments gave him the greater tendency to vexation.
Even that maid who tormented me sometimes took compassion on me, and came to fetch me as soon as I had gone into my
closet, saying, "Come to monsieur, in order that your mother-
in-law may not speak any more against you." I pretended to be
ignorant of all, but he could not conceal from me his annoyance, nor even endure me. My mother-in-law at the same time
no longer observed any measure, and all those who came to
the house were witnesses of the continual rudeness to which
I was subjected. What is surprising is that though I had the
sentiments of which I have spoken, and the pains I have
described and shall describe, I nevertheless suffered with
much patience; but this did not appear to me, owing to the
frightful revolt I felt within against all that was said to me,
and as I sometimes broke out in hastiness, but seldom, I
thought that this joined to the inward revolt was a crime.

My husband, some time before his death, had built a chapel
in the country where we spent part of the summer. I had the

advantage of hearing Mass every day, and communicating, but not daring to do it every day openly, the priest kept a wafer without their noticing it, and as soon as they had gone out, he gave me the Communion. The dedication of this little chapel was celebrated, and though I already was beginning to enter upon the state I have just described, as soon as the blessing was commenced, suddenly I felt myself seized within, and my seizure, which lasted more than five hours, the whole time of the ceremony, was that our Lord made a new consecration of me to himself. This chapel was only the figure of that one which our Lord made in me; but in a manner so powerful, so real, though very inward, that it seems to me I was for him a temple consecrated for time and for eternity. I said to you, "O my God, let this temple never be profaned"—speaking of both one and the other—"and let your praises be sung there for ever." It seems you promised it to me, although everything was at once taken away, and there did not remain even a memory that could console me.

When I was at this country house, which was only a small pleasure house, before the chapel was built, I used to pray in the woods and in closets. As I greatly loved the cross, I caused crosses to be put up in my places, and these served me as a hermitage.

As I became pregnant of my daughter, and it was thought I should die, I was for some time spared a little; for I was so extraordinarily ill the doctors had given me over. After having passed twelve years and four months in the crosses of marriage, as great as could be—except poverty, which I have never experienced, at least, that of worldly goods, though I have much desired it—you withdrew me from them, O my God, in the manner I am about to tell, to give me heavier ones to bear, and of a nature such as I had never experienced. I will say beforehand that in the great troubles I was subjected to, and when I was told I was in mortal sin, I had not a person in the world to speak to. I would have wished to have had some one as witness of my conduct; but I had none, being without any support, either confessor, director, friend, or councillor. I had lost all; and after, my God, you had deprived me of all, one after the other, you yourself also withdrew. I remained without a creature, and for crown of desolation, without you, my God, who alone could sustain me in so strange a state.

My husband's ailment became every day more obstinate, and he himself had a presentiment of death. His mind was made up for it, for the languishing life he led became every day more burdensome to him. To his other ailments was added a disgust for all kinds of nourishment, so great that he did not even take the things necessary for life. The little he took, there was no one but I had the courage to force on him. The doctors advised him to go to the country for change of air. The first few days he was there he appeared to be better, when suddenly he was seized by a colic and continued fever. I was well prepared for anything it might please Providence to ordain; for I saw some time back he could hardly live longer. His patience increased with his illness, and his illness was very crucifying for me; yet the good use he made of it softened all my troubles. I was extremely pained that my mother-in-law kept me away from his bedside as much as she could, and influenced him against me. I much feared he might die in this feeling, and it afflicted me extremely. I seized a moment, when my mother-in-law was not there, and approaching his bed, I knelt down and said to him, that if I had done anything which had displeased him, I asked his pardon. I begged him to believe it was not voluntarily. He appeared much touched, and as if he had recovered from a profound stupor, he said to me—what he had never said before—"It is I who ask your pardon. I did not deserve you." From this time not only had he no longer a dislike to see me, but he gave me advice as to what I should do after his death. He was eight days very resigned and patient; although, owing to the gangrene which increased, they cut him up with a lancet. I sent to Paris to fetch the best surgeon, but he was dead when he arrived.

It would be impossible to die with more Christian dispositions or courage than he did, after having received all the Sacraments in an edifying manner. I was not there when he died, for he had made me withdraw, not through hostility, but through tenderness, and he was more than twenty hours unconscious at the last. I believe, O my God, that you delayed his death only for my sake, for he was entirely eaten up with gangrene while he yet lived. You willed he should die on the eve of Magdalen's Day, in order to make me see I must be wholly yours. Every year on the Magdalen's Day I used to renew the contract I had made with you, my Lord, and I found myself free to renew it for good. I was at once enlightened that there was much mystery therein. It was the morning of the 21st of July, 1676, he died. The evening, when alone in my room in full daylight, I perceived a warm shade pass near me. The next day I went into my closet, where was the image of my dear and divine Spouse, Jesus Christ. I renewed my marriage, and I added to it a vow of chastity. After that a great interior joy seized me, which was the more novel to me as for a long time I had been in bitterness. It seemed to me our Lord wished to grant me some favor. Immediately I had a very great interior certainty that at the instant our Lord delivered my husband from purgatory. I have never since doubted it for a moment; although I have tried to be diffident. Some years after, Mother Granger appeared to me in a dream, and said to me: "Rest assured that our Lord, for the love he bears you, has delivered your husband from purgatory on the Magdalen's Day. He, however, entered heaven on the day of St. James, the 25th, which was his first day."

As soon as I learned my husband had expired, I said to you, "O my God, you have broken my bonds. I will offer to you a sacrifice of praise." After that I remained in a very great silence, exterior and interior; silence, however, dry and without support. I could neither weep nor speak. My mother-in-law said very beautiful things, at which everyone was edified, and they were scandalized at my silence, which was put down to want of resignation. A monk told me that every one admired the beautiful behavior of my mother-in-law; that as for me, they did not hear me say anything—that I must offer my loss to God. But it was impossible for me to say a single word, whatever effort I made. I was, besides, much prostrated, for although I had recently given birth to my daughter, I nevertheless watched my husband without leaving his room the twenty-four nights he was ill. I was more than a year in recovering from the fatigue of that. The prostration of body and the prostration of my spirit, the dryness and stupidity I was in, made me unable to speak. I, however, for some moments was in admiration at your goodness, O my God, which had set me free exactly on the day I had taken you for Spouse. I saw that crosses would not be wanting to me since my mother-in-law had survived my husband; and I could not understand your conduct, O my God, which, while setting me free, had yet more strongly bound me by giving me two children immediately before the death of my husband. This surprised me extremely, my God, that you set me at liberty only by making me captive. I have since learned that you had by your wisdom provided for me a means of being afterwards the plaything of your providence, for had I had only my eldest son, I would have placed him at college, and myself become a nun at the Benedictines. I should thereby have withdrawn myself from your designs regarding me.

I wished to mark the esteem I had for my husband by giving him the most magnificent burial that ever took place in the neighborhood, at my own expense. I also paid out of my own money the pious legacies he wished to make. My mother-in-law strongly opposed herself to everything I could do to secure my interests. I remained without any help; for my brother was very far from espousing my cause. I had no one from whom I could openly ask counsel. I knew nothing about business; but you, O my God, who, independently of my natural intellect, have always made me fit for all that it has pleased you, gave me so perfect an intelligence of it that I succeeded. I omitted nothing, and I was astonished that in these matters I knew all without having ever learned. I arranged all my papers and settled all my affairs without the help of anybody. My husband had a quantity of papers deposited with him. I made an exact inventory for each person with my own hand, and sent them to those to whom they belonged. This would have been very difficult for me, O my God, without your help, because, owing to the long time my husband had been ill, everything was in great disorder. This got me the reputation of a clever woman.

As soon as I was a widow my friends and people of the greatest distinction in the country came to advise me to separate at once from my mother-in-law; for, although I made no complaint of it, every one knew her temper. I answered them I had no ground to complain of her, and that I counted on remaining with her if she would allow me. It was the view you from the first gave me, O my God, not to descend from the cross, as you yourself had not descended from it. For this reason I resolved not only not to leave my mother-in-law, but even not to get rid of the maid of whom I have spoken. At the time of your greatest rigors towards me, O my Love, you prevented me from relieving myself of the exterior crosses, which, far from diminishing on the death of my husband, increased.

CHAPTER XXIII

I WAS in so strange a state of deprivation of all support, whether exterior or interior, that it would be difficult for me to describe it well or to make it fully understood. In order to acquit myself the best I can, I am about to describe successively the troubles through which during seven years I have passed, until it pleased you, O my God, to deliver me suddenly from them: then I will resume the thread of my narrative. I did not suddenly lose all support for the interior, but gradually, for during the lifetime of Mother Granger I had already suffered many interior troubles, but they were only like the forerunners of those I had afterwards to experience.

After you had wounded me in the profound manner I have described, you commenced, O my God, to withdraw from me, and the pain of your absence was so much the harder for me, the sweeter your presence and the more powerful your love had been in me. I complained of it to Mother Granger, and I thought I no longer loved you. One day, when keenly penetrated with this thought and this pain, I said to her that I no longer loved you, sole object of my love. Looking at me she said, "What! you no longer love God!" This word was more penetrating for me than a burning arrow. I felt so terrible a pain and such utter confusion I could not answer her, because that which was concealed in the central depth made itself at the moment so much the more apparent as I had thought it lost.

What persuaded me, O my God, that I had lost your love was, that in place of having found new strength in this love, so strong and so penetrating, I had become more weak and more powerless. For formerly I defended myself more easily from the leaning towards the creature; and then, though I had experienced how amiable you are, and your love had even banished from my heart all other love, and my soul had been so greatly elevated above the created, she found herself less capable of defending herself from a certain inclination for the creature: I did not then know what it was to lose our own strength to enter into the strength of God. I have learned it only by a terrible and long experience. I was the more afflicted at it, as this defect appeared to me the most difficult to conquer, and that into which I entered with the greatest facility, and of which I yet had the most horror; because it fills the heart, and seems to establish its dwelling in the same place where you, my God, previously made your residence. Although this was not actually so, my pain persuaded me of it.

Your conducting, O my God, before making me enter into the state of death was a conduct of dying life. Sometimes hiding and leaving me to myself in a hundred weaknesses, sometimes showing yourself with more clearness and love. The more the soul approached the state of death, the more long and tedious became her abandonments, and her weaknesses greater, and her enjoyments shorter, but more pure and more inward, until at last she fell into the total privation. It was an overthrow alike of the exterior and the interior: It seemed, my Love, your exterior providence and your interior guidance had challenged each other as to which would the sooner destroy her.

As soon as I saw the happiness of a state, or its beauty, or the necessity of a virtue, it seemed to me I incessantly fell into the contrary vice, as if that view—which, although very short, was always accompanied with love—had been given to me only to make me experience its opposite, in a manner the more terrible as I had preserved more horror of it. It was indeed then, O my God, I did the evil that I hated, and I did not do the good that I loved. There was given me a penetrating view of the purity of God, and I became still more impure as far as the sentiment; for as to the reality, this state is very purifying, but I was then very far from understanding it. It was shown me that uprightness and simplicity of heart were the essential virtue, and I did nothing but lie, without wishing it. I then thought they were lies, but, in truth, it was only pure mistake and hasty words without any reflection. I gave way to hastiness. I had never had anything but scorn for wealth. I felt attachments to it, and I would have liked to have back what I had lost; so it seemed to me. I could not control my words, nor hinder myself from eating what was to my taste. All my appetites awoke again, with an entire impotence to conquer them. Their revival, however, was only in appearance, for, as I have said, as soon as I ate things for which I felt so violent a desire, I lost the taste for them.

M. Bertot, without knowing my state, forbade austerities, which might have only served me for support. He told me I was unworthy of practicing them. I then believed, O my God, that you had made known to him my wicked state. I could no longer suffer anything, as it appeared to me—although I was quite surrounded by sufferings—owing to the extreme repugnance I felt to it. I entered into so strange a desolation that it is inexplicable, the weight of the anger of God was continual upon me. I used to lie on a rug, which was upon the landing, and cry with all my strength—when I could not be heard—in the sentiment I had of sin, and the inclination I believed I had to commit it, "Damn me, that I may not sin! You send others to hell through justice, give it to me through mercy." It seemed to me I would gladly cast myself into it in the apprehension I had of sin.

M. Bertot, on the reports made to him that I practiced great austerities—for people imagined it, owing to the extreme trouble I was in, which made me unrecognizable—though he had forbidden them to me, thought that I followed my own course. In this deplorable state, I could not tell him anything of myself, God not permitting it; for although I had such keen pains from sin, when I wished to write or speak of them, I found nothing, and I was quite stupid. Even when I wished to confess, I could not say anything, except that I had a sensibility for the creature. This sensibility was such that, during the whole time it lasted, it never caused me any emotion or temptation in the flesh. M. Bertot gave me up, and sent me word I should take another director. I no longer doubted God had made known to him my wicked state, and that this abandonment was the surest mark of my reprobation.

I continued so afflicted, I thought I should die of grief. I was pregnant of my daughter. I have often been astonished that I was not confined prematurely. My sobs were so violent I was on the point of suffocating. I should have been consoled at M. Bertot's abandonment if it was not that I regarded it as the visible mark of God's abandonment. My pain was so keen at the commencement I could hardly eat. People did not understand what I lived on, and I don't understand it myself.

CHAPTER XXIV

As soon as I was a widow my crosses, which one would have thought should have diminished, increased. That maid, whom I have spoken of, who ought to have been more gentle because she depended on me, became more violent. She had accumulated a great deal at the house, and I secured her a pension for the rest of her life, after the death of my husband, in consequence of the services she had rendered him. All this seemed bound to soften her; but quite the contrary happened. She was puffed up with vanity. The necessity of constantly watching an invalid had led her on to drink pure wine to keep up her strength; now as she became aged and feeble, the least thing went to her head. That became a habit with her. I endeavored to conceal this defect, but it became so strong it was impossible to put up with her. I spoke of it to her confessor, in order he might endeavor judiciously to correct it; but in place of profiting by the advice of her director, she became furious, and there was no violence she did not exhibit towards me. My mother-in-law, who up to that had had great trouble to endure this defect in the woman, and who had even spoken to me of it, joined her in blaming me and excusing her. It was, who would cause me the most trouble. If company came, she cried with all her strength, I had dishonored her; that I had driven her to despair; that I was damning myself, and would be the cause of her damnation. You gave me, O my God, despite the deplorable state I was interiorly in, a boundless patience towards her. I answered all her furies only with charity and gentleness, giving her even every mark of my affection. If any other maid came to serve me, she sent her away with fury, and reproached me that I hated her because she had faithfully served my husband: so that I had to make up my mind to be my own servant when it did not please her to come; and when she came, it was to cry and scold. These ways of acting, and many others, which it would be too long to tell, lasted up to a year before my departure. I had, besides, very severe and very frequent illnesses; and when I was ill this woman was in despair. I have always, therefore, thought you had caused all this only for me, O my Lord; for without a special permission she was not capable of such strange conduct. She did not even recognize faults so glaring, always believing she was in the right. All the persons you have used to make me suffer thought they did you service.

I went to Paris expressly to see M. Bertot. The urgent prayers I had caused to be made to him to direct me, joined to the death of my husband, at which he thought I should be very much afflicted, obliged him to conduct me anew. But it was very little use to me; for besides that I could not tell him anything of myself, or make myself known to him, because every idea was taken from me, even that of my wretchedness when I spoke to him, your providence, O my God, permitted that when I was eager to see him from the extreme need I thought I had of him, it was then that I could not see him. I went twelve or fifteen times to see him without being able to speak to him. In the space of two months I spoke to him only twice, and then for a short time, of what appeared to me most essential. I told him the need I had of an ecclesiastic to educate my son, and to remove his bad habits and the unfavor-

able impressions he had been inspired with against me. These
reached such a point that when he spoke of me he never called
me "my mother," but, "She has said;" "She has done." M.
Bertot found me a priest, who was a very good man, and who
had been very well recommended to him.

I went to make a retreat with M. Bertot and Madame de
C—— at P——. God permitted that at the most he spoke to me
less than ten minutes. When he saw I said nothing to him, and
knew not what to say—and, besides, I never told him of the
graces our Lord had bestowed on me (not through a desire of
concealing them, but because you did not permit it, O my
God)—he spoke to the souls that he thought more advanced
in grace, and left me as a person with whom he had almost
nothing to do. You concealed from him so well, O my God,
the state of my soul, in order to make me suffer, that he wished
to put me back into the considerations, thinking that I did not
use prayer, and that Mother Granger was mistaken when she
told him that I did. He even thought she had not had the gift
of discernment, as he let me know. I did what I could to obey
him, but it was entirely impossible for me. I was vexed with
myself for it, because I rather believed M. Bertot than all my
experiences. During my whole retreat, whatever efforts I
made, not a thought came to my mind. My inclination, which I
discerned only through the resistance I opposed to it, was to
remain in silence and nakedness; and I thought I was obedient
in so remaining. This made me still more believe I was fallen
from my grace. I kept myself in my nothingness, content with
my low degree of prayer, without envying that of others, of
which I deemed myself unworthy. I, however, would have
desired to do your will, O my God, and to advance in order
to please you, but I utterly despaired it could ever be; and as
I did not doubt it was through my fault I had lost my gift of
prayer, I was content to remain in my lowness. I was yet,
nevertheless, almost continually in prayer during this retreat;
but I did not know it, and nothing was said to me that could
lead me to think I was so: on the contrary, the lady who had
led me into the retreat said to me that I appeared not so much
defective as little advanced; and as she was reading a collec-
tion of the letters of M. Bertot, I recognized one he had
formerly written to me on my state. I told her it was to me, but

she would not believe me, asserting the contrary. The most spiritual writings were concealed from me, and I was told to apply myself to meditation; but it was impossible for me. O my God, how admirable was your providence to sink me in every way. Without this procedure I should still have subsisted in something.

In the place where I dwelt there was a person whose doctrine was suspected. He possessed a rank in the church which obliged me to show a deference to him. As he learned at once the opposition I had for all persons suspected, and he was satisfied I had some credit in the place, he used all his efforts to win me over to his opinions. I spoke to him with so much force that he could give me no answer. This only increased the desire he had of winning me, and forming friendship with me. For two years and a half he continued to urge me. As he had a very amiable temper, much cleverness, and was very civil, I had no distrust of him, and because I felt a great interior strength, and that while speaking to him God was very present to me, I thought it was an infallible mark God approved my seeing him. During the two and a half years I was obliged to see him, I felt very great troubles, for, on the one hand, I was led, as it were, in spite of myself, to see him and to speak to him; and on the other, there were many things in him I could not approve, and for which I felt an extreme repugnance.

I often kept away from him, but he came to ask me why I was no longer visible, and so managed with his attentions to my sick husband, that I could not avoid his conversations. I thought the shortest way was to break once for all, but M. Bertot would not permit me until after the death of my husband; then, seeing at last the hostility he had to the spiritual life, and that I could not gain anything over his mind, I broke the connection I had with him. When he saw he could not renew it, he caused me strange persecutions, stirring up all those of his party. These persons had at that time among them a method such, that in a very short time they knew those who were on their side, and those who were opposed to them. They sent circular letters to the nearest, which they passed on, the one to the other, so that in a very short time these persons decried me everywhere in the strangest manner. My name was known to them, but not the person. They loudly condemned my piety. They circulated secret reports to discredit me in all the places they knew I was held in repute. However, the joy I had at seeing myself freed from this connection was so great that I little felt what he could do to me. I enjoyed so greatly my new liberty that my trouble was counted for almost nothing. I said to myself, "I will never connect myself with any one, and I will maintain such a reserve I shall never more be at the trouble of breaking."

Fool that I was! I did not know that he who had freed me could alone hinder me from connecting myself. I still thought to be able to defend and guard myself, and my dismal experience had not yet perfectly convinced me of my powerlessness; for I fell again into a new connection, which lasted six months, but it did not cause me so much trouble, because this person was more devoted to God. The person with whom I had broken decried me then everywhere, which slightly injured my reputation. It was, O my God, the thing I most held to, and which cost me most to lose in the sequel. As I knew that people spoke of me, I watched myself with all my strength; but the blow was given, it had to take its course.

What I suffered was terrible, for the estrangement of my God was still greater. All creatures joined with you, O my God, to make me suffer; and I had such an impression it seemed to me they were avenging the outrages I had done to their Creator. I had neither relative, friend, nor confidante. It appeared to me every one was ashamed of me. I further bore a state of inexplicable humiliation; for the powerlessness in which I was of performing exterior acts of charity that I used to do, such as going to the holy Sacrament, burying the dead, remaining a long time at church, served as pretext to that person to condemn me. When he saw I no longer performed all these practices, he proclaimed it was through his means I had done them, and when I no longer saw him I had given up everything. He wished to attribute to himself the merit of what you made me do, O my God, by your grace alone. He went so far as publicly to preach of me as a person, who, after being an example for a town, had become its scandal. He, many times, preached hurtful things; and although I was present at his sermons, which were such as to overwhelm me with confusion (for they scandalized all who heard them), I could not feel pained: on the contrary, I rejoiced at them, for in my central depth I bore a condemnation against myself that I cannot express, and it appeared to me that this person, by the public confusion he procured me, repaired the faults and the infidelities I had committed. My reputation then suffered more and more by means of this person, and I inwardly suffered a greater confusion than if I had committed all possible evils. It was, who would cause me most insults. He turned against me all those who passed for being pious, after which he said, "You see, she has no one for her. So and so, who are saints, are all against her." I thought they were right in behaving thus. I did nothing whatever either to regain their esteem, or to show I was troubled at having lost it. On the contrary, I kept myself aloof and confused as a criminal who dares not lift his eyes. I was sunk before you, my God, in the deepest depth of abjectness. I regarded the virtue of others with respect, and saw the world without defect, and myself without any virtue.

I was often very ill, and in danger of death. I knew not what to do to prepare for death. I did not even see what I could do, and I let myself be devoured by grief. I hardly dared show myself, owing to my trouble. It seemed to me every one must know my abjectness, and the state from which I believed I had fallen. Even the pleasure of drinking my confusion was taken from me; there remained to me only the confusion itself, which I could no longer bear: for I did not feel, in myself, the least inclination to good, but, on the contrary, a tendency to every evil, and this involuntary tendency, without any effect, appeared to me a crime. God so permitted it. I deemed myself more filthy and ugly than the Devil, and yet at confession I knew not what to tell, except certain infidelities I committed, and that I felt natural sensibilities. For, as I have said, I did nothing marked. It was an experience of abjectness, and an inconceivable sentiment of my paltriness, which made me treat the sentiments of the heart as sins. I did not believe there was in the world a more wicked person than myself, and I suffered such confusion, I dared not show myself. One day I opened the New Testament without thinking what I was doing. I found these words: "Virtue is made perfect in weakness; My grace is sufficient for thee." This consoled me for some moments, but the consolation passed away in an instant, and served only to render the pain more severe, for there remained to me neither idea nor trace of these things.

CHAPTER XXV

YOU took from me, O my God, suddenly, all the sensibility I had for the creature, and you took it from me in an instant, as when one puts off a dress; so that from this time I have never had it for any one whatever. You were so far from me, O my God, and you appeared so angry, that there remained to me only the grief of having lost you, through my fault. The loss of my reputation, by means of the party of that person, increased each day, and became more sensible to my mind and to my heart, although it was not permitted me to justify myself, or complain. As I became still more powerless for all sorts of external works, and I could neither go to see the poor, nor remain at church, nor use prayer; and the more cold towards God, the more sensible I was to my ills—all this destroyed me more in my own eyes, and in the eyes of others. There were, however, suitors of high position, who sought me in marriage, persons who, according to ordinary rules, ought not to think of me. They presented themselves even at the height of my exterior and interior desolation, and it appeared to me it was a means of saving myself from the vexation I was exposed to. But it seemed to me then, in spite of all my troubles, that had a king presented himself, I would have gladly refused him, to make you know, O my God, that, with all my paltriness, I wished to be yours alone, and that if you did not want me, I should at least have the consolation of having been faithful to you in everything which depended on me. I never spoke of being asked in marriage, nor of the persons who asked me, although I well knew my mother-in-law used to say that there were no proposals, and that if I did not marry it was because I did not get the chance. It was enough for me, O my God, that you knew what I sacrificed for you, without telling it; especially one, whose high birth, joined to all external qualities, might have tempted my vanity, and my inclination. Yet, O my God, the more cruel you were to me, the more eager was I to make sacrifices to you. If in the sacrifices, and the terrible crosses, in which I was plunged, both from without and within, I could have hoped, O my Lord, to be pleasing to you, the hell I then endured would have been changed into paradise; but, alas! I was far from presuming, or hoping it. It seemed to me that a sea of affliction would have followed only by an eternal torment, O my God. I had even to submit to have lost you for ever—you, who alone could end my woes, which all creatures could only render more gnawing. I dared not desire to enjoy you, O my God, but I desired only not to offend you.

I was five or six weeks at the point of death. I often thought I should die from weakness, caused by a continual diarrhea, which had reduced me to such a state that I could not endure any nourishment. A spoonful of broth threw me into a faint; my voice was so weak that, however near my mouth the ear was placed, they could not distinguish my words. My dispositions were, that, in the extreme wretchedness to which I was reduced, I found nothing that could assure my salvation; on the contrary, my loss appeared inevitable. Yet I could not be unwilling to die, as I had a strong impression the longer I lived, the more I should sin, and that I could no longer avoid sin; that I would live only to commit it. Hell appeared to me more agreeable, and in my grief I cried out, "Hell, and not sin!" My other disposition was that, far from seeing any good in me, I saw only evil. All the good you had caused me to do in my life, O my God, was shown to me as evil. All appeared to me full of defects; my charities, my alms, my prayers, my penances, all rose up against me, and appeared to me objects of condemnation.

What I saw was inexplicable to me, and though I should have been able to explain it, my confessor would have understood nothing. He would have regarded as very great good and eminent virtue what your pure eyes rejected as unfaithfulness. It was indeed then, O most amiable Judge, while yet most rigorous—it was indeed then I understood what you say, that you will judge our righteousness. It was not my unrighteousnesses you judged, since they did not even appear in this judgment; it was all righteousnesses, but righteousnesses abominable in your eyes, as it appeared to me.

Ah! how pure you are! how chaste you are! Who will understand it? It was indeed then I turned my eyes on all sides to see whence help should come to me; but my help could only come from him who has made the heaven and the earth. When I saw there was no salvation for me in myself, I entered into a secret complaisance at not seeing in myself any good, on which to rest and assure my salvation. The nearer my ruin appeared, the more I found in God himself—all irritated as he appeared to me—something to increase my confidence. It seemed to me that I had in Jesus Christ all that was wanting to me in myself. I was, O divine Jesus, that lost sheep of the House of Israel that you were come to save. You were truly the Savior of her who could find no salvation out of you. O men, strong and holy, find salvation as much as you please in what you have done, that is holy and glorious for God; as for me, I make my boast only in my weaknesses, since they have earned for me such a Savior.

There were besides that two years when my ills were not so extreme, though great. All these ills, joined to the loss of my reputation, which I believed greater than it was—all this, I say, was sometimes so trying, with the inability to eat, that I knew not how I could live. In four days I did not eat enough for a single moderate meal. I was obliged to take to bed from pure weakness; my body could no longer bear so rude a burden. I would have liked to have been allowed to tell my sins to all the world. If I had believed, known, or heard, that it was a state, I should have been too happy; but I saw my pain as sin. Spiritual books, when I forced myself to read them, increased my trouble, for I did not see in myself those degrees which they mention. I did not even understand them, and when they spoke of the troubles of certain states, I was far from applying them to myself; I said, "These persons feel the pains that God operates, and as for me, I commit sin, and feel only my wicked state." What consoled me for some moments without consoling me, was, that you were not thereby less great, my God. I would have liked to separate the sin from the confusion of sin, and, provided I had not offended you, all would have been easy for me.

Here is a little sketch of my last wretchedness, which I am very pleased to make known, because I have therein committed many infidelities at the commencement, having yielded to the selfhood, to vain complaisance, long conversations really useless, although self-love and nature made them look in a way necessary; but at the end, I would not have endured a word too human, nor the least thing. You purified in me, my God, and my Divine Love, the real evil through an apparent evil. Could I not indeed sing with the Church, "Oh, happy guilt, which has earned for me such a Redeemer!"

CHAPTER XXVI

THE first monk whom you had used, O my God, to draw me to you, to whom I used to write at his own request, in the very depth of my desolation, wrote to me to cease writing to him; that he had nothing but repugnance for everything that came from me; that I greatly displeased you. O my God, you doubtless inspired him to write thus to me, in order that my desolation might be complete, and no hope might remain for me. A Jesuit Father, who had much esteemed me, wrote me something similar. I had not the least thought of justifying myself. I thanked them for their charity, and recommended myself to their prayers. I was at this time so indifferent to being universally condemned, and by the greatest saints, that I had no pain at it; for I gradually ceased to feel the loss of my reputation. Towards the end I would have liked everybody to have known me as I knew myself. The pain of displeasing you, O my God, without being able to remedy it, was too keen for me to feel the other crosses, although the domestic ones became daily more severe. The recollection of the time I had lost in talking and writing; infidelities I had committed; the strong impulse I felt in me to every kind of defect, was a far more sensible pain.

From the commencement you had accustomed me to dryness and privation. I even preferred it to abundance, because I knew it made me seek you above everything. I had even from the very commencement an instinct in my inmost depth to pass beyond everything, and to leave the gifts in order to run to the Giver; but at this time there was no longer question of that, nor even of losing you, for I no more wished to possess you in myself, having abused you. The abandonment of my director, and the coolness I remarked in persons he conduct-ed, no longer caused me pain, owing to the humiliation I felt within. My brother also joined himself to those who decried me, although he would not previously have looked at them. I believe, my Lord, it was you alone who brought things to this state; for he has virtue, and he surely believed he was doing good in behaving so. I was compelled by some business to go into a town where there are near relatives of my mother-in-law. When I had been there previously there was no civility I had not received from them, each vying with the other to entertain me. They treated me now with the utmost scorn, saying they thereby avenged the suffering I caused their relative.

When I saw the thing went so far, and that, despite my efforts, I had not been able to succeed in pleasing her, I resolved to have an explanation with her. I told her every one said I ill-treated her and made her suffer, although I labored for nothing else but to give her marks of my respect; that if it was so I begged her to consent to my withdrawing, as I had no intention of living with her in order to cause her trouble; that I lived there only to please her; that having the aversion she knew I had for the place where I dwelt, she could well believe I remained there only out of regard for her; that if I was burdensome to her I would withdraw. She answered me very coldly: I might do what I pleased; that she had not spoken of it; but that she was resolved to keep house separately. This was to give me my dismissal.

It was Advent. There was no house vacant in the town. The Benedictines offered me an apartment with them. I suffered inconceivable torture. On the one hand, I feared by withdrawing to withdraw from the cross; on the other, it did not seem right to remain with a person to crucify her, when I had no other desire than to please her. Yet, however careful I was, everything turned out equally ill. She complained I did things without consulting her; and when I consulted her, she would not answer me. When I asked her advice, she said I could do nothing myself; that at her age she was obliged to have the charge of everything. If I endeavored to forestall her inclinations, doing things as I believed she would have herself advised, she told me I despised her; that young persons had nothing but contempt for the aged; that they thought they knew everything better. When I went into the country for rest, she complained of it, saying I left her alone. If I begged her to come there, she would not. If I said I did not venture to ask her to come for fear of inconveniencing her and making her sleep away from home, she complained I did not wish her to come, and I went there only to escape from her. When I learned she was vexed at my being in the country, I returned to the town, and she could not endure me nor speak to me. None the less I conversed with her; for at that time, O my God, you gave me the grace of going counter to all my dislikes, though I did not know it. I conversed with her without appearing to see how she behaved. She did not answer me, and turned to the other side. I often sent her my carriage, and begged her to come and pass a day in the country; that it would amuse without inconveniencing her, since, being so near, she could return in the evening. She sent it back empty without an answer; and if I was some days without sending it to her, there were complaints. In short, all I did to please her, embittered her, God so permitting it. She had a very good heart, but her temper was perhaps there in spite of her, and I nevertheless have much obligation to her.

On Christmas Day, being with her, I said with much affection: "My mother, the King of Peace has been born this day to bring it to us. I ask of you peace in his name." I believe this touched her, though she did not let it appear. The ecclesiastic I had in the house, far from supporting and consoling me, served only to weaken and afflict me more, showing me I ought not to put up with certain things; and when in compliance I wished to introduce some order, as well in what concerned my mother-in-law as my domestics, besides being unsuccessful, it augmented my crosses and my troubles. For it is a strange thing that, no longer having a husband, when I ought to be mistress, I yet was unable to dismiss a servant, however faulty he might be. As soon as anyone ought to go she took his part, and all her friends mixed themselves up in it.

When I was ready to leave, one of the friends of my mother-in-law (a good man who has always esteemed me, without daring to let it appear to her), having learned of it, was very apprehensive I might quit the town, for some of my alms passed through his hands. He thought it would be a great injury to the neighborhood. He resolved to speak to my mother-in-law with the greatest caution he could, for he knew her. After he had spoken to her, she said that she would not turn me out of her house, but if I left it, she would offer no obstacle. He came to see me then, and begged me to go and make excuses to her, to satisfy her. I told him that I would do it a hundred times for one, although I knew not about what; that I was continually making them to her for whatever I saw vexed her; but that this was not the question, that I made no complaint against her, and that I was content to remain with her as long as it should please her; but that, being in her house, it was not right I should remain there to annoy her, that it was right I should secure her case. I nevertheless went with him into my mother-in-law's room. I said to her that I asked her pardon, if I had displeased her in anything, that it had never been my intention; that I begged her to tell me, in the presence of this gentleman, who was her friend, in what I might have caused her vexation, and if I had ever done anything designedly to offend her. You permitted, O my God, that she herself declared the truth in the presence of this man. She said she was not a person to allow herself to be offended, she would not have put up with it; that she had no other complaint against me except that I did not love her, and that I would have wished her dead. I answered her, these thoughts

were very far from my sentiments, and that, instead of ever
having this thought, I would have wished with all my heart to
have prolonged her life by my attentions to her; that my
affection was entire, but that she never would believe it,
whatever proof I tried to give her, as long as she listened to
persons who spoke to her to my disadvantage; that she even
had a servant who, far from showing respect to me, ill-treated
me to such a degree that she would push me when she wished
to pass—she had even done it in church, making me get out of
her way with as much violence as scorn, and many times in the
room even insulting me with words; that I had never complained of her, but that I was glad to let her know it, because
a spirit of that stamp might give her trouble some day, and put
into her mind things that would torment her.

She took the part of her servant; yet we kissed each other,
and it rested there. But you, O my God, who were the more
watchful over me the more you appeared to forget me, permitted
that, after I had gone to the country, this maid, having no
longer me to vent her vexation on, behaved so ill to her
mistress that she was obliged to dismiss her before my return. I
must mention here that the behavior of my mother-in-law was
rather God's conducting of me than a defect on her part; for
she had virtue and intelligence and, putting aside certain
failings, which people who do not use prayer keep ignorant
of, she had good qualities. Perhaps I have caused her crosses
without intending it. She has caused them to me, perhaps,
without knowing it, for the dislike she had for my manners
might have been a severe cross to her.

CHAPTER XXVII

ONE day, overwhelmed with troubles, and knowing not what
to do, it occurred to me to speak to a man of merit and

distinction, who often came to the neighborhood, and who is reputed very spiritual. I wrote him a note to fix a time, as I had need of his advice. As soon as I was before the Holy Sacrament I felt a terrible pain. "What!" (it was reproached me), "thou seekest to console thyself and to shake off my yoke." My husband was then living. I sent as quickly as possible another note to beg him to excuse me, and as I believed him spiritual, I said to myself. "If he is spiritual, he will not be offended; if he is not so, I should be sorry to speak to him." I told him that it had only been from self-love I had desired this conversation, and not from a true necessity; that, as I knew he understood what it was to be faithful to God, I had thought he would not be displeased that I used this Christian simplicity with him. He, however, was hurt; and this surprised me the more as I had conceived great ideas of his virtue. He certainly has it, but they are living virtues, which are ignorant even of the paths of death. You have been, O my God, my faithful conductor even in my abjectness, as I have discovered with wonder when it was past. Everlasting praise to you, O my God!

During the time of my experience of abjectness, I sought no outward recreations. On the contrary, they were disagreeable to me, and I wished not to see or to know anything. When the others went to see anything, I remained at home. My closet was my sole diversion. I found myself near the Queen, whom I had not seen, and whom I would have well enough liked to see, as well as Monseigneur, who was also there. I had only to open my eyes, and I did not do it. I loved to hear singing, yet I was once four days with a person who was reputed to have the most beautiful voice without asking her to sing; which astonished her, because she was not ignorant, that knowing her name, I must know the beauty of her voice. I have, nevertheless, committed striking infidelities in informing myself of what others said of me in blame. One of the things that caused me the greatest trouble in the seven years I have mentioned, especially the last five, was a strange folly of my imagination that gave me no repose; my senses kept it company, so that I could no longer shut my eyes in church, and thus, all the gates being opened, I had to look upon myself as a vine exposed to pillage, because the hedges that the husbandman had planted were torn down. I then saw all that was done, and all who came and went in the church—a state very different from the other. The same power that had drawn me inwards to concentrate me, seemed to push me outwards to dissipate me.

Overwhelmed then with abjectness of all kinds, crushed with vexations, wearied under the cross, I made up my mind to finish my days in this way; no hope was left me of ever emerging from this painful state. But, however, believing I had lost for ever grace and the salvation it earns for us, I would have liked at least to do what I could for a God whom I thought I should never love, and seeing the place whence I had fallen, I would have liked to serve him from gratitude, though I deemed myself a victim destined for hell. At another time the view of such a happy state gave rise in me to certain secret desires of returning to it; but suddenly I was cast back into the depth of the abyss, whence I did not utter even a sigh, abiding for ever in the state due to unfaithful souls. I remained some time in this state, like the eternally dead who must never live again. It seems to me that this passage suited me admirably: "I am like the dead, blotted out from the heart." It seemed to me, O my God, I was for ever effaced from your heart, and from that of all creatures. Gradually my state ceased to be painful. I became even insensible to it, and my insensibility appeared to me the final hardening of my reprobation. My coldness appeared to me a coldness of death. Such was the state of things, O my God, because you made me pass away lovingly into you, as I am about to tell.

To resume my narrative. It happened that one of my footmen wished to turn Bernabite, and I wrote of it to Father La Mothe. He told me that I must address Father La Combe, who was then Superior of the Bernabites at Tonon. This obliged me to write to him. I had always preserved a basis of respect and esteem for his grace. I was very glad of this opportunity of recommending myself to his prayers. As I could speak only of what was most real to me, I wrote him that I was fallen from the grace of my God; that I had repaid his benefits with the blackest ingratitude; in short, that I was abjectness itself and a subject deserving compassion; and that, far from having advanced towards my God, I had entirely alienated myself from him. He answered me as if he had known by a supernatural light, in spite of the frightful picture I drew of myself, that my state was one of grace. He wrote to me in this way, but I was very far from being convinced.

The letter I had received from Father La Combe, wherein he told me his present disposition, which was similar enough to that preceding my state of abjectness, had such an effect upon me because you thus willed it, O my God, that it brought peace to my mind and calm to my heart. I even found myself inwardly united to him, as to a person of great grace. Some time after this, at night, in a dream, a little deformed nun presented herself to me, who, however, appeared to me both dead and blessed. She said to me, "My sister, I come to tell you that God wishes you at Geneva." She said something more which I do not remember. I was extremely consoled, but I did not know what it meant. From the portrait of Mother Bon, which I have since seen, I have recognized it was she; and the time when I saw her corresponds with that of her death.

About eight or ten days before the Magdalen's Day, 1680, it occurred to me to write again to Father La Combe, and to beg him, if he received my letter before the Magdalen's Day, to say the Mass for me on that day. You caused, O my God, that this letter—unlike others which he received only very late, for want of messengers to fetch them on foot from Chambery— was handed to him the eve of the Magdalen's, and on the Day of the Magdalen he said the Mass for me. As he offered me to God at the first *memento*, it was said to him three times with much vehemence, "You shall both dwell in the same place." He was greatly surprised, as he had never had interior speech. I believe, O my God, that this is rather verified in respect to the interior and the identity of the crucifying circumstances to which we have alike been exposed, and in respect of yourself, O God, who are our dwelling-place, than with regard to temporal residence; for although I have been some time in the same country with him, and that your providence has furnished us with some occasions of being together, it appears to me it is much more verified by the rest, since I have the advantage as well as he of confessing Jesus Christ crucified.

CHAPTER XXVIII

IT was this happy Day of the Magdalen that my soul was
perfectly delivered from all her troubles. She already commenced after the first letter from Father La Combe, to recover
a new life, yet she was like a dead man brought back to life,
not yet released from his grave-clothes; but on this day I was
as if in perfect life. I found myself as much elevated above
nature as I had been rigorously captive under its load. I was
astonished at this new liberty, and to see returned, but with
as much magnificence as purity, him whom I thought I had lost
for ever. What I possessed was so simple, so immense, that I
cannot express it. It was then, O my God, that I found again
in you ineffably all that I had lost. You restored it to me with
fresh advantages. My trouble and my pain were changed into
a peace such that, the better to explain, I call it God-Peace.
The peace I possessed before this time was indeed the peace
of God—peace, the gift of God; but it was not God-Peace—
peace which he possesses in himself, and which is found only
in him.

At the commencement this liberty had less extent, but the
more I advanced, the more great the liberty became. I had
occasion to see M. Bertot for some moments. I told him I
believed my state much changed, without telling him the details, nor what I experienced, nor that which had preceded
it. I had very little time to speak to him, and further, he was
attending to something else. You, O my God, permitted that
he said to me, "No," perhaps without thinking of it. I believed
him, for grace made me believe what was said to me, in spite of
my lights and my experiences; so that when I was told the
contrary of what I thought, every other thought was banished from my mind, which remained so submissive to what was

said to it that it had not even a contrary thought of reflection. This caused me no trouble, for every state was indifferent to me. Every day, however, I felt increasing within me a species of beatitude. I was entirely delivered from all pain, and from all tendencies I thought I had to sin.

It seems to me I then performed all kinds of good, freed from self-hood or self-regard, and if a self-regard presented itself, it was at once dissipated. It seemed to me as if a curtain was drawn, which covered that thought, and made it no longer appear. My imagination was entirely fixed, so I had no longer trouble with it. I was astonished at the clearness of my mind and purity of my heart. I received a letter from Father La Combe, who wrote me that God had made him know he had great designs for me; whether they be of justice, or of mercy, all is alike to me. It had been said to him, "You shall both dwell in the same place." He knew no more, and God did not then let him know anything more particular. I had still Geneva in the bottom of my heart, without mentioning it to any one. I did not stop even to think of it, or of what Father La Combe had told me of the designs of God for my soul. I received all this with an entire indifference, without wishing either to occupy myself with it or to think of it; awaiting all, O my God, from your all-powerful will.

Oh, how truly have I experienced what you say in your Gospel, which is repeated in the four Gospels not without reason, and even said twice in one Gospel, that whoever shall lose his life shall find it, and whoever will save it, shall lose it. O happy loss, which a happy necessity forced me to make. When I believed myself lost without resource, it was then I found myself saved. When I no longer hoped anything from myself, I found all in my God. When I had lost every good, I found in him all kinds of good. When I had lost all created and even divine supports, I found myself under the happy necessity of falling into the Divine itself, and of falling into it through everything I thought separated me the further from it. In losing all the gifts I found the Giver. In losing you, my God, in me, I found you in yourself, in the immovable, to lose you no more. O poor creatures, who pass all your life in tasting the gifts of God, and who think thereby you are the most favored and the most happy; how I yet pity you, if you do not go to my God through the loss of those same gifts! How many souls pass all their life in this way, and believe themselves prodigies! There are other persons who, being destined by God to die to themselves, pass all their life in a dying life and in strange agonies, without ever entering into God through total death and loss, because they still wish under good pretexts to retain something, and never lose themselves in all the extent of the designs of God. For this reason they never enjoy God in fulness, which is a loss that will only be perfectly known in the other life.

O my Lord, what happiness did I not taste in my little solitude, and my little household, where nothing interrupted my repose! As I was a long time in the country, and the tender age of my children did not require too much of my attention, besides that they were in good hands, I withdrew all day into the wood, where I passed as many happy days as I had had there months of grief. For it was there I previously gave free course to grief to destroy me. It was also where in the commencement I gave place to love to consume me, and it was where now I let myself be more lost in an infinite and incomprehensible abyss. I can tell nothing of what took place in me, as it was too pure, too simple and too outside of me.

You treated me, O my God, like your servant Job, restoring to me double what you had taken from me, and delivering me from my crosses. You gave me a wonderful facility to please everybody, and what is more surprising, my mother-in-law, who up to that had always complained of me, whatever care I might have taken to satisfy her, declared that it was impossible to be more pleased with me than she was. Persons who had most decried me expressed sorrow at it, and became my panegyrists. My reputation was the more firmly established as it appeared the more lost. I continued in an entire peace both outward and inward. You did that, O my God, to render the sacrifice you were preparing to cause me to make both more painful and more perfect; for had I been obliged to break away during the time of persecution, it would have been a relief, and not a sacrifice; perhaps, also, I should never have been able to resolve to leave during the time of my troubles. I would always, doubtless, have been apprehensive of descending from the cross of myself and being unfaithful to it. It seems to me that one could not be more content and more happy than I was. As the cross had always been my faithful companion and friend, there awoke from time to time little pains at no longer suffering; but they were immediately absorbed in a central depth which could not admit any desires. Although the body suffered great pains, there was no longer pain, but a central depth which beatified everything. It seems to me that my soul was become like that New Jerusalem which is spoken of in the Apocalypse, where there is no more either crying or pain. The indifference in me was perfect, and the union to the good pleasure of God so great, that I did not find in myself any desire or tendency. What appeared then most lost in me was the will, for I did not find it for anything whatever. My soul could not incline herself more to one side than to another. All she could do was to nourish herself from the daily providences. She found another will had taken the place of her own—a will all divine, which yet was so her own and so natural, that she found herself infinitely more free in this will than she had been in her own.

These dispositions, which I describe as of a time past to avoid confusion, have ever since subsisted, and have even continually grown more strong and perfect up to the present hour.

O union of unity, asked from God by Jesus Christ for men, and earned by the same Jesus Christ, how powerful art thou in a soul that thou dost thus annihilate in her God! It is here, then, after the consummation of this divine unity, that the soul remains hidden with Jesus Christ in God. O happy loss, and so much the more happy as it is not one of those transitory losses that ecstasy produces, which are rather absorptions than losses, since the soul finds herself immediately after; but one of those permanent durable losses, which go on continually losing themselves in an immense sea, as a little fish would go continually sinking down into an infinite sea. But the comparison does not appear to me sufficiently accurate. It is rather like a little drop of water cast into the sea, which continually acquires more the qualities of the same sea. This soul was receiving, without power to incline herself or to choose. When I speak of power, I do not understand it of absolute power, but of that of a soul which has still elections and desires. She received in perfect indifference what was given or done to her. At the commencement she still committed some faults of precipitancy; but this was as if outside of her, without, however, her knowing her state.

CHAPTER XXIX

I was obliged to go to Paris for some business, and having entered a church, which was very gloomy, to make my confession, I went to the first confessor I found, whom I did not know, and whom I have never since seen. I simply made my confession—a very short one—and did not say a word to this confessor. I was greatly surprised when he said to me, "I know not who you are, whether you are maid, wife, or widow; but I feel a strong interior movement to tell you, that you should do what our Lord has made you know he desired of you. I have only that to say to you." I answered him, "My Father, I am a widow, who has little children four and six years of age. What else could God desire of me but to rear them?" He said to me, "I know nothing of it. You know whether God had made you recognize that he wished something of you. If it is so, there is nothing which should hinder you from doing his will. One must leave one's children to do it."

This greatly surprised me. I, however, said nothing to him of what I felt for Geneva. I, nevertheless, quietly prepared myself to leave everything if you wished it of me, O my God, and if you brought about the opportunities through your divine providence. I did not look upon it as a good to which I aspired, nor as a virtue I hoped to acquire, nor as an extraordinary thing, nor as an act which deserved some return on God's part. I did not embrace it as through zeal—this appeared dead in me; but I let myself gently go to what I was told was the will of God, to which mine could make no resistance—not through acquiescence as formerly, but as no longer existing, and no longer distinguishing or paying attention. While I was in this disposition, living in my family with extreme tranquillity, without troubling myself with all that, a monk of the Order of St. Dominic, one of my friends, had a great desire to go as a missionary to Siam. He dwelt at twenty leagues from us. When he was ready to make the vow that he had written out to repeat, it was not possible for him to do so. He was given to understand he ought to come and speak to me about it. He came immediately, and, as he had some repugnance to telling me, he went to say the Mass in my chapel, believing God would be satisfied if he should make his vow while celebrating the Mass in my hearing. But he was hindered; so that he left the chapel after he had put on the amice, which he took off to come and speak to me. He then told me his project. Although I had no feeling or thought of doing anything positive, I felt myself impelled to tell him what had happened to me, and the notion which I had a long time for Geneva. I related to him even a dream that appeared supernatural, which had occurred to me on the night of the Transfiguration, the 6th August, exactly one year before I made the vows, of which I will speak hereafter. I seemed to see the ecclesiastic of our house with my youngest son, looking with much admiration at the heaven. They cried out that the heaven was open. They begged me to come, that they saw Tabor and the heaven opened. I told them I did not wish to go there; that Tabor was not for me; that I needed only Calvary. They pressed me so strongly to go out that, unable to resist their importunity, I went. I saw only a remnant of light; and at the same time I saw descending from heaven a cross of immense size. I saw a number of people of all kinds—priests, monks— endeavouring to hinder it coming. I did nothing but remain quietly in my place, without trying to take it; but I was content. I perceived it approached me. With it there was a standard of the same color as the cross. It came and cast itself of its own accord into my arms. I received it with extreme joy. The Benedictines having wished to take it from me, it withdrew from their hands to cast itself into mine.

As I was conversing with the Father about this, I had a

strong movement to say to him, "My Father, you will not go to Siam. You will serve me in this business, and it is for this God has sent you here. I beg you to give me your opinion." (He is very learned.) He told me he would remain three days with me in the country, and that, after having recommended the business to God for these three days, and said three Masses, he would let me know his sentiment. After this time, then, he told me that he believed it was the will of God I should go to that country, but in order to be more sure, it was necessary to see the Bishop of Geneva; that if he approved my design, it was a mark that it was of God; that if he condemned it, I should think no more of it. I adopted this view, and he offered to go to Annécy, to see the Bishop of Geneva and speak to him, and to give me a faithful report of what they should have determined together. As he was advanced in years, we were discussing in what way he should make such a long journey without being inconvenienced, when there arrived two monks, passers-by, who told us the Bishop of Geneva was at Paris. This appeared to me, O my God, a miracle of your providence. The worthy monk resolved to go there. He counseled me to write to Father La Combe to know his sentiment, and to recommend the business to his prayers, for he knew he was of that country. He then spoke at Paris to the Bishop of Geneva, and as there occurred an affair, which Divine Providence arranged for me, to oblige me to go to Paris, I spoke myself to the Bishop of Geneva.

I told him my design was to go into that country, and there to employ my wealth in founding an establishment for all those who would truly turn to God and give themselves to him without reserve; that many servants of God, both male and female, assured me God demanded this of me; and although I did not feel any marked inclination for it, I yet thought myself bound to obey the voice of God, which was indicated to me, since so many different persons, mutually unacquainted, and far separated the one from the other, told me the same thing. The Bishop of Geneva approved of my design, and informed me that there were some New Catholics who wished to go and establish themselves at Gex, and that it was a providence. I answered him I had no vocation for Gex, but for Geneva. He told me I should be able to go thence to Geneva. I believed it was an opportunity which Divine Providence sent me, to make the journey with less difficulty, and as I knew nothing positive of what God wished of me, I would not offer any opposition. "Perhaps," I said, "he desires that I should merely contribute to this establishment."

I went to see the Superior of the New Catholics at Paris, to know how things were going on. She testified great joy, and assured me she would be one of the party. As she is a great servant of God, this confirmed me, for when I could reflect a moment, which was rare, I thought God would take her for her virtue and me for my money; for as soon as through unfaithfulness I regarded myself, I could not believe God wished to make use of me; but when I saw things in God, it seemed to me that the more insignificant I was, the more suited was I to his designs. As I did not see anything in me extraordinary, and believed myself in the lowest stage of perfection, and it appeared to me for want of light—for my soul was not perfectly established in the eternal light, which is you, O my God—as, I say, it appeared to me that extraordinary lights were needed for extraordinary designs, this made me hesitate and fear deception. I did not sufficiently understand that to follow step by step your divine providence was the greatest and purest light; and besides this, you gave me continual lights, and so much the more admirable as I the less sought them.

I had mysterious dreams which presaged only crosses, persecutions and griefs. My heart submitted itself to all that its God could will for it. I had one very significant. While engaged in some necessary work, I saw near me a very small animal which looked as if dead. This animal appeared to me to be the envy of some persons which seemed lately to be deadened. I caught this animal, and as I saw he exerted himself to sting me and grew bigger under my eyes, I threw him away. I found he had filled my fingers, as it were, with needles. I went up to a person I knew very well in order that he should remove them for me; but he stuck them deeper into me, and I continued full of these stings until a charitable priest of extraordinary merit (whose face is still before me, although I have never seen him; but I believe I shall see him before dying) caught that animal with pincers. As soon as he held it tight, my stings fell out themselves, and I found an easy entrance into a place which had previously appeared to me inaccessible; and although there was mud as deep as the waist in going to a deserted church, I passed over it without soiling myself. It will be easy from the sequel of my life to see what this signifies.

People, doubtless, will be astonished that, attaching so little importance to things extraordinary, I relate these dreams. I do it for two reasons: the first, through fidelity, having promised to omit nothing that should occur to my mind; the second, because it is the mode God makes use of to communicate with souls of faith, to give them intimations of the future in things that concern them; although there is a manner of knowing of extreme purity with which he endows them. These extraordinary dreams are found in numerous places in Holy Scripture. They have especial characteristics, such as, to leave a certainty they are mysterious, and that they will be realized in their time; of almost never escaping from the memory, though one forgets all others; of redoubling the certainty of their truth as often as one thinks of them or speaks of them; moreover, they produce for the most part on waking up a certain unction.

I received a letter from Father La Combe, who told me that he had caused some very holy women in that neighborhood to pray, and that all said God wanted me at Geneva. A nun of the Visitation, who is a very holy woman, told me that God had made the same thing known to her, and that it had been said to her, "She will be daughter of the Cross of Geneva." An Ursuline also informed me that our Lord had said to her, that he destined me to be the eye of the blind, the foot of the lame, etc. The ecclesiastic who was at our house greatly feared I might be deceived; but what finished in confirming him for that time was, that Father Claude Martin wrote me that God had made known to him after many prayers that he wanted me at Geneva, that he wanted me to make a generous sacrifice of everything. I answered him that perhaps God wanted only a sum of money from me to assist a foundation that was about to be established there; that I would furnish it without leaving my children. He answered me, that God had made known to him that he did not want my wealth, that he wanted my person. I received this letter and at the same time another from Father La Combe, who told me the certainty God had given him and numerous worthy servants of God, that God wanted me at Geneva. Although these two monks were more than a hundred and fifty leagues distant the one from the other, they wrote me almost the same thing. I was surprised, receiving at the same time these two almost identical letters from people so remote.

As soon as I believed it was your will, O my God, I did not see anything on earth capable of stopping me. My senses were nevertheless given over to the pain that such a determination must naturally cause a mother who loves her children, and as soon as I reflected, doubt seized my mind. I had no interior witness. I felt neither inclination nor desire, but rather repugnance; yet I surrendered myself against all hope, resting on faith in God, who does not permit those that trust him to be confounded.

I firmly believed that you would by your providence furnish all that was necessary for the education of my children, and this in pure faith; for the senses were without support. I made arrangements gradually, without eagerness, not wishing to do the least thing either to put off the business or to advance it, or to make it succeed. Providence was my sole guidance.

CHAPTER XXX

IT seemed, O my God, that while working by your providence to make me leave all, you daily made my ties stronger and my departure more blamable. For, in short, one could not receive greater kindness from one's own mother than what my mother-in-law showed me at this time. The least petty ailment I had threw her into mortal disquietude. She said she had veneration for the virtue you had placed in me. I believe that what not a little contributed to this change was that she learned from people, who, without thinking of it, addressed themselves to her, that three persons had sought me in marriage; and as I had refused them, although they were of a rank much above mine, and with great advantages, she was surprised at it; but what most struck her was that she remembered she had said to me at the time these persons were wooing me, that if I did not marry it was because I did not get the chance, and that I had not answered her a word to let her know it only depended on me to do so most advantageously. She thought that such harsh treatment as she had dealt me might perhaps induce me to yield to the proposals in order to deliver myself honorably from the tyranny. She well enough saw the injury this would be to my children. In short, you opened her eyes, and changed her harshness to tenderness.

I fell extremely ill. I thought, O my God, you were pleased with the will of my sacrifice, and you wished that of my life. It was in this illness my mother-in-law showed me the tenderness she had for me. She hardly stirred from my bedside, and the tears she shed showed the sincerity of her affection. I felt very grateful to her, and it seemed to me I loved her as a true mother. Why should I leave her when she loved me so much, and was so advanced in years? That maid, who hitherto had been my plague, took an inconceivable affection for me. She praised me everywhere, saying I was a true saint, although I was so far from it. She served me with extraordinary respect; begged my pardon for what she had made me suffer. She died of regret after my departure.

There was a nun in a convent I often went to. During six months I was in the country this woman had entered into a state of purification that every one in the house regarded as madness. They shut her up even with violence, and this nearly ruined her. All persons they had shown her to said it was madness. On my return I went into that house. They told me she had become mad. I knew she was a holy woman. I asked to see her. I understood at once it was not madness, but a state of purification. I said to the Superior, I begged they would not shut her up; that they would not show her to any one; and that she would have the kindness to trust her to me;

that I hoped things would change. I understood her greatest trouble was to pass as mad; that she had a very great repugnance for this; and that when the state of madness presented itself to her mind with the thought of sacrificing herself to it, far from doing so, she resisted and became quite furious. I counseled her to sacrifice herself to bear the state of madness, which Jesus Christ had been willing to bear before Herod. This sacrifice gave her at once more calm; but as God wished to purify this soul, he purified her from all things to which she had had most attachment. She had for her Superior a very strong attachment. She experienced as regards her a strange trouble, which was a desire of seeing her and being near her, and as soon as she approached her, a frightful hatred and opposition. It was the same in all her spiritual exercises for which she had had attachment. She formerly passed days before the Holy Sacrament; and now she could not continue there a single instant. This convinced them still more she was mad. I had in my central depth an instinct of just judgment, which did not deceive me, and I asserted the contrary. At last, after having suffered strangely, her Superior wrote me that I had been right, and that she had emerged from it purified as an angel. God permitted I was the only person who knew her state. You commenced to give me at this time, O my God, the discernment of spirits.

The winter preceding the year of my departure was one of the longest and most severe there had been for many years. It was in 1680. There was extreme want, which furnished me with the opportunity of exercising large charities; for besides what I gave in secret to respectable persons in poverty, who were very numerous, that which was done at the house in distributing bread to all the rest was very great. My mother-in-law shared in that of the house, and we joined together for the purpose. She contributed to it with much kindness and charity; and I found her so changed I was surprised and delighted at it. We used to give away at the house ninety-six dozen loaves every week; but the secret charities were larger. I had girls and little boys put to a trade. All this caused my departure to be much blamed, and the more so as my charities had been striking. At this time I did not find anything difficult, and you gave, O my God, such a blessing to my alms that

I did not find it cost anything to my family, which extremely surprised me. Previous to the death of my husband, my mother-in-law had told him I would ruin him through my charities.

What caused me still more trouble was the tenderness I had for my children, especially for my younger son, whom I had reason to love. I saw him disposed to good, and it seemed to me that everything in his natural disposition favoured the hopes I had conceived of him. It was a great risk to leave him to be educated by others, and this cost me more trouble in leaving him than all the rest. I would have wished to take my daughter with me. I did not think I ought to leave her, but she was suffering for three years from a triple-quartan fever, so that it appeared out of the question to take her. Yet, O my God, you, through your providence, caused her health to be restored so suddenly and so perfectly, four months before my departure, that I found her in a state to go with me.

What caused me the most trouble, was not so much going away, as binding myself to the New Catholics. I wished to find in myself an attraction towards them. I sought it and I found nothing. This institution was opposed to my mind and to my heart; not that I would not love to contribute to the conversion of erring souls, since I had for their conversion as much attraction as I was capable of, considering how very dead and annihilated I was as to my central depth; but the manner of life and spirit of this institution did not suit me, and when I wished to conquer myself in this point, and connect myself with them, my soul lost her peace. I might have thought I should have been well suited to them, since you had made use of me, O my God, before my departure to convert entire families, one of which was composed of eleven or twelve persons. Besides, Father La Combe had told me to make use of this opportunity for starting, and did not tell me whether I should bind myself to them or not; thus it was the providence of my God alone, to which I had given myself up without reserve, that hindered me from binding myself with them.

One day that through infidelity I reflected on this enterprise, I was a little disturbed by the fear of being mistaken, which increased when the house ecclesiastic, who was the only person to whom I had confided my secret, told me I was badly advised, that I certainly had not properly explained myself. Being a little cast down I had a movement to open Isaiah. On opening the book I found this passage: "Fear not, O Jacob, who art a little worm, and you Israel, who are as it were dead. It will be I who shall lead you. Fear not, for you are mine. When you shall walk through the waters I will be with you." I had a very great courage to go, but I could not persuade myself it was in order to be with the New Catholics. It was, however, necessary that, before setting out, I should see Sister Garnier, Superior of the New Catholics at Paris, in order to take measures with her; but I could not go to Paris because this journey would have prevented my making another at the time it would have been necessary for me to start. Although this person was very ailing, she resolved to come and see me; but, O my God, you conducted things in such a manner through your providence, to make everything come to the point of your will, that I saw every day new miracles which charmed me; for with paternal kindness you took care of the smallest things. When she was about to set out she fell ill, and you permitted it so to give time for a person who would have discovered everything to go on a journey. At last she started, still very weak, and, as she had informed me of the day of her departure, when on that day I saw it was excessively hot, and so close that I fancied, petted, as she was, in her own community, that she would not be let start. I addressed myself to our Lord to give some wind to moderate the heat, and enable the worthy woman to come. Hardly had I said this when there suddenly sprung up a wind so cool I was astonished at it, and this wind did not cease during her whole journey, until after her return.

I went to meet her, and took her to a country house, so that she was not seen or recognized by anybody. What embarrassed me a little was, I had two servants who knew her; but as I was engaged on the conversion of a lady, I led the conversation so that they easily thought it was for this purpose I had made her come, and that it was necessary to keep the secret in order this lady might not be deterred from coming by knowing who she was. You caused, O my God, that, although I was no controversialist, I yet answered all her doubts, so that she could not help yielding. Sister Garnier had much talent and grace, but her words did not produce in that soul the effect those you made me speak produced, as she has herself assured me. She could not even help saying so. I felt a movement to ask her from you as a testimony of your holy will. You granted her to me, O my God, although she did not make her abjuration until after my departure, and not before it; as you wished to make me start without other assurance than this, that the Divine Providence conducted all things. The Sister was four days without declaring her thoughts to me; on the fourth, she told me she would not come with me. I was the more surprised at it, as I had been persuaded, God, without having regard to my abjectness, would give to her virtue what he would refuse to my ill-deserts. Besides, the subjects she proposed to me appeared without supernatural grace, and quite human. This made me hesitate some moments; then, taking new courage through the abandonment of my entire self, I said to her, "I am not going there for you. I will, none the less, go there without you." She was surprised, as she confessed to me; for she thought as soon as she decided not to go I would be no longer willing. I arranged everything; and I wrote on a paper the terms of the contract of association with them. I had no sooner done it than, after the Communion, I felt dreadful burnings and trouble. I went to see Sister Garnier; and as I knew she had the Spirit of God, I made no difficulty of telling her my pain. I made her understand that I had no doubt God called me to Geneva; but I did not know if he wished me of their congregation. She asked until after the Mass and the Communion; and she would tell me what God wished of me. You made use of her, in spite of her own interests and against her inclination, to make me know your will, my Lord. She told me then I ought not to bind myself with her, and that it was not your design; that I should go simply with the Sisters; and when I should be there, Father La Combe would signify to me your will. I acquiesced at once in this advice, and my soul recovered her peace.

My first design, or, rather, my first thought had been, before learning that the New Catholics were going to Gex, to go to Geneva, where at that time there were Catholics in service and otherwise, and to settle in a small room, and without at first declaring myself; and as I knew how to make various ointments, to dress wounds, especially king's-evil, which was very prevalent in that place, and for which I had a very certain remedy, I would have thus quietly insinuated myself; besides the charities I would have given them. In this way I would have gained there many persons. I do not doubt if I had adopted this course things might perhaps have succeeded better. Yet I believed I would do better in following the opinion of the Bishop than my own lights. But what am I saying, O my God; has not your eternal design been realized and accomplished in me? We speak humanly because we are human; but, O God, when we regard things in you, we see them with other eyes. Yes, my Lord, your design was to give Geneva not to my labor and my words, but to my sufferings; for the more desperate I see things, the more I expect the conversion of that town, by a way known to you alone. Yes, Geneva, you will see within your walls the truth again flourish, which has been banished by error; and those beautiful words which are written on your Town Hall, "After darkness, Light," will be happily verified for you. And although at present you take them in a quite contrary sense, it is certain you will be one day illuminated with the light of truth, and that fine temple of St. Peter will again have the advantage of enclosing in its bosom our redoubtable mysteries. How true in one sense it is, O my Lord, that you have made me daughter of the Cross of Geneva, and that I would cheerfully give my blood to see your cross erected there. Father La Combe has since told me that he had had on his side a strong movement to tell me not to bind myself with the New Catholics; that he did not believe it was the will of God, but he forgot it. I could no longer consult M. Bertot, for he died four months before my departure.

The
Autobiography of
MADAME GUYON

———◆———

PART II

CHAPTER I

I SET out after the Visitation of the Blessed Virgin in a strange abandonment, unable to give an account of what made me set out, leaving my family, which I tenderly loved, and without any positive assurance, hoping, however, even against hope. I reached the New Catholics at Paris, where you worked miracles of providence to conceal me. They sent to fetch the notary who had drawn up the contract of engagement. When he read it to me I felt so strange a repugnance, that it was not possible for me to hear it finished, much less to sign it. The notary was surprised, but he was still more so when Sister Garnier came herself to tell him that there was no necessity for a contract of engagement. It was, O my God, your goodness alone that managed things in this way, for in my then disposition, it seems to me, I would have given the preference to Sister Garnier's views over my own. It was you, O my Lord, who made her thus speak, for she has been since much opposed to me, when they wished to bind me against my will and by force. You had done me the favor, my God, to put my affairs into perfect order, so that I was myself surprised at it, and at the letters you caused me to write, in which I had hardly any part beyond the movement of the hand. And it was at this time that it was given me to write by the interior spirit, and not by my intellect, which till then I had never experienced. So that my manner of writing was quite changed, and people were astonished, I wrote with such facility. I was not at all astonished; but what was then given me as a sample, has since been given to me with much more force and perfection. You began to render me unable to write in the ordinary human way.

I had with me two servants, to get rid of whom was very

147

difficult, for I did not think of bringing them with me; and if I left them they would have told of my departure, and people would have been sent after me, as was done when it was known. You so well arranged all things, O my God, by your providence, that they desired to go with me. And I have since clearly seen that you had done this only to prevent my being discovered; for, besides their being of no use to me, they very soon after returned to France. I set out from Paris.

I took with me my daughter and two maids to attend us both. We set out by water in order to escape being found if any one was looking for me. I went to Melun to wait for it. What was astonishing was that in the boat, my daughter, without knowing what she was doing, could not help making crosses. She kept a person employed in cutting rushes, and then she made them into crosses and quite covered me with them. She put more than three hundred on me. I let her do it, and I understood interiorly that there was a mystery in what she was doing. There was then given to me an inward certainty that I was going there only to reap crosses, and that this little girl was sowing the Cross for me to gather. Sister Garnier, who saw that whatever they did they could not prevent the child from loading me with crosses, said to me, "What this child is doing appears to me very mysterious." She said to her, "My little lady, put crosses on me also." She answered, "They are not for you; they are for my dear mother." She gave her one to please her, then she continued putting them on me. When she had put on a very great number, she had river flowers, which were found on the water, given to her, and making a wreath with them, she placed it on my head, and said to me, "After the Cross you will be crowned." In silence I wondered at all this, and I immolated myself to Love as a victim to be sacrificed to him.

Some time after my departure, a nun, who is a true saint, and a great friend of mine, related to me a vision she had about me. She said she saw my heart in the midst of a great number of thorns, so that it was quite covered with them, and that our Lord appeared in this heart, very well pleased; and she saw that the more strongly the thorns pricked, my heart, instead of being thereby disfigured, appeared more beautiful, and our Lord more pleased.

"She put more than three hundred crosses on me."

At Corbeil, on my way, I saw the Father of whom God had made use to draw me so strongly to his love. He approved my design to quit all for our Lord, but he thought that I would not be able to get on with the New Catholics; he even told me particular things on the point, to make me understand that their spirit, and that by which our Lord was conducting me, were almost incompatible. He said to me, "Above all, try that they shall not know you are walking by spiritual ways, for that will bring down on you persecutions." But, O my God, when it pleases you to make any one suffer, and he has yielded himself into your hands, it is idle to screen one's self and take precautions; it is hard to escape from your providence, especially when the soul has no longer any will, and her will is passed into yours.

While at Paris I gave the New Catholics all the money that I had. I did not reserve a penny for myself, being delighted to be poor, after the example of Jesus Christ. I brought from my house nine thousand livres, and I gave all to the New Catholics. A contract was drawn up for six thousand livres as a repayment, which they said they had need of; and as in the sequel they declared that they had this money on contract, and I had not reserved it for myself by my settlement deed, thinking it would not be known, it has been returned to my children, and I have lost it; at which I feel not the least vexation, for poverty constitutes my riches. The remainder I gave to the Sisters who were with us, both to meet the expenses of the journey, and to commence providing furniture. I gave them beside that the church ornaments, a chalice, a very beautiful sun of silver gilt, silver dishes, a ciboire, and everything needed by them. I did not even keep back my linen for my use, placing it in the common wardrobe. I had neither a locked cash-box nor a purse. Nevertheless, it was said that I had carried off large sums from my house, although that was very false. I had not even taken any linen but what was needed by me for a journey to Paris, for fear of rousing suspicion, and lest I should be discovered if I tried to carry away clothes. I had little eagerness for the riches of this earth; on the contrary, I had more desire to leave them than to possess them. Those whom God makes use of to torment me, have not hesitated to say that I had carried off large sums of money which I had injudiciously spent and given to the relatives of Father La Combe; but that is as false as it is true, that I had not a penny, and that when I arrived at Annecy, and a poor man asked alms, the inclination I had to give to the poor not being extinguished in my heart, and having nothing whatever, I gave him the buttons which fastened the sleeves of my chemise; and another time I gave to a poor man, in the name of Jesus Christ, a little ring, quite plain, which I wore as a token of my marriage with the Child Jesus.

We joined the diligence at Melun, where I left Sister Garnier, and took my place with the other Sisters whom I did not know. What is wonderful is that, although the carriages were very fatiguing, and I did not sleep during this long journey, while I was then so delicate that the loss of sleep used to make me ill, and my daughter, an extremely delicate child only five years of age, did not sleep either, we nevertheless bore the great fatigue without suffering; and this child had not one hour's trouble, although she was only three hours in bed each night. You alone, O my God, know the sacrifices you caused me to make, and the joy of my heart to sacrifice to you all things. If I had had kingdoms and empires, it seems to me I would have given them up with still greater joy to show you more my love. O my God, is it to give up anything when we give it up for you? As soon as we reached the inn, I used to go to the church to adore the Holy Sacrament, and I remained there until the hour of dinner. We held, O my Love, you and I, a conversation in the carriage (or, rather, you alone in me) which the others could not understand, therefore they perceived nothing of it; and the external gaiety I preserved even in the midst of the greatest dangers reassured them. I sang songs of joy to see myself disengaged from wealth, honor, and the embarrassments of the world. You helped us much by your providence, for you protected us in so singular a manner that it seemed you were the pillar of fire during the night, and the cloud during the day. We traversed an extremely dangerous pass between Chambéry and Lyons. Our carriage was broken at the exit of this dangerous pass; had it happened sooner we should have perished.

We reached Annecy, the eve of the Magdalen's Day, 1681;

and on the Day of the Magdalen the Bishop of Geneva said Mass for us at the tomb of St. Francis de Sales. There I renewed my marriage, for I used to renew it every year, and, according to my very simple disposition, without introducing anything formal or distinct; but you placed in my central depth, which was pure and freed from species and forms, all that is pleased you should be there. These words were impressed on me: "I will espouse thee in faith, I will espouse thee for ever;" and these others: "You are to me a husband of blood."

We set out from Annecy the same Day of the Magdalen, and the next day we went to hear Mass at Geneva, at the house of the French Resident. I had much joy in communicating; and it seems to me, O my God, that you there bound me more strongly to you. I asked of you the conversion of this great people. In the evening, late, we reached Gex, where we found only four walls, although the Bishop had assured us that there was furniture. Apparently he thought so. We slept at the Sisters of Charity, who had the kindness to give us their beds. I suffered a pain and agony, which can be better experienced than described, not so much on my own account, as for my daughter, who was visibly declining. I had a great desire to place her with the Ursulines at Tonon; and I was vexed with myself at not having taken her there in the first instance. Then all perceptible faith was taken from me, and a conviction remained that I had been mistaken. Pain took such possession of my heart that in my bed in secret I could not restrain my tears. The next day I said that I wished to take my daughter to Tonon, to the Ursulines, until I saw how we could arrange ourselves. My design was to leave her there. I was strongly opposed, and in a way cruel enough, and not honorable. I saw my daughter fade and grow thin, and in want of everything. I saw her as a victim, whom I had sacrificed by my imprudence. I wrote to Father La Combe, praying him to come and see me, to take measures thereon, not believing I could conscientiously keep her longer in that place. Many days passed away before I could have any answer. I was, however, very indifferent in the divine will of my God as to whether I received help or did not.

CHAPTER II

◆◆◆

OUR Lord had pity on my trouble and the deplorable state of my daughter, and caused the Bishop of Geneva to write to Father La Combe to come and see and console us, and that it would oblige him if he made no delay. As soon as I saw the Father I was surprised to perceive an interior grace, which I may call "communication," that I had never experienced with any one. It seemed to me that an influence of grace came from him to me by the very inmost of the soul, and returned from me to him, so that he experienced the same effect; but grace so pure, so unalloyed, so separate from all sentiment, that it made a kind of flux and reflux, and then went to lose itself in the Divine and Invisible Unity. There was in it nothing human or natural, but all pure spirit. And this union, so pure and holy, which has always subsisted and even increased, becoming ever more one, has never arrested or occupied the soul for a moment out of God, leaving her always in a perfect freedom; union which God alone effects, and which can take place only between souls who are united to him; union free from all weakness and all attachment; union which makes one rejoice over, rather than compassionate, the sufferings of the other, and the more we see ourselves overwhelmed with crosses and overthrows, separated, destroyed, the happier one is; union which for its subsistence has no need of bodily presence; which absence does not render more absent, nor presence more present; union unknown to any but those who experience it. As I had never had a union of this kind, it appeared to me then quite new, for I had never even heard that there was such; but it was so peaceable, so removed from all sentiment, that I have never had a doubt but that it was from God: for these unions, far from turning away from God, bury the soul more deeply in him. The grace which I experienced, and which caused this spiritual influence from him to me, from me to him, dissipated all my troubles and brought me into a profound calm.

God gave him from the first much openness with me. He told me the mercies which God had shown him, and many extraordinary things. I feared much this way of illumination. As my way had been by simple faith, and not in extraordinary gifts, I did not then understand that God wished to use me to withdraw him from the state of illumination, and to place him in the way of simple faith. These extraordinary things caused me fear at first. I dreaded illusion, especially in things which please, relating to the future, but the grace which came out from him, and which flowed through my soul, reassured me, besides that his humility was the most extraordinary I had yet seen; for I saw that he would have preferred the opinion of a little child to his own, that he did not cling to anything, and that, far from being puffed up, either by the gifts of God or his profound learning, one could not have a lower opinion of one's self than he had. It is a gift which God had bestowed on him in an eminent degree. He told me I should take my daughter to Tonon, and that there she would be very well off. He told me at once, after I had spoken to him of the internal repugnance I had for the manner of life of the New Catholics, that he did not believe God required me to join them, that I should remain there without an engagement, and that God would let me know by the course of his providence what he desired of me, but that I should remain until God himself by his providence withdrew me from it, or by the same providence established me there. He told me to ask our Lord to let me know his will. I could neither ask anything nor desire to know anything. I continued in my simple disposition. I had already commenced waking up so as to pray at midnight, but on this occasion I was roused up as if a person had awaked me; and on waking these words were suddenly put into my mind with some little impetuosity: "It is written of me that I will perform your will," and this insinuated itself into my soul with a flow of grace, so pure, yet so penetrating, that I have never experienced it more sweet, more simple, stronger, or more pure. I should remark here that although the then state of my soul was permanent in newness of life, that new life was not yet in the fixedness it has since been in; that is to say, properly, that it was an opening life and opening day, which goes on increasing and strengthening itself to the meridian of glory—day, however, where there is no night; life which fears no longer death in death itself, because death has conquered death, and he who has suffered the first death will never taste the second death.

After these words had been put into my spirit, "It is written of me that I will do your will," I remembered that Father La Combe had told me to ask God what he desired of me in this country. My recollection was my request; immediately these words were put into my spirit with much quickness: "Thou art Peter, and on this stone I will establish my church; and as Peter died on the cross, thou shalt die upon the cross." I was convinced this was what God wished of me; but to understand its execution was what I took no trouble to know. I was invited to place myself on my knees, where I remained until four o'clock in the morning in very profound and peaceful prayer. I said nothing about it in the morning to Father La Combe. The following night I was awaked at the same hour and in the same manner as the previous night, and these words were put into my mind: "Her foundations are in the holy mountains." I was put into the same state, which lasted until four in the morning, but I did not think at all on what this meant, paying no attention to it. The next day the Father told me that he had a very great certainty that I was "a stone which God destined to be the foundation of a great edifice," but he knew no more than I what that edifice was. In whatever way the thing is to be, whether His Divine Majesty wishes to use me in this life for some design known to him alone, or whether he wishes to make me one of the stones of the celestial Jerusalem, it seems to me that this stone is not polished except by blows of a hammer. Methinks that from this time out they have not been spared to it, as will be seen in the sequel; and that our Lord has indeed given it the qualities of stone, which are firmness and insensibility. I told him what had happened to me in the night.

I brought my daughter to Tonon. This poor child conceived a very great friendship for Father La Combe, saying that he was the good God's Father. On arriving at Tonon, I there found a hermit named Friar Anselm, of the most extraordinary holiness that had been known for a long time. He was from Geneva, and God had brought him out of it in a very miraculous manner at the age of twelve years, after having made known to him at the age of four years that he would turn Catholic. He had, with the permission of the Cardinal, then Archbishop of Aix in Provence, at nineteen years assumed the habit of an Augustinian hermit; he lived alone with another friar in a small hermitage, where they saw no one save those who came to visit their chapel. He had been for twelve years in this hermitage, eating nothing but vegetables and salt, sometimes with oil; he fasted continually without a moment's relaxation in the twelve years. Three times a week he fasted on bread and water, never drank wine, and ordinarily made only one meal in twenty-four hours. He wore a shirt of coarse hair, made with great cords of hair, which reached from top to bottom, and he lay only on a board. He had a gift of continual prayer. He prayed specially for eight hours a day, and said his offices—with all this submissive as a child. God had worked through him many striking miracles. He came to Geneva hoping to be able to gain his mother, but he found her dead.

This good hermit had many intimations of the designs of God for me and Father La Combe; but God made him see at the same time that he was preparing strange trials for us both. He knew that God destined us both to help souls. He once during his prayer, which was all in gifts and illumination, saw me on my knees, clothed in a brown mantle, and my head was cut off, but immediately replaced; and then I was clothed in a very white robe, with a red mantle, and a crown of flowers was placed on my head. He saw Father La Combe cut into two pieces, which were soon reunited; and while in his hand he held a palm, he was stripped of his clothes, and reclothed in the white garment with the red mantle; after which he saw us both near a well, and that we were quenching the thirst of numberless people who came to us.

A little after my arrival at the Ursulines of Tonon, Sister M——spoke to me with much openness, following the order Father La Combe had given her. She told me at once so many extraordinary things that I became suspicious, and I thought there was illusion in her case; and I felt angry with myself.

I commenced to feel exceedingly troubled at having brought my daughter; and with regard to her I thought myself indeed an Abraham when Father La Combe accosted me with the words, "You are welcome, daughter of Abraham." I saw no reason for leaving her there; and I could still less keep her with me, for we had no room, and the little girls they brought to make Catholics of were all mixed up with us, and had dangerous ailments. To leave her there also appeared to me madness, considering the language of the country, where they hardly understood French, and the food which she could not take, being quite different from ours.

I saw her daily grow thin and fade away. This put me in an agony, and I felt as if one was tearing my vitals. All the tenderness I had for her sprung up afresh, and I regarded myself as her murderer. I experienced what Hagar suffered when she put away from her in the desert her son Ishmael, that she might not see him die. It appeared to me that though I had been willing to expose myself without reason, I ought at least to have spared my daughter. I saw the loss of her education, and even of her life, inevitable. I did not mention my troubles on this head, and the night was the time which gave scope to my grief that daily became more violent: because you permitted, O my God, you who have always desired of me sacrifices without reserve, that during the whole time I was there, they provided her with nothing which she could eat. All that kept her alive were some spoonfuls of bad broth which I made her take against her will. I gave her up to you, O my God, an entire sacrifice; and it seemed to me that, like another Abraham, I was holding the knife to kill her. I was not willing to take her back, because I was told it was the will of God I should leave her there; and this will of God was for me preferable to everything, even the life of my daughter; besides, she would have been still worse off for food at Gex. Our Lord wished me to be utterly plunged in bitterness, and to make a sacrifice to him without alleviation.

On one side, he caused me to see the grief of her grandmother if she learned of her death, and that it seemed I had taken her away from her merely to kill her; on the other, the reproaches of the family. All her natural gifts were like arrows which pierced me. It would be necessary to experience what I suffered to understand it. With her natural disposition it seemed she would have done wonders if educated in France, and that I was depriving her of all this, and putting it out of her power to be fit for anything, or to find in the future proposals of marriage such as she might hope for, and that I could not without sin let her die thus. For thirteen days I suffered a trouble almost inconceivable; all that I had given up seemed to have cost me nothing in comparison with what the sacrifice of my daughter cost me. I believe that, O my God, you caused this to purify the too human attachment I had for her natural gifts; for after I had left the Ursulines they changed their mode of diet, and gave what was suitable for the delicacy of my daughter, so that she recovered her health.

CHAPTER III

As soon as it was known in France that I had gone away I was generally condemned. Those who attacked me most severely were the religious, in the world's sense, and especially Father La Mothe, who wrote me that all orthodox and pious persons, professional or gentlemen, condemned me. To alarm me the more, he told me that my mother-in-law, on whom I relied for the property of my children and for my younger son, had fallen into second childhood, and that I was the cause of it; this was, however, utterly false. Although there were times when my trouble was excessive, I let nothing of it be seen outwardly. I shut myself up as much as I could, and there I allowed myself to be penetrated by the pain, which appeared to me very profound. I bore it very passively, without being able, or even wishing, to alleviate it; on the contrary, my pleasure was to allow myself to be devoured,

without even wishing to understand it. This pain was as
peaceable as it was penetrating. Once I desired to open the
New Testament to console myself, but I was interiorly hindered; so that I remained in silence, without doing anything,
allowing myself to be devoured by the pain. It appeared to me
that I then commenced to bear troubles in a divine manner,
and that from this time forward, without any sentiment, the
soul could be at the same time very happy and very pained,
very afflicted and beatified. It was not at all in the same way
I had borne my first griefs, nor as I had borne the death of my
father. For then the soul was buried in peace, and in a peace
that was delightful, but she was not delivered over to pain;
what she suffered was only a shock to nature, a weight of
delightful pain. Here it is quite different; the same soul is
delivered entirely to suffering, and she bears it with a divine
strength; and this strength causes the soul to be divided without division from her entire self, so that her unchangeable
happiness does not prevent the most severe suffering. But
these sufferings are impressed on her by God himself as in
Jesus Christ; he suffered as God and man; he suffered in the
strength of God and in the weakness of a man; he was a
blessed God and a Man of sufferings; in short, God-Man,
suffering and rejoicing, without the beatitude diminishing anything of the pain, or the pain interrupting or altering the
perfect beatitude.

I answered all the violent letters they wrote me according
to the interior spirit's dictates, and my answers were found
very suitable; they were even much appreciated, so that, God
allowing, the complaints and thunders soon changed into
praise. Father La Mothe seemed to change his mind, and even
to esteem me, but this did not last long: self-interest was what
made him act so; but when he found that an annuity, which he
fancied I would give him, was not provided, he suddenly
changed. Sister Garnier from the first changed, and declared
herself against me; whether it was merely a pretense or a real
change. As to my body and my health, I took no trouble about
it. You gave me, my God, too much grace, for I have been two
months without almost any sleep, and the food which we had
was little suited to support me. The meat they served us was
rotten and full of maggots, for in that country the meat was

killed on Thursday for use on Friday and Saturday, and owing to the great heat, it was decayed by Sunday; so that what I once would have looked at with horror was my food. Nothing afflicted me then, for in giving me life you had given me capacity for everything. It seems to me I could do anything, without the necessity of doing it. I could do nothing, without at all minding. It is in you, O my God, that one recovers with increase all one has lost for you.

That intellect which I once thought I had lost in a strange stupidity, was restored to me with inconceivable additions. I was astonished at it myself, and I found that there was nothing for which it was not able, and in which it did not succeed. Those who saw me said I had a prodigious intellect. I knew well that I had but little intellect, but that in God my mind had taken a quality which before it was without.

Some time after my arrival at Gex the Bishop of Geneva came to see us. I spoke to him with the openness and impetuosity of the Spirit which guided me. He was so convinced of the Spirit of God in me that he could not refrain from saying so. He was even affected and touched by it, opened his heart to me about what God desired of him, and how he had been turned aside from fidelity and grace; for he is a good prelate, and it is the greatest pity in the world that he is so weak in allowing himself to be led by others. When I have spoken to him, he always entered into what I said, acknowledging that what I said had the character of truth; and this could not be otherwise, since it was the Spirit of truth that made me speak to him, without which I was only a stupid creature; but as soon as the people who wished to rule him and could not endure any good that did not come from themselves, spoke to him, he allowed himself to be influenced against the truth. It is this weakness, joined to some others, which has hindered him from doing all the good in his diocese that otherwise he would have done. After I had spoken to him he told me that he had had it in mind to give me as director Father La Combe; that he was a man enlightened of God, who understood well the ways of the spirit, and had a singular gift for calming souls—these are his own words—that he had even told him, the Bishop, many things regarding himself, which he knew to be very true, since he felt in himself what the Father said to him. I had great joy that the Bishop of Geneva gave him to me as director, seeing that thereby the external authority was joined to the grace which seemed already to have given him to me by that union and effusion of supernatural grace.

The wakefulness and fatigues, together with the indifferent climate of this country, caused me a great pulmonary inflammation, with fever and a retention in the stomach of all the water I drank, which caused me violent pains. The doctors thought me in danger, for besides that, I had taken many remedies which I did not pass off. You permitted, O my God, this malady doubtless both as an exercise for my patience and to glorify yourself in the striking miracle which you performed through your servant. As I was very weak, I could not raise myself in the bed without falling in a faint; and I could not remain in bed, for I was bursting from the waters and remedies I could not get rid of. God allowed that the Sisters neglected me utterly, particularly the one in charge of the housekeeping, who did not give me what was necessary for my life. I had not a shilling to provide for myself, for I had reserved nothing, and the Sisters received all the money which came to me from France—a very large sum. Thus I had the advantage of practicing a little poverty, and being in want with those to whom I had given everything.

They wrote to Father La Combe to come and take my confession. He very charitably walked all night, although he had eight long leagues; but he used always to travel so, imitating in this, as in everything else, our Lord Jesus Christ. As soon as he entered the house, without my knowing it, my pains were alleviated. And when he came into my room and blessed me, with his hands on my head, I was perfectly cured, and I evacuated all the water, so that I was able to go to the Mass. The doctors were so surprised that they did not know how to account for my cure; for, being Protestants, they were unable to recognize a miracle. They said it was madness, that my sickness was in the imagination, and a hundred absurdities, such as might be expected from people otherwise vexed by the knowledge that we had come to withdraw from error those who were willing.

A violent cough, however, remained, and those Sisters of themselves told me to go to my daughter, and take milk for a fortnight, after which I might return. As soon as I set out, Father La Combe, who was returning and was in the same boat, said to me, "Let your cough cease." It at once stopped, and although a furious gale came down upon the lake which made me vomit, I coughed no more at all. This storm became so violent that the waves were on the point of capsizing the boat. Father La Combe made the sign of the cross over the waves, and although the billows became more disturbed, they no longer came near, but broke more than a foot distant from the boat—a fact noticed both by the boatmen and those in the boat, who looked upon him as a saint. Thus I arrived at Tonon at the Ursulines, perfectly cured, so that instead of adopting remedies as I had proposed, I entered on a retreat which I kept for twelve days.

It was then I made perpetual vows of chastity, poverty, and obedience; to obey without resistance whatever I believed to be the will of God and the Church, and to honor Jesus Christ, the Child, in the way he wished. I admit that I do not know why nor how I made these vows. I did not find in myself anything to make a vow, and it seemed to me that I was so entirely yours, O my God, that I did not know where to find that which I vowed to you. I understood at the same time that the end of the vow and its consummation was given to my soul as well interiorly as exteriorly; that the soul, being in her entirety God's without reserve, without self-regard, without interest, had the perfect chastity of love, since she was even passed into this same love. It appeared to me that you, O my God, had endowed me with the perfect poverty, by the utter stripping you had effected on me as well interiorly as exteriorly, leaving me nothing of "the own." As to obedience, my will was so entirely lost in yours, that not only it found no resistance, but it had not even a repugnance; the same was its condition as regards the Church. And as to honoring the Childhood of Jesus Christ, I did not know by what means; for that which was proposed to me did not depend on me, but on you, O my God; and it appeared to me that the honor which I paid him was to bear himself in his states. I, however, made all these vows because I was told to make them, and I followed without choice, without inclination, and without repugnance, what I was told to do; and you have drawn from it your glory in a manner known to you alone, the effect of which soon appeared; for you took a new possession of my exterior, to make me the plaything of your providence, as you have since done. You despoiled me of my riches by a new poverty, and you deprived me of dwelling or place on earth, so that I have not where to rest my head. As to obedience, you made me practice it at one time, as will be seen, with the submissiveness of a child; but also how much have you obeyed me yourself; or rather, you, O my God, have rendered my wills wonderful, causing them to pass into you. In this unity the will of the soul so transforms itself into that of God as only to will that which God causes it to will, or rather, what he himself wills. Oh, it is then that this will is made wonderful, as well because it is made the will of God, the greatest of wonders, and its end, as that it works wonders in God; where, as soon as God causes it to will anything, since it is he who wills in it, this will has its effect; hardly has it willed, and the thing is done.

And as to that of the Holy Child Jesus, good God, to what a degree have I experienced its effects! Have you not placed me in a state of wonderful childishness? And have I not borne it in a singular manner? To honor Jesus, the Child, was for me to bear the Child Jesus Christ as he was willed me to bear him many times, and many of his states, as will be seen in the sequel.

I used to get up every night at midnight, and I had no need of an alarm, for by your goodness, O my God, as long as you desired it of me, I always woke sufficiently before midnight, to be up at that hour; and when through distrust or thoughtlessness I had set my alarm in the morning, I was never awakened. This led me to abandon myself more to your guidance, O my God, for I saw you had over me the care of a father and a husband. When I had any indisposition, and my body needed rest, you used not to awake me; but at that time, even sleeping, I felt a singular possession of you. For some years I had only a half sleep; my soul was awake to you with the more force as sleep seemed to withdraw her attention from everything else. Our Lord also made known to many persons that he destined me to be the mother of a great people, but a people simple and childlike. They understood these intimations literally, and thought that it related to some new foundation or society; but it appears to me that it means nothing but the persons whom God has willed I should afterwards gain for him, and to whom he has in his goodness willed that I should act as a mother, giving them the same union with me that children have with a mother, but a union much more strong and more inward, and giving me for them all that was necessary, that they might walk in the way by which God was guiding them, as I shall explain hereafter, when I speak of this state of maternity.

CHAPTER IV

BEFORE speaking of what remains for me to write (which, if I had anything of my natural selfhood, I would gladly suppress, as well owing to the difficulty of explaining myself, as that there are few souls able to appreciate a course of guidance so little known and so little understood that I have never read of anything like it) I will yet say something of the inner disposition I was then in, as far as I can make it intelligible—a matter of no small difficulty owing to its extreme simplicity. If this is of use to you, who desire to be among the number of my children; and if it is useful to my children in more thoroughly destroying self, and in leading them to allow God to glorify himself in them in his manner, not in theirs, I shall find my trouble well repaid; and if there is anything which they do not understand, let them truly die to themselves, and they will soon have a more powerful experience of it than I could give them; for description never does come up to experience. After I had emerged from the state of abjectness of which I have spoken, I understood how a state, which had appeared to me so criminal, and which was so only in my idea, had purified my soul, taking from her all selfhood. As soon as my mind was enlightened on the truth of that state, my soul was placed in an immense freedom. I recognized the difference between the graces which had preceded that state and those which have succeeded it. Previously everything was collected and concentrated within, and I possessed God in my center, and in the inmost of my soul; but afterwards I was possessed of him in a manner so vast, so pure, and so immense, that nothing can equal it. Formerly God was, as it were, enclosed in me, and I was united to him in my center; but afterwards I was submerged in the sea itself. Before, the thoughts and views were lost, but in a way perceived, though very slightly; the soul let them go sometimes, which is yet an act; but afterwards they had, as it were, entirely disappeared, in a manner so bare, so pure, so lost that the soul had no action of her own, however simple and delicate—at least, which could rise into consciousness.

The powers and the senses are purified in a wonderful manner: the mind is of a surprising limpidity; I was sometimes astonished that not a thought appeared in it. That imagination, once so troublesome, gives no longer any trouble whatsoever; there is no longer embarrassment, nor disturbance, nor occupation of the memory; everything is naked and limpid, and God makes the soul know and think whatever he pleases, without irrelevant species any longer inconveniencing the mind. This is of very great purity. It is the same in the case of the will, which, being totally dead to all its spiritual appetites, has no longer any taste, leaning, or tendency; it remains empty of all human inclination, natural or spiritual. It is this which enables God to bend it where he pleases, and how he pleases.

This vastness, which is not bounded by anything whatever, however simple, increases day by day, so that it seems that this soul, in sharing the qualities of her Spouse, shares especially his immensity. Formerly one was, as it were, drawn and shut up within; afterwards I experienced that a hand far more powerful than the first drew me out of myself, and plunged me, without view, or knowledge, in God, in a way which ravished me; and the more distant the soul thought herself from this state, the more ravished she was to find it. How sweet, then, is it to this soul, which is rather comprehended of it than comprehends it.

At the commencement of this state there happened to me a thing which I do not know how to name. My prayer was of a nakedness and simplicity beyond conception, and yet of an inexplicable depth. I was, as it were, held up high out of myself, and what particularly surprised me was, that my head felt as if violently lifted up. This was all the more unusual, because formerly its first movements were quite in the opposite direction, since I was quite concentrated. I believe that God wished me to have this experience at the commencement of the new life (which was so powerful, although very sweet, that my body fainted away)—I believe, I say, that our Lord permitted that to enable me to understand for the benefit of other souls, this passage of the soul into God; for after it had lasted with me some days, I no longer perceived this violence, although I have always since experienced that my prayer is no longer in me in the way that I formerly experienced it, when I used to say, "I carry in me the prayer that I offer to the God of my life." It will be difficult to understand what I wish to say without having experienced it. When I went to confession, I could hardly speak, not from internal recollection, nor as I have described when I was at the commencement; it was like an immersion. This is a word which I use without knowing if it is suitable. I was plunged down and raised up. Once, when at confession to Father La Combe at Gex, I felt this elevation so strong that I thought my body was about to be raised from the earth. Our Lord made use of it to let me grasp what that flight of the spirit is, which raised the bodies of some saints to a great height, and the difference there is between that and the loss of the soul in God. Before going on with the events which happened to me, I will say something about this.

The flight of the spirit is far more noble than the simple fainting away of ecstasy, although almost always the flight of the spirit causes weakness to the body, God drawing powerfully the soul, not in her center but in himself, in order to make her pass there, this soul not being yet sufficiently purified to pass into God without violence; a thing which can be brought about only after the mystical decease, where the soul veritably goes out of herself to pass into her Divine Object, which I call decease—that is to say, passage from one thing to another. That is indeed the happy Passover for the soul, and passage into the promised land. This spirit, which is created to be united to its principle, has such an impulse to return to it, that if it was not stopped by a continual miracle, it would, by its motive-power, carry the body wherever it wished, owing to its impetuosity and its nobleness; but God has given it an earthly body as counter-weight. This spirit, then, created to be immediately united to its principle, feeling itself drawn by its Divine Object, tends to it with extreme violence, so that God, suspending for a time the power which the body has to keep back the spirit, it follows with impetuosity; but as it is not sufficiently purified to pass into God, it returns gradually to itself, and the body reassuming gradually its quality, it returns to earth.

It is, then, certain that the soul, by death to herself, passes into her Divine Object, and this is what I experienced; and I found that the further I advanced, the more my spirit lost itself in its Sovereign, who drew it to him more and more; and he willed at the commencement I should know this for the benefit of others, not for myself. Daily this spirit lost itself more, and its principle attracted it continually more, until, owing to this drawing, it was so withdrawn from itself, that it lost itself completely from view, and no longer perceived itself. But the same Love which drew it to him brightened and purified it, that it might pass into him and be then transformed into himself. In the commencement of the new life I saw clearly that the soul was united to God without means or medium, but she was not completely lost in him. Each day she lost herself there, as one sees a river which loses itself in the ocean, at first unite with it, then flow into it, but so that the river may for a time be distinguished from the sea, until at last it gradually is transformed into the sea itself, which, while little by little communicating its qualities, changes it so entirely into itself, that it becomes one and the same sea with it. I have experienced the same in my soul, how God gradually makes her lose herself in him, and communicates to her his qualities, drawing her away from everything she has of the "*own*."

At the commencement of the new life I committed faults; and these faults, which would not have appeared anything on the contrary, would have been virtues in a different state, were little assertions of the selfhood, light, and on the surface—a haste, a slight emotion, but as slight as possible. I experienced at once that this raised a partition between God and my soul; it was like a speck of dust, but as this was only on the surface, the partition appeared to me finer than a spider's web. And then he willed me to go clear myself from it by confession, or else he himself purified me from it; and I saw clearly this partition, which was like a veil that did not break the union nor alter it, but covered it, and this slight partition made noticeable more of distinction between the Spouse and the Bride. I do not know if I make myself understood. The soul suffered from this little partition, but in a peaceable manner; she saw that she could indeed erect the partition, but could not take it away. Little by little all partition was lost, and the fewer and more delicate the partitions, the more union was lost in Unity, until at last there was only one where there had been two, and the soul lost herself so utterly that she could no longer distinguish herself from her Beloved, nor see him. It is that which caused her trouble in the sequel. As to her confession, she was astonished that she knew not what to say, that she no longer found anything; although one would think she must commit more faults, owing to the liberty she had to speak, talk, and act, which formerly she had not; but that no longer troubles her, nor is any more regarded as a fault. An inconceivable innocence, unknown and incomprehensible to those who are still shut up in themselves, is her life. But I must resume where I have broken off.

After I made my retreat at the Ursulines of Tonon, I returned by Geneva, and having no other means of traveling, the Resident lent me a horse. As I did not know how to use this means of conveyance, I made some difficulty, but they assured me it was very gentle, and I resolved to make the attempt. There was a kind of farrier present, who, regarding me with haggard eyes, as soon as I was mounted, struck the horse upon the crop. It made a frightful bound, and threw me to the earth with such a force that they thought I was killed. I fell upon my temple. I ought certainly to have been killed, for the bone of the cheek was broken in two, and I had two teeth knocked in. In my fall I was upheld by an invisible hand. Nevertheless, I remounted the best I could on another horse which they gave me to finish my journey, and my servant man placed himself beside me to hold me up. But a surprising thing happened; while on the road something was forcibly pushing me on the same side on which I had fallen off, and although I leant with all my strength to the other side, and I was held on firmly enough, I could not resist what was pushing me. I was every moment in danger of being killed, but quite content to see myself at the mercy of the divine providence. I at once understood it was the Devil, but I was quite confident he could do me no hurt but what my Master allowed him.

My relatives, after a slight attempt, left me in quiet at Gex. People even began to esteem me much, and as my miraculous cure had been written about to Paris, it made a great sensation. You permitted it, O my God, that I might fall the lower from the height to which you had elevated me. Almost all the persons then in repute for holiness wrote to me. The Demoiselles of Paris, who were renowned for good works, congratulated me. I received letters from Madame de Lamoignon and another lady, who was so pleased with my answer that she sent one hundred pistoles for our House, and told me when we were in want of money I had only to write to her, and she would send me whatever I wanted. At Paris they talked only of the sacrifice I had made. All approved and praised my action, so that they wanted an acccount of it printed, together with the miracle which had taken place. I do not know who prevented it. From this we may see the inconstancy of the creature; for the very journey which then brought me such praises is the same which furnished the pretext for such a strange condemnation.

CHAPTER V

MY relatives made no effort to bring me back. The first thing they proposed to me a month after my arrival at Gex was not only to relinquish my wardship, but also to give all my property to my children, reserving only an annuity for myself. Although the proposal, coming from persons who, as the sequel will show, had regard only for their own interests, ought to have appeared to me harsh, it by no means did so. I had neither friends nor advice. I did not know whom to ask as to the mode of effecting it; for as to willingness, I was perfectly ready. It seemed to me I had thus the means of accomplishing my vow and my extreme desire to be conformed to Jesus Christ, poor, naked, stripped of everything. It was necessary to send a power of attorney, which they had drawn up. Clauses which were inserted Our Lord did not allow me to notice, and I, believing it honestly prepared, signed. It was provided that when my children all died, I should not inherit my own property, but it was to pass to collaterals. There were other matters also equally to my disadvantage. Although what I reserved for myself was enough for the place where I then was, it is hardly sufficient to support me elsewhere. I gave up then my property, that I might be conformed to Jesus Christ, with more joy than those who demanded it of me could have from its possession. It is a thing which I have never either repented or regretted. O my God, what pleasure to lose all and to quit all for you! "Love of poverty, kingdom of tranquility."

Our Lord enlightened me to see that the external crosses came from him; so that I could not have any grudge against the persons who brought them on me—on the contrary, I felt a tender compassion for them, and I was more troubled from those I caused them innocently than at those they caused me. After the accident which befell me in my fall from the horse, which so injured me that I spat blood that came from the brain, and for eight days it also came from my nose (which, through your goodness, O my God, had no permanent consequence), the Devil commenced to declare himself more openly my enemy, and to break loose against me. One night when I least thought of it, he presented himself to my mind in a way so monstrous and terrifying that nothing could be more so; only a face was visible by means of a bluish light. I do not know if the flame itself composed this horrible face, for it was so mixed up and passed so quickly that I could not well distinguish. My soul remained unmoved and untroubled, understanding that it was the Devil. The sense were slightly alarmed, but as for the soul, she remained firm and immovable, without any motion of her own, and did not even allow the body to make the sign of the cross; because although this would have driven away the Devil for the moment, it would have shown I was afraid of him, or that I knew it was he. This way of despising is far more distasteful to him, so he never again appeared in that way; but he got into such a rage that every night, as I got up at midnight, he used to come at that hour and made a terrible knocking in my room. When I lay down it was still worse; he shook my bed for a quarter of an hour at a time. Then he used to go at the paper window-panes, which he broke; and every morning as long as this lasted the panes were found broken. I had no fear, not even a shiver in the senses. I used to get up and light my candle at a lamp which I kept lighted in my room, for I had accepted the office of sacristan, and the duty of waking the Sisters at the hour they should rise, ringing the "Aves;" and in spite of my indisposition I never failed to wake them or to be the first at all the duties. I made use of my little light to look all over the room, and at the window-panes at the very time the Devil was knocking more loudly than usual. As he saw I was not afraid of anything, he went off on a sudden, and did not attack me any more in person; but he did so by stirring up men against me, and this succeeded better for him, for he found them ready to do what he suggested, and to do it with the more zeal as they regarded it as a good deed.

One of the Sisters I had brought, who was a very beautiful girl, became connected with an ecclesiastic who had authority in this place. He inspired her from the first with an aversion to me, judging well that if she had confidence in me, I would not advise her to allow his frequent visits. She undertook a retreat. I begged her not to enter on it until I was there; for it was the time that I was making my own. This ecclesiastic was very glad to let her make it, in order to get entirely into her confidence, for it would have served as a pretext for his frequent visits. The Bishop of Geneva had assigned Father La Combe as director of our House without my asking, so that it came purely from God. I then begged this girl, as Father La Combe was to conduct the retreats, she would wait for him.

As I was already commencing to get an influence over her mind, she yielded to me against her own inclination, which was willing enough to make it under that ecclesiastic. I began to speak to her of prayer, and to cause her to offer it. Our Lord therein gave her such blessing that this girl, in other respects very discreet, gave herself to God in earnest and with all her heart. The retreat completed the victory. Now, as she apparently recognized that to connect herself with that ecclesiastic was something imperfect, she was more reserved. This much displeased the worthy ecclesiastic, and embittered him against Father La Combe and me, and this was the source of all the persecutions that befell me. The noise in my room ceased when that commenced. This ecclesiastic, who heard confession in the House, no longer regarded me with a good eye. He began secretly to speak of me with scorn. I knew it, but said nothing to him, and did not for that cease confessing to him. There came to see him a certain monk who hated Father La Combe in consequence of his regularity. They formed an alliance, and decided that they must drive me out of the House, and make themselves masters of it. They set in motion for this purpose all the means they could find. The ecclesiastic, seeing himself supported, no longer kept any bounds. They said I was stupid, that I had a silly air. They could judge of my mind only by my air, for I hardly spoke to them. This went so far that they made a sermon out of my confession, and it circulated through the whole diocese. They said that some persons were so frightfully proud that in place of confessing gross sins, they confessed only peccadillos; then they gave a detail, word for word, of everything I had confessed. I am willing to believe that this worthy priest was accustomed only to the confessions of peasants, for the faults of a person in the state which I was in astonished him, and made him regard what were really faults in me, as fanciful; for otherwise assuredly he would not have acted in such a manner. I still accused myself, however, of a sin of my past life, but this did not content him, and I knew he made a great commotion because I did not accuse myself of more notable sins. I wrote to Father La Combe to know if I could confess past sins as present, in order to satisfy this worthy man. He told me, no; and that I should take great care not to confess them except as passed, and that in confession the utmost sincerity was needed.

My manner of life was such that I had very few opportunities of committing faults, for I took not the least part in the affairs of the House, leaving the Sisters to dispose of the funds as they pleased, persuaded as I was that they made good use of them. A little after coming there I received a sum of eighteen hundred livres, which one of my friends lent me to finish our furnishing, and which I repaid on settling my property; they received this also. They managed as well as they could, and were good economists, but without experience, and they were without what was necessary for an establishment. I took no part in anything, except to perform my duty of sacristan, and to assist at all the offices, which we repeated—the Sister I have spoken of and I; there were only us two to repeat the offices, and we did it with as much exactitude as if we were many, and, with exception of meals and recreation, I remained all day shut up in my room. I let them receive and return all visits, and took no share therein. All I did was to speak an occasional word to those who were in seclusion, with a view to becoming Catholics; and our Lord gave such a blessing to what I said that we saw some whom previously they knew not what to do with, relish God in a wonderful manner, and acquire an incredible affection for remaining in the church. Living in this way, I had no opportunities for sinning.

This worthy gentleman gained over one of the Sisters, who had a weak mind—it was the one who was housekeeper— whereby they commenced causing me a few crosses. Some days before these persecutions were set on foot, at midnight, being with our Lord, I said to him: "It seems to me you promised me here only crosses; where are they, then? I do not see them." Hardly had this thought occurred to me when there came upon me such a number that, so to speak, they were tumbling one over the other.

Before continuing, I will mention that immediately on our arrival the Bishop of Geneva was so kind as to allow us to have the Holy Sacrament at our House. As soon as ever our chapel was in condition for it, we had this advantage; and as we wished to place it the day of the Holy Cross, which was our first day—and which name I had taken without knowing

why, to avoid recognition—the chapel not being yet sufficiently closed, for three nights I guarded the Holy Sacrament, lying by myself in the chapel. I never passed any with
greater satisfaction. I had a movement to pray for that unfortunate town which was the object of my tenderness, and
which was the occasion of all my disgraces. I had confidence,
as I have still more at present, that it would be one day, O my
Divine Spouse, the throne of your mercies. I cannot doubt it.

The Bishop, knowing I loved the Holy Child Jesus, sent
me to place in our little chamber a simple image of paper of a
Child Jesus, who held in his hands crosses for distribution.
On receiving it, I was struck with the thought that he came
with the hands full to distribute them to me, and I received
them with all my heart. For you have always shown this
kindness to me, my God, never to give me extraordinary crosses
without first having obtained my consent—not to the nature
of the cross in itself, but for the suffering an extraordinary
cross which was proposed to me; and at the same time those
words said of Jesus Christ, my divine model, came to my mind:
"For the joy set before him, endured the cross." It appeared
to me then, O my God, that I was offered the choice either of
the approbation of men and success, together with the assurance of my salvation; or of the cross, wretchedness, rejection,
persecution from all creatures, even privation of all creatures,
even privation of all assurance of salvation, and nothing but
YOUR GLORY ALONE. O Love, the latter was the object
of my choice and of my tender inclination. Yes; "for the joy
set before him, he endured the cross." I prostrated myself, my
face to the earth, for a long time, as it were, to receive all
your blows, O amiable justice of my God, with which from
that moment I felt myself inflamed. All self-interest having
perished and been destroyed in me, nothing remained but the
interest of your divine justice. Strike, O divine Justice, who
have not spared Jesus Christ, God-Man, who gave himself up
to death to satisfy you. Him alone you found worthy of you,
and in him you still find hearts which are fitted for you to
exercise your loving cruelties.

A few days after my arrival at Gex by night I saw in a
dream (but a mysterious dream, for I perfectly well distinguished it) Father La Combe fixed on a great cross of extraor-

dinary height. He was naked in the way our Lord is pictured. I saw an amazing crowd who covered me with confusion and cast upon me the ignominy of his punishment. It seemed he suffered more pain than I, but I more reproaches than he. This surprised me the more, because, having seen him only once, I could not imagine what it meant. But I have indeed seen it accomplished. At the same time that I saw him thus fixed to the cross, these words were impressed on me: "I will strike the shepherd, and the sheep shall be scattered;" and the others, "I have specially prayed for thee, Peter, that thy faith fail not. Satan has desired to sift thee."

This worthy ecclesiastic, as I have said, gained over that girl, and afterwards the Superior. I was of a very delicate constitution, and, however willing, that did not give bodily strength. I had two maids to serve me, but as the community needed one to cook and the other to attend the gate, and for other duties, I gave them up, thinking that they would not be unwilling I should have their services sometimes; since I besides allowed them to receive the whole of my income; for immediately after my settlement was made they received in advance the half of my annuity. I believed then that they would consent to these two maids rendering me the services which I could not perform myself. But our Lord permitted that they were unwilling. The church was very large to sweep. I had to sweep it by myself. Oftentimes I have fainted over the broom, and remained in corners utterly exhausted. This obliged me to ask sometimes that they would have it done by the grown peasant girls, who were there as New Catholics, and at last they had the kindness to allow this. What troubled me most was that I had never done washing, and it was necessary for me to wash all the linen of the sacristy. I took one of the maids I had brought to do it; for I had spoiled everything. These good Sisters came and dragged her out of my room by the arm, telling her to mind her own business. I did not appear to notice it, and in whatever manner they behaved I made no remonstrance. So the worthy ecclesiastic saw that I would not withdraw for all this. Besides, the other Sister attached herself more and more to our Lord through means of prayer, and contracted great friendship for me. This increased the ecclesiastic's trouble so that he could not keep in his rage against me. One day he thought proper to bring a very doubtful book to this girl. I handed it back to him, after having opened it, urgently requesting him not to bring books of this kind into the House. He was extremely offended, and set out for Annecy to make mischief.

CHAPTER VI

UP to that time the Bishop of Geneva had shown me much esteem and kindness, and therefore this man cleverly took him off his guard. He urged upon the Prelate that, in order to make certain of me for that House, he ought to compel me to give up to it the little money I had reserved for myself, and to bind me by making me the Superior. He knew well that I would never bind myself there, and that, my vocation being elsewhere, I would never give my capital to that House, where I had come only as a visitor; and that I would not be Superior, as I had many times already declared; and that even should I bind myself, it would be only on the condition that this should not be. I believe, indeed, that this objection to being Superior was a remnant of the selfhood, colored with humility. The Bishop of Geneva did not in the least penetrate the intentions of that ecclesiastic, who was called in the country the little Bishop, because of the ascendency he had acquired over the mind of the Bishop of Geneva. He thought it was through affection for me, and zeal for this House, that this man desired to bind me to it; consequently he at once fell in with the proposal, resolving to carry it through at whatever price. The ecclesiastic, seeing he had so well succeeded, no longer kept any bounds as regarded me. He commenced by stopping the letters I wrote Father La Combe. Afterwards he intercepted all those I wrote to Paris, and those which were written to me, in order to influence people's minds as he pleased, and that I might not be able either to know it, or defend myself, or tell how I was being treated. One of the maids I had brought wished to return, not being able to remain in that place, so that only one remained for me, and she was weak and too much occupied to aid me in many things I had need of. As Father La Combe was coming for the retreat, I thought he would soften the bitter spirit of this man, and would advise me. Meanwhile the proposal of binding myself, and becoming Superior, was made to me. I answered, that as for binding myself, it was impossible, my vocation being elsewhere, and for the Superiorship, I could not be a Superior before being a novice; that all of them had completed two years of novitiate before binding themselves, and when I had done as much, I would see what God inspired me. The Superior answered me sharply enough, that if I contemplated quitting them some day, I might do it at once. However, I did not withdraw for this; I behaved still in my usual way, but I saw the heavens grow dark gradually, and storms come from every side. The Superior meanwhile affected a more gentle air; she declared she also wished to go to Geneva, that I should not bind myself, but should promise to take her with me if I went there. She asked me whether I was not bound in some particular matter for Geneva. She wished to sound me, to see if I had not some plan, or perhaps some engagement under vow; but as I had not the advice of Father La Combe, I did not say anything to her. She professed even much confidence in me, and seemed united to me. As I am very frank, and our Lord has given me much uprightness, I believed she was acting in good faith: I even declared to her I was not attracted by the manner of life of the New Catholics, owing to their outside intrigues. I further let her know that certain abjurations and certain shufflings did not please me, because I desired people to be straightforward in everything; so that my refusal to sign things which were not true shocked them a little. She let nothing of it appear. She was a worthy person, and did these things only because that ecclesiastic told her it was necessary to act so, to bring the House into credit, and to attract the charity of Paris. I told her that if we acted uprightly God would not fail us; that he would sooner work miracles.

One day after the Superior had communicated, she came to

me and told me that our Lord had let her know how dear
Father La Combe was to him, and that he was a saint, that she
felt herself disposed to make a vow of obedience to him. She
appeared to say all this in perfect good faith, and I believe
she was then speaking sincerely. I told her she should not do
this: she said she wished it, and she was about to pronounce
the vow. I opposed it strongly, saying that these things
should not be done lightly, nor without consulting the person
whom one wished to obey, to ascertain if he would accept it.
She was satisfied with my reasons, and wrote to Father La
Combe all which she said had taken place in her, and how she
desired to vow obedience to him, that it was God who urged
her to it. Father La Combe answered her, and she showed me
the letter. He told her she should never make a vow to obey
any man; that he would never be her adviser; that the person
who is suitable at one time is not so at another; that one
should remain free, obeying, nevertheless, with love and charity, all the same as if bound by a vow; that as for himself, he
had never received such a vow from any one and never
would, that it was even forbidden him by their rules: that
none the less he would serve her to the best of his ability,
and that in a short time he would go to conduct the retreats.
She had also told him in that letter that she prayed he would
ask our Lord to let her know if he destined her for Geneva,
whether she should go with me; that she was content whatever the will of God, only that he should tell her exactly
what he knew in these things. He wrote her that on this
article he would simply tell her what he thought of it.

It is true that the characteristic of Father La Combe is
simplicity and straightforwardness. When he came for the
retreats, which was the third and last time he came to Gex, on
the first day she spoke to him with much eagerness. She asked
him if one day she would be united with me at Geneva. He
answered her with his usual candour: "My mother, our Lord
has let me know that you will never be established at Geneva;
as for the others, I have no light." (She is dead, so that was
well verified.) As soon as he made this declaration, she appeared enraged against him and me in a surprising way. She
went to find the ecclesiastic, who was in a room with the
housekeeper, and they together took measures to compel me

either to bind myself or to withdraw. They thought I would rather bind myself than withdraw. And they watched my letters more closely.

The Father preached at her request, which was only to lay a trap for him. He had in the parish made a sermon on charity, which had carried away every one. She asked him for a sermon touching the inner life. He preached one which he had preached at the Visitation at Tonon: "The beauty of the King's daughter comes from within." He explained what the inner life is, and what it is to act from it as a principle. That ecclesiastic, who was present with one of his confidants, said that it was preached against him, and that it was full of errors. He extracted eight propositions, which the Father had not preached, and after dressing them out as maliciously as he could, he sent them to a friend at Rome, in order, as he said, that they might be examined by the Sacred College and the Inquisition. Although they were very badly drawn up, they, nevertheless, passed as quite sound. His friend told him there was nothing whatever wrong in them. This vexed him, for he is not, as I hear, theologian enough to judge anything for himself. Moreover, he came the next day with surprising anger to Father La Combe, and attacked him, saying he had made the sermon to offend him. The Father drew it from his pocket, and showed him that he had thereon written the dates and the places where he had preached it; so that he was confounded, but not appeased. He became still more angry in the presence of many persons who were assembled there. The Father went on his knees, and in that position listened for half an hour to all the abuse which the ecclesiastic chose to utter. They came to tell me, but I did not choose to have anything to do with all that. The Father, after being treated in this way, said to the ecclesiastic with much sweetness and humility, that he was obliged to go to Annecy for some business of their convent, and that if he desired to send anything to the Bishop, he would take charge of his letters. The other answered for him to wait, that he would write. This good Father had the patience to wait for more than three full hours without hearing anything from him. They came and told me, "Do you know that Father La Combe has not started, but is in the church, where he awaits letters from M——?"

—mentioning the priest who had so illtreated him that he even tore from his hands a letter, which I had just given him for the good hermit I have mentioned. I went to the church to ask him to send the servant who was to accompany him to Annecy to see if the packet of that gentleman was ready; for the day was so far gone that he would have to sleep on the road. This man found mounted a servant of the ecclesiastic, who told him, It is I who am going there. And as he was going in, this same M—— said to another servant, to go as fast as he could so as to reach Annecy before the Father. He had kept him waiting merely to send off a man before him to prejudice the mind of the Bishop; and he sent back word to the Father that he had no letters to give him.

Father La Combe none the less went to Annecy, where he found the Bishop much prejudiced and embittered. He said to him: "My Father, it is absolutely necessary to bind that lady to give what she has to the House at Gex, and to become the Superior." "My lord," answered Father La Combe, "you know what she has herself told you of her vocation both at Paris and in this country, and therefore I do not believe she will consent to bind herself. It is not likely that, having given up everything in the hope of going into Geneva, she should bind herself elswhere, and thus render it impossible for her to accomplish God's designs for her. She has offered to remain with these good Sisters as a lodger. If they desire to keep her in that capacity she will remain with them; if not, she is resolved to withdraw into some convent until God shall dispose of her otherwise." The Bishop answered: "My Father, I know all that, but at the same time I know she is obedient, and if you so order her, she will surely do it." "It is for this reason, my lord, because she is obedient, that one should be very cautious in the commands one gives her," answered the Father. "It is not likely that I will urge a foreign lady, who has for her whole subsistence merely what she has reserved for herself, to rob herself of that in favor of a House which is not yet founded, and which, perhaps, never will be founded. If the House happens to fail, or to be no longer useful, on what shall the lady live? Shall she go to the almshouse?" The Bishop said: "My Father, all these reasons are good for nothing. If you do not cause the lady to do it, I will interdict you." That mode of speaking surprised the Father, who well enough knew the rules of the interdict, as not allowing it in matters of this nature. He said to him: "My lord, I am ready to suffer not only the interdict, but even death rather than do anything against my honor or conscience," and withdrew. He wrote me at the same time everything by an express, that I might take my measures thereon. I had nothing left but to withdraw into a convent, but before doing so I said again to these good Sisters that I was going away; for at the same time I received a letter that the nun to whom I had entrusted my daughter, and who was the one spoke French least corruptly, and was very virtuous, had fallen ill, and that she prayed me to go for a time to my daughter. I showed them the letter, and told them that I wished to withdraw into that community; that if they ceased persecuting me as they were doing, and if Father La Combe was left in quiet—who was deemed the apostle of the country because of the wonderful fruit of his missions—I would return as soon as the mistress of my daughter was recovered. It was my intention to do it. Instead of this, they persecuted me with more violence, and wrote against me to Paris, intercepted all my letters, and sent out libels.

This ecclesiastic and his friend went through all the places where Father La Combe had held his mission, to decry him and speak against him so violently that a woman was afraid to say her "*Our Father*" because she said, she had learned it from him. They made a fearful scandal through the whole country. Father La Combe was not in the country, for the day after my arrival at the Ursulines of Tonon, he set out in the morning to preach the Lent sermons at the Valley of Aosta. He came to say adieu to me, and at the same time told me he would go to Rome, and probably would not return, that his superiors might keep him there, that he was sorry to leave me in a strange country without help, and persecuted by every one. Did not that trouble me? I said to him: "My Father, I am not troubled at it. I use the creatures for God, and by his order; through his mercy I get on very well without them when he withdraws them. I am quite content never to see you again, if such be his will, and to remain under persecution." When he said that to me he did not know it would become so violent as it did. Afterwards he said he set out well pleased to see me in this disposition, and thus went away.

CHAPTER VII

As soon as Father La Combe was gone the persecution became stronger than before. The Bishop still showed me some politeness, as well to see if he could bring me over to his purpose as to gain time for ascertaining how things would go in France, and for prejudicing people against me, always taking care to prevent my receiving any letters. I let but very few be intercepted, and only those which were indispensable. The ecclesiastic and another had open on their table twenty-two letters which did not reach me; and in one of them was a very important power of attorney sent for my signature. This they were obliged to put in a new envelope to send to me. The Bishop wrote to Father La Mothe, and he had little trouble in making him embrace his interests. He was dissatisfied because I had not given him the annuity he expected, as he has many times plainly told me, and he was offended because I did not follow his advice in everything, added to which were some other personal causes. He from the first declared against me. The Bishop, who cared to humor only him, felt strong enough with Father La Mothe on his side, and even made him his confidant, while he circulated the news written by them. The general opinion was that what caused him and his brother to act in this way was the fear that I might cancel the deed of settlement if I returned, and that, having influence and friends, I might find the means of setting it aside. They were very much mistaken in this; for I never had the thought of loving anything else than the poverty of Jesus Christ. For some time the Father kept terms with me. He wrote me letters addressed to the Bishop; and they so well understood each other that he was the only person whose letters I received. Our Lord gave me very beautiful letters to write to him; but in place of being touched he was irritated at them.

The Bishop, as I said, kept some terms with me for a time, making me believe that he had consideration for me; but he wrote to people at Paris, and the Sister also wrote to all those pious people from whom I had received letters, in order to prejudice them against me, and to escape the blame that naturally would fall on them for having so shamefully treated a person who had given up everything to devote herself to the service of his diocese; and ill-treated her only after she had stripped herself of her property, and was no longer in a condition to return to France—to avoid, I say, a censure so just they invented every kind of false and fabulous stories. Besides that I was unable to make known the truth in France, our Lord inspired me to suffer everything without justifying myself. I did this with Father La Mothe. As I saw he twisted everything, and showed himself more bitter than the Bishop, I ceased to write to him.

I was in this convent. I had seen Father La Combe only on the occasion I have mentioned. Nevertheless, they circulated a story that I was running about with him; that he had taken me driving in a carriage at Geneva, that the carriage was overturned, and a hundred malicious absurdities. Father La Mothe himself retailed all this, whether he thought it true or otherwise.

All these calumnies turned to ridicule persons who were previously esteemed saints. It is here we must admire the dealings of God: for what cause had I given for them to speak in this way? I was in a convent a hundred and fifty leagues distant from Father La Combe, and nevertheless they made out the most disgraceful stories of him and of me.

I did not know that things were pushed so far and so violently, for I had no news. I saw I did not receive letters from any quarter, neither from my friends nor from persons of piety; but as I knew all my letters were intercepted, I was not surprised at it. I lived in this House with my daughter very peacefully, and it was a very great providence, for my daughter no longer could speak French; among the little girls of the mountains she had acquired a foreign air and objectionable manners. She had forgotten the little she had learned in France. As to cleverness and judgment, she was surprising, and had the best inclinations; but there were little tempers caused by certain unreasonable contradictions, and by caresses out of place. This arose from ignorance in education. God provided for everything in her case, as I will tell.

I could hardly say anything of the interior state I then was in, for it was so simple, so naked, so annihilated that things were in me as if natural. I could only judge of them by the effects. My silence was very great, and I had at the commencement leisure to taste God without distinct consciousness, in himself, in my little cell. Nothing, it seems, could interrupt me. All that tempest did not make the smallest alteration in my mind or my heart. My central depth was in a generality, peace, liberty, largeness, indestructible. And although I sometimes suffered in the senses owing to the continual upsets, that did not penetrate; they were only waves breaking on a rock. The central depth was so lost in the will of God that it could neither will nor not will. I remained abandoned, without troubling as to what I should do, or what I should become, or what would be the end of the frightful tempest, which was only commencing. The leading of providence for the present moment constituted all my guidance without guidance, for the soul in the state of which I speak cannot desire or seek a special or extraordinary providence; but I allowed myself to be led by the daily providence from moment to moment, without thinking of the morrow. I was like a child in your hands, O my God.

My soul was then, it seemed to me, like a leaf or a feather, which the wind carried where it pleases. She yielded herself to the operation of God, and all that he did externally and internally, in the same manner; allowing herself to be led without any choice, content to obey a child as readily as a man of learning and experience, seeing only God in the man in God, who never permits the soul entirely abandoned to him to be deceived.

Immediately on my arrival at the Ursulines of Tonon, our Lord made me see in a dream two ways by which he conducted souls under the figure of two drops of water. The one seemed to me of brilliance and beauty and clearness unequalled; the other seemed also to have brilliance, but it was all full of little fibers or threads of mud, and as I regarded them attentively it was said to me: "These two kinds of water are both alike good for quenching thirst, but this is drunk with pleasure, the other with something of disgust. The way of faith, pure and simple, is like this very brilliant and clear drop of water; it is highly pleasing to the Spouse, because it is utterly pure, without anything of the selfhood. It is not the same with the way of illumination which does not equally please the Spouse, and is not nearly so agreeable to him."

It was then shown me that this pure way was the one by which our Lord had had the goodness to conduct me hitherto; that the way of illumination was that by which some illumined souls were proceeding, and that they had led Father La Combe into it. Our Lord told me that without my knowing it, he had given him to me, drawing him to a more perfect life than hitherto he had led; that it was at the time of my attack of small-pox he had given him, and that the price to me was that illness and the loss of my younger son; that he is not merely my Father, but my son. The next day this Father, having come to say Mass at the Ursulines, and having asked me, I did not venture to tell him anything—though our Lord very strongly urged me to do it—owing to a remnant of selfhood, which formerly would have passed for humility in my mind. However, I spoke before the Sisters of the way of faith, how far more glorious to God, and more advancing to the soul it was, than all revelations and assurances, which still keep alive the soul in herself. This at first shocked them and him also, so much as to raise a feeling against me. I saw they were hurt, as they afterwards acknowledged. I said no more then, but as the Father is most humble, he ordered me to explain what I had wished to say to him. I told him a part of the dream of the two drops of water; he did not, however, then take in what I said to him, the hour not being yet come. But when he came to Gex to conduct the retreats, our Lord made me know, while I was praying at night, that I was his mother and that he was my son; he confirmed the dream I had had, and ordered me to tell it to Father La Combe.

My difficulty was to tell this to the Father, whom I hardly

had any acquaintance with. I wished to dissemble with myself, and say that it was presumption, although I perceived
very well that it was the self-love which desired to escape, to
avoid confusion. I felt myself painfully pressed to tell it to
him. I went to see him as he was preparing for the Mass, and
having approached him as if for confession, I said to him, "My
Father, our Lord desires me to say that I am your mother-
in-grace, and I will tell you the rest after the Mass." He
said the Mass, during which he was convinced of what I had
said to him. After the Mass he wished me to tell him all the
particulars of everything, and of the dream. I told them. He
remembered that our Lord had often made known to him that
he had a mother-in-grace, whom he did not know, and having
asked me the time I had had the small-pox, I told him on St.
Francis' Day, and that my younger son died a few days
before All Saints. He recognized that it was the very time
when our Lord touched him in such an extraordinary way
that he was near dying of contrition. This caused him such an
interior awakening that, having retired to pray, he was seized
with an interior joy and great emotion, which made him enter
into what I had said of the way of faith.

As soon as I left Gex they commenced tormenting in a
strange way that good girl who had given herself to God, and
on account of whom the whole tragedy was played. The
ecclesiastic attacked her more vigorously than ever, and to
succeed the better, he depicted me in a contemptible aspect in
order that, as she has cleverness, the ridicule into which he
turned me should make her lose the esteem she entertained for
me, and lead her to give herself to his guidance. She still
confessed to him, but she was not willing to enter into anything more special with him; on the other hand, the Sisters
represented the friendship she had for me as a frightful crime.
They tried to make her say what was not fact; she was
persecuted incessantly. The Bishop wrote to her to put full
confidence in that ecclesiastic. She said that in the height of
her trouble she used to see me every night in a dream, that I
encouraged her to suffer, and told her what answers she
should make. As they have no vows, particularly in the matter
of obedience, and she had not been forbidden, she found
means of writing a note to me. They discovered her. There

was nothing in it beyond a little friendship. The ecclesiastic refused her for a month both absolution and the Communion owing to that note. The Sisters, on the other hand, caused her very great troubles, but God gave her the grace to suffer all. We could have no communications; however, our Lord still supported her.

After Easter of the year 1682 the Bishop came to Tonon. I had an opportunity of speaking to him when by himself, and our Lord caused that when I had spoken he was satisfied; but the people who had stirred him up against me returned to the charge. He strongly pressed me to return to Gex, and become Superior. I answered him that as to the Superiorship, none could be Superior without having been novice, and as for the binding myself, he himself knew my vocation, and what I had told him both at Paris and Gex; that, notwithstanding, I spoke to him as a Bishop, who held the place of God, and he should be careful to think only of God in what he should say to me; that if, holding this place, he told me to bind myself, I would do it. He remained quite confused, and said to me, "Since you speak to me in this way, I cannot advise it. You cannot go against your vocation; but I pray you confer benefit on that House." I promised to do so, and when I received my annuity I sent a hundred pistoles, intending to continue the same as long as I remained in the diocese. He withdrew, well pleased, for surely he loves good, and it is a pity he allows himself to be governed as he does. He even said, "I love Father La Combe; he is a true servant of God. He has told me things I cannot doubt, for I felt them in myself. But," continued he, "when I say this, I am told I deceive myself, and that he will be mad before six months." It was the discontented monk, the friend of the ecclesiastic, who had said that. This weakness astonished me. He told me he was very well satisfied with the nuns whom Father La Combe had conducted, and was as far as possible from finding any such thing as had been told him. I took the opportunity thereupon to say to him he should in all things rely on himself, and not on others. He agreed. Hardly, however, had he returned, when he again took up his former suspicions. He sent me word by the same ecclesiastic that it was his opinion I should bind myself at Gex. I requested that ecclesiastic to tell him I held to the advice he had given me; that he had spoken to me as from God, and at present they were making him speak as man.

CHAPTER VIII

MY soul was in an entire self-surrender, and very great contentment in the midst of these violent tempests. She could do nothing but continue in her former indifference, desiring nothing even of God, whether grace or disgrace, sweetness or cross.

A soul in this state has no sweetness nor spiritual relish. It would be unseasonable. She remains such as she is in her nothingness as to herself, and this is her place; and in the all as to God, without reference to, or reflection on, herself. She knows not if she has virtues, gifts, and graces in him who is the author of all that; she does not think of it, and can will nothing, and everything that concerns her is, as it were, foreign. She has not even the desire of procuring the glory of God, leaving to God the care of procuring it for himself, and she is in regard to it as pleases him. In this state God sometimes sets her to pray for some soul; but this is done without choice or premeditation, in peace, without desire for success. What does this soul, then? one will ask.

She lets herself be led by providences and by creatures without resistance. Her outside life is quite common, and as for within, she sees nothing there; she has no assurance, either internal or external, and yet she never was more assured. The more hopeless everything, the more is her central depth tranquil, in spite of the ravage of the senses and of creatures, which for some time after the new life makes some slight cloud and partition, as I have said. I should remark that the reason why there occurs a partition is because the soul is only immediately united, not yet transformed; for as soon as she is mingled and entirely passed into her original Being, there is no longer a partition.

At the commencement of the way of faith the soul profits from her defects, being by them humiliated through a reflection, simple, peaceful, tranquil, loving the abjectness which she reaps from them. The more she advances the more this simple action, without action, becomes simplified. At last there is no longer a question of this; the soul remains motionless and unshaken, bearing without movement the trouble her fault causes her, without any action whatsoever. It is what God requires from the soul from the time she is completely passive; and this is the conduct he has observed with me from the early years, long before the state of death. But, however faithful the soul to perform no sensible action to get rid of her trouble, there was yet an almost imperceptible action which the soul then did not know, and which she has become acquainted with only because she afterwards has found herself in a state exempt from this simple—nay, very simple action. It is impossible to understand me without experience.

In this state the soul commits no voluntary fault: that is my belief; for it is not likely that, having no will for anything whatsoever, great or small, pleasant or bitter—for honor, wealth, life, perfection, salvation, eternity—she should have a will to offend God; therefore it is not so. All her imperfections are in nature, not in herself; therefore it is on the surface, and that is lost gradually. It is true our nature is so deceitful that it insinuates itself everywhere, and the soul is not incapable of sin; but her greatest faults are her reflections, which are here very injurious, as she then wishes to regard herself under pretext even of telling her state. For this reason one should be in no trouble at all to tell one's state, or to take any count of it, if God does not put into the mind what he wills one to say of it.

The same firmness which keeps her from stirring under the troubles of her defects, the soul should preserve under temptations. The Devil greatly fears to approach such souls, and he leaves them at once, no longer daring to attack them. He attacks only those who yield, or who fear him. Souls conducted by faith are not ordinarily tried by the demons; that is for souls conducted by illumination. For it is necessary to know that the trials are always suited to the state of the soul. Those who are conducted by illumination, by extraordinary gifts, ecstasies, etc.,have also extraordinary trials which are effected by the intervention of demons; for, as everything with them is in the line of assurance, the trial even is an assurance. But it is not the same with the souls of simple faith: as they are conducted by nakedness, self-annihilation, and by what is commonplace, their trial is also quite commonplace; but that is far more terrible, and destroys the selfhood more. That which causes its death for them is nothing extraordinary, it is only the disturbance of their own temperament; they are troubles they regard as veritable faults, which give them no assurance unless it be that of their total self-annihilation.

I say, then, that the same firmness which one should have in regard to defects and temptations, so as not to give an opening to the Devil, one should have in regard to gifts and graces. In this state everything is so inward that nothing is perceived. But if anything falls upon the senses the soul is steadfast in letting the grace come and go, making no movement, however simple, either to relish or to recognize it. She leaves everything as though it was passing in another, without taking any part in it. At the commencement, and for a considerable time, the soul sees that nature wishes to take its part, and then her fidelity consists in restraining it, without permitting it the least expansion; but after the habit of restraining it has enabled her to remain immovable, and as if it were a thing that did not affect her, she no longer regards anything, she no longer appropriates to herself anything, and she lets all flow by into God in purity, as it has come forth from him. Until the soul be in this state, she always in some degree defiles by her intermixture the operation of God, like those streams which contract corruption from the places through which they flow; but as soon as the same streams flow in a pure place, they then continue in the purity of their source.

For this reason she knows not what to choose, neither state nor condition, however perfect they may be. She is content with everything she has; she keeps herself at peace wherever she is placed, high or low, in one country or in another; all that she has is all that is needed for her to be fully content; she could not be in trouble at the absence, nor rejoiced at the presence, of persons the most devoted to God, and who might seem most necessary to her, and in whom she has entire confidence; because she is entirely satisfied, and she has all that is needed, though everything be wanting to her. It is this which makes her not seek to see people or to speak, but receive the providences; both for the one and the other, without which there is always something of the human, however fair the pretext with which we cover ourselves. The soul feels very well that all which is done by choice and election, and not by providence, instead of aiding, hurts her, or at least brings her little fruit.

But what is it which makes this soul so perfectly content? She knows not. She is content without knowing the subject of her contentment, and without wishing to know it, but content in a way that is vast, immense, independent of external events; more content in the humiliations of her own neediness and the rejection of all creatures in the order of providence, than upon the throne, by her own choice.

O you alone who conduct these souls, and who can teach these ways, so self-annihilating, and so contrary to the ordinary spirit of devotion, full of itself and its own discoveries, conduct thus souls without number, that you may be loved purely! These are the souls which alone love you as you wish to be loved. These souls are the delight of God, who says, "His delight is to be with the children of men;" that is to say, these souls quite childlike and innocent. They are very far from pride, being unable to attribute to themselves aught but nothingness and sin, and they are so one with God that they see only him, and all things in him.

When we allow ourselves to be led by the Spirit of God, he makes us enter into the liberty of his children adopted in Jesus Christ and by Jesus Christ, for "where the Spirit of the Lord is there is liberty," because "he gives not his Spirit to us by measure;" for those whom he has predestinated to be his free children, them he has called, and those whom he has called he has justified. It is, then, he who operates in them that righteousness which is conformable to their call. But to what has he destined those cherished souls? "To be conformed to the image of his Son." Oh, it is here is the great secret of that call and that justification, and the reason why so few souls arrive at that state. It is because there one is predestinated to be conformed to the image of the Son of God. But some one will say, Are not all Christians called to be conformed to the image of the Son of God? Yes, every one is called to be conformed to it in something, for if a Christian did not bear on him the image of Jesus Christ he would not be saved, since he is saved only by this character. But the souls of which I speak are destined to bear Jesus Christ himself, and to be conformed to him in all, and the more perfect their conformity, the more perfect are they.

But is every one called to this state? Very few, as far as I can understand, and even of the few who are called to it, few walk in it in true purity. The souls in passive illumination and extraordinary gifts, though holy and quite seraphic, do not enter into this way. There is a way of illumination—a holy life, where the creature appears quite admirable. As this life is more apparent, it is also the more esteemed by those who have not the purest lights. These persons have striking things in their life; they have a fidelity and a courage which astonish, and it is this which wonderfully adorns the life of the saints. But the souls which walk in this other path are little known. God despoils them, weakens them, strips them naked bit by bit, so that, depriving them of every support and every hope, they are obliged to lose themselves in him. They have nothing great which is apparent, hence it comes that the greater their interior is, the less they can speak of it, because for a very long time they can see there only want and poverty; afterwards they no longer see themselves.

CHAPTER IX

BEING at the Ursulines of Tonon, after I had spoken to the Bishop of Geneva, and saw how he changed as he was influenced by others, I wrote some letters to him and to Father La Mothe; but as I saw it was useless, and he was thereby more embittered, and the more I tried to clear up matters, the more trouble the ecclesiastic took to embroil them, I let things be, without further action. I saw the tempest about to break upon our heads without being able to prevent it. I had dreamed that I was drawing a cord which at first seemed of diamond, and afterwards appeared to me to be if iron, and at the same time seeing a terrible storm fall upon my head, I gave myself up to the mercy of the waves. I saw clearly the crosses which were springing up from every side, and my soul remained in a profound peace, waiting for the blows which she could not avoid. I had not done the least thing to draw it upon me, and I watched the torrent rushing down without having contributed to the storm. As I saw I had not contributed to it, and that there was nothing for me to do but to suffer, I kept quiet, without troubling myself as to success. One day they came and told me that this ecclesiastic had again gained over the poor girl I much loved, and who had already cost me much; at the same time they gave me a means of hindering him, but this human mode of acting was repugnant to my inmost spirit, and those words, "Except the Lord," etc., were suggested to me. I sacrificed her as well as the rest to God. But our Lord, who had permitted this only to detach me from a love I had for her perfection, provided for the matter himself, and prevented her connecting herself with him in a manner the more admirable as it was more natural, and more contrary to their intentions. Afterwards God made this worthy girl see that he had extricated her with a quite fatherly goodness. I did not conceal from her what she had cost me, for assuredly the case was such that I would not have felt so much the death of one of my children as her destruction. While I was with her she was always vacillating, and one could not make sure of her, so that as regards her, one had to live by trust; but—O goodness and infinite power of my God, to save without us what we should lose without you!—no sooner was I at a distance from her than she became steadfast.

For me, there was hardly a day passed that they did not put upon me new insults, and make attacks quite unexpected. Every day they invented some new calumny; there was no trick or invention they did not use against me. They came to see me, to try and surprise me in my words, but God guarded me so well that they were themselves taken. I had no consolation from creatures, for the Sister who was in charge of my daughter became my greatest cross. She said I had come too late. The maid I had brought, and who remained with me, gave me very great troubles; she was unhappy, and wished to return; she opposed and condemned me from morning to night, representing the wealth I had given up, and that I was useless there. She made me bear all the ill-tempers her discontent gave birth to. Father La Mothe wrote me that I was rebelling against my Bishop, that I remained in his diocese only to cause him trouble. Besides, I saw that there was nothing for me to do in this diocese as long as the Bishop should be opposed to me. I did what I could to win him, but it was impossible to succeed without entering into the engagement he desired, and that was impossible for me. This, joined to the defective education of my daughter, sometimes threw my senses into agony; but the central depth of my soul was so tranquil that I could neither wish nor resolve on anything, letting myself be as though these things had no existence. When some little ray of hope came to me, it was at once taken away, and despair constituted my strength.

During this time Father La Combe was at Rome, where, far from being blamed, he was received with so much honor, and his doctrine so esteemed that the Sacred Congregation did him the honor to take his views on certain points of doctrine, and found them so sound and clear that it followed them. While he was at Rome the Sister would not look after my daughter, and when I undertook the care of her, she was offended; so that I knew not what to do. On the one hand I did not wish to hurt her, and on the other I endured much in seeing my daughter as she was. I urgently entreated this Sister to look after her, and not to allow her to acquire bad habits; but I could not even get her to promise me to exert herself. I thought when Father La Combe returned he would put everything to right, or would give me some consolation; not that I wished for him, for I could neither be afflicted at his absence, nor wish for his return.

When it was known at home that I was at the Ursulines,

and had left Gex, and that I was much persecuted, M. de Monpezat, Archbishop of Sens, who had a great kindness for me, knowing that my sister, an Ursuline of his diocese, was obliged to go to the waters for a species of paralysis, gave her his authority to go there, and also to go into the diocese of Geneva, to remain with me at the Ursulines, or to bring me back with her. On the other hand, the Ursulines of Tonon expressed a wish to adopt the constitutions of those of Paris, and that my sister should bring them. She came then, and God made use of her to bring me a maid whom he desired to give me of his own pleasure, to fashion in his mode, and to be suitable for me. My sister came to me with this good girl in the month of July, 1682. Our Lord sent her to me quite at the right moment for teaching my daughter to read, and looking after her a little. I had already taught her so that she read even in Scripture, but during the time I had left her they had given her such a bad accent that it was piteous. My sister mended all that; but if she procured me this advantage in the care of my daughter, she caused me many crosses, for from the first she took a dislike to the Sister who looked after my daughter, and the Sister to her, so that they could not agree. I did what I could to reconcile them, but besides that I could not succeed, the very care I took made my sister believe I had more affection for that Sister than for her, which hurt her extremely; although it was not at all the case, for I had much to suffer from her myself, of which I said nothing; but it grieved me to see a disturbance where I had tasted so profound a peace. The maid I had brought, and who was discontented with that Sister and with being there, because she wanted to return to her relatives, embroiled things still more. She made my sister share in her disgust. It is true my sister practiced virtue, and endured certain things which seemed to outrage reason; for she could not understand that, seeing she was a very aged Sister and a stranger, she ought to submit to a Sister still in noviciate, who was in her own House and of very humble origin. I made her see what Jesus Christ had suffered. What astonished me extremely was, that I succeeded better with my sister, who was not at all spiritual, than with the other, who thought herself very exalted in gifts and illumination, and yet whom it was impossible to make change when she had once taken up an idea.

I have learned, O my God, from her, that it is not the greatest gifts which sanctify, if they are not accompanied by a profound humility, and that death to all things is infinitely more useful to us; and this very girl, who believed herself at the height of perfection, has seen from the experiences which afterwards befell her, that she was very far from it. O my God, how true it is that one may have your gifts and be yet very imperfect and full of self; but how necessary it is to be pure and small to pass into you, O true Life!

The Bishop of Geneva wrote to Father La Mothe to engage him to cause me to return. Father La Mothe sent me word of it, but the Bishop assured me that it was not so. I did not know whom to believe. When Father La Combe proposed to me to return, I felt some slight repugnance in the senses, which did not last long. The soul cannot but allow herself to be led by obedience, not that she regards obedience as a virtue, but it is that she can neither be otherwise, nor wish to do otherwise; she allows herself to be drawn along without knowing why or how, as a person who should allow himself to be carried along by the current of a rapid river. She cannot apprehend deception, nor even make a reflection thereon. Formerly it was by self-surrender, but in her present state it is without knowing or understanding what she does, like a child whom its mother might hold over the waves of a disturbed sea, and who fears nothing, because it neither sees nor knows the danger.

CHAPTER X

MY daughter recovered her health. I must tell how this happened. She had smallpox, and the purples. They brought a doctor from Geneva, who gave her up in despair. They made Father La Combe come in to take her confession; he gave her his blessing, and at the same instant the smallpox and the purples disappeared, and the fever left her. The doctor, though a Protestant, offered to give a certificate of a miracle. But although my daughter was restored, my crosses were not lessened, owing to her bad education.

Father La Combe introduced order in many things regarding my daughter; but the mistress was so hurt that the friendship she had for me changed into coolness and distance. However, as she had grace, she readily got over it; but her natural character carried her away. I told her my thoughts on the defects I perceived in her because I was ordered to do so; and although at the moment God enlightened her to see the truth of what I said, and that she was afterwards still more enlightened, it all the same made her grow cool. The discussions between her and my sister became stronger and more bitter. Herein I admired the conduct of God and the cleverness he gave my daughter, who was only six and a half years of age: she found out by her little attentions the means of pleasing them both, preferring to do her little exercises twice over so as to do them first with the one, then with the other. This did not last long, for as the mistress generally neglected her, and at one time did things, another time not, she was reduced to learning merely what my sister and I taught her. It is true that the vivacity of my sister is so excessive that it is difficult without a special grace to get on with her; but it seemed to me that she conquered herself in many things. Formerly I had difficulty to put up with her ways, but in the end I loved all in God.

All souls have desires more or less strong except those which are in the divine moment. There are even great souls which only have them almost imperceptible; others who have them so great that they are the admiration of those who know them. Some languish upon the earth because they burn to go to see God; others long for suffering—are consumed with an ardor for martyrdom; others for the salvation of their neighbor. All this is very excellent; but he who contents himself with the divine moment, although exempt from all these desires, is infinitely more content, and glorifies God more.

CHAPTER XI

AFTER Father La Combe had returned from Rome much praised for his doctrine, he performed the duties of preaching and confessing as usual, and as I had for myself a permission from the Bishop of Geneva to confess to him, I made use of him. He at once told me I should return. I asked him the reason. It is, he said, because I believe God will do nothing by you here, and my lights are deceptive. What made him speak thus was that while at Loretto, he was suddenly withdrawn from the way of illumination and put into the way of simple faith. Now, as this state causes a failure of all distinct light, the soul which finds herself plunged in it finds herself in a trouble so much the greater as her state had been more full of lights. It is this which makes her think all the lights on which she previously supported herself to be nothing but deceptions. This is true in one sense, and not in another, since the lights are always good and true lights when they come from God; but it is that in resting on them we understand them or interpret them ill: and it is in this lies the deception, for they have a signification known to God, but we give them a different sense; then the self-love, disgusted that things do not happen according to its lights, accuses them of falsity. They are, nevertheless, very true in their sense.

I gave an account to Father La Combe of what I had done and suffered in his absence, and I told him the care that you, O my God, took of my affairs. I saw your providence even in the smallest matters, unceasingly spread itself over me. After having been many months without any news of my papers, and when people even pressed me to write, blaming me for my indifference, an invisible hand held me back, and my peace and confidence were so great that I could not interfere in anything. Some time after I received a letter from our domestic ecclesiastic, telling me he was ordered to come and see me, and bring my papers. I had sent to me from Paris a considerable package for my daughter. It was lost on the lake, and I could get no news of it, but I gave myself no trouble. I believed still it would be found. The man who had put it on board had for a month made search in all the neighbourhood, without being able to learn any news of it. At the end of three months a person had it brought to us. It was found in the house of a poor man. He had not opened it, and did not know who had brought it there.

Once when I had sent for all the money which had to supply my wants for an entire year, the person who had been to cash the letter of exchange, having placed the money in two bags on a horse, forgot that it was there, and gave his horse to a boy to lead. He let the money fall from the horse in the middle of the market-place of Geneva. I arrived at that moment, coming from the other side, and having got out of my litter, the first thing I found was my money, over which I walked; and what is surprising is that, though there was a great crowd on that spot, no one had seen it.

The Bishop of Geneva continued to persecute me, and when he wrote to me it was always with expressions of politeness and thanks for the charities I bestowed at Gex; on the other hand, he said I gave nothing to that House. He even wrote against me to the Ursulines, where I was staying, commanding them to prevent my having conference with Father La Combe, "for fear of disastrous results." The Superior of the House, a man of merit, and the Prioress, as well as the Community, were so indignant that they could not avoid declaring it to himself. He excused himself by an outward professed respect, and a "I did not intend it in that sense." They wrote him that I saw the Father only at the confessional, not in conference, that they were so edified by me that they were very happy to have me, and that they considered it a great favor from God. What they said out of pure love was displeasing to the Bishop, who, seeing I was loved in this House, said that I gained over every one, and he wished I was out of the diocese. Although I knew all this, and that these good Sisters were much pained at it, I could feel none,

owing to the fixedness of my soul, your will, my God, rendering everything alike to me. I find you as well in one thing as
in another, and since your will is yourself, everything in this
will is to me you, O my Love; so that all the pains which
creatures can cause, however unreasonable, and even passionate
they may appear, are not regarded in themselves, but in
God—not that the soul has this actual view, but it is so: and
the habitual faith makes everything be seen in God without
distinction. So when I see poor souls give themselves so much
trouble for idle talk, being always on the watch beforehand,
or clearing up matters, I pity them for their lack of enlighten-
ment; and the more of grace souls have, the more strange that
appears to me.

To relieve me a little from the fatigue which continual
conversations caused me, I asked Father La Combe on his
arrival to allow me a retreat, and to say that he wished me to
make one. He told them so, but they could hardly leave me in
repose. It was then that I allowed myself the whole day to be
devoured by love, which had no other operation but to
consume me little by little. It was then also that I felt the
quality of "spiritual Mother," for God gave me a something for
the perfection of souls, which I could not conceal from Father
La Combe. It seemed to me that I saw into the depth of his
soul, and the minutest recesses of his heart. Our Lord made me
see that he was his servant, chosen among a thousand to
honor him in a special degree, and that there was not a man
upon the earth at that time on whom he looked with such
complaisance as on him, but that he wished to conduct him by
total death and entire annihilation, that he wished me to help
in it, and he would make use of me to cause him to travel the
road, by which he had first made me pass, only that I might be
able to conduct others by it, and to tell them the routes by
which I had passed; that at present my soul was far more
advanced than his, that God wished to render us one and
comfortable, but that one day he would pass her by a bold
and impetuous flight. God knows what joy I had at it, and
with what pleasure I would see my children surpass their
mother in glory, and that I would willingly give myself over in
any way that it might be so.

In this retreat there came to me such a strong movement to

write that I could not resist it. The violence I exercised over myself not to do it made me ill, and took away my speech. I was very much surprised to find myself thus, for this had never happened to me. It was not that I had anything particular to write. I had absolutely nothing, not even an idea of any kind. It was a simple instinct with a fulness I could not support. After much resistance I told Father La Combe the disposition in which I found myself; he answered that on his side he had had a strong movement to command me to write, but owing to my weak state he had not ventured to prescribe it for me. I told him the weakness was only due to my resistance, and I thought it would pass away as soon as I wrote. He asked me, "But what do you wish to write?" "I know nothing about it," I replied. "I wish nothing, I have no idea, and I think I should commit a great infidelity in giving myself one, or thinking for a moment on what I might be able to write." He ordered me to do it. On taking up the pen I did not know the first word of what I was about to write. I set myself to write without knowing how, and I found it came to me with a strange impetuosity. What surprised me most was that it flowed from my central depth, and did not pass through my head. I was not yet accustomed to this manner of writing, yet wrote an entire treatise on the whole interior way under a comparison with streams and rivers. Although it was tolerably long, and the comparison was kept up to the end, I have never formed a thought, nor even taken any care where I left off, and, in spite of continual interruptions, I have never read over anything, except at the end, where I read over a line or two owing to a word having been left out; even then I thought I had committed an infidelity. Before writing I did not know what I was going to write. When it was written I thought no more of it. I should have committed an infidelity in retaining any thought to put it down, and our Lord gave me grace that this did not happen. As I wrote I found myself relieved, and I became better.

As the way by which God was leading Father La Combe was very different from that by which he had hitherto walked, which had been all light, ardor, knowledge, certitude, assurance, feelings, and that now he made him go by the narrow path of faith and of nakedness, he had very great trouble in adapting himself to it; which caused me no small suffering, for God made me feel and pay with extreme rigor all his resistance. Who could express what he has cost my heart before he was formed according to yours and according to your will? Only you, O my God, who have done it, know. The more precious that soul is in your eyes, the more dearly have you made me pay. I can indeed say that it is upon me the robe of the new life you have given him has been remade. I was subjected to a double pain; the one was that the possession which God had of my soul became every day more strong, so that sometimes I passed the day without it being possible for me to pronounce a word: for God then wished to bury me more deeply into himself, and to annihilate me more in him, in order to make me pass into him by a complete transformation. Although my state was without sensibility, it was so profound, and God became more and more so powerfully the master, that he did not leave me a movement of my own. This state did not prevent me from condescending to my sister and the other nuns; however, the useless things in which they were occupied could hardly suit my taste, and this was the reason which led me to ask for keeping a retreat, that I might let myself be possessed to the good pleasure of him who held me closely clasped in an inexpressible manner. At this time he purified a remnant of nature, very subtle and delicate, so that my soul found herself in extreme purity.

It was then it was given me to write in a purely divine manner. All I had written formerly was tested, was condemned to the fire by Love, the examiner, who found defects in all that appeared the most perfect. I resisted, as I have said, but God became so powerfully the master that he harrassed me to death when I resisted in the least thing.

You desired, O my God, in order to accustom me to the suppleness of your Spirit, to exact of me for a time things which cost me much and caused me serious crosses. Our Lord bound me more closely with Father La Combe, but by a union as pure as it was spiritual. He willed that I should tell him the minutest of my thoughts, or write them to him; for as he was often absent either on missions, which he was continually engaged in, or for the business of the House, he was not often at Tonon. This cost me much, for it was a thing I had never done when formerly I might have conveniently done it, while I was still in myself, and when I could speak to directors; but now it appeared to me mere loss of time. I imagined even for lack of experience that it could not be done without reflection, and as reflection was entirely opposed to my state, it would be very injurious to me. I was surprised to see that the need of writing to him increased each day in the design and order of God: but what reassured me was, that I was so disengaged from any feeling or attachment in respect of him, that I was astonished. The more powerful the union became, the more we were united to God, and removed from human sentiments. I was still more led to pardon nothing in him, and to desire his self-annihilation, that God alone might reign. With much fidelity I told him all that God gave me to know he desired of him, and this I would gladly have evaded. The obligation God imposed on me to tell him the radical defects of the Sister who had charge of my daughter (as he was prejudiced in her favor, owing to the illumination she had told him she had) irritated him against me several days. When I told him anything, this produced in him disgust for me and alienation. Our Lord made me painfully feel it, although he said nothing to me. I experienced that our Lord obliged me to keep hold on him, and made me pay by suffering for his infidelity. On the other hand, if I wished to say nothing to him, and to keep back views which only served to offend him, our Lord harassed me to death, and gave me no rest until I had declared to him both my pain and my thought; so that I suffered thereby a martyrdom exceeding anything that can be told, and which has been very protracted.

CHAPTER XII

Our Lord, willing that I should bear him in all his states, from the first to the last and willing to make me perfectly simple, gave me in regard to Father La Combe such a miraculous obedience that, in whatever extremity of illness I might be, I grew well when, either by word of mouth or by letter, he ordered it. I believe our Lord did it to make me express Jesus Christ the Child, and also to be a sign and evidence to this good Father, who, having been conducted by evidences, could not leave that way; and in whatever was told him, or which God made him experience, he still kept seeking evidences.

My sister had brought me a maid, whom God wished to give me to fashion in his manner, not without crucifying me—a thing that I expect will never be; for when our Lord gives me persons, he always gives them at the same time the means of making me suffer, whether to direct those persons themselves to the interior way, or in order that I should never be without a cross. She was a girl to whom our Lord had given singular grace, and who was so highly reputed in her country that she passed for a saint. Our Lord brought her to me to make her see the difference of sanctity conceived and comprised in gifts—with which she was then endowed—and sanctity which is acquired by our entire destruction, by the loss of those very gifts, and of that which we are. This girl fell seriously ill. Our Lord gave her the same dependence on me as I had on Father La Combe—with some distinction, however. I helped her to the best of my ability, but I found that I had hardly anything to say to her, except to command her ailment and her disposition; and whatever I said was done. Then I learned what it is to command by the Word, and to obey by the same Word. I found in me Jesus Christ commanding and likewise obeying.

As I saw she was too much crushed, and her weak body could no longer endure the torment they caused her, I forbade the demons approaching her for a time; they left at once. But the next day at waking I had a strong impulse to allow them to visit her; they returned with so much fury that they reduced her to extremity. After having thus given some relaxation at different intervals, and allowed them to return, I had a strong movement to forbid them to attack her any more. I forbade them: they returned no more. Nevertheless she still continues ill, until one day she had received our Lord in such weakness that she could scarcely swallow the sacred Host. After dinner I had a strong impulse to say to her, "Get up, and be no longer ill." The nuns were very much astonished, and as they knew nothing of what was going on, and they saw her on foot after having been in the morning at extremity, they attributed her illness to the vapors.

As soon as the devils were withdrawn from this girl, I felt as if by an impression the rage they were in against me. I was in my bed, and I said to them, "Come and torment me if your Master allows it;" but, so far from doing this, they fled from me. I understood at once that the devils fear worse than hell a soul that has been annihilated. I felt in myself such an authority over the devils that, far from fearing them, it seemed to me I would make them fly from hell if I was there. It should be known that the soul of whom I speak, in whom Jesus Christ lives and acts, does not perform miracles as those who perform them by a power in them of performing miracles. They are performed by the annihilation of the soul, for as she is no longer anything, nothing of all this can be attributed to her; therefore when the movement urges, she does not say, "Be healed in the name of Jesus Christ," for this "Be healed in the name of Jesus Christ" is a power in the person of performing miracles in the name of Jesus Christ. Here it is not the same; it is Jesus Christ who performs the miracle, and who says through that person, "Be healed," and the man is healed; "Let the devils depart," and they depart. When one says this, one knows not why one says it, nor what causes one to say it; but it is the Word who speaks and operates what he says. "He spoke, and they were made." One does not utter prayers beforehand, for these miracles are performed without any previous design, and without the soul looking upon it as a miracle. One says quite naturally what is given one to say.

Hereupon I must remark two things: one, that the souls of whom I speak do not ordinarily perform miracles by giving anything, or by simply touching; but it is by the word, although they sometimes accompany it with touching. It is the all-powerful Word. The other thing is that these miracles require the consent, or at least that there should be no opposition, in the person on whom they are performed. Our

Lord Jesus Christ asked the good people he healed, "Do you wish to be healed?"

There was a worthy nun afflicted with a violent temptation. She went and told a Sister, whom she believed very spiritual and in a state to help her: but, far from finding help, she was violently repulsed. The other despised her, and even harshly treating her because she had temptations, said to her, "Do not come near me, I pray, since you are of that kind." This poor girl came to see me in terrible distress, believing herself lost, owing to what the Sister had said to her. I consoled her, and our Lord relieved her at once; but I could not refrain from saying that assuredly the other would be punished, and that she would fall into a worse state. The one who had so used her came to see me, very well satisfied with herself; and she told me what she had answered, adding that she had a horror of persons who are tempted, that for herself she was safe from all this, and that she never had had a bad thought. I said to her, "My Sister, for the friendship I have for you, I wish you the trouble of her who has spoken to you, and even a more violent one." She answered me proudly enough, "If you ask it of God for me and I ask the contrary, I think I shall be as soon heard as you." I answered her firmly, "If it is my own interest I regard, I shall not be heard; but if it is the interest of God only and yours, he will do it sooner than you fancy." I said this without reflection. The same night—it was evening when we were speaking—she entered into such a violent and furious temptation, the like of which was hardly ever seen; it continued with the same strength for a fortnight. It was then she had full opportunity to recognize her weakness, and what we should be without grace. At first she conceived an excessive hatred for me, saying I was the cause of her trouble; but as it served, like the mud which enlightened the man born blind, she saw very well what had brought on her such a terrible state.

I fell exceeding ill. This illness was a means to cover the great mysteries which God desired to operate in me. Never was there a malady more extraordinary or more continued in its intensity. It lasted from Holy Cross Day of September to that of May. I was reduced to the state of a little child, but a state which was apparent only to those who could understand; for as to the others, I appeared in an ordinary condition. I was reduced to the dependence of Jesus Christ, the Child, who wished to communicate himself to me in his state of childhood, and that I should bear him as such. This state was communicated to me almost immediately on my falling ill, and a dependence corresponding to the state. The further I advanced, the more was I set free from this dependence, as children gradually emerge from dependence in proportion to their growth. My illness at first was a continuous fever of forty days. From the Holy Cross of September up to Advent it was a less violent fever, but after Advent it seized me in a more violent manner. In spite of my illness the Master willed I should receive him at Christmas midnight. Christmas Day my childhood became greater, and my illness increased. The fever intensified so that I was delirious; besides, there was an abscess at the corner of the eye, which caused great pain. It opened entirely at this time, and they dressed it, for a long time passing in an iron up to the bottom of the cheek. I had such burning fever and so much weakness that they were obliged to allow it to close again without healing, for my exhausted body could not endure the operations without danger of instantly expiring. I suffered with extreme patience; but it was like a child, who knows not what is done to him, I experienced at the same time both the strength of a God and the weakness of a little child, with a corresponding dependence. This mode of action was so foreign to my natural character that nothing less than the power of a God was needed to make me enter into it. I gave myself up to it, however, for my interior was such and was so powerfully urged by God, that I could not resist him. They often brought me the Eucharist; the Superior of the House having ordered that this consolation should be allowed me, seeing the extremity I was in. As Father La Combe often brought it to me, when the confessor of the House was not there, he remarked, and the nuns who were familiar with me also remarked it, that I had the face of a little child. In his astonishment he several times said to me, "It is not you; it is a little child that I see." For myself, I saw nothing within but the candor and innocence of a little child. I had its weaknesses; I sometimes wept from pain, but this was not known. I played and laughed in a way that charmed the girl who attended me; and those good nuns, who knew nothing about it, said that I had something which surprised and charmed them at the same time.

Our Lord, however, with the weaknesses of his childhood gave me the power of a God over souls, so that with a word I cast them into trouble or peace, according as was necessary for the good of those souls. I saw that God made himself obeyed in me and through me, as an absolute Sovereign, and I no longer resisted him. I took no part in anything; you might have performed, O my God, in me and through me the greatest miracles, and I should not have been able to reflect upon it. I felt within a candor of soul, without taint, which I cannot express. Moreover, I had to continue telling my thoughts to Father La Combe, or else writing them to him and aiding him, according to the light that was given to me. I often was so weak that I could not raise my head to take food, and when God desired I should write to him, either to aid and encourage him, or to explain what our Lord gave me to know, I had the strength to write. As soon as my letters were finished, I found myself in the same weakness. I was very much surprised to understand by experience that what you had wished of me, O my God, in obliging me thus to tell all my thoughts, had been to perfect me in simplicity, and to make Father La Combe enter into it, rendering me supple to all your wishes; for whatever cross it was to me to tell my thoughts, and although Father La Combe often was offended to the point of disgust at serving me, and he let me know it, I never for that ceased from telling them to him.

Our Lord had made us understand that he united us by faith and by the cross, so that it has indeed been a union of the cross in every way; as well from what I have made him suffer himself, and he in turn has made me suffer, as from the crosses which this has drawn upon us from outside. The sufferings I had in respect of him were such that I was reduced to extremity, and they endured many years; for although I have been longer at a distance from him than near him, this has not relieved my ill, which has continued until he has been perfectly annihilated and reduced to the point God wished for him. This operation has made him suffer pains and

more severe in proportion as the designs God had for him
were the greater, and he has caused me cruel pains. When I
was a hundred leagues away from him, I felt his disposition. If
he was faithful in allowing himself to be destroyed, I was in
peace and free; if he was unfaithful, in reflection or hesitation, I suffered strange torments until it was over. There was
no necessity for him to tell me his state, that I should know it.
I was often laid upon the ground the whole day, without
being able to move, in agony, and after having for a fortnight
in this way endured sufferings which surpassed all I ever
suffered in my life, I received letters from him, by which I
learned his state to be such as I had felt it. Then suddenly I
felt that he had re-entered on the state in which God wished
him; and then I experienced that gradually my soul found a
peace and a great freedom, which was more or less, according
as he gave himself up more or less to our Lord. This was not a
voluntary thing in me, but compulsory; for if nature could
have shaken off this yoke, more hard and painful than death,
it would have done so. I said, O union necessary, and not
voluntary, thou art not voluntary only because I am not any
more mistress of myself, and I must yield to him who has taken
so powerful a possession of me after I have given myself to him
freely and without any reserve.

CHAPTER XIII

MY sister was in no way capable of understanding my state,
so that often she was offended at it. She got vexed when one
concealed one's self in the least from her, and she could not
appreciate a state that many persons more spiritual than she
would have been unable to understand; so that I suffered
much from every quarter in this malady. The distress from the
great pain was the least; that from the creature was very

different. My only consolation was to receive our Lord, and sometimes to see Father La Combe; moreover, I had to suffer much from him, as I have said, bearing all his different dispositions. I was strangely exercised by my sister, by that nun, and by the maid who wanted to return to France. Whatever extremity I might be in, I had to listen to their differences, which they told me, the one after the other; then they quarrelled with me for not taking their side. They did not let me sleep—for as the fever was more intense at night, I could only sleep for an hour, and I would gladly have slept by day: but they would not have it, saying it was only to avoid speaking to them—so that I required very great patience to bear with them. It lasted more than six months. I think this partly was the cause of a revery I had for two days together; for I did not sleep, and I continued to hear a noise, with a terrible headache. I complained of nothing, and I suffered gaily, like a child. Father La Combe commanded them to give me some rest: for some days they did so, but it did not last; they recommenced immediately.

I cannot express the mercies which God showed me in this illness, and the profound lights he gave me on the future. I saw the Devil let loose against prayer and against me, and that he was about to stir up a strange persecution against people of prayer. I wrote all this to Father La Combe, and unless he has burned the letters, they ought to be still in existence. The Devil did not dare attack me myself; he feared me too much. Sometimes I defied him, but he did not venture to appear, and I was for him like a thunderbolt. I understood then what power a self-annihilated soul has.

The day of the Purification, when I had relapsed into a very severe fever, the Father ordered me to go to the Mass. For twenty-two days I had had continued fever, more violent than ordinary. I did not give a single thought to my state, but I got up and attended at the Mass, and returned to my bed much worse than before.

It was a day of grace for me, or, rather, for the Father. God showed him very great grace in regard to me. Near Lent the Father, without giving attention to the fact that he had to preach at Lent, when he saw me so ill, said to our Lord to relieve me, and that he would bear a part of my disease. He told our maids to ask the same thing, namely, that he might relieve me in the way he meant.

It is true I was a little better, and he fell ill, which caused great alarm in the place, seeing he had to preach. He was so much run after that people used to come from five leagues' distance and pass several days there to hear him. When I learned he was so ill on Shrove Tuesday that they thought he would die, I offered myself to our Lord to become more ill, and that he would restore health to him, and enable him to preach to his people, who were hungering to hear him. Our Lord heard me, so that he mounted the pulpit on Ash Wednesday.

It was in this illness, my Lord, that by degrees you taught me that there is another way than by speech for conversing with the creatures, who are entirely yours. You made me conceive, O Divine Word, that as you are always speaking and working in a soul, although you there appear in a profound silence, there was also a means of communication in your creatures, and by your creatures in an ineffable silence. I learned then a language unknown to me before. I perceived gradually that when Father La Combe was brought in either to confess me or give me the Communion, I could no longer speak to him, and that there took place in my central depth towards him the same silence which took place towards God. I understood that God wished me to learn that even in this life men might learn the language of the angels. Little by little I was reduced to speaking to him only in silence; it was then that we understood each other in God, in a manner ineffable and quite divine. Our hearts spoke and communicated to each other a grace which cannot be told. It was an altogether new country for him and me, but divine beyond expression.

We passed hours in this profound silence, still communicating, without being able to say a single word. It was there we learned by our experience the communications and operations of the Word, in order to reduce souls into his unity, and to what purity one may attain therein. It was given me to communicate in this way with other good souls, but with this difference, that for the others I alone communicated the grace with which, in this sacred silence, they were filled from me, communicating to them an extraordinary strength and grace; but I received nothing from them. In the case of the Father, I experienced that there was a flux and reflux of communication of graces, which he received from me and I from him; that he gave to me and I him the same grace in an extreme purity.

It was then I understood that we were created to participate during this life in the ineffable happiness of intercourse with the Trinity, and in the flux and reflux of the divine Persons, which end in Unity of principle, and become again Unity without ever for a moment arresting the fruitfulness and communication between them; principle without principle, which incessantly communicates, and receives all it communicates; that it was necessary to be very pure to receive God in simplicity, and to allow him to flow back in himself in that purity; and that it was necessary also to be very pure to receive and communicate the Divine Word, and then to distribute him by a flux and reflux of communication upon the other souls which God gives us. It is this which makes us one in God himself, and perfects us in the divine Unity, where we are made one same thing in him from whom all originates.

It was in this ineffable silence I understood the manner in which Jesus Christ communicated himself to his intimates, and the communication of St. John on the breast of our Lord at the Last Supper. It was not the first time that he had so placed himself, and it was because he was very fit to receive those divine communications that he was the chosen and loved disciple. It was at this great banquet that Jesus Christ, as Word, flowed into John, and discovered to him the most profound secrets, before communicating himself to him in the mastication of his body. And it is then there was communicated to him that wonderful secret of the eternal generation of the Word, because he was rendered a participator in the ineffable intercourse of the Holy Trinity. He knew that therein is the characteristic of the true children of God, and how the silent speech operated; for this speech in silence is the most noble, the most exalted, the most sublime of all operations. It was then he learned the difference of being "born of the flesh, of the will of man, or of the will of God."

CHAPTER XIV

IN this long sickness, your love alone, O my God, constituted my occupation without occupation. I was consumed night and day. I could not see myself in any way, so was I lost in you, O my Sovereign Good, and it seems indeed to my heart that it has never gone out from this Divine Ocean, although you have dragged it through the mud of the most severe humiliations. Who could ever comprehend, O my Love, that you made your creatures to be so one with you, that they so lose sight of themselves as no longer to see anything but you? O loss, which is the blessing of blessings, although all is effected in crosses, deaths, and bitterness!

Jesus the Child was then all living in me, or rather, he was existing alone; I was no longer. You taught me, O my Love, that your state of childhood would not be the only one I must bear; you impressed upon me these words as of a real state, into which you wished me to enter: "The birds of the heaven have nests, and the foxes have holes, but the Son of Man has not where to rest his head." You have indeed made me experience this state in all its extent since that time, having never left me even an assured dwelling, where I could rest for more than a few months, and every day in uncertainty as to being there on the morrow; besides this, in a total deprivation of all creatures, finding refuge neither with my friends, who were ashamed of me, and who openly renounced me when they saw me decried, nor among my relatives, the greater part of whom have declared themselves my adversaries and my greatest persecutors. The rest have never regarded me but with contempt and indignation. My own children ridiculed me in society.

One night that I was quite awake you showed me to myself under the figure—who says figure does not say reality; the

brazen serpent which was the figure of Jesus Christ was not
Jesus Christ—you showed me, I say, under the figure of that
woman in the Apocalypse, who has the moon under her feet,
encircled with the sun, twelve stars upon the head, who,
being with child, cried in the pains of childbirth. You explained to me its mystery. You made me understand that the
moon, which was under her feet, signified that my soul was
above the vicissitude and inconstancy of events; that I was
surrounded and penetrated by yourself; that the twelve stars
were the fruits of this state, and the gifts with which it was
honored; that I was pregnant of a fruit, which was that spirit
you wished me to communicate to all my children, whether in
the manner I have mentioned, or by my writings; that the
Devil was that terrible dragon who would use his efforts to
devour the fruit, and cause horrible ravages through all the
earth, but that you would preserve this fruit of which I was
full in yourself, that it should not be lost—therefore have I
confidence that, in spite of the tempest and the storm, all you
have made me say or write will be preserved—that in the rage
in which the Devil would be at not succeeding in the design
he has conceived against this fruit, he would attack me, and
would send a flood against me to swallow me up; that this
flood would be that of calumny, which would be ready to
sweep me away, but the earth would open—that is to say, the
calumny would little by little subside.

During my illness I was often at the point of death, as I
have said. One day, when they thought me almost well, at
four o'clock in the morning I perceived the Dragon, not under
any form. I did not see him, but I was certain it was he. I had
no fear, for, as I have said, I could not fear him, because my
Lord protects me, and keeps me safe under the shadow of his
wings. He emerged as if from the place between the side of my
bed and the wall, and gave me a furious blow on the left foot.
I was immediately seized with a great shivering, which lasted
continuously four hours; it was followed by a very sharp
fever. Convulsions seized me, and the side on which he had
struck was half dead. The attacks came every morning at the
same hour as the blow, and the convulsions increased in a
marked way every day. On the seventh day, after having
been all the night sometimes without pulse and without speech,

and sometimes a little better, in the morning I felt the convulsions were coming on. I felt at the same time that life left the lower parts in proportion as the convulsions came higher: they fixed themselves in my entrails. I felt then very great pains, and a movement in my entrails, as if I had thousands of children, who all moved at the same time. In my life I have never felt anything approaching that. This lasted a very long time with extreme violence. I felt little by little my life was contracting itself round the heart. Father La Combe gave me the Extreme Unction, the Prioress of the Ursulines having prayed him to do so, as they had not their ordinary priest. I was very glad to die, and he was not troubled at it. It would be difficult to understand without experience how a union, so close that there is nothing like it, can bear, without feeling any pain, a division such as that of seeing a person die to whom one is so firmly attached; he himself was astonished at it. But, nevertheless, it is not difficult to conceive that, being united only in God himself, in a manner so pure and so intimate, death could not divide us; on the contrary, it would have united us still more closely.

It is a thing I have many times experienced, that the least resistance he made to God caused me to suffer inexplicable torments; and to see him die, a prisoner, at a distance for ever, did not cause me the shadow of pain. He showed then great contentment at seeing me die, and we laughed together at the moment which constituted all my pleasure; for our union was different from any that can be imagined. However, death still drew near my heart, and I felt the convulsions which seized my entrails mount up there. I can say I have felt death without dying. The Father, who was on his knees near my bed, remarked the change in my face, the clouding of my eyes; he saw I was on the point of expiring. He asked me, Where was death and the convulsions? I made a sign that they were reaching the heart, and I was about to die. O God, you did not want me yet; you reserved me for far other pains than those of death, if one can call pains what one suffers in the state in which you have placed me by your goodness alone. You inspired Father La Combe to place his hand over the coverlet in the region of my heart, and with a strong voice, heard by those in the room (which was almost full), he said to death to pass no further. It obeyed his voice, and my heart, recovering a little life, came back. I felt those same convulsions descend again into my entrails, in the same way as they had mounted up, and they continued all the day in the entrails with the same violence as before, then descended gradually to the place where the Dragon had struck, and this foot was the last revivified. For two months on that side a very great weakness remained, and even after I was better, and in a condition to walk, I could not support myself on that foot, which could hardly bear me. I continued still ill, and in languor, and you gave me, my God, yet new evidence of your love. How many times did you make use of your servant to restore life to me, when I was on the point of expiring!

As they saw that my ailments did not cease, it was thought the air of the lake, on which the convent was built, was entirely unsuited to me, and was the cause of so many mishaps. It was settled that I must leave it. While I was thus ill, our Lord gave Father La Combe the idea of establishing a hospital in this place, where there was none, to receive the sick poor, and also of instituting a Congregation of Dames of Charity, to furnish those who could not quit their family to go to the hospital with the means of living during their sickness—such as we have in France; no institution of the kind being in this country. I readily entered into it, and without any capital but providence and some useless rooms that the authorities of the town gave, we commenced it. It was dedicated to the Holy Child Jesus, and he willed to give the first beds there from the money of my annuity which belonged to him. He gave such a blessing that many other persons joined. In a little time there were about twelve beds, and for the service of this hospital he gave three persons of great piety, who, without any payment, consecrated themselves to the service of the sick. I gave them ointments and remedies which they distributed to rich people, who paid, to the profit of the sick poor, and to the poor of the town they gave them without charge. These good Dames are so well disposed that through their charity, and the care of these nuns, this hospital is very well maintained. These Dames formed a union also to provide for the sick who could not go to the hospital; and I gave them some little rules I had observed when in France. They have kept this up with love and charity.

All these trifling things, which cost little, and which succeeded only in the blessing that you gave them, O my God, drew upon us new persecutions. The Bishop of Geneva was more offended than ever, and because he saw that these little things made me to be loved, he said I gained over every one. He openly declared that he could not endure me in his diocese, where, however, I had done nothing but good, or, rather, you through me. He commenced even to extend his persecutions to the worthy nuns who had kindness for me. The Prioress had severe crosses through me, but they did not last long; for as I was obliged, owing to the air, to withdraw, after having been there about two years and a half, they had greater quiet. On the other hand, my sister was very tired of that House, and as the time for the mineral waters approached, the occasion was seized to send her back, together with the maid I had brought, and who tormented me so much during all my illness. I kept with me only her whom Providence had sent me by means of my sister; and I have always believed that God had permitted her journey merely that she might bring her to me, God having chosen her for me, as suitable for the state he wished me to bear.

While I was still ill at the Ursulines, the Bishop of Verceil, who was a very great friend of the Father General of the Bernabites, urgently asked him to select among his monks a man of merit, piety, and doctrine, in whom he could have confidence, and who might serve him as theologian and adviser; that his diocese was in great want of this help. The General at once cast his eyes on Father La Combe. This was the more feasible, as his six years of priorship were coming to an end. The Father General, before engaging him with the Bishop of Verceil, wrote to him to know if he would have any objection, assuring him he would do only what was pleasing to him. Father La Combe answered that his only wish was to obey him, and he might give whatever order he pleased. He told me of this, and that we were about to be entirely separated. I had no chagrin thereat. I was very well content that our Lord should make use of him under a Bishop who knew him, and did him justice. There was still some delay in sending him off, as well because the Bishop was still at Rome, as that the period of the Father's priorship was not yet completed.

CHAPTER XV

I LEFT then the Ursulines, and a house at a distance from the lake was sought for me. The only empty one available had every appearance of the utmost poverty. There was no chimney except in the kitchen, through which we had to pass to reach the room. I took my daughter with me, and gave the largest room to her and the maid who attended her. I was placed in a little hole with some straw, which we went up to by a wooden ladder. As I had no furniture but our bedsteads, which were white, I bought some rush-seated chairs, with plates and dishes of earthenware and wood. Never have I tasted such contentment as I found in this little spot; it seemed to me so in harmony with Jesus Christ. I relished everything better on wood than on silver. I made all my little provisions, thinking to live there for a long time. But the Devil did not allow me to enjoy so sweet a peace. It would be difficult to tell the persecutions I was subjected to. Stones were thrown through my windows, falling at my feet. I had got the little garden put in order; at night people came, tore up everything, broke the trellis-work, and overturned everything, as if soldiers had been through it. All night long they came to the door and abused me, making a show of breaking in the door. These persons have since told who had set them on. Although from time to time I gave in charity at Gex, I was none the less persecuted. I can say I have never tasted an equal pleasure to that in this poor and solitary little place where I lived; I was happier than kings. But, O my God, it was still a nest for me, and a place of repose, and you willed I should be like you.

The Marquise de Prunai, sister of the chief State Secretary and Minister of His Royal Highness, had sent an express from Turin during my illness, to invite me to go to her; that, being persecuted as I was in this diocese, I should find an asylum with her; that meantime things would soften down; and when people should be well disposed, she would return with me, and join me and my friend from Paris, who also wished to come to work there according to the will of God. I was not then able to carry out what she desired, and I made my account to remain at the Ursulines until things changed. She spoke no more of it. This lady is of the most extraordinary piety, having quitted the Court for retirement and to give herself to God. At twenty-two years of age, with good natural advantages, she remained a widow, and has refused all offers in order to consecrate herself to our Lord, whose she is without any reserve.

It was settled I should go to Turin, and that Father La Combe should escort me, and go thence to Verceil. I took in addition, in order to do things with perfect propriety, and deprive our enemies of all subject for talk, a monk, a man of merit, who for fourteen years was teaching theology. I further took with me a boy I had brought from France, who had learned the trade of tailor. They hired horses, and I had a litter for my daughter, my maid, and myself. But all these precautions are useless when it is God's pleasure to crucify. Our adversaries wrote at once to Paris, and they invented a hundred ridiculous stories—pure fictions, and utterly false— about this journey. It was Father La Mothe who set all that going—perhaps he believed it true; even had it been so, out of charity he should have concealed it, but, being as false as it was, he was still more bound to do this. They said that I had gone alone with Father La Combe, running from province to province, and a thousand malicious fables. We suffered all in patience without justifying ourselves or complaining. Hardly had we arrived at Turin when the Bishop of Geneva wrote against us. He persecuted us by his letters, being unable to do it any other way.

Father La Combe went to Verceil, and I remained at Turin, in the house of the Marquise de Prunai. What crosses had I not to endure from my family, the Bishop of Geneva, the

Bernabites, and numberless persons? My elder son came to see me on the subject of my mother-in-law's death, which was a very serious addition to my crosses; but after we had heard all his reasons—seeing without me they had sold all the movables, elected guardians, and settled everything independently of me—I was quite useless. It was not thought well for me to return, owing to the severity of the season. You alone, O my God, know what I suffered; for you did not make me know your will, and Father La Combe said he had no light to guide me.

I felt myself dependent on him. We have been a real cross, the one to the other; we have truly experienced that our union was in *faith* and in *cross*, for the more we were crucified, the more were we united. It is fancied that our union was natural and human: you know, O my God, that we both found in it only cross, death, and destruction. I avow that the crosses which have come to me from this quarter have been the greatest of my life. You know the purity, the innocence, and the integrity of that union, and how it was all founded on you yourself; as you had the goodness to assure me. My dependence became greater every day; for I was like a little child who neither can nor knows how to do anything. When Father La Combe was where I was, I could not exist long without seeing him, as well owing to the strange ills which overwhelmed me suddenly, and reduced me to the point of death, as owing to my state of childhood. When he was absent, I was not troubled at it, and I had no need. I did not even think of him, and I had not the slightest desire to see him, for my need was not in my will, nor in my choice, nor even in any leaning to him or inclination; but you were the author of it, and as you were not contrary to yourself, you gave me no need of him when you took him away from me.

At the commencement of my stay at Turin, Father La Combe remained there some time waiting for a letter from the Bishop of Verceil; and he availed of the opportunity to pay a visit to his intimate friend the Bishop of Aosta, who was acquainted with my family. As he knew the bitter persecution which the Bishop of Geneva set on foot against us through the Court at Turin, he made me an offer to go into his diocese, and he sent me the kindest letters possible by Father La Combe. He wrote that previous to his acquaintance with St. Paulina, St. Jerome was a saint; but how was he spoken of afterwards? He wished me thereby to understand how Father La Combe had always passed for a saint before that persecution that I had innocently brought on him. At the same time he showed me that he preserved a very great esteem for him. He even desired, as he was very old, to give up the Bishopric in his favor. The Marquise de Prunai, who had so much wished for me, seeing the great crosses and the abjectness of my state, became disgusted with me: my childlike simplicity, which was the state God then kept me in, seemed to her mind stupidity, although in that state our Lord made me utter oracles; for when it was a question of helping any one, or of anything our Lord wished of me, with the weakness of a child, which appeared only in the candor, he gave me a divine strength. Her heart remained closed for me all the time I was there. Our Lord, however, made me tell what would happen to them, and which, in fact, has happened, not only to her, but also to her daughter and the virtuous ecclesiastic who lived with her. She, nevertheless, towards the end, took to me with more friendship, and she saw that our Lord was in me. She was obliged for family reasons to quit Turin, and go to her estate. She strongly urged me to go with her, but the education of my daughter did not permit me. It was out of the question to remain at Turin without the Marquise de Prunai, and the rather, as having lived very retired in that place, I had made no acquaintances. I knew not what to do. Father La Combe, as I said, lived at Verceil. The Bishop of Verceil had written to me most kindly, strongly urging me to go to Verceil and live near him, promising me his protection and assuring me of his esteem, adding that he would look upon me as his own sister, that from the account he had received of me he extremely desired to have me.

It was his sister, a nun of the Visitation at Turin, a great friend of mine, who had written to him about me; also a French gentleman he knew. But a certain point of honor prevented me. I did not wish that any one could say that I had been running after Father La Combe, and that it was with a view to going there I had come to Turin. His reputation was also at stake, which would not allow him to consent to my going there, however strongly the Bishop of Verceil urged it. If, however, he and I had believed it was the will of God, we would have got over all other considerations. God kept us both in such a dependence on his orders that he did not let us know them; but the divine moment determined everything. This served much to annihilate Father La Combe, who had very long walked by certainties. God in his goodness deprived him of them all, for he willed him to die without reserve.

CHAPTER XVI

ONE night our Lord made me see in a dream that he wished also to purify the maid he had given me, and to make her truly enter upon the death of Self, but that it was necessary this also should be done through me, and by means of suffering. I, therefore, had to make up my mind to suffer for her what I suffered for Father La Combe, although in a different manner. She has made me suffer inconceivable torments. As she resisted God much more than he, and the selfhood was far stronger in her, she had more to purify; so that I had to suffer martyrdoms that I could not make conceivable should I tell them: but it is impossible for me. What augmented my trouble was that Father La Combe never understood this as long as it lasted, always attributing it to defect and imperfection on my part. I bore this torment for that girl three entire years. When the resistances were strongest, and the Father approved her, without my knowing it, I entered into torments I cannot tell. I fell sick from it, so I was almost continually ill. Sometimes I passed whole days upon the ground, supported against the bedstead, without being able to stir, and suffering torments so excessive that had I been upon the rack I think I should not have felt it, so terrible was the internal pain. When that girl resisted

God more strongly, and came near me, she burned me; and when she touched me I felt so strange a pain that material fire would have been only its shadow. Ordinarily I allowed myself to burn with inconceivable violence; at other times I asked her to withdraw, because I could not any longer support the pain. She sometimes took this for aversion, and told Father La Combe, who was angry at it, and reproved me. However, when herself, she could not judge altogether in that manner, for our Lord made me constantly perform miracles for her. I had absolute power over her soul and her body. However ill she was, as soon as I told her to be cured, she was so; and as to the interior, as soon as I said to her, "Be at peace," she was so; and when I had a movement to deliver her to pain, and I delivered her to it, she entered into an inconceivable pain; but almost all her pain it was I bore, with inexpressible violence.

O my God, it seems to me you have made me understand by my own experience something of what you have suffered for men; and it seemed to me, by what I suffered, that a part of what you have suffered for men would have consumed ten thousand worlds. It needed no less than the strength of a God to bear that torment without being annihilated. Once, when I was ill, and this girl was in her resistances and her selfhood, she approached me. I felt so violent a fire that I could not, it seemed to me, bear it without dying. I told her to withdraw, owing to what I suffered. As she thought it was only opposition to her, she persisted, out of friendliness, in remaining. She took me by the arms. The violence of the pain was so excessive, that without paying any attention to what I did, being altogether beside myself from the excess of pain, I bit my arm with such force that I almost took out the piece. She saw the blood and the wound I had caused myself before perceiving the manner. This made her understand that there was something extraordinary in it. She informed the Father, as he was then at Turin, and for some time he had not come to see me, because he was in division and in trouble. He was much surprised at the hurt I had caused myself: he could not understand what caused me to suffer; and I had difficulty to explain myself to him, and make him know it. In the evening she wished to approach me. I commanded the pain which I suffered for her to seize upon her. At once she entered into so strange a pain that she believed she was about to die, and I was delivered from it for the moment; but as she could not bear it, I took it back away from her, leaving her in peace.

She exteriorly entered into a state which might have passed for madness. She was no longer fit to render me any service; in continual anger, everything offended her without rhyme or reason—jealousy of everybody, and a thousand other defects. Although she exercised me enough for the exterior, all this gave me no trouble; it was only that extreme pain which made me suffer. She became frightfully awkward, breaking and destroying everything, not being able to endure any one. All who saw me served in this way, pitied me, for she had the disgrace that, whatever eagerness she had to do well, she did everything ill; our Lord so permitting it. If I was ill in a sweat or a shivering fit, she, without thinking, threw pots of water over me; if any one, or she herself, had prepared anything, hoping to give me an appetite, she threw it in the cinders; if I had anything useful, she broke or lost it; and I never said anything to her, although things went so far that there was reason to think my income would not suffice for the half year. She was greatly distressed because I never said anything to her about what concerned me; for her affection for me was such that she was more grieved at this than at other faults which did not affect me, while for me it was the contrary. I had not the shadow of trouble from this. What I could not suffer in her was the self-love and the selfhood. I strongly reproved her for it, and I said to her, "All which concerns me gives me no trouble, but I feel such a terrible opposition for your self-love and selfhood, I could not have greater for the Devil." I saw clearly that the Devil could not hurt us, but for our self-love and selfhood; and I had more aversion and more horror for that self-love and that selfhood than for all the devils. At the beginning I was pained at the opposition I had for this girl, whom I otherwise so loved, that it seemed to me I would rather have sent away my own children than get rid of her. Father La Combe, not understanding this, reproved me, and made me suffer much. However, it was not in me from myself, but from God; and when the Father supported her, it made me suffer doubly, for I suffered from the infidelity of the one and the selfhood of the other. Our Lord made me understand that this was not a defect in me, as I persuaded myself; that it was because he gave me the discernment of spirits, and my central depth would reject, or acept, that which was of him, or was not.

Since that time, although I have not borne the purification of other souls, as in her case, I nevertheless recognize them not by any light, nor by what they tell me, but by the central depth. It is well to say here that one must not mistake; and souls which are still in themselves, whatever degree of light and ardor they may have arrived at, should not apply this to themselves. They often think they have this discernment, and it is nothing but the antipathy of nature. It has been seen that our Lord had previously destroyed in me all sorts of natural antipathy. It is necessary that the central depth be annihilated—that it depend on God alone, and that the soul no longer possess herself, for these things to be from God. This lasted three years.

In proportion as this soul was purified the pain diminished, until our Lord made me know that her state was about to change, and that he would have the goodness to harmonize her to me. So it suddenly changed. Although I suffered such strange torments for the persons our Lord desired to purify, I did not feel all the persecutions from without; and yet they were very violent. The Bishop of Geneva wrote to different kinds of persons: to those who he thought would show his letters to me he spoke well of me, and in the letters which he thought I should not see he wrote much evil. Our Lord permitted that those persons, having mutually shown each other the letters, were indignant at a procedure so contrary to good faith. They sent them to me, that I might be on my guard. I kept them for more than two years; then I burned them, in order not to do harm to that prelate. The strongest battery was that he opened through one of the Ministers, co-Secretary of State, with the brother of the Marquise de Prunai. Moreover, he took all the trouble imaginable to render me an object of suspicion, and to decry me. For this he used certain Abbés; and although I did not go out, and did not show myself, I was well-known from the unflattering portrait the Bishop made of me. It did not make as much impression as it would have done had he stood better with the Court; but certain letters, which Madame Royale found after the death of the Prince, which he had written him against her, made her for her part attach no weight to what the Bishop of Geneva wrote; on the contrary, she sent me friendly messages, and invited me to go and see her. I went to pay my respects; she assured me of her protection, and that she was very glad I was in her State.

My interior state was continually more firm and immovable, and my mind so clear, that neither distraction nor thought entered it, save those it pleased our Lord to put there. My prayer, still the same—not a prayer which is in me, but in God—very simple, very pure, and very unalloyed. It is a state, not a prayer, of which I can tell nothing, owing to its great purity. I do not think there is anything in the world more simple and more single. It is a state of which nothing can be said, because it passes all expression—a state where the creature is so lost and submerged, that though it be free as to the exterior, for the interior it has absolutely nothing. Therefore its happiness is unalterable. All is God, and the soul no longer perceives anything but God. She has no longer any pretense to perfection, any tendency, say partition, any union; all is perfected in unity, but in a manner so free, so easy, so natural, that the soul lives in God and from God, as easily as the body lives from the air it breathes. This state is known of God alone, for the exterior of these souls is very common, and these same souls, which are the delight of God, and the object of his kindness, are often the mark for the scorn of creatures.

CHAPTER XVII

WHILE I was still in Savoy God made use of me to draw to his love a monk of merit, but one who did not even dream of taking the road to perfection. He sometimes accompanied Father La Combe when he used to come to assist me in my illness, and the thought occurred to me to ask him from our Lord. The evening that I received the Extreme Unction he came near my bed. I said to him that if our Lord had pity on me after my death, he would feel the effects of it. He felt himself internally so touched as to weep; he was one of those who were most opposed to Father La Combe, and he who, without knowing me, had made out the most stories against me. Quite changed, he returned home, and could not help wishing to speak to me again, being extremely moved because he believed I was about to die. He wept so much that the other monks rallied him on it. They said to him, "Can anything be more absurd? A lady of whom only two days ago you said a thousand bad things, now that she is about to die, you weep for her as if she was your mother!" Nothing could prevent his weeping, nor take away the desire of again speaking to me. Our Lord heard his wishes, and I grew better. I had time to speak to him. He gave himself to God in an admirable manner, although he was advanced in age. He changed even as to his natural character, which was cunning and insincere, and became simple as a child. He could not call me anything but his mother. He also acquired confidence in Father La Combe, even making his general confession to him.

A year after, while I was with Father La Combe, I said to him, Father N—— is certainly changed, for our Lord has made me feel it. When he gives me any one specially I must always suffer something. O my God, how indeed true is it that I have brought forth children only with pain! But also, when they became unfaithful I felt that they were taken away, and that they were no longer anything to me; but for those whom our Lord did not remove from me, who were only wavering or unfaithful for a time, for them he made me suffer. I clearly felt that they were unfaithful, but they were not removed from me, and I knew that in spite of their infidelities, they would one day return. When, then, I said to Father La Combe that he was changed—and I had told him more than a year before that he would change—he said to me that it was my imagination. A few days after he received from him a letter full of friendship, and he said to me, "See how he is changed." While reading the letter I had again a very strong certitude that he was changed, and that a remnant of respect and shame made him continue to write thus, and that he would yet do so for some time. It happened exactly; he continued still for some time forced letters; then he ceased to write; and Father La Combe learned that the fear of losing certain friends had changed him. There are some for whom our Lord makes me pray, or makes me take some steps to aid them, and others for whom it is not even given me to write a letter to strenghten them.

While I was with the Marquise de Prunai, undecided whether I should place my daughter at the Visitation of Turin, to go with her, or whether I should take some other step, I was much surprised, when I least expected it, to see Father La Combe arrive from Verceil, and tell me that I must return to Paris without a moment's delay. It was evening. He told me to set out the next morning. I confess this unexpected news surprised me, without, however, disturbing me in the very least. It was for me a double sacrifice, to return to a place where I knew I had been so grievously decried, to a family which had nothing but scorn for me, and had represented my journey as a voluntary tour caused by the human attachment I had for Father La Combe; although it was strictly true that providential necessity alone had led me to it. You alone, O my God, knew how far we were from such sentiments, and that we were equally ready never to see each other, should it be your will, or to see each other continually should that be your will. Here, then, was I, without answering a word, ready to set out together with my daughter and a maid-servant, without any person to escort me; for Father La Combe was resolved not to accompany me, even across the mountains; because the Bishop of Geneva had written everywhere that I had gone to Turin, running after him.

But the Father Provincial, who was a man of quality of Turin, and who knew the virtue of Father La Combe, told him that I must not be allowed to go among those mountains, especially as I had my daughter with me, without some one I knew, and that he ordered him to accompany me. The Father admitted to me that he had some repugnance, but his duty of obedience and the danger to which I should have been exposed in going alone, made him get over his objections. He was to accompany me as far as Grenoble, and thence return to

Turin. I set out then with the intention of going to Paris to suffer all the crosses and submit to all the confusion it might please God to make me suffer.

What made me pass by Grenoble was the wish I had to spend two or three days with a great servant of God, a friend of mine. When I was there, Father La Combe and this lady told me to go no further, and that God wished to glorify himself in me and through me in that place. Father La Combe returned to Verceil, and I let myself be led by providence, like a child. This worthy Mother at first took me to a window, not having found room at the inn, and I expected to spend only three days there; but as they told me to remain at Grenoble, I remained in her house. I placed my daughter in a convent, and resolved to employ all this time in giving myself up in solitude to him who is absolutely master of me. I made no visit in that place, no more than in any of the other places where I had dwelt; but I was very much surprised when, a few days after my arrival, many persons came to see me, who made profession of being in an especial manner devoted to God. I at once became aware of a gift of God, which had been communicated to me without my understanding it— namely, the discernment of spirits, and the giving to each what was suitable to him. I felt myself suddenly clothed with an Apostolic state, and I discerned the state of the souls of the persons who spoke to me, and that with such facility that they were astonished, and said one to the other that I gave to each that of which he had need. It was you, O my God, who did all these things.

It reached such a point that ordinarily from six in the morning until eight in the evening I was occupied in speaking of God. People came from all sides, from far and near—monks, priests, men of the world, girls, women, and widows—all came, the one after the other, and God gave me wherewith to satisfy all in an admirable manner, without my taking any thought, or paying any attention to it. Nothing in their interior state, nor what passed in them, was concealed from me. You made, O my God, an infinity of conquests that you alone know. There was given them a surprising facility for prayer, and God gave them great graces and worked marvellous changes. I had a miraculous authority over the bodies and souls of these persons whom our Lord sent to me; their health and their interior state seemed to be in my hand. The more advanced of those souls found near me that, without speech, there was communicated to them a grace which they could not comprehend, nor cease to wonder at. The others found an unction in my words, and that they operated in them what I said to them. They had not, said they, ever seen, or rather, ever experienced anything similar. I saw monks of different orders, and priests of merit, to whom our Lord gave very great graces; and God gave grace to all, without exception—at least, to all who came in good faith.

What is surprising is, that I had not a word to say to those who came to surprise and to spy on me; and when I wished to force myself to speak to them, besides being unable, I felt that God did not desire it. Some went away, saying, "People are mad to go and see that lady: she cannot speak;" others treated me as stupid, and I did not know those persons had come to spy on me. But when they had gone out, some one came and said to me, "I was not able to come soon enough to tell you not to speak to those persons; they came from So-and-so to spy on you, and to catch you." I said to them, "Our Lord has been beforehand with your charity, for I have been unable to say a word to them."

I felt that what I said came from the fountain-head, and that I was merely the instrument of him who made me speak. In the midst of this general applause our Lord made me understand what was the Apostolic state with which he had honored me, and that to be willing to give one's self up to aid souls in the purity of his Spirit, was to expose one's self to cruel persecutions. These very words were impressed upon me: "To sacrifice yourself to aid your neighbor is to sacrifice yourself to the gibbet. Those who now say of thee, 'Blessed be he who cometh in the name of the Lord,' will soon say, 'Take away; crucify.' " One of my friends speaking of the general esteem in which I was held, I said to her, "Notice what I say to you this day, that you will hear curses proceed from the same mouths which are giving blessings."

CHAPTER XVIII

————◆•◆————

BEFORE I came to Grenoble, on the road, I went into a convent of the nuns of the Visitation. Suddenly I was struck by a picture of Jesus Christ in the garden, with these words: "Father, if it be possible, let this cup pass; however, your will be done." At once I understood that this was addressed to me, and I sacrificed myself to the will of God. There I experienced a very extraordinary thing; it is, that among so great a number of souls all good and with grace, and for whom our Lord, through me, did much, some were given me as simple plants to cultivate, in whom I did not feel our Lord desired me to take any interest. I knew their state; but I did not feel in myself that absolute authority, and they did not in especial manner belong to me. Here I understood better the true maternity. The others were given to me as children, and for these I always had something to pay, and I had authority over their souls and their bodies. Of these children some were faithful, and I knew they would be so, and they were united with me in charity. Others were unfaithful, and I knew that of these last some would never recover from their faithlessness, and they were taken away from me; as for others, that it would be merely a temporary straying. For both the one and the other I suffered heart-pains that are inconceivable, as if they were being drawn out of my heart. These are not those heart-pains which are called failure or faintness of the heart. It was a violent pain in the region of the heart, which was yet spiritual, but so violent that it made me cry out with all my strength, and reduced me to my bed. In this state I could not take food, but I had to allow myself to be devoured by a strange pain. When these same children left me, and by cowardice, lack of courage to die to themselves, they gave up everything, they were torn from my heart with much pain.

I have never in my life had so much consolation as in seeing in that little town so many good souls who vied with each other in giving themselves to God with their whole heart. There were young girls of twelve and thirteen years of age, who worked all day in silence in order to converse with God, and who had acquired a great habit of it. As they were poor girls, they joined in couples; and those who knew how to read, read out something to those who could not read. It was a revival of the innocence of the early Christians. There was a poor washerwoman, who had five children and a husband paralyzed in the right arm, but more halt in his spirit than in his body: he had no strength except to beat her. Nevertheless, this poor woman, with the sweetness of an angel, endured it all, and gained subsistence for that man and her five children. This woman had a wonderful gift of prayer, preserving the presence of God and equanimity in the greatest miseries and the most extreme poverty. There was also the wife of a shopkeeper greatly influenced by God, and the wife of a locksmith. They were three friends. Both of them sometimes read for that washerwoman, and they were surprised how she was instructed by our Lord in all they read for her, and how she spoke of it divinely.

One day that I was ill a friar, who is well versed in the treatment of sick persons, came begging, and having learnt I was ill, came in. Our Lord made use of him to give me the proper remedies for my illness, and permitted that we entered into a conversation, which woke up in him the love which he had for God, and which was, according to him, stifled by his important occupations. I made him understand that there is no occupation which could hinder him from loving God, or thinking of him. He had no trouble in believing me, having already much piety and disposition for spiritual religion. Our Lord showed him great grace, and gave him to me as one of my true children. What is admirable is, that all those whom our Lord has given me in this way, I felt that he accepted them in me to be my children; for it is he who accepts them, and who gives them.

When our Lord gives me some children of this kind, he

gives them, without my having ever exhibited anything of this, very great inclination for me; and without themselves knowing why or how, they cannot help calling me their mother—a thing which has happened to many persons of merit, priests, monks, pious girls, and even to an ecclesiastical dignitary, who all, without my having ever spoken to them, regard me as their mother—and our Lord has had the goodness to accept them in me, and to give them the same graces as if I was in the habit of seeing them. One day a person who was in a very trying state, and in manifest danger, without thinking what she did, cried aloud, "My mother, my mother!" thinking of me. She was at once delivered, with a fresh certainty that I was her mother, and that our Lord would have the goodness to succor her in all her needs through me. Many whom I knew only by letters, have seen me in dreams answer all their difficulties, and those who are more spiritual took part in the conversation, or intimate union of unity; but these last are few in number, who at a distance have no need for letters nor for discourses to understand; the others are interiorly nourished from the grace which our Lord abundantly communicates to them through me, feeling themselves filled from that outflow of grace.

For when our Lord honors a soul with spiritual fecundity, and associates her in his maternity, he gives her what is necessary to nourish and sustain her children according to their degree.

I say, then, that when Jesus Christ associates any one in spiritual maternity he provides a means of communicating himself; and it is this communication of pure spirit which forms the nourishment and essential support of souls, but a sustenance which they taste, and which they find by experience to be all they need. I know that I shall not be understood, for only experience can make this intelligible. I was sometimes so full of these pure and divine communications, which flow out from "that fountain of living water which shall spring up to eternal life," mentioned by St. John the Evangelist, that I used to say, "O Lord, give me hearts on whom I may discharge from my abundance, otherwise I must die," for these outflowings from the Divinity into the center of my soul were sometimes so powerful that they reacted even on the body, so that I was ill from it. When some of those whom our Lord had given me as children approached, or he gave me new ones in whom grace was already strong, I felt myself gradually relieved, and they experienced in themselves an inconceivable plenitude of grace and a greater gift of prayer, which was communicated to them according to their degrees.

CHAPTER XIX

THERE were some worthy girls here who were specially given to me, in particular one, and over her I had great power, both over her soul and her body, to establish her health. At the commencement, when this girl came to me, she felt a great attraction to come, and our Lord gave her through me all she had need of; but as soon as she was at a distance, the Devil excited in her mind a frightful aversion to me, so that when it was necessary for her to come and see me, it was with repugnance and terrible efforts that she did it, and sometimes when half way she turned back through faithlessness, not having the courage to continue; but as soon as she was faithful to persist she was delivered from her trouble. When she came near me it all vanished, and with me she experienced that abundance of grace which has been brought to us by Jesus Christ. It was a soul greatly influenced by God from her childhood, to whom our Lord had given much grace, and whom he had led with great gentleness. One day she was with me I had a movement to tell her she was about to enter on a serious trial. She entered on it the next day in a very violent manner. The Devil put into her mind a terrible aversion to me. She loved me by grace, and hated me through the impression, which in a strange manner the Devil made on her; but as soon as she came near me he fled, and left her in quiet. He put into her mind that I was a sorceress, and that it was by this means I drove off the devils, and that I told her what was about to happen, in consequence of which things happened as I had told them to her. She had a continual vomiting, and when I told her not to vomit, and to retain the food, she retained it. One day before entering on the trial which I shall tell, she came to see me in the morning. She could hardly speak to me, such was her then aversion for me, and the Devil did not wish her to tell it, lest I should drive him off. He closed her mouth, and put into her mind that all I said or did was by sorcery. As she did not say a word, I knew her trouble, and I told it to her. She acknowledged it. When I was in the church I said to her: If it is through the Devil I act upon you, I give him the power to torment you; but if it is another spirit who possesses me, I will that during the Mass you participate in that spirit. The little time we were there before they commenced the Mass, the Devil made use of his interval, and more forcibly impressed on her that I was a sorceress, and it was this which made me act, and that she saw how she was worse since I had said that to her. While she was in the crisis of her pain, and an aversion to me that amounted to rage, the Mass commenced. As soon as the priest made the sign of the cross, she entered into a heavenly peace, and so great a union with God, that she knew not whether she was on earth, or in heaven. We communicated in the same manner, and she was saying to herself during this time, "Oh, how certain I am it is God who moves and leads her!" After the Mass was over, she said to me, "O my mother, how have I felt what God is in you! I have been in Paradise." These are her words. But as I had only said "Until after Mass," the Devil came to attack her with more rage than before.

The greatest mischief he did was hindering her from telling me her state, for although our Lord made me well enough acquainted with it, he yet wished her to tell it to me. She was very ill; she thought she had an abscess, and the faints she fell into, joined to a pain of the head, made the doctor think so. She believed that when I touched the place on her side the abscess broke; but our Lord gave me no knowledge that it was so. I said nothing to her about it, and I have not attached faith to it, although she tried to persuade me; but what is certain is that our Lord made use of me many times to cure her.

The Devil attacked her violently, and not being content alone, he took as allies a fine gang, and caused her much trouble. I drove him away when I had the movement for it, or I handed her over as I had done before, according as our Lord inspired me; but always as soon as she approached me and kept herself in silence to receive grace, he left her in repose. In my absence he thought he would be revenged to his full; as many as sixteen of them came to torment her. She wrote it to me. I told her when they came to torment her more violently, to threaten them that she would write to me. They left her for moments.

Then I forbade them for a time to approach her, and when they presented themselves at a distance she said to them, "My mother has told me that you should leave me in quiet until she permits it." They did not approach her. At last I forbade them once for all, and they left her in quiet. She was faithless to God, and practiced on me evasions and deceptions, which only came from self-love. I at once felt it, and that my central depth rejected her, not that she ceased for that to be among the number of my children; but it is that our Lord could not endure her deception or her duplicity. The more she concealed things, the more our Lord made me know them, and the more he rejected her from my central depth.

CHAPTER XX

THIS worthy friar of whom I have spoken, and who had already previously received from God sufficient grace to dispose him to spiritual views, though for want of help and, perhaps of faithfulness, he had not advanced—this good friar, I say, felt himself led to open his heart to me like a child. Our Lord gave me all that was necessary for him, so that, not being able to doubt the impression of his grace, he said to me,

without knowing what he was saying, "You are my true
mother." From that time our Lord had the goodness to show
him much mercy through this petty nothing, and I felt indeed
that he was my son, and one of the most united and faithful.
Whenever he came to see me, our Lord showed him fresh
mercies, and he used to go away full, strengthened, encouraged to die really to himself, and certified of the power of
God in me, which he experienced with his dependence. Our
Lord gradually taught him to speak in silence, and to receive
grace without the intervention of words; but this took effect
in him only in proportion as he died to himself. Our Lord had
promised that where several should be assembled in his name,
he would be in the midst of them. It is in this way the promise
takes effect very really.

This same worthy friar had occasion to bring to me some of
his companions, and God took them all for himself. Not that
they were my children, as he was; they were only conquests.
And it was at the very time God was giving me these worthy
monks, that the other monks of the same order were committing
ravages and endeavoring to destroy spiritual religion. I marveled how our Lord compensated himself on these worthy
monks—in pouring out his Spirit upon them with fulness—for
what the others tried to make him lose, but without much
effect; for those other good souls which were persecuted
were strengthened by the persecution, instead of being shak-
en.

The Superior and the master of the novices of the House
where this worthy friar was declared against me without
knowing me, and were vexed that a woman, they said, should
be so sought after. As they regarded things in themselves and
not in God, who does what he pleases, they had only scorn
for the gift which was contained in so miserable a vessel, in
place of esteeming only God and his grace, without regard to
the baseness of the subject in which he pours it out. This
worthy friar contrived that his Superior came to thank me for
the charities, he said, that I gave them. Our Lord permitted
that he found in my conversation something which pleased
him. At last he was completely gained over, and it was he
who, being made Visitor some time afterwards, distributed so
great a quantity of books, which they, out of extreme charity,

purchased at their expense. How admirable are you, O my God, in your conduct, all wise and all loving, and how well you know how to triumph over the false wisdom of men and over all their precautions!

In the Noviciate there were several novices. He who was the senior of them was so disgusted with his vocation that he did not know what to do. The temptation was such that he could neither read, nor study, nor pray, nor perform almost any of his duties. The begging friar, one day that he acted as his companion, had a movement to bring him to me. We talked a little together, and our Lord made me discover the cause of his trouble and the remedy. I told it to him, and he set himself to pray, but a prayer of affection. He suddenly changed, and our Lord gave him great grace. In proportion as I spoke to him, an effect of grace was produced in his heart, and his soul opened herself like a parched land to the dew. He felt he was changed and freed from his trouble before leaving the room. He performed at once with joy, and even to perfection, all his exercises, which previously he performed with disgust, or did not perform at all. He studied and prayed with ease, and discharged all his duties, so that he no longer knew himself, nor did the others. But what astonished him more was a germ of life which had remained with him, and a gift of prayer. He saw that there was given to him without trouble what previously he could not have, whatever trouble he took; and that vivifying germ was the principle which made him act, and gave him grace for his occupations and a root of God's presence, which brought with it all good. He gradually brought to me all the novices, who all felt the effect of grace, but differently and according to their degree; so that never did Noviciate appear more flourishing.

The Father, who was master, and the Superior, could not help wondering at so great a change in their novices, although they did not penetrate the cause; and one day as they spoke of it to the begging friar, and said to him—for they had him in great esteem, being men of merit and virtue—that they were surprised by the change in the novices, and the blessing that the Lord had given to their Noviciate, he said to them, "My Fathers, if you permit me, I will tell you the cause. It is that lady, against whom you cried out so strongly without knowing her, of whom God has made use for this." They were very much surprised, and that Father, although very aged, had the humility, as well as his Guardian, to use prayer in the way taught in a little book which our Lord had made me compose, and of which I shall speak immediately. They so much profited by it that the Guardian said, "I am a new man. I could not pray because my reasoning was dulled and exhausted, and now I do it without trouble as much as I wish, with much fruit and a quite different presence of God." The other Father said to him, "For forty years I am a monk, and I can say that I have never known how to pray, nor known and tasted God until this time." As my true children I had only the first of the novices of whom I have spoken, the begging friar, and another Father, nephew of the begging friar. There were many others won for God in a special manner. I saw clearly that they were gained, but I did not feel in their case that maternity and that inward flowing out of which I have spoken, although they were, however, our Lord's through my means. I do not know if I can make myself understood.

Our Lord gave me a very great number of children, and three famous monks, from an order by which I have been, and am still, much persecuted. These are very closely bound to me, especially one. He made me help a great number of nuns and virtuous girls, and even men of the world, among others a young man of rank, who has given himself to God, and is his in a very special manner. He is a man very spiritually minded, and who, while married, is very holy. Our Lord sent me also an Abbé of rank, who had left the Order of Malta, to take up that of the priesthood. He was relative of a Bishop of that neighborhood, who had plans for him. Our Lord gave him great grace, and he is very faithful to prayer. I could not write the great number of souls then given to me—maids and wives, monks and priests; but there were three curés, and one canon, who were more especially given to me, and a grand vicar. There was also a priest who was given to me very intimately, for whom I suffered much; but as he was not willing to die to himself, and too much loved himself, he was entirely torn away from me, and I suffered terribly. I suffered before he was torn from me, and I knew by my suffering that he was about to be torn from me, and to fall. As for the others, some remained unshaken, and others were a little shaken by the tempest, but they are not torn away; although these stray, they still return; but those who are torn away never return.

CHAPTER XXI

YOU were not content, my God, with making me speak, you further gave me an impulse to read the Holy Scripture. There was a time that I did not read, for I found in myself no want to fill up; on the contrary, rather too great a plenitude. As soon as I commenced reading the Holy Scripture, it was given me to write out the passage I read, and immediately the explanation of it was given to me. In writing out the passage I had not the least thought on the explanation, and as soon as it was written out it was given to me to explain it, writing with inconceivable quickness. Before writing I did not know what I was going to write; while writing I saw that I was writing things I had never known, and during the time of the manifestation light was given me that I had in me treasures of knowledge and understanding that I did not know myself to possess. As soon as I had written I remembered nothing whatever of what I had written, and there remained to me neither species nor images. I could not have made use of what I had written to aid souls; but our Lord gave me while I spoke to them all that was necessary for them. In this way our Lord made me explain all the Holy Scripture. I had no book except the Bible, and that alone I used without searching for anything. When, in writing on the Old Testament, I took passages from the New to support what I was saying, it was not that I sought them out, but they were given to me at the same time as the explanation; and exactly the same with the New Testament. I there made use of passages from the Old, and they were given to me without my searching for anything. I had no time to write except at night, for I had to speak all day, without reflection any more for speaking than for writing, and as little careful of my health, or of my life, as of myself. I used to sleep only one or two hours every night, and with that almost every day I had fever, ordinarily a quartan, and yet I continued to write without inconvenience, without troubling myself whether I should die or live.

I continued to write, and with incredible quickness, for the hand could hardly follow the spirit which dictated, and during this long work I did not change my conduct, nor make use of any book. The copyist could not, however diligent, copy in five days what I wrote in a single night. What is good in it comes from you alone, O my God; and what is bad comes from me. I mean to say, from my unfaithfulness and the mixture which, without knowing it, I have made of my impurity with your pure and chaste doctrine. At the commencement I committed many faults, not being yet broken in to the operation of the Spirit of God, who made me write. For he made me stop writing when I had time to write and I could conveniently do it, and when I seemed to have a very great need of sleeping, it was then he made me write. When I wrote by day there were continual interruptions, and I had not time to eat, owing to the number who used to come. I had to give up everything as soon as I was asked for, and in addition I had the maid who served me in the state of which I have spoken, and she without cause used to come and suddenly interrupt me, according as her whim took her. I often left the meaning half finished, without troubling myself whether what I was writing was connected or not. The places which may be defective are so only because sometimes I wished to write as I had the time, and then it was not grace at its fountain head. If these passages were numerous it would be pitiable. At last I accustomed myself to follow God in his way, not in mine. I wrote the Song of Songs in a day and a half, and in addition received visits. The quickness with which I wrote was so great that my arm swelled up and became quite stiff. At night it caused me great pain, and I did not believe I could write for a long time.

There came to see me a counselor of the Parliament, who is a model of holiness. This worthy servant of God found on my table a "Method of Prayer," which I had written a long time before. He took it from me, and having found it much to his taste, he gave it to some of his friends, to whom he thought it would be useful. All wished to have copies of it. He resolved with that worthy friar to have it printed. The printing commenced and the approbation given, they asked me to put a preface to it. I did so, and it is in this way that the little book, which has been made the pretext for my imprisonment, was printed. This counselor is one of my closest friends, and a great servant of God.

This poor little book, notwithstanding the persecution, has nevertheless been printed five or six times, and our Lord gives a very great blessing to it. These worthy monks took fifteen hundred copies. The begging friar wrote perfectly, and our Lord inspired him to copy my writings, at least a part. He also gave the same idea to a monk of a different order, so that each of them took some to copy. Being one night engaged in writing something which he thought urgent (for he had misunderstood what had been said to him), as it was extremely cold, and his legs were naked, they so swelled that he could not move. He came to see me, quite sad, and as if disgusted with writing. He told me his ailment, and that he could not go on his begging rounds. I told him to be cured; he was so on the instant, and went away very well pleased and very desirous of transcribing that work, through which he declares our Lord has bestowed on him great graces. There was also a worthy girl, but very fickle; she had a great pain in the head. I touched it for her, and she was immediately cured.

CHAPTER XXII

A poor girl came to see me one day quite distressed. She said to me, "O my mother, what strange things I have seen!" I asked her what it was. "Alas!" she cried, "I saw you like a lamb in the midst of a pack of furious wolves. I have seen a terrible gang of people of all kinds, of every age, sex, and condition—priests, monks, married people, maids, wives—with pikes, halberts, naked swords, who were trying to stab you. You let them do so without stirring, or showing astonishment, or defending yourself. I looked on all sides if any one would come to assist or defend you, but I have not seen any one." Some days after those who through envy were preparing a secret battery against me suddenly broke out like a thunderbolt. Libels commenced to circulate everywhere, and letters were shown me of the most dreadful character, which, without knowing me, envious persons had written. They said that I was a sorceress; that it was by magic I attracted souls; that whatever was in me was diabolic; that if I bestowed charities, it was with false money I did so; and a thousand other crimes they accused me of, which were as false and as ill founded the one as the other. As the tempest each day increased, and they in truth said "Crucify!" exactly as our Lord had at the first let me know, some of my friends advised me to withdraw for a time. The Almoner of the Bishop of Grenoble told me to go to St. Baume and to Marseilles, to spend some time; that they wished for me there, where were some very spiritually minded persons; that he would accompany me, together with a worthy maid and another ecclesiastic, and meantime the tempest would pass off. But before speaking of my departure from Grenoble, I must say something more of the state which I bore in that country.

Before writing on the Book of Kings of all that refers to David, I was put into such a close union with this holy patriarch that I communicated with him as if he had been present, not in images, species, or figures—my soul was far removed from these things—but in a divine manner, in an ineffable silence, and in perfect reality. I understood what this holy patriarch was; the greatness of his grace, the conduct of God with him, and all the circumstances of the states through which he had passed; that he was a living figure of Jesus Christ, and a shepherd chosen for Israel. It seemed to me that all our Lord made me, or would make me, do for souls, would be in union with this holy patriarch, and with those to whom I was at the same time united in a manner similar to what I had been with David, my dear King. O Love, did you not make me know that the wonderful and real union between this holy patriarch and me would never be understood by any one? for none was in a state to understand it. It was then you taught me, O my Love, that by this admirable union it was given me to carry Jesus Christ, Word-God, into souls. Jesus Christ is born of David according to the flesh. Oh, how many conquests did you cause me to make in this quite ineffable union! My words were efficacious, and produced effects in hearts. It was the formation of Jesus Christ in souls. I was in no way the mistress of speaking or saying things; he who led me made me speak them as he wished, and for as long as was pleasing to him. There were souls to whom he did not let me say a word, and others for whom there were deluges of grace. But that pure love did not suffer any superfluity nor trifling. Sometimes there were souls who asked several times the same things, and when they were answered according to their need, and it was only a desire of speaking, without my paying any attention to it, I could not answer them. They then said to me, "You said this last; must we hold to this?" I used to say to them, "Yes," and then I was enlightened that because the answer would have been useless, it was not given to me. It was exactly the same with those whom our Lord was leading through the death of themselves, and who came to seek for human consolation. I had for them merely the strictly neces-sary, after which I was unable to speak. I would rather have spoken of a hundred indifferent matters, but as for his Word, he himself is the dispenser of it. Oh, if preachers spoke in this spirit, what fruit would they not have! There were others, as I have said, to whom I could communicate myself only in silence, but a silence as ineffable as efficacious. These last are the most rare, and it is the special characteristic of my true children. It is the communication of the Blessed Spirits.

O God, who will ever comprehend the pure and holy unions which you form among your creatures! The carnal world only judges of them carnally, attributing to a natural attachment that which is the highest grace. You alone, O God, know what I have suffered on this head. All the other crosses, although very hard, appeared to me shadows beside

that. Our Lord made me one time understand that when Father
La Combe should be established in him in a permanent state, and
he should have no more interior vicissitudes, he would have
none also in regard to me, and that he would remain for ever
united to me in God. That is so at present. I saw that he felt
the union and the division only owing to his weakness, and
that his state was not yet permanent. I felt it only because he
divided himself, and that I had to bear all this; but ever since
the union has been without contrariety, without hindrance
and in its perfection, he has no longer felt it, no more than I;
except by an awakening in interior conversation in the manner of the Blessed.

The union of the soul with God is felt only because it is
not entirely perfect; but as soon as it is consummated in unity,
it is no more felt: it becomes, as it were, natural. One does not
feel the union of the soul and the body. The body lives and
operates in this union without one thinking, or paying attention to the union. It exists—we know it; and all the functions
of life which the body performs do not allow us to be ignorant
of it—yet one acts without attention to that. It is the same for
the union with God and with certain creatures in him, for
what shows the purity and eminence of this union is that it
follows that with God; and it is so much the more perfect as
that soul to God and in him is more perfected. Yet were it
necessary to break this pure and holy union, one would feel
it the more, in proportion as it is more pure, perfect, and insensible; as one very well feels when the soul is about to
separate from the body by death, although one does not feel
the union.

CHAPTER XXIII

THE Almoner of the Bishop of Grenoble persuaded me to go
and pass some time at Marseilles, to let the tempest blow over,

and said that I should there be very well received, that it was his country, and that many good persons were there. I wrote to Father La Combe, that I might have his approval. He permitted it. I might have gone to Verceil, for the Bishop of Verceil had sent me by express the strongest, most pressing, and most attractive letters possible, to induce me to go into his diocese; but deference to man's opinion and the fear of giving opportunity to my enemies (when I use the term enemy it is not that I consider any person such, nor that I can look upon those whom God makes use of otherwise than as the instruments of his justice, but it is to explain myself)—these two reasons, I say, made me extremely unwilling. Besides, the Marquise de Prunai, who since my departure had been more enlightened by her own experience, having found true some of the things which I had believed were about to happen to her, had conceived for me a very strong friendship, and a very intimate union, so that the most united sisters could not be more so than were we. She wished extremely I should return to her as I had before promised; but I could not resolve upon it, lest it should be thought I was going where Father La Combe was. But, O my God, how this remnant of self-love was overthrown by the action of your adorable providence! I had still this interior support of being able to say that I had never been running after Father La Combe, and that this could not be said of me, nor could I be accused on this head of any attachment to him, since when it depended only upon me to live near him, I did not do so. The Bishop of Geneva had not failed to write against me to Grenoble, as he had done elsewhere. His nephew had been from house to house decrying me. All this was indifferent to me, and I nevertheless procured for his diocese all the good I could. I even wrote politely to him; but his heart was too wounded in the matter of worldly interest, he said, to give in. These were his own words.

I embarked, then, on the Rhone, with my maid and a worthy girl of Grenoble, to whom our Lord had through my means given much grace. She was to me a genuine source of crosses. The Almoner of the Bishop of Grenoble accompanied me, together with another ecclesiastic, a very excellent man. We had many adventures, and were near perishing; for in a very dangerous place the cable broke, and the boat went right against a rock. The master pilot fell overboard at the shock, and would have been drowned but for the gentlemen who saved him. Another accident also happened to me. Having with the gentlemen gone down the Rhone in a small boat managed by a child, in expectation of finding a large boat, without success, we had to return to Valence, after having gone down more than a league. Every one got out of the boat because it was too heavy to reascend the river, and as I could not walk I remained in it at the mercy of the waves, which bore as where they pleased without resistance; for the child who managed the boat, and did not know his business, took to tears, saying we were about to be drowned. I encouraged him, so that, having contended for more than four hours with the waves, while those who were on the bank believed us at one time utterly lost, then again saved, at last we arrived.

These manifest dangers, which frightened the others, far from alarming me, increased my peace—a thing which astonished the Bishop's Almoner, who was in a horrible fright when the boat ran against the rock and split; for, attentively looking at me in his emotion, he noticed that I did not frown, and that my tranquillity was not in the least altered. It is true that I did not feel even the first movements of surprise, which are natural to every one on these occasions, and which do not depend on us. What caused my peace in these perils that suddenly surprise, was my inmost center being in an abandonment always fixed and firm in God, and because death is to me far more agreeable than life; I should need much more abandonment to God for living than for dying, if I could have any wish. I am indifferent to everything, and that is why nothing alters my central depth.

On leaving Grenoble a man of rank, a great servant of God and an intimate friend of mine, had given me a letter for a very devout Knight of Malta, whom I have always regarded since I knew him as a man our Lord destines to be very useful to the Order of Malta; to be its example and support through his holy life. I told him even that I believed he would go to Malta and that God would assuredly make use of him to inspire with piety many of the Knights. He has, in fact, gone to Malta, where at once the highest offices were given to him. That man

"As I could not walk, I remained alone in the boat at the mercy of the waves."

of rank sent him the little book on prayer entitled, "A Short Method," printed at Grenoble. This knight had an almoner very much opposed to spirituality. He took the book and at once condemned it, and set about stirring up a party in the town, among others seventy-two persons who openly called themselves the seventy-two disciples of M. de St. Cyran. I had only arrived at ten o'clock in the morning, and a few hours after noon everything was in commotion against me. They went to see the Bishop of Marseilles, telling him that, owing to that little book, he must drive me away from Marseilles. They gave him the book, which he examined with this theologian, and which he found very good. He sent to fetch M. Malaval and a worthy Recolet Father who he knew had been to see me a little after my arrival, to ascertain from them whence arose this great tumult. M. Malaval and the monk told the Bishop what they thought of me, so that he expressed great displeasure at the insult which had been put on me. I was obliged to go and see him. He received me with extreme kindness, and asked my pardon. He prayed me to remain at Marseilles, that he would protect me; he even inquired where I lodged, that he might come and see me. The next day the Almoner of the Bishop of Grenoble, with that other priest who came with us, went to see him. The Bishop again expressed to them the vexation he felt at the insults which had been cast upon me without cause, and he said that it was the usual practice of those persons to insult all who were not of their faction; that they had insulted himself. They were not content with that; they wrote me the most offensive letters possible, although these persons did not know me.

I understood that our Lord was commencing in earnest to deprive me of any dwelling-place, and these words came afresh to me: "The birds of heaven have nests, and the foxes have holes, and the Son of Man has not where to lay his head." I willingly entered upon that state.

Our Lord nevertheless made use of me during the short time I remained at Marseilles to aid in supporting some good soul.

As soon as I had left Grenoble those who, without knowing me, hated me, set in circulation libels against me. One person for whom I had had a very great charity, and whom I had even withdrawn from an engagement in which she was for

many years, having contributed to remove to a distance the
person to whom she was attached, became so furious thereat
that she went herself to see the Bishop of Grenoble, to speak
to him against me, going so far as to say that I had advised her
to do an evil which I had broken off even at my expense; for it
cost me money to get away the person. They had lived together
for eight years, and I knew her only for one month. She went
from confessor to confessor saying the same thing, in order to
excite them against me. The fire was kindled in all directions:
only those who knew me and who loved God supported my
side, and they found themselves more bound to me by the
persecution. It would have been very easy for me to destroy
the calumny, as well with the Bishop as the town. It was only
needed to say who the person was and to exhibit the fruits of
her disorder, for I knew everything; but as I could not
declare the guilty one without making known her accomplice,
who was very repentant and touched by God, I thought it
better to suffer everything and remain silent. There was a
very holy man who thoroughly knew the whole story; he
wrote to her that if she did not retract her lies he would
publish her evil life, so as to make known her wickedness and
my innocence. That poor girl persevered still for some time in
her malice, writing that I was a sorceress, and that she knew
it by revelation and many other things. However, some time
after she had, according to her account, such cruel remorse of
conscience that she wrote to the Bishop and others to retract.
She got a letter written to myself, that she was in despair at
what she had done, that God had punished her in such a
manner that never had she been treated in a similar way. After
her retractation the rumour subsided, the Bishop was disabused,
and from that time he has shown me great kindness. This
creature had said, among other things, that I caused myself to
be worshipped, and such strange absurdities that the like
were never seen. As she had been formerly mad, I believe
there was more weakness than malice in what she did.

Being then at Marseilles, I knew not what to do, for I saw
no possibility either of remaining there or returning to Grenoble, where I had left my daughter in a convent. On the
other hand, Father La Combe had written me that he did not
think I ought to return to Paris. I felt even great repugnance

to it, without knowing the reason, which made me think that it was not yet the time. One morning I felt myself interiorly urged to depart. I took a litter to go and visit the Marquise de Prunai, who was, it seemed to me, the most respectable refuge for me in the state things were. I thought to be able to go by Nice, as I had been assured by people; but I was very much astonished, when at Nice, to learn that the litter could not pass the mountain to go where I wanted. I knew not what to do, nor what side to turn to, being alone, abandoned by all the world, without knowing, O my God, what you wished of me. My confusion and my crosses increased each day. I saw myself without refuge or retreat, wandering and vagabond. All the workmen that I saw in their shops appeared to me happy in having a dwelling-place and a refuge, and I found nothing in the world so hard for a person like me, who naturally loved honor, as this wandering life. While I knew not what course to take, I was told that next day a small sloop was about to start, which would go to Genoa in a single day, and that if I wished they would land me at Savona, whence I could be carried to my friend the Marquise de Prunai. I consented to this, having no possibility of other conveyance. I had some joy in embarking on the sea. A storm came on in a place dangerous enough for a small boat, and the sailors were very bad. The turbulence of the waves constituted my pleasure, and I was delighted to think that these mutinous waters would serve perhaps for my grave. O God, perhaps I committed some infidelity in the pleasure I took at seeing myself beaten and tossed by these raging waves. I thought I saw myself in the hands of your providence: it seemed to me I was its plaything; and I said to you, O my God, in my language, "Let there be, then, in the world victims of your providence, and let me be one. Do not spare me." Those who were with me saw my intrepidity, but they were ignorant of its cause. I asked of you, O my Love, a little hole in a rock, to place myself there and to live separated from all creatures. I pictured to myself that a desert island would have ended all my disgraces, and would have placed me in a state to perform infallibly your will; but, O my Love, you destined me to another prison than a rock, another exile than that of the desert isle. You reserved me to be beaten by waves more irritated than those of the sea. Calumny was the mutinous and pitiless sea to which you desired I should be exposed, to be thereby beaten without mercy: blessed for ever, O my God, be you for this!

We were stopped by the storm, and in place of a short day's journey, the proper time to reach Genoa, we were eleven days on the way. How peaceable was my heart during this great agitation! The tempest of the sea and the fury of the waves were only the symbol of that which all creatures had against me. I said to you, "O my Love, arm them all to avenge yourself on my infidelities and those of all creatures." I saw with pleasure your arm raised against me, and I loved more than a thousand lives the strokes it gave me. We could not disembark at Savona; it was necessary to go to Genoa. We arrived there in the Holy Week. I had to endure the insults of the inhabitants, owing to their irritation against the French for the injuries caused by the bombardment. The Doge had just left, and he had taken with him all the litters; for this reason I could not get one. I had to remain several days at an excessive expense, for these people demanded exorbitant sums, and as much for each person as would be charged in Paris at the best inn for the whole party. I was almost without money; but the fund of providence could not fail me. I begged most earnestly, at whatever cost, that I might be supplied with a litter, so as to be able to go and spend Easter with the Marquise de Prunai; yet there were only three days remaining to Easter, and I could not make myself understood. Owing to my entreaties, a bad litter was brought me, the mules belonging to which were lame, and I was told that for an exorbitant sum they would take me to Verceil, which was two days' distance, but not to the Marquise de Prunai; because they did not even know where her estate was. I was strangely mortified, for I did not wish to go to Verceil, and yet the nearness of Easter, and the want of money in a country where they practiced a sort of tyranny, left me no choice, but under an absolute necessity of allowing myself to be taken to Verceil.

You led me, O my God, by your providence, where I did not wish to go. Although the sum I had to give for such a bad conveyance for two days' journey was ten louis d'or, each sixteen livres of that country, nevertheless I accepted the unreasonable bargain from extreme necessity, and that in a country where conveyances are very cheap. The voiturier was the most cruel man possible, and for crown to our trouble, I had sent on the ecclesiastic, who accompanied us, to Verceil, in order to break the surprise of their seeing me after I had protested that I would not go there. This ecclesiastic was very badly treated on the road, from hatred against the French, and part of the journey he had to do on foot, so that, although he had set out in advance, he reached only a few hours before me. The man, then, who led us, seeing that he had only women to deal with, insulted us in every way possible.

We passed through a wood full of robbers. The muleteer was afraid, and told us that if any one met us on the road we were lost, and that they spared no one. Hardly had he told us this, when four well-armed men appeared. They at once stopped the litter. The muleteer was very much terrified. They came to us and looked at us. I made them a bow with a smile, for I had no fear, and I was so abandoned to providence, that it was equal to me to die in that way or another, in the sea, or by the hand of robbers. But, O my God, what was your protection over me, and what was my surrender into your hands! How many dangers have I run on the mountains, and on the edge of precipices! How many times have you stopped the foot of the mule, already sliding over the precipice! How many times have I expected to be precipitated from those frightful mountains into terrible torrents, which were hid from view by the depth, but which made themselves heard by their fearful noise! Where the dangers were more apparent, it was there my faith was stronger, as well as my intrepidity, which sprung from an inability to desire anything else but what would happen, whether it should be to be smashed on the rocks, to be drowned, or to be killed—all being alike in your will, O my God. The people who led me said they never saw a similar courage, for the most terrifying dangers, and where death seemed most certain, were those which pleased me more. Was it not you, O my God, who held me back in the danger, and prevented me from rolling into the precipice, to which we were already slipping down? The more reckless I was of a life, which I endured only because you yourself endured it, the more did you take care to preserve it. It was,

O my God, like a challenge between us two: I to abandon myself to you, and you to preserve me. The robbers then came to the litter, but I had no sooner saluted them than you made them change their purpose, one pushing the other to hinder him from hurting me. They saluted me very politely, and with an air of compassion, unusual in such persons, they withdrew. I was at once impressed, O my Love, that it was a stroke of your right hand, which had other designs for me than to make me die by the hands of robbers.

The muleteer, seeing me alone with two maids, thought he could illtreat me as much as he pleased, perhaps imagining to extort money. Instead of taking me to the inn, he took me to a mill, where there was no woman; there was only a single room, with several beds, where the millers and the muleteers slept together. It was in this room he wanted to compel me to remain. I said I was not a person to lie down where he had brought me, and I tried to oblige him to take me to the inn. He would do no such thing. I had to set out on foot at ten o'clock at night, carrying a part of my clothes, and travel more than a quarter league of that country in the midst of darkness, without knowing the road, crossing even one end of the robbers' wood, to go and find the inn. That man, seeing me leave the place where he had wanted to make us sleep, not without wicked intentions, cried out after us, abusing and ridiculing us. I bore my humiliation with pleasure, not without seeing and feeling it; but your will, my God, and my abandonment made everything easy to me. We were very well received at the inn, and those worthy people did their best to refresh us from our fatigue, assuring us that the place where we had been taken was very dangerous. The next day we had again to return on foot to find the litter, that man refusing to bring it to us. On the contrary, he poured out insults, and for crown of disgrace, he sold me to the post, and forced me thereby to go in a post-chaise, instead of in the litter.

I reached Alexandria in that conveyance. It is a frontier town dependent on Spain, on the side of the Milanais. Our postilion wished to take us, as usual, to the post. I was much astonished to see the mistress of the house come to meet him, not to receive, but to hinder him entering. She had been told that there were women, so, thinking us other than we were, she did not wish for us. The postilion wished to persist. Their dispute grew so warm that a number of officers of the garrison, with a great crowd, assembled at the noise, astonished at the strangeness of the woman not wishing to lodge us. They thought she knew us for persons of bad livelihood, so that we had to submit to insults. However I urged the postilion to take us elsewhere; he would not do it, and persisted obstinately in trying to enter, assuring the mistress that we were honorable and even pious persons, the signs of which he had seen. By his persistence he compelled the woman to come and see us. As soon as she had looked at us she did like the robbers, allowed herself to yield, and made us come in. I had no sooner got out of the chaise than she said to me, "Go and shut yourself in that room, and do not stir, that my son may not know you are there, for if he knows it, he will kill you." She said this to us with so much emphasis, and her servant also, that if death had not for me the many charms it has, I should have died of fear. The two poor girls were in terrible alarm; when any one stirred, or came to open the door, they thought that our throats were about to be cut. In short, we remained between death and life until the next day, when we learned that the young man had taken an oath to kill all women who should lodge at his house, because a few days before he had a very serious business which threatened his ruin; a woman of evil life having assassinated a respectable man at their house. This had cost them much, and with reason he feared similar persons.

CHAPTER XXIV

AFTER such adventures, I arrived at Verceil the evening of Good Friday. Going to the inn, I was very badly received, and I had the opportunity of passing a genuine Good Friday, which lasted very long. I sent to find Father La Combe, believing him already informed by the ecclesiastic I had sent in advance, but the latter had only just arrived. I had many genuine mortifications to swallow for the time I was without this ecclesiastic, which I should have escaped had I had him; for in this country, when ladies are accompanied by an ecclesiastic they are regarded with veneration, as persons of respectability and piety. Father La Combe was strangely displeased at my arrival, God so permitting; he even could not hide it from me. Thus I saw myself at the moment of arrival on the point of setting out again; and I would have done this, notwithstanding my extreme fatigue, but for the Easter festival. Father La Combe could not prevent himself showing his mortification. He said that every one would think I had come to see him, and this would injure his reputation. He was in very high esteem in that country. I had no less pain in going there, and it was necessity alone which had made me do it, in spite of my objections; so that I was placed in a state of sufferings, and our Lord adding his hand, made them very severe. The Father received me coldly, and in a manner which showed me his sentiments, and this redoubled my pain. I asked him if he wished me to return, that I would set out on the moment, although I was overwhelmed with the fatigues of such a long and dangerous journey; besides that I was much weakened by the Lent fast, which I kept as strictly as if I had not been travelling. He told me he did not know how the Bishop of Verceil would take my arrival, when he had ceased to expect it, after I had so long obstinately refused the obliging offers he had made me; that he no longer showed any desire to see me since that refusal. It was then, it seemed to me, that I was cast out from the surface of the earth, without the means of finding any refuge, and that all creatures were combined together to crush me. I spent the rest of the night in this inn, without being able to sleep, and without knowing what course I should be compelled to take, being persecuted to the degree I was by my enemies, and a subject of shame to my friends.

As soon as they knew at the inn that I was an acquaintance of Father La Combe they treated me very well, for he was there esteemed as a saint. The Father did not know how to tell the Bishop of Verceil that I was come, and I felt his trouble more keenly than my own. As soon as the Prelate knew I had arrived, as he thoroughly understood the proprieties, he sent his niece, who took me in her carriage and brought me to her house; but things were only done for appearance, and the Bishop, not having yet seen me, did not know how to take such an inopportune journey, after my having three times refused to go there, although he had sent expresses to ask me to do so. He was disgusted with me. However, as he was informed that my design was not to remain at Verceil, but to go to the Marquise de Prunai, and that it was necessity owing to the festival which detained me, he let nothing appear; on the contrary, he took care that I was very well treated. He could not see me until after Easter, as he officiated all the Vigil and on the day. In the evening, after all the duty of Easter Day was over, he had himself carried in a chair to his niece's house to see me, and although he understood French no better than I did Italian, he was none the less very well satisfied with the conversation that he had with me. He seemed to have as much kindness for me as he previously had indifference. The second visit finished in gaining him entirely.

One could not be under greater obligations than I was to this good Prelate. He conceived as much friendship for me as if I had been his sister, and in the midst of his continual occupation, his sole diversion was to spend a half-hour with me, speaking about God. He began a letter to the Bishop of Marseilles to thank him for having protected me in the persecution. He wrote also to the Bishop of Grenoble, and there was nothing he left undone to mark his affection. He no longer thought of anything but devising means to keep me in his diocese. He was not willing to let me visit the Marquise de Prunai; on the contrary, he wrote to her, inviting her to come herself with me into his diocese. He even sent Father La Combe expressly to urge her to come, assuring her that he wished to unite us all and form a small Community. The Marquise de Prunai entered into it readily enough, and her daughter also, and they would have come with Father La Combe but for the Marquise having fallen ill. She thought of sending her daughter to me, and the matter was deferred until she should be in better health. The Bishop commenced by hiring a large house, which he even treated for the purchase of, in order to locate us in it. It was very suitable for a Community. He wrote also to a lady at Genoa, an acquaintance of his, sister to a cardinal, who expressed much desire to unite with us, and the matter was considered already settled. There were also some devout girls, who were quite ready to set out to come to us. But, O my God, your will was not to establish me, but rather to destroy me.

The fatigue of the journey made me fall ill; the girl I had brought from Grenoble also fell ill. Her relatives, persons very full of self-interest, got into their heads that if she died in my hands I might cause her to make a will in my favor. They were much mistaken; for, far from wishing for the property of others, I had even given away my own. Her brother, full of this apprehension, came as quickly as possible, and the first thing he spoke to her of, although he found her recovered, was to make a will. This caused a great fracas at Verceil; for he wanted to take her away, and she was not willing to go. However, as I noticed little solidity of character in this girl, I thought it was an opportunity which divine providence offered me of getting rid of her, as she was not suited to me. I advised her to do what her brother wished. He formed friendship with some officers of the garrison, to whom he told ridiculous stories, that I wanted to ill-use his sister, whom he represented as a person of quality, although she was of quite humble birth. This brought me many crosses and humiliations. They commenced to say, what I had always dreaded, that I had come for the sake of Father La Combe. They even persecuted him on account of me.

The Bishop of Verceil was extremely vexed, but he could not apply any remedy; for he could not make up his mind to let me go, besides that I was in no state to do so, being ill. The friendship he had for me increased each day, because, as he loved God, he had a friendship for all those he believed wishing to love him. As he saw me so ill, he came to see me constantly, when he was free from his duties and occupations. This caused him and me also no slight crosses. He used to make me little presents of fruit, and other things of that nature. His relatives became jealous, saying I had come to ruin

him, and carry away into France the money of the Bishop. It
was what was furthest from my thoughts. This worthy Bishop
swallowed all the crosses, through the friendship he had for
me, and still confidently calculated on keeping me in his
diocese as soon as I was recovered.

Father La Combe was his theologian and his confessor: he
esteemed him greatly; and the Father did a great deal of good
in that garrison, God making use of him to convert many of the
officers and soldiers. Some of very scandalous life became
models of virtue. He induced the subaltern officers to make
retreats; he preached and instructed the soldiers, who profited
greatly, and as a consequence made general confessions. In
this place there was a constant mixture of crosses and of souls
gained for our Lord. There were some of his brother monks,
who, after his example, were working for their perfection,
and, although I hardly understood their language and they
did not at all understand mine, our Lord brought it about that
we understood each other in what regarded his service. The
Father Rector of the Jesuits, having heard me spoken of, took
the opportunity of Father La Combe's absence from Verceil to
come and, as he said, try me. He had studied theological
subjects that I did not understand, and put numbers of
questions to me. Our Lord gave me the means of answering,
and he went away so satisfied that he could not help speaking
of it. Father La Combe stood well then with the Bishop of
Verceil, who looked on him with veneration.

But the Bernabites of Paris, or rather Father La Mothe,
bethought himself of bringing him away from there, to make him
go and preach at Paris. He wrote of it to their General,
saying that they had none at Paris qualified to uphold the
House; that their church was deserted; that it was a mistake
to leave a man like Father La Combe in a place where he was
merely corrupting his language; that his great talents should
be exhibited at Paris; that for the rest, he could not bear the
burden of the House of Paris, if he was not given a man of
that stamp. Who would not have believed that all this was
sincere? The Bishop, who was a great friend of the General,
hearing of it, offered opposition, and wrote to him that it was
to do him the very greatest injury to take away a man who was
so useful to him, and at a time when he had the greatest need

of him. He was right, for he had a Grand Vicar whom he had brought from Rome, who, after having been Nuncio of the Pope in France, had by his evil life been reduced to live off his Masses, even in Rome itself, where he was in such great need as to attract the compassion of the Bishop of Verceil, who took him, and gave him very good allowances for acting as his Grand Vicar. This Abbé, far from gratitude to his benefactor, following the whim of his humor, was constantly in opposition to the Bishop, and if any ecclesiastic was disorderly or discontented, it was with him the Abbé took part against his Bishop. All those that complained against the Prelate or insulted him, were at once friends of the Grand Vicar, who, not content with this, labored with all his might to embroil him with the Court of Rome; saying he was entirely devoted to France, to the prejudice of his Holiness's interests, and as a proof, that he had several Frenchmen with him. He also by his secret intrigues embroiled him with the Court of Savoy; so that this worthy Bishop had very severe crosses from this man. Not being able to bear it, the Bishop requested him to retire, and with great generosity gave him all that was necessary for his return journey. He was extremely offended at having to leave the Bishop, and turned all his anger against Father La Combe, against a French gentleman, and against me.

The General of the Bernabites was not willing to grant Father La Mothe's request, for fear of hurting his great friend the Bishop, and to take away from him a man who in that conjuncture of affairs was very necessary to him. As for me, my ills increased day by day. The air, which there is extremely bad, caused me a constant cough, together with the fever which I often had, accompanied with inflammation of the chest, so that I had to be severely bled. I became swollen. In the evening I would be swollen to a great size, in the morning nothing was apparent; the fever which I had every night consumed the humors. It was all the right side which first swelled; at first only the right arm, afterwards it extended and became so considerable that it was thought I should die. The Bishop was very much distressed, for he could not make up his mind to let me go, nor yet to see me thus die in his diocese. But after having consulted the doctors, who told him that the air of the place was fatal to me, he said to me with many tears,

"I prefer you should live away from me rather than to see you die here."

He gave up his design for the establishment of a Community; for my friend was not willing to settle there without me, and the Genoese lady could not leave her town, where she was highly thought of. The Genoese prayed her to do there what the Bishop wished to do at his place. It was a Community something like that of Madame de Miramion; for in that country there are only cloistered nuns. From the beginning, when the Bishop proposed the matter to me, I had a presentiment that it would not succeed, and that it was not what our Lord desired of me. Nevertheless, I gave in to all that was wished of me in recognition of the Prelate's kindness, sure as I was that our Lord would be able to prevent anything he did not desire of me. When this good Prelate saw that he must resolve to let me go, he said to me, "You would like to be in the diocese of Geneva, and the Bishop persecutes and rejects you; and I, who would so gladly have you, am not able to keep you." The Bishop wrote to Father La Mothe that I would go away in the spring, as soon as the season would allow; that he was very distressed at being obliged to let me go; and he said of me things that might throw me into confusion, if I could take to myself anything. He wrote that he regarded me in his diocese as an angel, and a thousand other things which his goodness suggested. From this out I made my account for returning; but the Bishop expected to keep Father La Combe, and that he would not go to Paris. That would have been the case, indeed, but for the death of the General, as I shall tell hereafter.

While I still was at Verceil I had a movement to write to Madame de C——. It was some years since she had ceased writing to me. Our Lord made me to know her disposition, and that he would make use of me to help her. I asked Father La Combe if he would approve of my writing to her, telling him of the movement I had; but he did not wish it. I remained submissive, and at the same time assured that our Lord would unite us, and would provide me one way or another with the means of serving her. Some time after I received a letter from her, which not a little surprised Father La Combe, and he then left me free to write to her whatever I wished. I did it

with great simplicity, and what I wrote was like the first
foundation of what our Lord desired of her, having willed to
use me afterwards to help her, and to cause her to enter into
his ways; for she is a soul to whom I am closely tied, and
through her to others.

CHAPTER XXV

THE Father-General of the Bernabites, the friend of the
Bishop of Verceil, died. As soon as he was dead Father La
Mothe wrote to the person who was Vicar-General, and who
held his place until a new election. He told him the same
things he had told the other, and the necessity there was to
have at Paris men like Father La Combe; that he had no one to
preach the annual sermon in their church. This worthy Father, who believed Father La Mothe was acting in good faith,
having learned that I was obliged to return to France owing
to my indisposition, sent an order to Father La Combe to go to
Paris, and to accompany me the whole journey, Father La
Mothe having asked him to do so, on the ground that as he
would accompany me, their House at Paris, which was already poor, would be saved the expenses of such a long
journey. Father La Combe, who did not penetrate the venom
concealed under this fair appearance, consented to accompany
me, knowing that it was my custom to take with me ecclesiastics
or monks. Father La Combe set out twelve days before me, in
order to attend to some matters of business, and to accompany
me only at the crossing of the mountains, which appeared to
him the place where I had most need of escort. I set out in
Lent, the weather being very fine, to the grief of the Prelate,
who excited my compassion by the trouble he was in at losing
Father La Combe, and seeing me go away. He had me taken at

his expense to Turin, giving me a gentleman and one of his ecclesiastics to accompany me.

As soon as the resolution was taken that Father La Combe should accompany me, Father La Mothe at once set going everywhere the story that he had been obliged to do it, in order to make me return to France; although he knew very well that I was intending to return before we knew that Father La Combe would return. He exaggerated the attachment I had for him, making himself out a subject of pity; and on this every one said that I ought to put myself under the direction of Father La Mothe. However, he dissimulated towards us, writing to Father La Combe letters full of esteem and of tenderness to me, praying him to bring his dear sister, and to serve her in her infirmity on such a long journey, and that he would be deeply obliged for his care, and a hundred similar things.

I could not bring my mind to leave without going to see my friend the Marquise de Prunai, notwithstanding the difficulty of the journey. I had myself carried, for it is impossible to go there otherwise, except on horseback, owing to the mountains, and I could not go in that way. I spent twelve days with her. I arrived exactly the Eve of the Annunciation, and as all her tenderness is for the mystery of the childhood of Jesus Christ, and she knew the part our Lord gave me in it, she received extreme joy at seeing me arrive to spend that festival with her. Nothing could be more cordial than what passed between us with much openness. It was then she told me that all I had said to her had happened, and a worthy ecclesiastic who lived with her, a very holy man, told me the same. We together made ointments, and I gave her the secret of my remedies. I encouraged her, and so did Father La Combe, to establish a hospital in that place, which she did while we were there. I gave the little contribution of the Holy Child Jesus, who has always made successful all the hospitals which have been established in reliance on providence. I think I forgot to say that our Lord also made use of me to establish a hospital near Grenoble, which subsists without other capital than providence. My enemies have made use of this subsequently to calumniate me, saying that I had spent my children's property in establishing hospitals; although the truth is, that, far from having expended their money, I had even given them my own, and that these hospitals have been established merely on the capital of divine providence, which is inexhaustible.

As soon as it was determined that I should come into France, our Lord made me know that it was in order to have there the greatest crosses I had ever yet had, and Father La Combe also had knowledge of it; but he said to me, that I must immolate myself to all the divine wishes and anew be a victim immolated to new sacrifices.

At Chambéry we saw Father La Mothe, who was going to the election of a General. Although he affected friendship, it was not difficult to see that his thoughts were other than his words, and that he had formed in his mind the design of destroying us. I speak of the behavior of this Father only in obedience to the command which has been laid upon me to omit nothing. I shall be obliged, in spite of myself, to speak often of him. With all my heart I would gladly suppress what I have to say. If what he has done regarded only myself, I would willingly suppress it; but I think it a duty I owe to truth and the innocence of Father La Combe, who has so long been grievously oppressed and overwhelmed by calumny and by an imprisonment of many years, which according to all appearance will continue as long as his life. I feel myself, I say, obliged to expose all the artifices made use of to blacken him and render him odious, and the motives which have led Father La Mothe to adopt such a course. Although Father La Mothe appears heavily charged in what I say of him, I protest before God that I yet omit many facts.

I saw, then, very clearly his design. Father La Combe also remarked it, but he was resolved to sacrifice himself and to immolate me to all which he believed the will of God. Some even of my friends informed me that Father La Mothe had evil designs, but yet they did not imagine them so extreme as they were in reality. They thought he would send away Father La Combe after having made him preach, and that for this purpose he would get him into trouble. At Chambéry it was interiorly said to Father La Combe, in the same way as it had been told him that we should be together, that "we should be separated." We separated at Chambéry. Father La Mothe went to the Chapter after begging Father La Combe with affected urgency every day not to leave me, but to accompany me as far as Paris. Father La Combe asked his permission to leave me alone at Grenoble, because he was very desirous of going to Tonon to see his family, and he expected to rejoin me at Grenoble after three weeks. It was with difficulty this was granted, such was the affectation of sincerity.

I set out for Grenoble and Father La Combe for Tonon. As soon as I arrived I fell ill of a continued fever, which lasted fifteen days, when that worthy begging friar had an opportunity of practicing his charity. He gave me remedies, and these, joined to the fever and the change of climate, gradually consumed my disease. All those whom God had given me on my first visit to Grenoble came to see me during my illness, and exhibited extreme joy at seeing me again. The Bishop of Grenoble expressed more kindness than ever. They again pressed me to remain at the General Hospital, but it was not where you wished me, O my God; it was upon Calvary. Father La Combe and I were so penetrated by the cross that everything announced to us *Cross*.

The
Autobiography of
MADAME GUYON

———◆———

PART III

CHAPTER I

HARDLY had I arrived at Paris when it was easy for me to discover, by the conduct of the persons, the evil designs they had against Father La Combe and against me. Father La Mothe, who directed all the tragedy, dissimulated as much as he could, and in his usual manner, giving secret blows and making semblance of flattering while he was dealing the most dangerous strokes. Through self-interest they desired to make me go to Montargis, hoping thereby to seize upon the wardship of my chidren, and to dispose of my person and my property. All the persecutions which have befallen me from the side of Father La Mothe and of my family have been solely due to selfish motives. Those which have been directed against Father La Combe have been only due to the fact that he did not oblige me to do what they wished of me, and also to jealousy. They threatened to deprive me of the fief that I had reserved for myself by my deed of settlement. As I never betrayed the sentiments of my heart, I replied that I would not litigate, but if they wished to take away the little I had reserved for myself, though so trifling in comparison with what I had given up, that I would yield it cheerfully; being delighted to be not only poor, but in the extremity of want, in imitation of our Lord Jesus Christ.

After our Lord had made Father La Combe suffer much in our union, in order to purify it thoroughly, it became so perfect as to be henceforth an entire unity; and this in such a way that I can no longer distinguish him from God. I cannot in detail describe the graces God has given me, for everything passes in me in a manner so pure that one can tell nothing of it. As nothing falls under the senses, nor can be expressed, it must all remain in him, who himself communicates himself in himself; as well as an infinity of circumstances, which I must leave in God with the rest of the crosses.

I had arrived at Paris the Eve of St. Magdalen, 1686, exactly five years after my departure thence. Shortly after his arrival Father La Combe was very much run after and applauded for his sermons. I perceived, indeed, some little jealousy on the part of Father La Mothe, but I did not think that things would go to such a length. Doubtless it will be a matter of surprise that the greater part of the Bernabites of Paris and the neighboring Houses should join against Father La Combe. There were two causes for it. First, the selfish motives and the jealousy of Father La Mothe, which made him invent all sorts of artifices. He told them all that in ruining Father La Combe they would have a pretext for shaking off the yoke of the Savoyards; for it should be known that every six years the Bernabites had a Savoyard as Provincial. This, he said, was an insult to the French nation. They all fell in with it, and for this purpose betrayed their brother, without, however, obtaining what they desired, except for a few years; for, as a fact, they had at present a Savoyard as Provincial. The second reason was the special jealousy of their Provincial, who, owing to a Lent service taken away from one of his friends and given to Father La Combe, became his enemy, though previously his friend. That united the interests of the Provincial and of Father La Mothe.

This latter pushed artifice so far as to say that Father La Combe had accompanied me from Turin to Paris without entering their Houses, and that he remained in the inn with me to the great scandal of their Order. He did not tell them that there was no convent of their Order on the route; but, on the contrary, he made it to be understood that there were, and that it was to the shame of these Houses that he had not been there. Who would not have believed a calumny told with such art? This began to stir up every one against me; but the excellent sermons of Father La Combe and his success in the conduct of souls, counterbalanced these calumnies.

I had deposited a small sum with Father La Combe (his superiors permitting), which I destined for the dowry of a girl professing as a nun. I thought I was bound in conscience, for owing to me she had left the New Catholics. She is the young woman of whom I have spoken, that the priest of Gex tried to gain over. As she is beautiful, although extremely discreet, there is always ground for fear when one is exposed without any fixed settlement. I had then assigned this moderate sum for that worthy girl. Father La Mothe desired to have it, and made Father La Combe understand that if he did not cause me to give it for a wall that he wished to rebuild in his convent, they would get him into trouble. But Father La Combe, always upright, said that he could not conscientiously advise me to do anything else than what he knew I had resolved to do in favor of the girl. All this, joined to jealousy at the success of Father La Combe's sermons, made him determine to unite with the Provincial, and to betray Father La Combe to satisfy the grudge of each.

They no longer thought except of the means to arrive at their end, and to do it successfully they sent to confession to Father La Combe a man and a woman who were united in practicing all sorts of villainy with impunity, and persecuting God's servants. I believe there never were such artifices as theirs. The man writes all kinds of hands, and is ready to execute anything one desires. They pretended devotion, and amongst so great a number of worthy souls who came from all parts to Father La Combe for confession, he never discerned those devilish spirits.

Previous to this, when I was alone in my room on my knees before an image of the Child Jesus, where I usually prayed, suddenly I was, as it were, cast back from this image, and sent to the Crucifix: all that I had of the state of childhood was taken away from me, and I found myself bound anew with Jesus Christ Crucified. To tell what this bond is would be very difficult for me, for it is not a devotion, as is commonly supposed. It is no longer a state of suffering by conformity with Jesus Christ; but it is the same Jesus Christ borne very purely and nakedly in his states. What passed in this new union of love to what Divine Object he alone knows; but I understood it was no longer a question for me of bearing him, the Child, or in his states of nakedness: that I must bear him Crucified; and it was the last of all his states. For in the commencement I had indeed borne crosses, as may be seen in the narrative of my life, which is quite full of them; but they were my own crosses, borne through conformity with Jesus Christ. Then, my state becoming more profound, it was given me to bear the states of Jesus Christ, which I have borne in the middle of my life in nakedness and crosses. And whilst one bears in this manner the states of Jesus Christ one does not think on Jesus Christ—he is then removed; and even from the commencement of the path of faith one has him no longer thus objectively. But the state I am now speaking of is quite different; it is of a vastness almost infinite, and few souls bear him in this way. It is to bear Jesus Christ himself in his states. Only experience can make intelligible what I wish to say.

At this period I received a letter from Father La Combe, who wrote me in these terms: "The weather is very lowering" (speaking of Father La Mothe's humor towards him). "I do not know when the thunderbolts will fall, but all will be welcome from the hand of God." Meantime the husband of this wicked creature who counterfeited the saint ceased coming to confession to Father La Combe, in order the better to play his game. He sent his wife, who said she was very sorry for her husband having left this Father; that her husband was a fickle man; that she did not resemble him. She counterfeited the saint, saying that God revealed to her future events, and that he was about to have great persecutions. It was not difficult for her to know this, since she plotted them with Father La Mothe, the Provincial, and her husband.

During this time I went to the country to the Duchess of C——. Many extraordinary things happened to me, and God gave me great graces for my neighbor; it seemed as if he desired to dispose me thereby for the cross. Father La Combe wrote to me while I was in the country that he had found an admirable soul (meaning that woman who counterfeited the saint), and mentioned certain circumstances which made me apprehensive for him. However, as our Lord gave me nothing special on the subject—and, besides, I feared that if I told him my thoughts it would be ill taken, as at other times; and as our Lord did not urge me to say anything, I wrote to him that I abandoned him to God for that as for the rest.

While this woman was counterfeiting the saint, and exhibiting great affection and esteem for Father La Combe, her husband, who imitated all kinds of writing, was induced

(evidently by the enemies of Father La Combe, as the sequel
has shown) to write defamatory libels, to which they attached
the propositions of Molinos, which for two years were circu-
lating in France, and said these were the sentiments of Father
La Combe. They had them carried everywhere amongst the
Communities, and Father La Mothe and the Provincial, who
was more tricky, caused these libels to be sent back to themselves; then assuming the rôle of persons much attached to the
Church, they themselves carried these libels to the Official,
who was in their plot, and brought them to the notice of the
Archbishop. They said that zeal urged them, and that they
were in despair that one of their monks should be heretic and
execrable. They also slightly mixed me up in the matter, saying
that Father La Combe was always at my house. This was
utterly false, for I could hardly see him, except at the confessional, and then only for a moment. They renewed their old
calumnies about the journeys, and went from house to house
among honorable families, saying that I had been on horseback
behind Father La Combe—I, who was never so in my life!—
that he had not been to their Houses along the road, but that
he remained at the inn.

They forged a letter from a person of Marseilles (I even
believe I heard it said, from the Bishop of Marseilles), addressed to the Archbishop of Paris, or to his Official, in
which they stated that at Marseilles I had slept in the same
room with Father La Combe; that there he had eaten meat in
Lent and behaved very scandalously. This letter was carried,
this calumny was retailed everywhere, and after having circulated it, Father La Mothe and the Provincial, who had concocted it together, resolved to tell it to me. Father La Mothe
came to see me, apparently to make me fall into the trap and to
make me say in the presence of people he had brought with
him, that I had been to Marseilles with Father La Combe. He
said to me, "There are horrible stories against you sent by the
Bishop of Marseilles, that you have there committed frightful
scandals with Father La Combe; there are good witnesses of
it." I began to smile, and said to him, "The calumny is well
imagined, but it ought to have been first ascertained if Father
La Combe had been to Marseilles, for I do not believe that he
has ever been there in his life; and when I passed through it

was Lent. I was with such and such persons and Father La Combe was preaching the Lent sermons at Verceil." He was dumbfounded, and withdrew, saying, "There are, however, witnesses that it is true;" and he went immediately to ask Father La Combe if he had not been at Marseilles. He assured him he had never been in Provence, nor further than Lyons and the road from Savoy to France; so that they were somewhat taken aback. But they devised another expedient. Those who could not know that Father La Combe had never been to Marseilles, they left in the belief that it was Marseilles, and to the others they said that it was Seissel in the letter. This Seissel is a place where I have never been, and where there is no bishop.

Father La Mothe and the Provincial carried from house to house the libels and those propositions of Molinos, saying they were the errors of Father La Combe. All this did not prevent Father La Combe from making a wonderful harvest by his sermons and at the confessional. From all sides people came to him. It was gall to them.

The Provincial had just held his Visitation, and had passed quite close to Savoy without going there; because he did not wish, he said, to hold the Visitation that year. They plotted together, Father La Mothe and he, to go there in order to collect some reports against Father La Combe and against me, and to gratify the Bishop of Geneva, whom they knew to be very bitter against me and against Father La Combe, for the reasons I have mentioned. The Provincial set out, then, immediately on his return from the Visitation of Provence, to go into Savoy, and gave orders to Father La Mothe to do everything he could to ruin Father La Combe.

They plotted with the Official, a man skilful and clever in this sort of affair; but as it would have been very difficult to mix me up in the business, they instigated that woman to ask to see me. She told Father La Combe that God made known to her admirable things of me, that she had an inconceivable love for me, and wished very much to see me. As besides she said she was very much in want, Father La Combe sent her to me to give her something in charity. I gave her a half louis-d'or. At first she did not strike me in her true character; but after half an hour's conversation with her, I had a horror of her. I hid it from myself, for the reasons I have mentioned. Some days from that—three days after, I think—she came to ask me for the means of getting herself bled. I told her that I had a maid very skilful at bleeding, and if she wished I would have her bled. She indignantly refused, and said she was not a person to allow herself to be bled by any one but a surgeon. I gave her fifteen sous. She took them with a scorn which made me see she was not what Father La Combe believed her. She immediately went and threw the fifteen-sous piece before Father La Combe, asking if she were a person to be given fifteen sous. The Father was surprised; but as in the evening she had learned from her husband that it was not time for breaking out, but for feigning, she went to see Father La Combe, asked his pardon, and said it was a strong temptation that had made her act so, and that she asked back the fifteen sous-piece. He told me nothing of all this, but several nights I suffered strangely owing to this woman. In sleep sometimes I saw the Devil, then suddenly I saw this woman; sometimes it was the one, sometimes it was the other. This made me wake with a start. For three nights I was thus, with a certainty that she was a wicked woman who counterfeited devotion to deceive and to injure. I told it to Father La Combe, and he reprimanded me very severely, saying it was my imagination, that I was wanting in charity, that this woman was a saint. I therefore kept quiet. I was very much astonished when a virtuous girl, whom I did not know, came to see me, and told me that she felt bound to warn me, knowing that I was interested in Father La Combe, that he confessed a woman who was deceiving him; that she knew her thoroughly, and she was, perhaps, the most wicked and the most dangerous woman in Paris. She related to me strange things this woman had done and thefts committed at Paris. I told her to declare it to Father La Combe. She said that she had told him something of it; but that he made her acknowledge it as a fault in confession, on the ground that she was uncharitable, so that she no longer knew what to do. That woman was overheard in a shop speaking evil of Father La Combe. It was told to him, but he would not believe it. She sometimes came to my house. I, who am without natural antipathy, had such a violent one, and even such horror for this creature, that the force I put upon myself to see her, in obedience to Father La Combe, made me turn so extraordinarily pale, that my servants perceived it. Among others, a very worthy girl—she who made me suffer so much for her purification—felt for her the same horror that I felt. Father La Combe was again warned that there was one of his penitents who went about decrying him to all the confessors, and saying execrable things of him. He wrote them to me, and told me at the same time that I should not imagine it was this woman; that it was not she. I was perfectly certain it was the same. Another time she came to my house; the Father was there. She told him something of the intimations she had that he was about to have great crosses. I had an immediate conviction that it was she who was causing them. I told it to Father La Combe; but he would not believe me, our Lord so permitting it, to render him like to himself. One thing which seemed extraordinary, is that Father La Combe, so soft and so credulous to any other who did not tell him the truth, was not at all so for me. He himself was astonished at it, yet I am not astonished, because in God's conducting of me my nearest are those who crucify me the most.

CHAPTER II

One day a monk, at one time my confessor, to whom this woman went to retail her calumnies, sent to ask me to come and see him. He related to me all that she had told him, and the lies in which he had detected her. As for me, I continually detected her in falsehood. I at once told Father La Combe. He was suddenly enlightened, and, as if scales had fallen from his eyes, he no longer doubted the villainy of this woman. The more he recalled what he had seen in her, and what she had said to him, the more convinced he was of her villainy, and avowed to me there must be something diabolic in the woman to enable her to pass as a saint. As soon as I returned home she came to see me. I gave orders not to let her in. She wanted me to give her alms, to pay for the hire of her house. I was very ill that day, and in consequence of an excessive thirst my body was swollen. One of my maids told her plainly that I was ill, that they were alarmed because I had been dropsical, and that for two days I had been swollen. She wanted to enter in spite of the maid, when the one who knew something of her villainies came to prevent her, and told her that nobody could speak with me. She wrangled with them, but they patiently bore it. She straightway went to see the Superior of the Premontrés and retailed to him frightful calumnies. She said that I was pregnant. This man, who hardly knew me, believed her, and sent for my daughter's maid whom he had given me. He told her this frightful calumny. She, who perfectly knew the thing was impossible, said to him, "My Father, by whom? she never sees a man, and she is very virtuous." This astonished him. She told me of it. That wretched creature went everywhere retailing the same story, thinking that I should be a long time swollen, and it would be easy for her to make it believed; but as the swelling passed away in a couple of days, owing to a trifling remedy, this calumny had no consequence. Besides, they knew that if they had recourse to calumny they must reckon with secular judges, and they would find it a bad bargain. They determined therefore to attack me also in the matter of faith, in order to throw me into the hands of the Official, and that by means of a little book, entitled "Short Method, etc.," to which my name did not appear, and which had been approved by doctors of the Sorbonne appointed for that purpose at Lyons and also at Grenoble. But before turning to myself, I must tell how they went to work.

Father La Mothe came to see me, and said that at the Archbishop's office there were frightful reports against Father La Combe, that he was a heretic and a friend of Molinos. I, who well knew he had no acquaintance with Molinos, assured him of this. I further said to him, that I knew he had great power with the Archbishop, and I begged him to take Father La Combe there, that, as soon as the Archbishop had spoken to him, he would be undeceived. He promised he would next day, but he took very good care not to do so. I told him of the villainy of this woman, and what she had done to me. He coldly answered that she was a saint. It was then I commenced to discover that they were acting in concert.

I went to see Father La Combe at the confessional, and told him what Father La Mothe had said to me, and that he should ask to be taken to the Archbishop by him. He went to Father La Mothe, who said that he would take him to the Archbishop, but there was no hurry; that the reports were not against him, but against me: and for nearly a month he played see-saw with us, saying to Father La Combe that the reports were not against him but against me, and to me that they were against him, and that I was not mentioned in them. Father La Combe and I were confounded when we spoke of all these things and this deceit. Nevertheless Father La Combe preached and heard confession with more applause than ever, and this augmented the vexation and jealousy of those people. Father La Mothe went for two days into the country, and Father La Combe, being senior, remained as Superior in his absence. I told him to go to the Archbishop, and to take the opportunity when Father La Mothe was not there. He answered me that Father La Mothe had told him not to leave the House during his absence; that he saw clearly that it would be very necessary for him to see the Archbishop, and that perhaps he would never have this opportunity again; but that he wished to die observing his obedience, and, since his Superior had told him to remain in his absence, he would do so. It was merely to prevent his going to the Archbishop, and making him acquainted with the truth, that this had been said to him.

There was a doctor of the Sorbonne, Monsieur Bureau, who came to see me two or three times, on the occasion of a visit from the Abbé de Gaumont, a man of wonderful purity, nearly eighty years of age, who has passed all his life in retreat, without directing, preaching, or hearing confession: he had known me formerly, and brought Monsieur Bureau to see me. Against this latter Father La Mothe was indignant, because one of his penitents, who had left him, had been to see Monsieur Bureau, who is a very honorable man. With reference to him, Father La Mothe said to me, "You see Monsieur Bureau; I do not wish it." I asked him the reason, telling him that I had not been to seek him, but that he had come to see me, and that rarely; that I did not think it proper to turn him out of my house, that he was a man in high repute. He told me that he had done him a wrong. I wished to know what this wrong was. I learned it was because that penitent, who had given much to Father La Mothe and had left him only because he was grasping, had been to Monsieur Bureau. I did not deem this reason sufficient to alienate a man who had done me service, and to whom I was under obligation, and who was, besides, a true servant of God. Father La Mothe himself went to the Official's office to depose that I held assemblies with Monsieur de Gaumont and Monsieur Bureau; that he had even broken up one of them—an utter falsehood. He said it also to others, who repeated it to me; so that I learned it from the Official and from others. Without any regular process they attacked Monsieur Bureau, the Official being delighted to have this opportunity of illtreating a man whom he had hated for a long time. They set to work the scribe, husband of that wicked woman, against Monsieur Bureau, and in a short time there were counterfeit letters from Superiors of religious Houses where Monsieur Bureau directed and heard confession, who wrote to the Official, that Monsieur Bureau preached and taught errors, and introduced trouble into the religious Houses. It was not difficult for Monsieur Bureau to prove the falseness of these letters, for the Superiors disavowed them. Madame de Miramion, friend of Monsieur Bureau, herself proved their falsity; yet, far from doing justice to Monsieur Bureau, they made His Majesty believe he was guilty, and exiled him, as I shall tell hereafter, abusing the King's zeal for religion by making his authority subservient to the passion of these people.

One day Father La Mothe came to me, and said it was absolutely true that there were horrible reports against Father La Combe, and insinuated that I should get him to withdraw, hoping thereby to make him appear guilty; for it was hard to find the means of ruining him, because, whether they judged him themselves, or sent him to their General, the latter would have knowledge of everything, and the innocence of Father La Combe, as well as the wickedness of the others, would have been known. They were very much embarrassed to discover something. I said to Father La Mothe, that if Father La Combe was guilty he should be punished (I spoke very boldly, knowing thoroughly his innocence), and therefore there was nothing for him to do but to wait in patience what God would bring about; that, for the rest, he ought to have taken him to the Archbishop to let his innocence be seen. I even asked him to do this with all the urgency I could. Father La Combe on his side besought him to let him go, if he was unwilling to take him. He always said he would take him to-morrow or some other day; then he had business to prevent him; and yet he many times went there by himself.

Seeing that Father La Combe patiently waited his evil fortune, and not having yet discovered the last expedient, by which they have succeeded in ruining him, Father La Mothe raised the mask. He sent to warn me at church, where I was, to come and speak to him, and, having brought with him Father La Combe, he said to me, in his presence, "My sister, it is you who now must think of flying: there are against you execrable reports; you are accused of crimes that make one shudder." I was no more moved, nor confused by it, than if he had told me an idle tale that in no way touched me. With my ordinary calmness I said to him, "If I have committed the crimes of which you speak I could not be too severely punished, and therefore I am far from desiring to fly; for if, after having all my life professed to be in an especial manner devoted to God, I made use of piety to offend him—him that I would give my life to love and to make loved by others—it is right that I should serve as an example, and that I should be punished with the utmost rigor: but if I am innocent, flying is not the means to make it believed." Their design was to incriminate Father La Combe by my flight, and to make me go to Montargis as they had planned.

When he saw that, far from entering into his proposal, I remained unmoved, and firm in the determination to suffer everything rather than fly, he said to me, quite in anger, "Since you will not do what I tell you, I will go and inform the family" (meaning that of my children's guardian) "in order that it may compel you to do it." I said to him that I had told nothing of all this to my children's guardian, nor to his family, and that it would surprise them; that I begged him to allow me to go the first to speak to them, or at least to consent that we should go together. He agreed that we should go together next day. As soon as I had left him, our Lord, desiring me to see the whole conduct of this affair, in order that I might not remain ignorant of it—our Lord, I say, at once inspired me, suggesting that Father La Mothe was hurrying off to prejudice the family against me, and tell them whatever he pleased. I sent my footman to run and see if my suspicion was true, and to get a carriage for me to go there myself. Father La Mothe was already there before me. When he knew I had discovered he was there, he became so furious he could not prevent its appearing, and, as soon as he had returned to the convent, he discharged his vexation on poor Father La Combe. He had not found the guardian of my children; but he had spoken to his sister, the wife of a Maître des Comptes, a person of merit. When he told her that I was accused of frightful crimes, that they must induce me to fly, she replied, "If Madame," meaning me, "has committed the crimes you say, I believe I have committed them myself. What—a person who has lived as she has lived! I would answer for her with my own life. To make her fly! Her flight is not a matter of indifference, for if she is innocent it is to declare her guilty." He added, "It is absolutely necessary to make her fly, and it is the sentiment of the Archbishop." She asked him where I should fly to. He answered, "To Montargis." That aroused her suspicion. She told him her brother must be consulted, and that he would see the Archbishop. At this he was quite confounded, and begged they would not go to see the Archbishop; said he was more interested than any other; that he would himself go there." I arrived just as he had left. She told me all this, and I related to her from beginning to end all he had said to me. As she is very clever, she understood that there was something in it. He came back, and contradicted himself many times before us both.

The next day, the guardian of my children, having ascertained the Archbishop's hour, went there. He found Father La Mothe before him, but he had not been able to get admitted. When he saw the guardian of my children, a Counselor of Parliament, he was much disturbed; he grew pale, then he grew red, and, at last accosting him, he begged that he would not speak to the Archbishop—that it was his place to do so, and that he would do it. The Counselor remained firm that he would speak to him. The Father, seeing he could not prevent it, said, "You forget, then, what my sister has done this winter," referring to a misunderstanding that he himself had caused. The Counselor very honorably answered him: "I forget all that, in order to remember that I am obliged to serve her in a matter of this nature." Seeing that he could gain nothing, he besought him that at least he might be the first to speak to the Archbishop. This made the Counselor believe he was not acting straightforwardly. He said to him, "My Father, if the Archbishop calls you the first, you will go in the first, otherwise I will go in." "But, sir," added he, "I will tell him that you are there." "And I," said the Counselor, "will tell him that you are there." Upon that the Archbishop, knowing nothing of this tangle, called the Counselor, who said to him that he was informed there were strange reports against me; that he knew me for a long time as a woman of virtue, and that he answered for me with his own person; that if there was anything against me it was to him they should address themselves, and he would answer for everything. The Archbishop said he knew nothing at all about it; that he had not heard mention of me, but of a Father. Upon this the Counselor told him that Father La Mothe had said that his Grace had even advised me to fly. The Archbishop said this was not true, he had never heard a word about it. Upon which the Counselor asked him if he would consent to cause Father La Mothe to be called to say this to him. He was brought in, and the Archbishop asked him where he had picked up that; as for himself, he had never heard a word about it. Father La Mothe defended himself very badly, and said he had it from the Father Provincial. On leaving the Archbishop's he was quite furious, and came to look for Father La Combe to discharge his anger, telling him they should repent of the affront put upon him, and that he would find means to make them repent.

CHAPTER III

SOME days after, having consulted with Monsieur Charon, the Official, they discovered the means of ruining Father La Combe. Since I had been unwilling to fly, it was what seemed the most hopeful. They caused His Majesty to be informed that Father La Combe was a friend of Molinos, and of the same opinions, pretending even, on the evidence of the scribe and his wife, that he had committed crimes which he had never done; whereupon His Majesty, believing the thing true, with as much justness as kindness, ordered that Father La Combe should not leave his convent, and that the Official should go and inform himself as to his opinions and his doctrines. There was never an order more equitable than this, but it did not suit the enemies of Father La Combe, who well knew it would be very easy for him to defend himself against matters so false. They concerted a means of withdrawing the affair from the cognizance of the General, and interesting His Majesty in it. The only one they found was to make him appear disobedient to the commands of the King, and, in order to succeed, they resolved to conceal the order from Father La Combe; so that, going out for some exercise of charity or obedience, he should appear rebellious. Father La Combe preached and heard confession as usual, and even gave two sermons, one at the Grand Cordeliers at St. Bonaventura, and another at St. Thomas de Villeneuve at the Grand Augustinians—sermons which carried away everybody. They carefully concealed for him, I say, the orders of the King, and plotted with the Official in all that they did; for they could avail nothing in this matter unless they were in concert.

Some days previously Father La Mothe told me that the Official was his intimate friend, and in this business would not do anything but what was pleasing to him. He pretended to make a spiritual retreat in order not to absent himself from the House, and the better to accomplish his business, and also to have a pretext for declining to serve Father La Combe, and take him to the Archbishop. One afternoon news was brought to Father La Combe that a horse had passed over the body of one of his penitents, and that he must go and take her confession. Without delay the Father asked permission from Father La Mothe to go and take the woman's confession: it was willingly given. Hardly had he set out, when the Official arrived. He said officially that he had not found Father La Combe; that he was disobedient to the orders of the King (which were never told him). Quite openly they told the Official he was at my house, although they well knew the contrary, and that it was more than six weeks since he had been there. They informed the Archbishop that he was constantly at my house; but, as a single exit by the order of his Superior was not sufficient to make Father La Combe appear as black to His Majesty as they desired to make him appear, it was necessary to have other instances. However, Father La Combe, having learned that during his absence the Official had come to speak to him, resolved on no account to go out. This slightly embarrassed them: so they made the Official come one morning, and, as soon as he entered, they told Father La Combe, who knew not that he was there, to go and say Mass. He was surprised, because it was not his turn. No sooner had he finished the Mass, than he saw the Official leaving. He went to his Superior, and said to him, "My Father, is it that they wish to entrap me? I have just seen Monsieur Charon, the Official, leaving." The Superior said to him, "He wished to speak to me. I asked him if he wished to speak to you; he said 'No.' " Yet that very morning there had been drawn up a second official statement that Father La Combe was not present, that he was again disobedient to the orders of the King. The Official came a third time. Father La Combe saw him from the window, and asked to speak to him. He was not allowed to appear, on the ground that the business was with the Superior, and that he had not come for Father La Combe. The latter came to see me at his confessional, where I was waiting, and told me that he much feared a snare; that the

Official was there; and they would not let him speak to him. A third official statement was drawn up, that Father La Combe was for a third time disobedient to the orders of His Majesty.

I asked for Father La Mothe, and I said to him that I begged him not to behave thus; that he had told me he was very much the friend of the Official, and that assuredly they were trying to use strategem. He said to me coldly, "He did not wish to see Father La Combe; he had not come for that." I advised Father La Combe to write to the Official, and to beg him not to refuse him the favor which is not refused to the most guilty—that of hearing them; to do him the kindness to come and ask for him. I myself sent the letter by an unknown person. The Official said he would go in the afternoon without fail. Father La Combe was somewhat troubled at having written this letter without the permission of his Superior, for he could not believe things were at the point they were: he went and told him. As soon as he knew it, he sent two monks to the Official, to request him not to come, as the event proved. As I passed by, on my way to a house I had hired, I met these two monks. I had a suspicion of the fact (for our Lord willed I should be witness of all): I had them followed. They went to the house of the Official. I felt certain Father La Combe had confided to Father La Mothe the letter he had written. I went to see Father La Combe, and asked him. He admitted it to me. I told him I had met these two monks on the road, and had had them followed. We were still speaking when Father La Mothe came to say the Official would not come, that things were changed. Father La Combe from this saw clearly that the affair would be one of simple trickery.

However, Father La Mothe pretended to be anxious to serve him. He said to him, "My Father, I know you have attestations of your doctrine from the Inquisition and the Sacred Congregation of Rites and the approbation of Cardinals for your security. These documents are beyond reply, and, since you are approved at Rome, a mere Official has nothing to say to you on the subject of doctrine." I was still at the Bernabites when Father La Combe went to look for those documents, and to draw up a memorial. Believing that Father La Mothe was acting in as good faith, as he protested, and seeing that he assured me that the Official would only do what he pleased, that he was his friend, and that he wished to serve Father La Combe, that Father in his simplicity believed him, and brought him his papers, which were unanswerable on the point of doctrine—as to morals, that was not within the province of the Official. After Father La Combe had given these necessary papers, they were suppressed, and in vain did the poor Father ask them back again. Father La Mothe said he had sent them to the Official. The Official said he had not received them. They were no more heard of.

On St. Michael's Day, five days before the imprisonment of Father La Combe, I was at his confessional. He could only say these words to me: "I have so great a hunger for disgrace and ignominy I am quite languishing from it. I am going to say the Mass: listen to it, and sacrifice me to God, as I myself am going to immolate myself to Him." I said to him, "My Father, you will be satiated with them." And, in fact, on October 3, 1687, the Eve of St. Francis his patron, when at dinner, they came to carry him off, to place him with the Fathers of Christian Doctrine. During this time his enemies piled falsehood upon falsehood, and the Provincial sent for the Abbé who had been Grand-Vicar to the Bishop of Verceil and dismissed by him. He came express to Paris to make false depositions against Father La Combe; but this was cut short, and served merely as a pretext for putting him into the Bastille. The Provincial had brought some unsigned reports from Savoy, and boasted everywhere that he had the means of putting Father La Combe in the Bastille. In fact, two days afterwards, he was put in the Bastille, and although he was found perfectly innocent, and they have been unable to support any judgment, they have been able to persuade His Majesty that he is a dangerous spirit; therefore, without judging him, he has been shut up in a fortress for his life. And when his enemies learned that in the first fortress the officers esteemed him and treated him kindly, not content with having shut up such a servant of God, they have had him removed to a place where they believed he would have more to suffer. God, who sees all, will render to each according to his works. I know by the spirit communication that he is very content and abandoned to God.

After Father La Combe was arrested, Father La Mothe was more eager than ever to make me fly. He urged it upon all my friends; he urged it upon me myself, assuring me that, if I went to Montargis, I should not be involved in this business: if I did not go, I should be involved in it. He then conceived the notion that, to dispose of me and the little that remained to me, and to exculpate himself in the eyes of men for thus having handed over Father La Combe, it was necessary that he should be my director. He skilfully proposed it to me, at the same time holding out threats. He added, "You have no confidence in me, all Paris knows." I admit this stirred my pity. Some of his intimate friends came to see me, and said that, if I consented to put myself under his direction, I should keep out of the trouble. Not content with this, he wrote in all directions and to his brothers to lower me in their esteem. He so well succeeded that they wrote me the most outrageous letters imaginable, and especially that I should be ruined if I did not place myself under Father La Mothe. I still have the letters. There is a Father who prayed me to make a virtue of necessity; that if I did not put myself under his direction I should expect nothing but utter discomfiture. There were even some of my friends weak enough to advise me to pretend to accept his direction, and to deceive him. O God, you know how far I am from evasions and disguises, and trickery, especially in this matter. I replied that I was incapable of treating direction as a farce, that my central depth rejected this with a fearful force. I bore all this with extreme tranquillity, without care or anxiety to justify or defend myself, leaving to my God to appoint for me what he should please. He augmented my peace in proportion as Father La Mothe exerted himself to decry me, and this to such a degree I dared not show myself; every one cried out against me, and regarded me as an infamous character. I bore it all with joy, and I said to you, O my God, "It is for love of you I suffer these reproaches, and that my visage is covered with confusion" (Ps. 43:16). Every one without exception cried out against me, save those who were personally acquainted with me, who knew how far removed I was from these things; but the others accused me of heresy, sacrilege, infamies of every kind, the nature of which I am even ignorant of, of hypocrisy, knavery. When I was at church I heard people behind me ridiculing me, and once I heard priests say that I ought to be thrown out of the church. I cannot express how content I was inwardly, leaving myself entirely without reserve to God, quite ready to suffer the last penalty if such was his will.

I did not take a step, leaving myself to my God, yet Father La Mothe wrote everywhere that I was ruining myself through my solicitations for Father La Combe. I have never, either for him or for myself, made any solicitation. O my Love, you know that I wish to owe everything to you, and that I expect nothing from any creature.

There was not a day passed without a new attack on me, and sometimes many in the day. Reports were brought of what Father La Mothe was saying of me: and a Canon of Notre Dame told me that what made the ill he said of me so very credible was that he pretended to love and esteem me; he exalted me to the clouds, then he cast me down to the abyss. Five or six days after he had said that horrible reports against me had been brought to the Archbishop, a pious girl went to the scribe Gautier, and, not finding him, his little boy of five years of age said to her, 'There is great news. My papa is gone with papers to the Archbishop." In consequence of this, I learned that in fact the reports of which Father La Mothe had spoken had been carried to the Archbishop after the arrest of Father La Combe.

They still kept pressing me to fly, although the Archbishop had told me myself not to quit Paris, and they wished to incriminate me and Father La Combe also by my flight. They did not know how to work to get me into the hands of the Official, for if they accused me of crimes I must have other judges, and any other judge that might have been assigned me would have seen my innocence, and the false witnesses would have incurred risk. Yet they wished to make me pass for guilty to be master of me and shut me up, in order that the truth of this business might never be known; and for this purpose it was necessary to put me out of the way of ever being able to make it heard. They still circulated the same rumor of horrible crimes, although the Official assured me there was no mention of them, for he feared I should withdraw myself from his jurisdiction. They then made known to His Majesty that I was a heretic, that I had constant correspondence with Molinos—I, who did not know there was such a person as Molinos in the world until I learned it from the Gazette; that I had written a dangerous book; and that therefore His Majesty should place me in a convent, in order that they might interrogate me; that, as I was a dangerous spirit, it was necessary I should be shut up under key, cut off from all intercourse either without or within; that I had held assemblies. This they strongly maintained, and therein was my greatest crime; although this was utterly false, and I have never held one, nor seen three people at the same time. In order to better support the calumny about the assemblies, they counterfeited my writing, and concocted a letter in which I wrote that I had great designs, but that I much feared they would come to nothing, owing to the detention of Father La Combe; that I no longer held my assemblies at my own house; that I was too closely watched; but that I would hold them in such and such houses, and in such streets, at the house of persons whom I did not know and never heard named. It was on this fictitious letter, which was shown to His Majesty, that the order to imprison me was given.

CHAPTER IV

THEY would have executed it two months sooner, but I became very ill with excessive pains and fever. It was thought I had an abscess in the head, for the pain there during five weeks was enough to make me lose my senses; besides this, I had a pain in my chest, and a violent cough. Twice I received the Holy Sacrament as for one dying. As soon as Father La Mothe knew I was ill, he came to see me. I received him in my usual way. He asked if I had not some papers; that I ought to entrust them to him, rather than to any one else. I told him that I had none. He had learned from one of my friends, who, knowing who he was, but not that he was the author of this business, told him that he was sending me the attestation of the Inquisition for Father La Combe, having learned that his own had been lost. This attestation was a very important document, for they had informed His Majesty that Father La Combe had avoided the Inquisition.

Father La Mothe was very much alarmed to know I had this document, and, making use of his ordinary artifice and of the opportunity of my extremity, he came to see me. He assumed the role of the affectionate and joyous person, telling me that Father La Combe's matters were getting on very well (though he had just caused him to be put into the Bastille); that he was on the point of coming out victorious, at which he was extremely glad; that only one thing was wanting—that it had been said he had fled from the Inquisition, and they needed an attestation of the Inquisition: if he had that, he would be set free at once. He added, "I know you have one. If you give it to me, this will be done." At first I made a difficulty about giving it to him, having such good cause for distrust; but he said to me, "What! you wish to cause the ruin of that poor Father La Combe, when you might save him, and you will cause us this affliction for want of a document that you have under your hand." I gave way, and sent for this document and placed it in his hands. He immediately suppressed it, and said that it was gone astray; and however I urged him to restore it to me, he has never done so. As soon as I had given the attestation to Father La Mothe, he went out, and the Ambassador of Turin sent a page to ask me for this attestation, which he would have an opportunity of using to the advantage of Father La Combe. I asked him if he had not seen two monks go out as he came in. He said, "Yes." I told him I had just given it into the hands of the elder. He ran after, and asked it from him. Father La Mothe denied that I had given it to him, asserting that I had an affection of the brain, which made me imagine it. The page came to tell me his answer. The persons who were in my room bore witness that I had given it to him. It could not be recovered from his hands.

When Father La Mothe saw that he had nothing more to fear from this quarter, he no longer observed any measure in insulting me, dying as I was. There was hardly an hour passed that they did not put upon me new insults. They told me that they were only waiting for my recovery, to imprison me. He wrote still more strongly against me to his brothers, informing them that I persecuted him. I wondered at the injustice of creatures. I was alone, deprived of everything, seeing nobody; for since the imprisonment of Father La Combe, my friends were ashamed of me; my enemies triumphed; I was abandoned and generally oppressed by all the world. On the other hand, Father La Mothe, in credit, applauded by all, doing what he pleased, and oppressing me in the most extraordinary manner; and he complains I illtreat him at the very time I am at the gates of death! He is believed, and I, who do not utter a word and preserve silence, am illtreated. His brothers wrote to me all in concert—one, that it was for my crimes I suffered; that I should place myself under the direction of Father La Mothe, or I should repent of it: and with that he said to me the most insulting things of Father La Combe. The other told me that I was mad, and must be tied; lethargic, and must be roused up. The first wrote to me again that I was a monster of pride and such like, since I was unwilling to be cleansed, directed, and corrected by Father La Mothe: and the other let me know that I wished to be thought innocent while I did everything that resembled sin. This was my daily fare in the extremity of my ills; and with this, Father La Mothe cried with all his force against me, that I illtreated him. To all these insults I opposed only kindness, even making him presents. I had not a friend, nor any corporal relief. I was accused of every crime, of infamy, error, sorcery, and sacrilege. It seemed to me that I had only one business henceforth, which was to be for the rest of my life the plaything of providence; continually tossed about, and after that an eternal victim of divine justice. In all this my soul is unresisting, having no longer an "own" interest, and unable to desire to be anything but what God shall cause her to be, for time and eternity. Let those who read this reflect a little on the meaning of a state of this kind, when God appears to range himself on the side of creatures; and, with that, a perfect steadfastness which never belies itself. It is indeed your work, my God, where the creature avails nothing.

As soon as I was in a condition to have myself carried to the Mass in a chair, I was informed that I must speak to M. the Theologian. It was a trap arranged between Father La Mothe and the Canon, at whose house I lodged, in order to furnish a pretext for arresting me. I spoke with much simplicity to that man, who is quite of the party of the Jansenists, and whom M. N—— had gained over to torment me. We only spoke of things within his grasp, and of which he approved. Nevertheless, two days afterwards, it was reported I had declared many things and accused many persons; and they used this to exile all the people who displeased them. A great number were exiled, who they said had formed assemblies with me. They were all persons whom I never saw, whose names are unknown to me, and who never knew me. This is what has been most painful to me, that they should have made use of this invention to exile so many men of honor, although they well knew I had no acquaintance with them. One person was exiled because he said that my little book was good. It is to be remarked that nothing has been said to those who have formally approved it. Far from condemning the book, it has been reprinted since I am a prisoner, and advertised at the Archbishopric and throughout all Paris. Yet this book is the pretext which has been seized upon to bring me under the jurisdiction of the Archbishop. The book is sold, is distributed, is reprinted, and I am still kept a prisoner. In other cases when anything bad is discovered in books, they are content to condemn the books and leave the persons at liberty. In my case, it is the exact opposite; my book is approved anew, and they detain me a prisoner. The same day that all those gentlemen were exiled, a letter was brought commanding me to go to the convent of the Visitation in the Faubourg St. Antoine. I received the letter with a tranquillity which extremely surprised the person who brought it. He could not help showing his astonishment, as he had seen the grief of those who were only exiled. He was touched even to tears, and though he had an order to carry me with him, he left me the whole day on my promise. That day many of my friends came to see me. I spoke of it only to some of them. All that day I had an extraordinary gaiety, which astonished those who saw me, and who knew the business. I was left free all the day, and they would have been very well pleased had I fled; but our Lord gave me quite other sentiments. I could not support myself on my legs, for I still had fever every night. I could not, I say, stand when I had to sustain so rude a shock. I thought that my daughter would be left to me, and a maid to attend me. My heart clung the closer to my daughter for the trouble she had cost me to rear, and that I had endeavored, with the help of grace, to uproot her faults, and to bring her to the disposition of having no will, which is the best disposition for a girl of her age: she was not twelve years.

CHAPTER V

ON the 29th of January, 1688, the Eve of St. Francis de Sales, I had to go to the convent of the Visitation. As soon as I was there it was signified to me that I could not have my daughter, nor any one to attend upon me; that I should be a prisoner, confined by myself in a room. This was the entertainment I had to restore me in my extreme feebleness; but I keenly felt the separation when they tore from me my daughter. I asked that she might be left in the same house, and that I would not see her. Not only was this refused; but they had, further, the harshness to forbid any news of her being given to me. My trouble was that I feared her exposure in the world, and lest she should in a moment lose what I had with so much care endeavored to secure to her. From this moment I had to sacrifice my daughter as if she no longer belonged to me.

They selected the House of the Visitation in the street of St. Antoine, as being the one where I had no acquaintance, and in which they had most confidence. They thought I should there be kept with more rigor than in any other; and they were not mistaken, for they knew the zeal of the Mother

Superior in executing the King's orders. Besides, such a frightful portrait of me had been given to them, that the nuns regarded me with horror. It is a House where faith is very pure, and God is very well served, and for this reason, believing me a heretic, they could not regard me with favor. In the whole House they chose for my jailer the person who they knew would treat me rigorously. To make my cross complete this girl was needed.

As soon as I had entered they asked me who was my confessor since the imprisonment of Father La Combe. I named him. He is a very good man, who even esteems me, yet terror had so seized upon all my friends, owing to my imprisonment, that this worthy monk, without realizing the consequences, renounced me; saying he had never heard my confession, and he never would. That had a bad effect, and having detected me, according to their story, in falsehood, there was no further doubt of all the rest. This made me pity that Father, and wonder at human weakness. My esteem for him was not lessened, yet there were many persons who had seen me at his confessional, and who might have served as witnesses. I was content to say, "Such a one has renounced me. God be praised!"

The girl I had by me was gained over by my enemies to torment me. She wrote all my words, and spied everything. The smallest thing could not reach me but she ripped it entirely. She used her whole endeavor to catch me in my words. She treated me as a heretic, deceived, empty-headed. She reproached me for my prayers, and a hundred other things. If I was at church she gave great sighs, as if I was a hypocrite. In short, she regarded me with only horror and indignation. This girl was the intimate of the Superior of the House, so that he saw her almost every day, and this Superior was in the party of Father La Mothe and the Official; so that, although this girl was ready enough to obey him from the inclination she had for him, he made it a matter of conscience for her to illtreat me. God alone knows what she made me suffer. Moreover, the Official said I should be judged on the testimony of the Prioress; yet she never saw me, and only knew me through this girl, who perpetually told her ill of me; and being prejudiced against me, the most innocent words appeared to her crimes, and actions of piety, hypocrisy. I cannot express to what point her aversion for me went. As she was the only person of that Community I saw, being always locked into a small room, I had matter for the exercise of patience. Our Lord has not permitted me to lose it.

Yet I committed an infidelity, which caused me strange suffering: it is that when I saw her eagerness to make me speak in order that she might catch me in my words, I tried to watch myself. O God, what torment for a soul become simple as a child! I tried to guard my words that they might be more exact; but the only result of this was to make me commit more faults, our Lord permitting it so, to punish the care I had wished to take of myself—I, who am his without reserve, and who ought to regard myself only as a thing that belongs to him, with no more thought of myself than if I had no existence. Therefore, so far from my precaution serving me, I was surprised into faults in my words, which but for that I would not have committed; and, owing to the care I had wished to take of myself, I was for some days thrown back upon myself with a torment that I cannot better compare than to that of hell.

Immediately after I came into this House, Monsieur Charon, the Official, and a Doctor of the Sorbonne came to interrogate me. They commenced by asking me if it was true that I had followed Father La Combe, and that he had taken me from France with him. I answered that he was ten years out of France when I left it, and therefore I was very far from having followed him. They asked me if he had not taught me to practice prayer. I declared I had practiced it from my youth; that he had never taught it to me; that I had no acquaintance with him except from a letter of Father La Mothe, which he had brought me on his way to Savoy, and that, ten years before my departure from France. The Doctor of the Sorbonne, who was acting in good faith, who has never known anything of the knaveries (for I was not allowed to speak in private to him), said aloud that there was no ground there for a serious inquiry. They asked me if it was not he who had composed the little book, "Short and Easy Method." I said, "No;" that I had written it in his absence, without any design it should be printed; that a Counselor of Grenoble, a friend of mine, having taken the manuscript from my table, found it useful, and desired it might be printed; that he asked me to make a preface for it and to divide it into chapters, which I did in a single morning. When they saw all I said tended to acquit Father La Combe, they no longer questioned me about him. They commenced by interrogating me on my book. They have never interrogated me on my faith, nor on my prayer, nor on my morals.

I at once made a formal protest, written and signed with my own hand, that I had never wandered from the sentiments of the Holy Church, for which I would be ready to give my blood and my life; that I had never joined with any party; that I had all my life professed the most orthodox sentiments; that I had even labored, all my life, to submit my intellect and destroy my own will; that if anything were found in my books that might be ill interpreted, I had already submitted all, and I again submitted it, to the opinion of the Holy Church, and even to that of persons of doctrine and of experience; that if I answered to the interrogatories upon the little book it was merely through obedience, and not to support it, as my only design had been to help souls, not to hurt them. That was the first interrogation. I was interrogated four times. On my coming into the House they told the Prioress that I would be there only ten days, to the end of my interrogation. I was not at first surprised that I was prohibited from all communication outside the house or within, because I thought the motive was that I might not have any advice in the interrogation.

The second interrogation was on the little book; whether I had desired to do away with vocal prayer from the church, and particularly the Chaplet, referring to the place where I had taught the saying of *Our Father* with application, and had explained the *Our Father*, and that an *Our Father* so repeated was worth more than many said without attention. It was not difficult to answer this, for to teach a prayer with attention and application is not to destroy prayer; on the contrary, it is to establish it, and to render it perfect. They then put to me other questions on the same book, which I then had not; and I have so little memory, that I did not even know if what they asked me was in the book. Our Lord gave me the grace that he promised to the Apostles, which was to give me a much better answer than I could have found for myself. They said to me,

"If you had explained yourself like this throughout the book, you would not be here."

Suddenly I remembered I had put at the foot of the chapter the same reason that they approved, and I stated it. They would not write it down. After this, I saw they had simply taken the passages of the book that were not explained, and they had omitted their explanation; and it was merely to serve as a pretext for persecution, as the sequel has shown. After I had declared to them the explanations were in the book, and if there was anything wrong in it, they should not hold responsible me, a woman without learning, but the doctors who had approved it even without my asking them, since I was not acquainted with them; from that time they no more interrogated me on this book, nor on that on "The Song of Songs," being satisfied with the submission I had made.

The last interrogation was on a forged letter, where I was made to write, that I had held assemblies in houses that I was not acquainted with. They read the letter to me, and as the writing was not at all like mine, I was told it was a copy, and that they possessed the original, which was similar to my writing. I asked to see it, but it has never appeared. I said I had never written it, and that I had no acquaintance with the Minim, to whom it was addressed. To understand the malignity of this letter, it should be known that a worthy Minim Father came to see me on behalf of certain nuns of my acquaintance. One of the hostile persecutors said to me, "You see then Minims also." Father La Mothe and the woman saw him, and one of the two asked me his name. I did not know it, for I was not acquainted with him, so I was unable to tell it. They concocted then a letter to a Minim to whom they gave the name Father Francis, although I have since learned his name to be quite different. They made me, then, write to this Father, on the 30th of October, a letter in which I wrote to him as if he were residing at Paris, the Place Royale, "My Father, do not come to see me at the Cloister Notre Dame." The reason why they had put this was, that they had watched that he had not come to the Cloister Notre Dame, and were ignorant of the cause. It continued, that I no longer held assemblies because I was being spied on. This letter convicted me also of designs against the State, cabals, and assemblies;

and they added, "I do not sign because of the evil times." As they were reading this letter to me, I maintained I had never written it. The very style would have shown this to all who have seen or received my letters. As to the assemblies, I always said I had no acquaintance with those persons; that I knew no other Minim but one, who had come to me on behalf of certain nuns; that he did not belong to Paris, that he was Corrector of Amiens. At the time, I did not recollect other reasons to mention, and the Official would not even let these reasons be written. He made them merely put that I said it was not mine. After having read this letter, he turned to me, and said, "You see, Madame, that after a letter like this there was good reason to put you in prison." I answered him, "Yes, Sir, if I had written it." He maintained still, in the presence of the Doctor, it was my writing. But our Lord, who never fails at need, made me remember, as soon as they were outside, that the worthy Father was at Amiens from the commencement of the month of September, and it was impossible for me to have written to him as being in Paris on the 30th of October; that he had gone away five weeks before I lodged at the Cloister Notre Dame, and therefore I could not have written to him from there before his departure, on the subject of that arrest, and pray him to come and see me on the 30th of October, in such and such houses with which I was not acquainted, and where I never was—the more so as he was at Amiens. I sent all this in writing to the Official, who took very good care not to show it to the Doctor. I further wrote him that, if he was unwilling to take the trouble to prove its falseness, he should give a commission to the guardian of my children, who would willingly do it. But far from this, what did they do? I am shut up more closely than before. I am accused and defamed everywhere, and they deprive me of the means of justifying myself. They fabricate letters for me, and they are unwilling I should prove my innocence of them. For two months after the last interrogation not a word was said to me, while the same rigor was practiced towards me; that Sister treating me worse than ever.

Up to this I had not written anything for my justification to the Archbishop or to the Official; for I had no liberty to write to others, no more than I have at present. I had been, up to the time that I tried to watch myself in the manner I have mentioned, without any sensible or perceptible support, but in a peace of paradise, leaving myself as a mark for all the malice of men. My diversion was to express my state in verse. It seemed to me that, though shut up in a close prison, my soul had the former liberty, larger than the whole earth, which appeared to me but as a point in comparison with the vastness I experienced; and my contentment was without contentment for myself, because it was in God alone, above every *own* interest. Twelve days before Easter I went to confession. I raised my eyes without knowing why, and I saw a picture of our Lord fallen under his cross, with these words: "See if there is any sorrow like unto my sorrow." At the same time, I received a powerful impression that crosses were about to fall on me in greater crowds. I had always, until then, entertained some hope justice would be done me; but when I saw that the more I appeared innocent the more they endeavored to obscure my innocence, and the more closely I was kept confined, I concluded they sought not my innocence, but only to make me appear guilty. What happened confirmed me still more in this thought.

The Official came to see me by himself, without the Doctor, who had been present at the interrogations, and he said to me, "We must not talk about the false letter; it was nothing" (after having previously told me it was for that I was imprisoned). I said to him, "What, Sir, is it not the point in question—the counterfeiting the writing of a person and making her pass for one who holds assemblies and has designs against the State?" He immediately said to me, "We will seek the author." I said to him, "He is no other than scribe Gautier," whose wife had told me he counterfeited all sorts of writing. He saw well I had hit the mark. Then he asked me where were the papers I had written on the Scripture. I told him I would give them when I should be out of prison. I did not wish to say to whom I had confided them. He said to me, "If we happen to ask them from you, say the same thing," making me offers of service. Yet he went away very pleased thinking he had a means of ruining me beyond remedy, and satisfying Father La Mothe's desire that I should never be let out of prison.

He drew up a formal complaint as if he had interrogated me judicially, although it was nothing but a simple conversation. He charged I had rebeled when they had demanded my papers. I knew nothing of all this. I wrote a very strong letter to the Official on what he had said to me, that the letter they had forged was nothing. I also wrote to the Archbishop, who is himself mild enough, and who would not have been led to treat me with so much rigor if he had not been solicited by my enemies. He gave me no answer. But the Official thought he had found a means of ruining me by saying I had been rebelious, and I would not give up my writings. Three or four days before Easter he came with the Doctor of the Sorbonne and his formal charge. To the latter I answered that I had made a great difference between a private conversation and an interrogation, and that I had not deemed myself obliged to tell a thing which had been asked me only hypothetically, and that the papers were in the hands of my maid. They asked me if I was willing to hand them over to be disposed of as they pleased. I said, "Yes; that having written only to do the will of God, I was as content to have written for the fire as for the press." The Doctor said nothing could be more edifying. The copies of my writings were placed in their hands, for as to the originals they had long ceased to be at my disposal. I do not know where those who took them from me have placed them; but I have this firm faith, that they will all be preserved in spite of the tempest. As for me, I had no more of them than I gave, and I did not know where were the others; thus I could say it with truth.

The Prioress of the House where I am a prisoner asked the Official how my affair went, and if I would soon be let out of prison. It escaped him to say to her (and perhaps he did it owing to the Doctor, the better to screen himself): "My Mother, what could one do to a person that does and says all that one desires and in whom nothing is found? She will be released on a very early day." Yet they did not justify me. The Archbishop declared himself well satisfied with me, and my release and innocence were openly spoken of. Father La Mothe was the only one who had apprehensions. They sought to catch me by surprise.

The more I was innocent, the more troubles I had. I was

informed my affair went well, and I should be released at Easter. In the depth of my soul I had a presentiment to the contrary.

CHAPTER VI

UP to this I had been in a state of inexplicable contentment and joy at suffering and being a prisoner. It seemed to me that the captivity of my body made me better taste the liberty of my spirit. The more I was confined externally, the more I was large and extended within. My prayers still the same, simple and nothing; although there are times when the Spouse clasps more closely and plunges deeper into himself. I had been in this way up to the time that I committed the infidelity of trying to watch myself in the manner I have told. On St. Joseph's Day I was introduced into a more marked state, one rather of heaven than of earth. I went to the Calvary, which is at the bottom of the garden; my jailer having had permission to take me there. It was in this place (which has always been my delight), and there I remained a very long time; but in a state too simple, pure, and naked for me to be able to speak of it. The most elevated dispositions are those of which one can say nothing.

By this state—so much above anything that can be told, although in the same central depth which does not change—I understood there was some new cup for me to drink; like as the Transfiguration of Christ, where he conversed on his sufferings, was, as it were, the pledge of that which he had to suffer, and an introduction into his Passion.

For the day of St. Joseph, a saint with whom I am in a very intimate manner united, was as a day of Transfiguration for me. It seemed to me that I had no longer anything of the creature, and from this time a sort of suspension has taken place, so that I have been as much abandoned by God as persecuted by creatures: not that I have any pain or trouble at this abandonment or that my soul has the least inclination for anything else—that can no longer be, for she is without inclination or tendency for anything whatsoever; but nevertheless she is in such an abandonment that I am sometimes obliged to reflect to know if I have a being and subsistence. The whole of St. Joseph's Day I was the same, and it began to diminish gradually up to the day of the Annunciation, which is the day my heart rejoices in: yet on that day it was signified to me that I must enter upon new bitterness, and drink to the dregs of the indignation of God. The evening of the Annunciation I was put into an agony I cannot express. The fury of God was entire, and my soul without any support from heaven or from earth. It seemed to me that our Lord desired to make me experience something of his agony in the Garden. This lasted until Easter, after which I was restored to my former tranquillity with this difference, that all co-operation is removed, and that I am, whether in regard to God or in regard to creatures, as that which no longer exists. I have to make an effort to think if I am and what I am; if there are in God creatures and anything subsisting.

Although I have been treated in the manner I have said, and I shall hereafter tell, I have never had any resentment against my persecutors. I have not been ignorant of the persecution they caused me. God has willed that I have seen all and known all; he gave me an interior certainty that it was so, and I have never had a moment's doubt of it: but although I knew it, I had no bitterness against them. Loving the blows which God inflicts, one cannot hate the hand he uses to strike us, although one well sees which it is.

On Holy Thursday the Official came to see me by himself, and told me he gave me the freedom of the cloister—that is to say, that I could go about in the House; that he would not give any liberty for outside. I could not even obtain permission to speak to the guardian of my children. Yet they did not cease continually urging my daughter to consent to a marriage which would have been her ruin; and, in order to succeed, they had put her into the hands of the cousin of the gentleman to whom they wished to give her. That would have caused me great anxiety if I was capable of feeling it; but I had all my trust in God, and that he would not permit it to take place, the person in question having no tincture of Christianity, and being utterly ruined. The Official told me, at the same time, that I was entirely acquitted; that I was left here only for a short time for form's sake, that they might have the opinion of the Prioress, whose merit and uprightness was long known. The Prioress and all the community gave me the best character that one can give of a person, and the community conceived a very great affection for me, so that the nuns could not help speaking good of me to everybody. Had I my choice of all the convents in Paris, even those where I am known, I could not be better than in this one. It was there, O my Love, that I recognized yet more your providence over me, and the protection you afforded me; for they had chosen this Community as the one where they believed I should be treated with the greatest rigor, after having in the strongest manner prejudiced it against me.

As soon as Father La Mothe learned they spoke well of me in this House, he persuaded himself they could not speak well of me without speaking ill of him; and although I saw nobody, he wrote and complained to all the world, that I decried him everywhere, and that the community were speaking much ill of him; so that he embittered anew against me the minds of the Archbishop and of the Official, whose confessor he is. Far from releasing me at the end of ten days, as they had said, they left me there many months without saying anything to me. They even circulated new calumnies and, after having said I was innocent, they blackened me worse than ever. The Archbishop said I must expect nothing but from my repentance. He told Père de la Chaise that I had errors, and that I had even retracted them with tears, but that there was good ground to believe it was only through dissimulation, and therefore it was necessary to keep me shut up. On this I demanded only one thing, that they should punish me if I was guilty, but that they should exhibit my interrogation. It was what they never would do: on the contrary, the only answer was fresh calumnies.

What has been most painful to me in all this affair, is that it was impossible to take any measures. I was continually tossed between hope and despair. They suddenly came to tell me my persecutors had the upper hand, that they had made His Majesty believe I was guilty of all the crimes of which I was accused. Practically all my friends withdrew, and said they did not know me. My enemies cried Victory! and redoubled their rigors and severities against me. I continued content and resigned to remain in disgrace, believing I must there end my days, and no longer thought but of remaining all my life a prisoner. Then suddenly there came days of hope, which showed the business almost concluded in my favor, and that I was on the point of being declared and recognized as innocent. When the matter seemed settled and hope revived, there came a new turn, and a fresh calumny of my enemies, who made it believed they had found new documents against me, and that I had committed new crimes. This was continual, so that I regarded myself in the hands of God as a reed beaten by the wind, laid flat then suddenly lifted up, unable to continue either in disgrace or in hope. My soul has never changed her position from being incessantly beaten: she was always in the same state.

I was suddenly told that Father La Mothe had succeeded in having me placed in a House of which he is the master, and where it was believed he would make me suffer extremely, for he is very harsh. He so fully believed it, that he had given orders to keep a room ready to shut me up in. They brought me this news, which was of all what I should dread. All my friends were weeping bitterly. I did not feel even the first movement of trouble or pity for myself; my soul did not even for an instant change her position. Another time a person of weight offered to speak for me, and was confident of my immediate deliverance. The thing seemed done. I had not a first movement of joy at it. It seems to me my soul is in an entire immobility, and there is in me so entire a loss of all which regards myself, that none of my interests can cause me pain or pleasure. Besides, I belong so entirely to my God, that I cannot wish anything for myself but what he does; death, the scaffold, with which numberless times I have been threatened, does not make the least alteration. Shall I say it, O my Love, that there is in me a sovereign love for you alone above all love, which even in Hell would make me content myself or afflict myself with anything which should be my own, but with the sole contentment of God.

A lady of the world whom Providence caused me to meet in this House, and who has conceived much affection for me, and has rendered me all the services she was able, seeing the injustice done to me, resolved to ask a Jesuit Father of her acquaintance to speak to Père de la Chaise. This worthy Father did it: but he found Père de la Chaise much prejudiced against me, because they had made him believe that I was in errors, and that I had even retracted them, but that many still clung to me; so that this worthy lady advised me to write to Père de la Chaise. I wrote him this letter:

"My Reverend Father,

"If my enemies had attacked only my honor and my liberty, I would have preferred silence to justifying myself, it being my habit to adopt this course; but at present, when they attack my faith, saying that I have retracted errors, and when I am even suspected of having still more, I have been obliged, while asking the protection of your Reverence, to inform you of the truth. I assure your Reverence I have done nothing of the kind, and what surprises me is, that, after the Official himself has acknowledged that the memoirs which were given in against me were false, and that the letter forged against me was recognized as coming from a forger, as a consequence of the incontestable proofs I gave him it was not mine: after those who have been given me for examiners, who have never demanded from me a retractation, but petty explanations, with which they appeared satisfied, have declared me innocent, and I have even placed in their hands writings which I had only made for my own edification, offering them to their judgment with all my heart—that after, I say, these things, I have reason to believe your Reverence is not informed of my innocence. I cannot, my Reverend Father, dissimulate that, for any other article but that of faith, it would be easy for me to suffer calumny, but how could I keep silence for the most righteous grief that ever was? I have all my life made so open a profession of the most orthodox sentiments, that I have even thereby attracted enemies. If I dared open my heart to your Reverence with the secrecy of a perfect confidence, it would be very easy to prove to you, by incontestable facts, that it is temporal interests which have brought me where I am. After having refused things which in conscience I could not do, I was threatened with being involved in trouble. I have seen the menaces; I have even felt their effects, without being able to defend myself, because I am without intrigue and without party; and how easy is it, my Reverend Father, to oppress a person destitute of all protection! But how can I expect your Reverence to believe me, when, unfortunately, I am only known to you by calumny? However, I advance nothing that I cannot prove, if you consent to be informed of it. It would be a favor that would win the eternal gratitude of your, etc."

This letter had an effect the exact opposite of what was anticipated. I wrote it only through complaisance and to avoid scandal; for they regarded as obstinacy my resolution to make no step for my justification. They said that I was expecting God to do everything, and that this was to tempt him. I felt within that this letter and all they made me write would be without effect; that, on the contrary, they would do more harm than good. Yet our Lord willed I should write, to make them see that all one does for a soul given up to God is an exceedingly small thing, if he does not himself do it. I had known from the commencement that our Lord wished to be my sole deliverer. Therefore I had a joy that cannot be expressed when I saw all the intrigues of the best-intentioned creatures only serve to spoil everything. Père de la Chaise spoke of me to the Archbishop. This only served to give rise to new falsifications and new persecutions. The Archbishop assured him I was very criminal, and, the better to prove it, he feigned to wish to show me favor. He sent here a Bishop, one of his friends, to solicit the Prioress underhand that she should make me write a letter of submission and civility, in which I should declare that I was criminal and that I had retracted, promising that, if I wrote this letter, they would release me at once.

I forgot to say that, a month previous to this, the Official came with the Doctor to see me, and, in the presence of the Mother Superior, proposed to me that, if I would consent to the marriage of my daughter, I should be released from prison before eight days. I said I would not purchase my liberty at the price of sacrificing my daughter; that I was content to remain in prison as long as it should please our Lord. He answered that the King would not do any violence but he desired it. I said that I knew the King was too just and too equitable to act otherwise. Yet, a few days afterwards, they reported to Père de la Chaise, that I had said that the King wished to keep me in prison until I had consented to the marriage of my daughter; that the Archbishop had himself told the guardian of my children that I should not be released until I had consented to it; and, although I saw nobody and had no communication with outside, they accused me of having invented this, and they said I was a State criminal, and should again be shut up under key. But before this they made another attempt to see if I would write the letter they desired of me, as preliminary to my deliverance. They had no intention to deliver me, but a strong wish to have an incontestable proof against me, in order to confine me for the rest of my days—the one object my enemies had in view.

CHAPTER VII

THE Official and the Doctor came to tell the Prioress that I must again be shut up under key. She represented to them that the room I was in was small, opening only on the side where the sun shines all day; and in the month of July, how was it possible? it was to cause my death. They paid no attention to this. The Mother asked why they shut me up again. They told her I had done frightful things for a month back in her House, that I had had strange bursts of violence in this same House and that I scandalized the nuns. In vain the Mother protested the contrary, and assured them the whole community were edified by me, and they could not tire of admiring my patience and my moderation. The Official said he knew it at first hand, and I had done terrible things in her House. The poor woman could not restrain her tears at seeing an invention so utterly remote from the truth.

They then sent to fetch me, and they maintained to me that I had done horrible things in this House for a month back. I asked what they were. They would not tell me. I asked who could give an account of what I had done beside the Prioress and the nuns, yet they would not accept their testimony; that I would suffer as long as it pleased God: that they had commenced this business on forgeries, and would continue it on the same. The Doctor said to me I ought not to embitter matters, nor do the horrible things they said I had done. I answered him that God was witness of all. He told me that, in this sort of affairs, to take God for a witness was a crime. I told him that nothing in the world could prevent me having recourse to God. I then withdrew, and I was shut up more closely than the first time; and because they had not got a key, they fastened the room with a wooden bar across. All who passed by there were astonished. I had much joy at this new humiliation. Oh, what pleasure, my Love, to be, for you, in the most extreme abjections!

When the Official was asked why he had caused me to be shut up, he said, he did not know; that they must ask the Prelate. The guardian of my children went to see the Archbishop, and asked him why they had imprisoned me, since he himself had said I was exonerated. He answered him, "You, Sir, know, being a Judge, that ten documents do not condemn, but a single one may be found which condemns absolutely." The Counselor said to him, "But, my Lord, what has my cousin done anew?" "What," says he, "you do not know it! She has done frightful things for a month back." He, very greatly surprised, asked what they were. He said to him, "After having declared she was innocent, she has written with tears, and as if under force, a retractation, in which she states that she recognizes she has been in error and in evil sentiments, that she is guilty of the things of which they accuse her, and that she cursed the day and the hour she became acquainted with that Father"(meaning Father La Combe).

The Counselor was strangely surprised, but he suspected it was an invention. He requested to see that, and also my interrogations. The Archbishop told him it was a thing which would never be shown, and that it was the affair of the King. The Counselor, for greater certainty came here to see my friend, to know if I had written and signed anything. My friend assured him that neither the Official nor the Doctor had come here for four months—that is, since the Holy Thursday, when they came to propose the marriage of my daughter, on which occasion the Counselor was present. Thus he saw I had signed nothing, and that I had written nothing, except, at the instance of the Mother, one letter to the Archbishop, of no importance, the copy of which she had and showed him. Here it is:—

"MY LORD,
"If I have so long preserved a profound silence, it is, not to be troublesome to your Greatness, but at present the necessity of my temporal concerns indispensably requires me: I earnestly pray your Greatness to ask my liberty from His Majesty. It will be a favor for which I shall be under infinite obligations to you. I am the more hopeful of obtaining it, because the Official told me, before Easter, that I should not remain longer here than ten days, although many times that period has since passed; but I shall in no way regret this if it has served to persuade you, my Lord, of my perfect submission and of the profound respect with which I am, etc."

This letter said nothing at all; yet he asserted he had a frightful one which I had written against the King and against the State. It was not difficult for the scribe who had written the first false letters to write others.

It was, then, these frightful counterfeit letters, which were shown to Père de la Chaise, for which I was shut up. O God, you see all this, and my soul was content in the face of such falsities and such knaveries. As soon as I was again shut up, a fresh rumor was set going that I had been convicted of crimes, and that I had committed fresh ones. Every one broke out against me; even my friends found fault with me, and blamed me for the letter I had written to Père de la Chaise. They commenced, also, in the House to have doubts of me; and the more desperate I saw everything, the more content was I, O my God, in your will. I said, "O my Love, now they will no longer oblige me to have recourse to creatures. I await everything from you alone. Do with me, then, for time and for eternity, whatever is pleasing to you. Gratify yourself with my trouble." The guardian of my children was not firm. He was sometimes for me, but as soon as Father La Mothe spoke to him he was against me; so that he was continually wavering.

Three days before I was shut up, Father La Mothe had said that they would shut me up again, and he wrote to my sister, the nun, a violent letter against me. He also said, "We have learned that, in the place where Father La Combe is imprisoned, there is a commandant who is one of his friends. They will take care to imprison him." It should be known that when Father La Combe was transferred to the Isle of Oleron, the commandants did justice to his virtue. As soon as they saw him they recognized he was a true servant of God. Consequently the commandant, full of love for the truth, wrote to Monsieur de Chateauneuf, that this Father was a man of God, and that he begged some alleviation of his imprisonment might be granted. De Chateauneuf showed the letter to the Archbishop, who showed it to Father La Mothe, and they decided he must be transferred from there. This has been done. He was tkaen to a desert isle, where he cannot see those commandants. O God, nothing is concealed from you. Will you for long leave your servant in ignominy and grief?

Before I was arrested, M. —— had sent for a woman, who is a person of honor, but who did not know me, to tell her that she must go to the Jesuits and depose against me many things which he mentioned to her. She answered him, that she did not know me. He said that was of no importance, it must be done; that his design was to destroy me. Thereupon this woman went to consult a virtuous ecclesiastic, who told her it was a sin and a falsehood. She did not do it. He then proposed it to another person who excused himself. Another, a monk, against whom there were subjects of complaint, to bring himself into credit, wrote against me. It was he who would write most violently. A relative, who is at Saint-Cyr, spoke on my behalf to Madame de Maintenon. She is the only person who has spoken for me. Madame de Maintenon found the King much prejudiced, Father La Mothe having been even with him to speak against me. There was, therefore, nothing to be done. They came to tell me there was no more hope, and all my friends said that the only thing which could be expected was perpetual prison.

I fell dangerously ill, and the physician considered me in great peril. It could not be otherwise, as I was shut up in a place where the air was so hot it was like a stove. They wrote to the Official to procure for me the necessary alleviations, and even the Sacraments, and to permit some one to enter my chamber to attend me. He gave no answer, and but for the Superior of the House, who thought they could not in conscience allow me to die without treatment, and who told the Mother Superior to give it to me, I had died without help; for when it was mentioned to the Archbishop, he said: "What, she is ill, is she, at being shut up within four walls after what she has done!" and although the Counselor asked it of him, he would yield nothing. I had a very violent continuous fever, inflammation of the throat, a cough, and a continual discharge from the head upon the chest, which, it seemed, must suffocate me. But, O God, you did not want me, since you inspired the Superior of the House to give orders I should be seen by the physician and the surgeon; for I should have died but for the promptness with which they bled me.

The martyrs of the Primitive Church have suffered for the message of God, which was announced to them by the Word. The martyrs of the present time suffer for dependence on the Spirit of God. It is this Spirit, which is about to be poured out on all flesh, as is said in the prophet Joel. The martyrs of Jesus Christ have been glorious martyrs, Jesus Christ having drunk all confusion and disgrace. But the martyrs of the Holy Spirit are martyrs of shame and ignominy. And as the Holy Spirit is the consummation of all graces, so the martyrs of the Holy Spirit will be the last martyrs, after which, during a very long time, this Holy Spirit will so possess hearts and minds, that he will cause his subjects to do through love all that is pleasing to him. O Holy Spirit, Spirit of Love, make, then, of me all that pleases you for time and for eternity. Let me be slave to your will, and as a leaf is moved at the pleasure of the wind, may I allow myself to move at your divine breath: but as the impetuous wind breaks and tears away all that resists it, break all that opposes itself to your empire, break the cedars, as your prophet expresses it,—yes, the cedars shall be broken, all shall be destroyed; but "Send out thy Spirit, and thou wilt renew the face of the earth." It is this same Spirit which destroys, that will renew the face of the earth.

This is very certain. Send your Spirit, Lord; you have promised it. It is said of Jesus Christ, he expired, "breathed out his spirit;" marking thereby the consummation of his sufferings and the consummation of the ages. Also, it is said, he gave up his spirit after having said, "It is consummated," which shows us the consummation of all things will be effected by the extension of that same Spirit through all the earth; and that this consummation will be that of eternity, which will never be consummated, because it will no more subsist but by the vivifying and immortal Spirit. Our Lord in expiring gave up his spirit into the hands of his Father, as if to let us know that after this Spirit (which is, which was, and which will be, the will and love of God communicated to men) had come out from God to visit the earth, it would return to God almost entirely withdrawn from earth and continuing immovable for a time.

O Spirit, Consummator of all things, reduce everything to one! But before that can be, you will be a Spirit-Destroyer. Accordingly, Jesus Christ, speaking of the Spirit that he is about to send, says: "I am not come to bring peace, but the sword. I am come to bring fire. What do I wish, but that it should burn?" It is necessary to be re-born of the Spirit and of water. The message (speech) is like water that flows away; but it is the Spirit which renders it fruitful. It is this "Spirit, which will teach us all things;" as Jesus Christ says, "He will take of mine:" for it is by the Holy Spirit the Word is communicated to us.

CHAPTER VIII

ALTHOUGH the Archbishop had told the Counselor, who is guardian of my children, that I had written to him those retractations and those dreadful letters of which I have spoken, which, as the Lord showed me in a dream, they had got written by the forger who had done the first one, they did not cease, in an underhand way, urging me to write something similar, promising me complete liberty. They wished to draw from me retractations, and yet neither in the interrogations nor judicially had they ever required them of me, because the Doctor, who is an honorable man, was witness to it, and there was nothing which called for them, as I was never interrogated upon anything of this kind. But they hoped, in procuring this letter from me, to declare me guilty to posterity, and to show thereby they had reason for imprisoning me; thus covering all their artifices. They further wished a pretext which might appear, and which would prove it was with justice they had caused Father La Combe to be imprisoned; and they tried by menaces and by promises to make me write that he was a deceiver. To this I answered, that I was not unhappy in the convent nor in prison, however rigorous it might be; that I was ready to die, and even to ascend the scaffold, rather than write a falsehood; that they had only to show my interrogations; that I had spoken the truth as I had sworn to speak it.

As they saw they could extract nothing from me, they composed an execrable letter, wherein they make me accuse myself of all sorts of crimes, even of those our Lord has given me the grace to be ignorant of: that I recognize Father La Combe has deceived me; that I hate the hour I knew him. O God, you see this, and you keep silence: you will not always keep silence. When Father La Mothe saw that people were beginning to believe he was the author of the persecution and of the imprisonment of Father La Combe, in order to excuse himself to the world, he caused it to be conveyed to Father La Combe that I had accused him. He said, "I have intreated the Archbishop to show me the interrogations of my monk. I even wished to follow this up, and to demand the reason why he was a prisoner, but the Archbishop told me that they were matters concerning the King, with which I should not meddle." He published to all the world that I was on the point of ruining their House: that I tried to make them Quietists—I, who never spoke to them. He bethought him of another trick, in order it might never be known to His Majesty that he was the author of our persecutions. He made the Archbishop, whose director he is, consult him to know if in conscience he, the Archbishop, could set me free; because he feared Madame Maintenon might speak in my favor. To an answer making me appear guilty, Father La Mothe, in a concerted letter, writes as if in my interest; "I think, my Lord, you may let my sister go, notwithstanding all that is past; and I answer you after having consulted God, and I do not find any objection to it." This letter is carried to His Majesty to show the probity of Father La Mothe, and to arrest any suspicion touching him. Yet they did not cease to say openly, notwithstanding the consultation, that they do not believe in conscience they could set me at liberty, and it is on this footing they speak of it to His Majesty; making me appear so much the more criminal as they make Father La Mothe the more zealous. A Bishop, speaking of me one day to one of my friends, who tried to defend me: "How," said he, "do you wish to make us believe her innocent,—I, who know that Father La Mothe, her own brother, has been compelled by zeal for the good of the Church and by a spirit of piety, to carry frightful reports against his sister and his monk to the Archbishop? He is a good man, who has done this only through zeal." This Bishop is intimate with the Archbishop: a Doctor of the Sorbonne, who is everything with the Archbishop, said the same.

Although Father La Combe is in prison, we do not cease to communicate together in God, in a wonderful manner. I have seen a letter of his where he writes it to a person in his confidence. Many spiritual persons to whom our Lord has united me by a kind of maternity, experience the same communication, although I be absent, and find in uniting themselves to me the remedy for their ills. O God, you who have chosen this poor insignificant creature to make her the throne of your bounties and of your rigors.

I experience at present two states both together. I bear Jesus Christ Crucified and Child. As a consequence of the one, crosses are in great number, very severe and without cessation; there being few days I have not many of them. As a consequence of the other, I have something childlike, simple, candid; something so innocent that it seems to me, if my soul were put under a press, only candor, innocence, simplicity and suffering would issue from it. O my Love, it seems to me you have made of me a prodigy before your eyes for your sole glory.

Written this 21st of August, 1688, aged forty years, from my prison which I love and cherish.

I will write the memoirs of the rest of my life through obedience, with a view to completing them one day, if it is deemed suitable.

I forgot to say that I believe I felt the state of the souls who approached me, and that of the persons who were given to me, however distant these were. I call "feeling" an interior impression of what they were; especially in the case of those who passed for spiritual. I knew at once if they were simple or dissimulating; their degree and their self-love, for which things I had a repugnance to them. I recognized when they were strong in themselves, and resting on the virtue they believed themselves to have, and by which they measured others, and condemned in their mind those who were not like them, although more perfect. These persons, who believe themselves and are believed righteous, are much more disagreeable to God than certain sinners through weakness; whom the world regards with horror, and to whom, nevertheless, God shows very great mercies. This will only be seen at the Day of Judgment. Yet God suffers with difficulty these strong souls, of themselves so full, although they think themselves humble, because they practice certain forms of humility; which most often only serve to augment their self-opinion. If these souls had to suffer some real humiliation, whether for some unexpected fall or public infamy, where would they be? Then one would know their lack of solidity. If it were known how God loves true littleness, men would be astonished at it. When people speak to me of some persons of piety, my central depth rejects those who are not in the littleness of which I speak, and it admits those who are devoted to God as God wishes them, without my knowing how this takes place. I find there is in me something which rejects the evil and approves the true good.

The 21st of August, 1688, it was thought I was about to be released from prison, and everything seemed arranged for it. Our Lord made me feel in my central depth that, far from intending to deliver me, it was new snares they were spreading for me, and that they were taking counsel together the better to destroy me; that all they had done was only to make the King acquainted with Father La Mothe, and to give him an esteem for him.

The 22nd at my waking, I was put into a state of agony, like that of Jesus Christ agonizing and seeing the counsel of the Jews against him; and the certainty of that plot was again given to me. I saw that there was none but you, O my God, who could withdraw me from their hands. I comprehend that you will one day do it by your right hand; but I am ignorant of the manner, and I abandon all things to you. I am yours, O my Love, for time, and for eternity.

The Official came with the Doctor, the guardian of my children, and Father La Mothe, to speak to me of the marriage of my daughter. Father La Mothe, who heard all this, did not say a word, except that he whispered to me (believing thereby to hide his part in the persecutions, and to persuade me he had no part in them) that I was detained in the convent only about the marriage of my daughter. I made little answer to him, and I treated him as civilly and as cordially as was possible; our Lord giving me the grace easily for love of himself to treat him so. They said to Father La Mothe I had received him very well and they were edified at it. He answered that, while I was showing him outward civility, I was abusing him under my breath. He wrote the same to my brothers, saying I had strangely illtreated him. I declare I was surprised at such an invention, and I would not have believed that one could invent in such a way.

God, who never abandons those who hope in him, has done that which he had made me know he would do for me by the hand of Madame de Maintenon. It happened in the way I am about to describe: which should make us marvel at the conduct of God, and the care he takes of those who are his, while he appears most to abandon them.

God had permitted the affairs of my only uncle to fall into disorder. He had a daughter, a canoness of intelligence and merit. She had a very pretty little sister, and, as Madame de Maintenon had lately established a House for girls whose fathers were ruined in the service of the King, the canoness went to present her sister to Madame de Maintenon, who was very much pleased with her, and also with her own cleverness. She begged her to remain at the House until her little sister got used to it; but when she had become acquainted with the cleverness and the capacity of the canoness, she engaged her to remain altogether, or at least for some time, begging her to see the House fairly started. Shall I say, oh my Love, that I believe you have done this only for me? My cousin wished to speak in my favor to Madame de Maintenon, but she found her so prejudiced against me by calumny that she had the grief to see nothing could be done in this quarter. She let me know it. I remained very content in the will of God, with this rooted conviction, that nothing would be done except through Madame de Maintenon, and that this was the way of which God had resolved to make use.

I remained then very peaceful, waiting the moment of the good God, when Madame de Miramion, who had been very much prejudiced against me, and who believed me very criminal, because my enemies had persuaded her of it, came by pure providence to the convent where I was. She had much esteem for the Prioress. She asked her if she believed me misled, as she had been told. The Prioress and the nuns told her a thousand good things about me, which their charity made them see. She was amazed, for she had been assured I caused great evils in this House. She resolved to serve me through pure charity, and to speak to Madame de Maintenon, and this had a good effect. But that which above all makes us marvel at the providence of God with regard to me is that the Abbess with whom I had placed that worthy girl, the nun, who has caused me so many crosses both at Gex, and because Father La Mothe's desire to get the money I had given for her dowry has been in part, the cause of the persecution he stirred up against me—this Abbess, I say, found herself obliged to come to Paris for some business. She is a relative of Madame de Maintenon; and as she had need of arranging with me for the dowry of that girl, she complained of the Archbishop's refusal to allow me to speak to her, and she explained it was a business of charity I was doing in favor of a poor girl, whom I was making a nun in her House. This gave an opportunity to Madame de Maintenon to speak for me, that I might be able to arrange with this Abbess. Being again entreated by my cousin, she spoke to the King, who said they should present him with a petition. It was brought to him, and, as it was the eve of St. Louis, I had an instinct to pray for the King that he might be enlightened as to the truth. He ordered the Archbishop to set me at liberty; which not a little surprised and vexed him. I marveled, O my God, at your divine providence, and the markedly special springs of your adorable control; since this same money, which has been the first source of all my troubles, through Father La Mothe's desire to have it, you have made, O my God, the means of my liberty. This Abbess did much more, for by her authority she caused to be given to Father La Mothe, as it were in spite of himself, and while fearing his practices were discovered, a letter of esteem for my piety and the pious life I had led.

CHAPTER IX

As the Archbishop was not willing to have the worst of it, and my enemies, on seeing themselves powerless to hurt me, were only the more embittered, they resolved to inform the King that I could not be released until certain formalities had been observed. They wished to draw up a deed such as to make it appear that they were in the right, and to screen themselves from all inquiries that might hereafter be made against them; and also to avoid the lie being given to them as to the forgeries and the reports they boasted of having against me, and their assertions that I had written and executed acts of retractation. The Official came on Wednesday, September 1, 1688. After having taken the testimony of the Mother Superior as to my conduct in their convent, which she gave in the most distinct and favorable manner possible, he sent for me, and told me I must sign a deed which he had previously drawn up, and which he had had copied by his secretary. He produced two papers I had in truth myself given him on the 8th of February of the same year, 1688, which had been used by me as memoirs, to answer certain things he asked me, and which papers he had inserted at full length in my interrogations; but these he would never publish, lest my innocence should thereby be known, and people should see the frightful falsehoods which had been concocted against me, and for which reparation was due. Moreover, these papers contained the assurance and the protestations I had made of never having wandered from the sentiments of the Holy Church. In the deed which they presented to me, he had inserted that I had given him two deeds. I refused to sign it, and, on my refusal, the Doctor, who accompanied him, told him that this word "deed" was not proper for simple papers; that they must put "papers." He would not consent. It was necessary to put "memoirs" that I had recognized as coming from me. I saw clearly there was here some trick, and it was only for some evil purpose they brought me back two papers otherwise useless, since they were inserted at full length in my interrogation. Wherefore reproduce the two papers and suppress all the interrogations, unless to overreach me in some way? I said I would willingly sign that I had placed in his hands two memoirs of the 8th of February, 1688, provided they wrote the contents of the said memoirs; but to say simply that I had given two memoirs, without explaining what they were, I would not do it; that after all they had forged in my name, I

ought to fear everything. He would not allow any explanation. He gave way to fearful violence against me, saying I
should sign it, and swearing I was ruined if I did not do so. I
had to waive this, in spite of all my reasons, to avoid their
violence and withdraw myself from their hands. I requested
that at least the Doctor who accompanied him should sign my
papers, in order that they might not be able to substitute
others in their place. He would not allow this. He signed
them himself; but what use was that to me, since they remained
in his hands? They told me if I signed all they requested of me
the door of the convent would infallibly be opened, but if I
refused there was no longer any safety for me. They wished
to put into their deed that I had been in error; and, in order
to oblige me to sign a thing which I would rather have given
my life than sign, they told me that every one makes mistakes—
that this is what is meant by errors. I asked him if he meant to
say "errata," as we read in books; I would willingly do this,
but as for "errors" I would never consent to that. He said to
me gently enough, I should not make any difficulty; that it
was for my good; that he asked this of me as the infallible
means of withdrawing me from prison. But when he saw I
persisted in saying that I had never been in error, and that I
would never sign if they inserted the word "error," he got
into a frightful fury, declaring by his faith I should sign, or
he would know the reason why, with frightful outbursts of
violence to prove to me I was in error.

The Doctor, who saw the Official rise up in a strange
fury, told me to let it pass, making me understand it was more
important for me to get out of their hands. He told me afterwards he would give me, if I wished, a deed signed with his
own hand, to the effect that he had advised me to sign. I was
about then to sign, and I skipped one side of the sheet in
order to have time for consultation.

As the Abbess had permission to come and bring to me any
one she pleased, I took advice; for they had brought me back
the paper which I had signed on one side, thinking it was a
mistake. I was told I must at any price be got out of their
hands, provided I did not insert that I had been in error. I
said this was not in the deed, but that "if in my books and
writings there was error, I condemned them with all my heart."

They had thought to take me by surprise, but my God has not allowed it, making me see their end, in all they demanded of me. They wished to make me put, that if there was error in my books, as well those which openly appeared as in those which did not appear, I detested them. I said I had not written any book which did not appear. I knew they had set going a rumor that I had printed books in Holland, and they desired by this deed to make me admit that it was so. I said, then, I had not made any other book. To excuse himself, the Official said, that my writings were thick enough to pass for books, and he put "writings." The Doctor, who hardly dared to speak, told him, however, I was right. If he had insisted upon putting "I had errors" I would rather have let my head be cut off than sign it.

Here are the contents of the paper I had given them February 8, 1688, of which, through the mercy of God, I had kept a duplicate, in order that those into whose hands these writings may fall may see the difference there is between these and those which have been foisted upon me.

"I urgently intreat you, gentlemen, to write two things: first, that I have never deviated from the most orthodox opinions of the Holy Church; that I have never had private opinions of my own; that I have never taken up with any party; that I am ready to give my blood and my life for the interests of the Church; that I have labored all my life to strip myself of my own opinions, and to submit my intelligence and my will. The second, that I have never pretended to write anything which was not conformable to the opinions of the Holy Church; that if through my ignorance anything not comformable to its opinions has slipped in, I renounce it, and I with all my heart submit to its decision, from which I never wish to deviate. That if I answer the interrogations put to me upon the little book, it is purely through obedience, and not to maintain or defend it, as I submit it with all my heart."

I have forgotten to say that, when it was seen the nuns spoke much good of me and declared their esteem, my enemies and some of their friends came and told them that the fact of their having esteem for me was very injurious to their House: that it was said, I had corrupted them all and made them Quietists. They took alarm at this. The Prioress forbade the

nuns to speak good of me; so that, when I was again imprisoned, it was thought they had discovered much evil, and that
made even my friends doubtful. I then saw myself rejected by
all, and so abandoned by the whole world that it was only
with pain they tolerated me in the House; and even my friend,
fearing the esteem she had for me might be injurious to her,
gradually withdrew and became cold. It was then, O my God,
that I could well say you were all things to me. I saw the
nature of human respect, which leads one to betray the known
truth; for at heart they esteemed me, yet, to keep themselves in
repute, they pretended the opposite. Father La Mothe went
and carried to the Jesuits forged letters of a frightful character that he said were from me; and he said he was in despair at
being obliged to speak against me; and that it was through
zeal for religion he renounced the friendship he owed me.
Thereby he gained over Père de la Chaise and almost all the
Jesuits.

I have again forgotten to say that, when I told the Official
that with reason I was not willing they should insert that
word "error," because I felt certain it was a snare, owing to
their boasting they had in their hand a retraction, he told me
he must have been a great fool not to make me put it in, and
that the Archbishop would dismiss him, trying to make me
understand they wanted that word for their justification.
Five days from that, he came to make me sign the second page.
I would not have done it, being quite indifferent whether I
remained as I was, provided I did your will, O my God: but
Madame de Maintenon sent me word to sign, and that she
would inform the King of their violence; that it was necessary
to get me out of their hands. I signed then. After which I had
the liberty of the cloister.

The guardian of my children went to expedite my formal
release. You permitted, O my God, by your providence, this
paper to go astray for five days through a misunderstanding:
that caused me again in this House ups and downs; as for my
heart and my soul they remained always at the same level. I
have even had more perceptible joy on entering my prison
than on leaving it. At last, on the eve of the Exaltation of the
Holy Cross, the release was brought to me. I saw clearly, O
my Love, you wished the Cross to be exalted in me.

I have learned since I am at liberty, and even before, that a person who persecuted me had obtained an order to send me two hundred leagues from here, into a prison where I should nevermore have been heard of. You waited to save me, O my God, until things were utterly desperate. I learned one morning that no one was willing to meddle in my affair—neither Madame de Maintenon nor my cousin. From that I received a very great joy; and when the affair has been most desperate, then I have felt again a renewal of joy. Here, then, was I very happy, even when I learned they were striving to have me placed in perpetual imprisonment—and the measures were so well taken for it, that when the release was demanded from the secretary, after His Majesty's order had been given to set me free, he inquired if it was not for that lady whom they were about to transfer. O God, how you overthrow the designs of men!

The Abbess and my children's guardian came to fetch me, and manifested great joy; as did all my friends. It was only the others who were extremely vexed at it. I went out, without feeling I was going out, and without being able to reflect on my deliverance. On leaving the convent they took me to the Archbishop, as a matter of form to thank him. It was indeed due to him for what he had made me suffer, for I do not doubt my God has been glorified by it. Then I went to see Madame de Miramion, who indeed was rejoiced at a thing to which she had not a little contributed. I there providentially found Madame de Montchevreuil, who manifested much joy at seeing me delivered, and assured me Madame de Maintenon would have no less: which Madame de Maintenon herself showed every time we met. I wrote to her to thank her. A few days after my release, I went to St. Cyr to salute her. She received me most kindly, and in a marked manner. A few days before, she had declared to my cousin how much my letter had pleased her, and that in truth our Lord gave her for me sentiments of particular esteem. I returned to see the Archbishop. He begged me to say nothing of what had passed. Father La Mothe, however, was in despair at my release; but he always pretended the contrary to those who had access to me. He sent persons to spy me, and to surprise me in my words. I do not yet know what effect this will have. The Official begged Madame de

Miramion not to receive me into her Community, and he came to tell me not to go there. That had not much effect, for this lady still declared her intention to take me to her House, where I am at the present moment. If God wills it, I shall one day write the continuation of a life which is not yet finished. This 20th of September, 1688.

The desire I have had to obey and to omit nothing will have doubtless caused some repetitions; they will at least serve to show you my exactness in what you order me, and that if I have omitted anything, it is either because I have not been able to express it, or through forgetfulness.

Some days after my release, having heard mention of the Abbé de F——, I was suddenly with extreme force and sweetness interested for him. It seemed to me our Lord united him to me very intimately, more so than any one else. My consent was asked for. I gave it. Then it appeared to me that, as it were, a spiritual filiation took place between him and me. The next day I had the opportunity of seeing him. I felt interiorly this first interview did not satisfy him: that he did not relish me. I experienced a something which made me long to pour my heart into his; but I found nothing to correspond, and this made me suffer much. In the night I suffered extremely about him. In the morning I saw him. We remained some time in silence, and the cloud cleared off a little; but it was not yet as I wished it. I suffered for eight whole days; after which, I found myself united to him without obstacle, and from that time I find the union increasing in a pure and ineffable manner. It seems to me that my soul has perfect rapport with his, and those words of David regarding Jonathan, that "his soul clave to that of David," appeared to me suitable for this union. Our Lord has made me understand the great designs he has for this person, and how dear he is to him.

CHAPTER X

I SHOULD be unable to write anything more regarding my inner state; I will not do it, having no words to express what is entirely disconnected from all that can fall under feeling, expression, or human conception. I shall only say that, after the state when I came back to life, I found myself for some years, before being placed in what is called the Apostolic state—that of a Mission to help others, the selfhood having been entirely consumed—I found myself, I say, in a happiness equal to that of the Blessed, save for the Beatific Vision; nothing here below affected me; and neither at present do I see anything in heaven or in earth which can trouble me as regards myself. The happiness of a soul in this state cannot be understood without experience, and those who die without being employed in helping their neighbors, die in supreme felicity; although overwhelmed with external crosses. But when it pleased God to honor me with his Mission, he made me understand that the true father in Jesus Christ, and the Apostolic pastor, must suffer like him for men, bear their languors, pay their debts, clothe himself with their weaknesses. In truth, God does not do these sorts of things without asking from the soul her consent; but how sure he is this soul will not refuse him what he asks! He himself inclines the heart for that he wishes to obtain. It seems he then impresses upon it these words: "I was happy, I possessed glory, I was God; but I have quitted all that, I have subjected myself to pain, to contempt, to ignominy, to punishment. I became man to save man. If thou art willing to finish what remains lacking of my Passion and that I should make in thee an extension of my quality of Redeemer, it is necessary thou consent to lose the happiness thou dost enjoy; to be subjected to wants, to weaknesses, in order to bear the languors of those with whom I shall charge thee, to pay their debts, and finally to be exposed, not only to all the interior pains from which thou hast been delivered for thyself, but to all the most violent persecutions. If I had remained in my private life, I should never have suffered any persecution; only those are persecuted who are employed to help souls." There was needed, then, a consent of immolation to enter into all the designs of God regarding the souls he destines for himself.

The nature of this suffering is something most inward, most powerful, and most special. It is an excessive torment, one knows not where it is, nor in what part of the soul it resides. It is never caused by reflection, nor can it produce any. It causes neither disturbance, nor embarrassment; it does not purify: and, for this reason, the soul finds it gives her nothing. Its excess does not hinder an enjoyment, without enjoyment, and a perfect peace. It takes away nothing from the sense of largeness. One is not ignorant that it is for souls one is suffering, and very often one knows the person: one finds one's self during this time united to him in a painful manner. One often bears the weaknesses that those persons ought to feel; but ordinarily it is a general indistinct pain, which oftentimes has a certain relation to the heart causing extreme pain to the heart, but violent pains, as if one pressed it, or pierced it with a sword: this pain, purely spiritual, has its seat in the same place which is occupied by the Presence of God. It is more powerful than all corporal pains, and it is yet so insensible, and so removed from sentiment, that the person who is overwhelmed by it, if he was capable of reflection, would believe that it has no existence, and that he is deceiving himself. Since God willed me to participate in the Apostolic state, what have I not suffered!

When I am suffering for a soul, and I merely hear the name of this person pronounced, I feel a renewal of extreme pain. Although for many years I am in a state equally naked and void in appearance, owing to the depth of the plenitude, nevertheless, I am very full. Water filling a basin to the utmost limits it can contain, offers nothing to distinguish its plenitude; but when one pours in more upon it, it must discharge itself. I never feel anything for myself, but when anything stirs that depth, infinitely full and tranquil, this makes the plenitude felt with such excess that it gushes over on the senses. This is the reason that makes me avoid hearing certain passages read or repeated: not that anything comes to me by external things, but it is that a word heard stirs the depth: anything said of the truth, or against the truth, stirs it in the same way, and would make it break out if continued.

Oh divine wisdom, oh savory knowledge, you flow incessantly from the heart and from the mouth of these souls, like a stream of divine sap, which communicates life to an infinity of branches, although one sees only a coarse and moss-covered bark. "What do you see in the Shulamite," this choice soul, you others who are watching her, says the sacred Bridegroom, "except the companies of an army in array?" No, you will only see that in her. Do not therefore form any judgment, oh you who are not thus far, and be assured that, "although I am black I am very beautiful; that my sun, by his burning looks, his discolored me in this way to preserve me for himself, and to withdraw me from the sight of all creatures." To attack those souls is to wound the heart of God. To judge them is to judge God.

All the greatest crosses come in this Apostolic state (if one can call them crosses), because hell and all men are stirred up to hinder the good which is being done in souls. If Jesus Christ had not come out from his private life, he would not have been persecuted and crucified. If God left these souls concealed in the secret of his countenance, they would be secure from the persecution of men. But how cheerfully would one suffer the wheel or the fire even for a single soul! We must not be astonished if the devils stir up all the regions of their dominion against Apostolic souls. It is because the Devil well knows that one soul of this kind, once listened to, would destroy his empire. All devotions hurt him but moderately, for in the self-love of the devout he gets compensation for what they make him lose by their regulated practices; but there is nothing to be gained by him from a soul devoted to the truth of God and to his pure love, who allows herself to be annihilated by the sovereign dominion of God, and who, no longer subsisting in herself, gives full power to God continually to extend more widely his empire. The Devil cannot approach these souls except at a distance. The rage with which he is animated against them has no bounds. Oh, how mistaken we are when we judge devotion by exterior actions! To be devout, or to be devoted to God, we must have neither choice nor preference for one action more than for another. People form ideas and imagine that a soul which is God's in a certain manner, ought to be such and such; and when they see the opposite to the ideas they had formed for themselves, they conclude God is not there; while it is often where he especially is.

There are the saints of the Lord, who are sanctified, not like other saints by the practice of virtues, but by the Lord himself, and by an unlimited suppleness, which is the real possession of all virtue. They are all the more the saints of God, since they are only holy in him and for him. They are holy in his style, not in the style of men. O my Love, you have so many souls who serve you in order to be holy: make for yourself a troop of children who serve you because you are holy; who serve you in your style!

The souls of which I speak are incapable of any sort of preference or predilection: but they are moved by a necessity, which, not being in them, for they are free, has its seat in God himself, after the sacrifice of this same liberty. They have not any natural love, but an infinite charity, applied and stirred more powerfully for certain subjects than for others, according to the design of God, the need of the persons, and the closeness of the union that God wills they should have with them. This strong, even apparently ardent love, is not in the powers as other inclinations; but in that same central depth which is God himself. He governs as a sovereign and inclines this same central depth, indistinguishably from himself, towards the thing he wishes one should love, and to which one is united; and this love is he; so that it cannot be distinguished from God, although it terminates in a particular subject.

It is well to explain here a matter which might cause great mistakes to souls. It is, that the soul sunk in God, and become infinitely supple in relation to God, may seem either reserved, or to have difficulty in saying certain things to others. It is not now a defect which is in her in regard to herself, but this

constraint comes from the person to whom one should speak:
for God makes felt as if by anticipation, all the dispositions
of the soul to whom one should speak: and although that soul,
if one asked, would assert confidently, there was no repugnance to receive what should be said (because, in fact, the
will is so disposed), yet it is certain that, whatever the good
will, the matters are repugnant, whether because they exceed
the present scope of that person, or because there are still
lurking secret ideas of a virtue based on reason. It is, therefore,
the narrowness of the person to whom one speaks which
causes the repugnance to speak. Moreover the exterior state
of childhood has a thousand little things which might pass for
unfaithfulnesses, similar to those of persons who through
self-love do not say the things which are distasteful to them;
but it is easy to see that this is not the case, because they
have passed through a state which did not permit them reserve
of a thought, whatever it might cost. Souls of this state must
be judged by that which God has made them pass through,
rather than by what one sees; for otherwise one would judge
them in relation to one's own state, and not by that which
they are. That which is weak in God is stronger than the
greatest strength, because this weakness does not come from
not having acquired all strength, virtuous and understood by
reason; but because, having infinitely passed beyond this, it
is lost in the divine strength, and this it is which causes those
opposites, that unite so well although they appear incompatible,
of the divine strength and of the child's weakness.

A.D. 1688.

CHAPTER XI

ON leaving St. Mary's I went to Madame de Miramion. Those
who were the cause of my having been placed at St. Mary's

opposed this, and told me it was more suitable that I should retire into a private house. As I penetrated their intention, which was no other than to commit new forgeries, in order to have the opportunity of causing me fresh trouble, I remained firm in the resolution to enter into the Community of that lady. As soon as they saw they could not succeed with me, and that I wished to live in a Community, they bethought themselves to write to Madame de Miramion, assuring her that they themselves saw me go, at least once a week, to Faubourg St. Marceau, into discredited houses, and that I held assemblies. Father La Mothe was the author of these letters, and maintained that, being unwilling to credit it, he had been there several times during the last month, and that he had always seen me enter those houses. It is to be remarked that I had never been to the Faubourg St. Marceau, and that for three months I was confined to bed, where every day an abscess I had in the eye was dressed; besides I had a very severe fever during that time. Madame de Miramion, who was almost always present when they treated me, and who knew I did not leave the bed, was very indignant at this proceeding; so that when Father La Mothe came to see her, to confirm what he had written, and to add still further calumnies, as to things which, he said, I had done within eight days, she spoke very strongly to him on the blackness of his accusations, assuring him she believed all that had been told her of the malignity he had practiced on me; as she herself was witness that, for three months, I had not been able even to leave the bed, and since I was with her I had not gone out four times; and then, it was a responsible member of my family who had come to fetch me in the morning and bring me back in the evening. When he saw himself so ill received, he endeavored to put other machines in motion. He complained everywhere, I had caused him to be ill-treated by Madame de Miramion; although I was then ignorant of what passed, and only knew it some times afterwards, when, being recovered, Madame de Miramion showed me the letters.

My daughter was married at Madame de Miramion's, and, owing to her extreme youth, I was obliged to go and remain some time with her. I lived there two years and a half. What made me leave her was the desire I had to withdraw into a convent and to live there unknown; but God, who had other designs for me, did not permit it, as I shall tell in the sequel. While I was with my daughter the persecution did not cease. They were constantly inventing something against me. When I was in the country with her, they said I instructed the peasants, although I saw none of them. If I was in the town, according to their story, they made me receive persons, or else I went to see them; and yet I neither saw them, nor knew them. All these things joined to the inclination I had all my life to pass it in retreat, determined me to write to the Mother Prioress of the Benedictines of Montargis, that I wished to end my days with her, unknown to everybody, without seeing there even any nun but her; and without the outside world, or my family, or any one in the world knowing anything of it. We had agreed upon the matter, and I was to be given a small apartment, where there was a closet with a lattice opening over the altar, and a little garden at the foot. It was what I wanted. The confessor was to be trusted, and I would have communicated in the morning by a little lattice on the days I should have made my devotions. This project made and accepted, I sent my furniture in advance; but as the Mother Prioress spoke of it to her Archbishop, he did not keep the secret. My friends and my enemies, if so one may call persons to whom one wishes no ill, opposed my project with very different views: the former, not to lose me altogether; and the latter, in order to ruin me, and not allow their prey to escape. They considered that a life such as I wished to lead would give the lie to all the calumnies they had hitherto invented, and take from them all means of persecuting me more. I saw myself, then, obliged by both, who prayed the Archbishop to forbid my being received, to live in the world, in spite of my aversion for the world; and to be still the mark for the contradiction of men, the object of their calumnies, the plaything of Divine Providence. I then knew God was not content with the little I had suffered, and that he was about to raise against me strange hurricanes: but as it is almost impossible for me not to desire all that God desires, I submitted cheerfully, and I made him an entire sacrifice of myself; too happy to pay by such slight pains what I owed to his justice, and too honored by being in some sort conformed to the image of his Son.

It may be thought strange that I say I made a sacrifice to God, after having in so many places noticed that I no longer found a will in me, or repugnance for anything that God would desire. Yet it is certain when God wishes to charge the soul with new crosses, different from those she has had, and to make her bear heavier ones, however conformed she may be to the will of God, yet, as he respects the freewill he himself has given man, he still obtains her consent, which never fails to be given.

Some time before the marriage of my daughter, I had become acquainted with the Abbé F——, as I have already said, and the family into which she had entered being among his friends, I had the opportunity of seeing him there many times. We had some conversations on the subject of the inner life, in which he offered many objections to me. I answered him with my usual simplicity, and I had reason to believe he had been satisfied. As the affairs of Molinos were making great noise at that time, people had conceived distrust on the most simple things, and on terms the most common with those who have written on these matters. That gave me opportunity to thoroughly explain to him my experiences. The difficulties he offered only served to make clear to him the root of my sentiments; therefore no one has been better able to understand them than he. This it is which, in the sequel, has served for the foundation of the persecution raised against him.

Having left my daughter, I took a small secluded house, to follow there the disposition I had for retreat. I confined myself to seeing my family, who hardly inconvenienced me, and a small number of friends, whom I saw there only at long intervals—the greater part not ordinarily residing at Paris. Since my release from St. Mary's, I had continued to go to St. Cyr, and some of the girls of that House having declared to Madame de Maintenon that in the conversations I had with them they found something which led them to God, she permitted them to put confidence in me; and on many occasions she testified, owing to the change of some with whom hitherto she had not been satisfied, that she had no cause for repenting it.

She then showed me much kindness, and, during three or four years that this lasted, I received from her every mark of esteem and confidence; but it is this very thing in the sequel which has drawn down upon me the greatest persecution. The *entrée* Madame de Maintenon gave me at St. Cyr, and the confidence shown me by some young ladies of the court, distinguished by their rank and by their piety, began to cause uneasiness to the persons who had persecuted me. They stirred-up the directors, to take offence, and, under the pretense of the troubles I had had some years before, and of the great progress, as they said, of Quietism, they engaged the Bishop of Chartres, Superior of St. Cyr, to represent to Madame de Maintenon that I disturbed the order of her House by a private Direction; and that the girls whom I saw were so strongly attached to what I said to them, that they no longer listened to their Superiors. Madame de Maintenon caused me to be told in a kindly way. I ceased to go to St. Cyr. I no longer answered the girls who wrote to me, except by open letters, which passed through the hands of Madame de Maintenon.

A person of my acquaintance, a particular friend of Monsieur Nicole, had heard him often declaim against me, without knowing me; and he thought it would be easy to make him get over his prejudice if I could have some interviews with him, and by this means to disabuse many persons with whom he had relations, and who declared themselves in the most open manner hostile to me. That person urged me strongly to it, and, notwithstanding the repugnance I at first felt, certain of my friends, to whom I made known the urgency employed with me for this purpose, advised me to see him. As his ailments did not permit him to go out, I promised, after some civilities on his part, to pay him a visit. He at once referred to the "Short Method," and told me that little book was full of errors. I proposed to him we should read it together, and begged him to kindly tell me those which struck him, and that I hoped to remove his difficulties. He told me he was quite willing, and commenced to read the little book, chapter by chapter, with much attention; and when I asked him if there was nothing in what we had just read which struck him, or caused him trouble, he answered, "No; that what he was looking for was further on." We went through the book, from one end to the other, without his finding anything that struck him. Oftentimes he said to me, "Here are the most beautiful comparisons possible." At last, having long sought the errors he thought he had seen in it, he said to me, "Madame, my talent is to write, and not to hold such discussions, but if you will see one of my friends, he will state his difficulties to you, and you will perhaps be very glad to profit by his light; he is very clever, and a very good man. You will not be sorry to make his acquaintance, and he understands all this better than I. It is Monsieur Boileau, of the Hotel Luines." I excused myself for some time, to avoid controversies, which did not suit me, not pretending to defend the little book, and letting it pass for what it was worth. But he pressed me so strongly, I could not refuse him. Monsieur Nicole proposed to me to take a house near him, and to go to confession to Father de la Tour, and spoke to me as if he had much wished me to be of his friends, and connected with his party. I answered all his proposals as civilly as possible; but I let him know that the little property I had kept for myself did not allow me to hire the house he proposed; that, wishing to live in a perfect retreat, the distance of that I occupied put it beyond my power to see there much society, which was in accordance with my inclination; and that, not having a carriage, the same distance offered an obstacle to the proposal he made me of going to confession to Father de la Tour, because he lived at one end of Paris, and I at the other. We parted none the less good friends, and I knew he greatly praised me to some persons to whom he had spoken of my visit.

A few days after, I saw M. Boileau, as he had wished it. He spoke to me of the "Short Method." I repeated to him what I have so often said, of the disposition in which I had composed that little book, and of that in which I still was regarding it. He told me he was truly persuaded of the sincerity of my intentions, but that this little book, being in the hands of a great many people, might injure many pious souls, through the mischievous consequences that might be deduced from it. I begged him to be so kind as to tell me the passages which caused him trouble, and I said I hoped to remove his difficulties. We read the little book, and while reading he told me the difficulties he found. I explained the matter to him, so that he appeared to be satisfied; after which he no longer insisted. Thus we went through the whole book—he insisting more or less on the passages that stopped him, and I explaining to him simply my thoughts and my experience, without disputing on matters of doctrine, in which I relied on him entirely, as more capable than I of deciding.

This discussion finished, he said to me, "Madame, there would have been no difficulty with regard to this little book, if you had explained things somewhat more fully, and it might be very good if you explain in a preface that which is not clear in the book;" and he urged me strongly to work at it. I answered him, that never having had the intention of making public this little book (which was properly only a private instruction I had written at the entreaty of one of my friends, who had asked it from me, in consequence of some conversations we had had together on the matter), I had not been able to foresee either that it would be printed, or that the meanings he had just explained to me could be put upon it; but that I would always be ready to give the explanations that should be desired, in order to remove objections that might be taken to it. He greatly praised me, and made me promise that I would explain, in a sort of preface, the difficulties he had proposed, after which, he assured me, the book might be good and useful. I did this some days afterwards, and sent him an explanation, with which he appeared very well satisfied. I saw him again, once or twice, and he urged me to have the little book reprinted with this preface. I represented to him, that this little book had furnished the pretext for the persecution and troubles I had been exposed to; that it was not suitable for me to put myself forward as the author; that I did not think I ought to contribute to the printing of this any more than of the former; but the strongest reason I had, was the promise I had given the Archbishop not to write any more on this subject. He approved my resolution, and we separated very well satisfied with one another.

I fell ill some time after, and as the nature of my ailment was little understood by the doctors, they prescribed the waters of Bourbon, after having in vain tried to cure me by ordinary remedies. It was a very strong poison, which had been given me: a servant had been gained over for the purpose. Immediately after he gave it, I suffered such violent pains that, without prompt help, I should have died in a few hours. The lackey at once disappeared, and has not since been seen. That he had been instigated to do it, many circumstances proved.

While I was at Bourbon, the water I threw up burned like spirits of wine. As I take no care of myself I should not have thought I had been poisoned, if the Bourbon doctors, after throwing the water on the fire, had not assured me of it. The mineral waters gave me little benefit, and I still suffered for seven years and a half. Since then people have three or four times tried to poison me. God preserved me through his goodness, and by the presentiments he gave me of it. This illness and the journey to Bourbon caused me to lose sight of M. Nicole, of whom I no longer heard mention, except that, about seven or eight months afterwards, I learned he had composed a book against me on the subject of that little book we had read together, with which both he and his friend had appeared satisfied by the explanations I had given them: I believe his intentions were good; but one of my friends, who read that book, told me that the quotations were not exact, and that he had little understanding of the subject on which he had written. Shortly afterwards, I learned that Dom Francis L'Ami, a Benedictine of merit, well known, with whom I was not acquainted, a friend of M. Nicole, struck by the little solidity in his book, had undertaken to refute it, and, without having any knowledge of the "Short Method," in order to justify it from M. Nicole's imputations, he made use only of passages from his own book and what he quoted: he himself not having the little book. He has not printed that refutation; but it is still in existence, being in the hands of one of his friends. I let everything pass without thinking of justifying myself.

CHAPTER XII

THE directors of St. Cyr having succeeded in what they wished, and I no longer going there, the matter made some noise. I adopted the plan of seeing nobody, expecting this would put an end to the talk. Thus the love of retirement, together with the desire I had to deprive those who hated me so gratuitously, of the opportunity of attacking me anew, made me go and spend some days in the country, in a house nobody knew; and after having let my family, my friends, and those who persecuted me believe that I would no more come back to Paris, I returned to my house, where I saw none of them for the rest of the time I remained there. M. Fouquet, uncle to my son-in-law, was the only person who knew where I was. I needed some one to receive the little income I had reserved for myself, when parting with my property, and also an upright witness who knew how I was living in my solitude. They no longer then saw me: I was, it seemed, beyond reach. But who can avoid the malice of men when God wills to use it to make us enter into his eternal designs of crosses and ignominy?

The course I had adopted ought, it would seem, to have put an end to the murmurs, and calmed the minds: but quite the opposite happened. My retirement, then, did not produce the effect that had been expected. It was suggested that from a distance I was spreading the poison of Quietism, as I had done near at hand; and, to give countenance to the calumny, they stirred up a number of pretended "devotees," who went from confessor to confessor, accusing themselves of crimes which they said were due to my principles. There were those I had tried to save from their irregularities, to whom, some years before, I had forbidden my house, after having failed in my endeavors.

Before I had entirely secluded myself, a very extraordinary thing happened. M. Fouquet had a valet, very well educated and a very worthy man, and a girl who lived in the house became madly in love with him. I do not tell here anything which numbers of persons of honor and probity have not learned from M. Fouquet himself. She declared her passion to that man, who was horrified. One day she said to him, "Wretch; I have given myself to the Devil that you might love me, and you do not love me." He was so frightened at this declaration he went and told his master, and he, after having questioned the girl, who told him horrible things, turned her out. As the valet was well educated, the horror of what that wretched creature had done, led him to become a Father of St. Lazare. M. Fouquet did not neglect that unfortunate. He engaged numbers of persons, suitable alike from their learning and their virtue, to have a care of her. All gave her up, for she was so hardened that they saw no remedy but in a miracle of grace. This valet of M. Fouquet, become a Father of St. Lazare, fell mortally ill. He sent for M. Fouquet, begging him not to let him die without seeing him. He recommended that unfortunate to him, and said, "When I think it is owing to me she has withdrawn herself from Jesus Christ to give herself to the Devil, I am afflicted beyond belief." M. Fouquet promised him again to do what he could. I do not know what moved him to bring the creature to me; but it is certain that it was to make known, at least for a time, the power of God: and that, as the Devil had not been able to make M. Fouquet's valet consent to sin, so that Spirit of lies has no power over those who are God's, but what God permits him to exercise. M. Fouquet then brought this girl to me, and, on seeing her, without knowing the cause, I had a horror of her. She was not less distressed at being near me; but, nevertheless, God overthrew the Devil. This girl, while with me, often said to me, "You have something strong that I cannot endure," which I attributed to a piece of the true cross I had on my neck. Although I attributed it to the true cross, I nevertheless saw that God operated through me, without me, with his divine power. At last this power obliged her to tell me her frightful life, which makes me tremble as I think of it. She related to me the false pleasures that Spirit of Darkness had procured for her; that he made her pass for a saint in the place where she lived; that he allowed her to perform visible austerities; but that he did not allow her to pray: that, as soon as she wished to do it, she appeared to her under a hideous form, ready to devour her; that in the other case, he appeared to her under a form as amiable as possible, and that he gave her all the money she wished. I said to her, "But amid all these false pleasures he procures for you, have you peace of heart?" She said to me in a terrible tone, "No; I experience a hellish trouble." I answered her, "In order that you may see the happiness there is in serving Jesus Christ, even in the midst of pain, I pray him to make you taste for one moment that peace of heart, which is preferable to all the pleasures of earth." She was immediately introduced into a great peace. Quite transported with this, she said to M. Fouquet, who was present, "Ah, Sir, I am in Paradise, and I was in Hell."

These good moments were not lost; M. Fouquet took her immediately to M. Robert, Grand Penitentiary, to whom she made a general confession and promised amendment. She was well enough for six months; but the Devil enraged, caused, I believe, the death of the Penitentiary, who died suddenly. Father Breton, a Jacobin, who had many times endeavored to rescue her from the abyss into which she had cast herself, also died. I then became very ill, and this creature, who was allowed admittance to me because M. Fouquet begged it, came to see me. She said to me, "I knew that you were very ill. The Devil told me. He said he did all he could to cause your death, but it was not permitted to him; he will none the less cause you such evils and persecutions you will succumb to them." I answered her, there was nothing I was not ready to suffer provided she was thoroughly converted; that she should not listen to the Devil any more, whom I had forbidden her to answer, after having made her renounce him and renew the vows of her baptism. Because he had commenced by making her renounce her baptism and Jesus Christ, I made her do the contrary, and give herself anew to Jesus Christ. She said to me, "You must have great charity to be willing still to contribute to my conversion; for he told me he would do you so much

ill, and stir up so many against you that you would succumb."
At this moment I seemed to see, in the imagination, a blue flame
which formed a hideous face: but I had no fear of it any more
than of the threats he sent me; for God for many years keeps
me in this disposition, that I would cheerfully give my life,
even all the repose of my life, which I value much more, for the
salvation of a single soul. One day that M. Fouquet suspected nothing, a priest came to see him and asked him news of
this creature. As he thought it was a good design brought
him, M. Fouquet told him that they hoped for her entire
conversion, and that they saw much progress towards it. This
priest, or this devil in the form of a priest, asked where she
lodged. He told him, and when M. Fouquet came to see me a
little after, and spoke to me of the priest, it occurred to me it
was that wicked priest of whom she had spoken to me, and
with whom she had committed so many abominations (for she
had told me her life and her crimes), and this proved only too
true. She came no more. The Penitentiary died, as I have said,
and M. Fouquet fell into a languishing illness, that terminated
only with his life; but the girl came no more to see us.

I had been led, as I have mentioned, to see M. Boileau on
the subject of the "Short Method." I had reason to believe he
was satisfied with my conduct, from the things he repeated to
some of my friends, of our conversations; but he was, a little
after, one of my most eager persecutors. An extraordinary
woman, who passed for a very devout person, having placed
herself under his direction, on her arrival in Paris, made him
change his sentiments. He apparently spoke of me to her on
the subject of the visits I had paid him. She assured him I was
wicked, and I would cause great evils to the Church. She
excited then, as she has since done, much attention in Paris.
She was brought to visit people of every character and position,
bishops, magistrates, ecclesiastics, women of rank—in a word,
under pretext of a pretended miraculous ailment, they established her reputation to such a point that they could do
nothing but talk of the extraordinary things that appeared in
her. I could not imagine what this woman could be, nor what
motive led her to speak of me in the manner she did. She
seemed to have fallen from the clouds, for nobody knew who
she was, nor whence she came; and it has always been a

puzzle for all those who have heard her spoken of, except M. Boileau, and perhaps some one in his most intimate confidence. As her name was entirely unknown to me, I did not believe myself any more known to her; but some years after, having learned that she had borne the name of Sister Rose, it was not difficult for me to divine the reasons why she had thus spoken of me. This woman, about whom there was in fact something very extraordinary persuaded M. Boileau, and persons of virtue and probity with whom he was in relation, that the greatest service they could render God was to decry me, and even to imprison me, owing to the ills I was capable of causing. What made her desire I should be imprisoned was the apprehension that I might proclaim what I knew of her. If she still lives, she will see by my silence that, being God's to the degree I am, she had nothing to dread; the history of her life having been confided to me under the pledge of secrecy by herself.

Immediately there was an inconceivable outburst. Had I even known all these details, which only came to my knowledge later, and had I even then known who this woman was, I believe I should have failed in any effort to disabuse minds so prejudiced: I should not have been believed, and perhaps I should not have been willing to say anything against her; because God then kept me in that disposition of sacrifice, of suffering everything, and receiving from his hand all that might happen to me through this person, and those whom she had led away by her pretended extraordinary power. Nevertheless, she stated one circumstance which ought to have changed the opinion of so many good persons, if they had been willing to be enlightened; but the prejudice was such that they would not even examine into the truth, let alone believe it.

This circumstance was, that God had made known to her the excess of my wickedness, and that he had given her as an assured sign of the truth she advanced, that in my writings I had merely copied those of Mademoiselle Vigneron; and that it would be easy to see their correspondence with my books. A person of great consideration, to whom M. Boileau confided this, wished to prove the matter for himself. He went to the Minims and asked them for those writings. They made a great deal of difficulty, assuring him that they had never left their hands. However, not being with civility able to refuse that person, who promised to bring them back in a few days, he examined them himself; but far from seeing in them any relation with what I had written, he found a total difference. In order to disabuse M. Boileau of his prejudice, he proposed to him to satisfy himself with his own eyes, and to read for himself those writings, to see their contrariety. But, in spite of all his urgency on two different occasions, and the deference due from M. Boileau to that illustrious person, he would never do it, assuring him this woman had told him the truth, and that, knowing her as he did, he could not suspect her of the contrary. The truth is, I had never seen those writings of Mademoiselle Vigneron, and I had never heard her name pronounced up to that time.

On which side might deceitfulness be looked for—from a person always submissive and obedient, who so willingly gives up her judgment and her will, who has renounced all for God, who is known for a long time by so many good people, that have followed her in all the ages of her life and offer for her a testimony little open to suspicion: or, from a person unknown, who changes her name in most of the places where she has lived (for there are at least four that have come to my knowledge),—from a person whom devotion elevates from the dust; poor, whom devotion raises and enriches: while mine, if I have any, and God knows it, has only brought me humiliations, the strangest confusions, and universal discredit? O my Lord, it is there I recognize you; and since, to please you, it is necessary to be conformed to you, I value more my humiliation at seeing myself condemned by all the world than if I saw myself at the summit of glory.

This woman persisted always in saying I must be imprisoned, I would ruin everybody. Those whom I have ruined, you know it, Lord, are full of love for you. What made this woman speak in that way was, as I have said, the fear that, if I had seen her, or had known her name, I might have spoken of things she had a great interest in keeping hid. Yet this creature attracted such credit, and stirred up against me such persecutions, that every one had pleasure in inventing new fables against me.

Some ecclesiastics, led away by M. Boileau, or by views and motives which charity does not permit me to speak of, but known to a small number of friends who remained to me, co-operated in all this. There were also some directors vexed because some persons who appeared to have a kindliness for me had left them for Father Alleaume (who was my intimate friend), with which, however, I had nothing to do. However it be, every device was used to decry me, and in order to render what they called my doctrine suspected, they thought it was necessary to decry my morals. They omitted nothing to attain their purpose, and, after having persuaded the Bishop of Chartres of the pretended danger to the Church by endless stories, he set to work to persuade Madame de Maintenon, and those of the Court he knew to be my friends, of the necessity of abandoning me, because I was wicked, and capable of inspiring them with wicked sentiments. Madame de Maintenon held out some time. The part she had taken in my release from St. Mary's, my conversation, my letters, the testimony of those of her friends in whom she had most confidence, made her suspend her judgment. At last she gave way to the reiterated urgency of the Bishop of Chartres and of some others he employed in the direction of St. Cyr. He did not succeed equally with some persons of rank, who, having been many years witnesses of my conduct, knew me for themselves, and were acquainted with the different springs that had been put in motion to ruin me. I owe them the justice to make known that it was no fault of theirs that the authority of the King was not employed to shield me from so much injustice. They drew up a memoir likely to influence him in my favor, giving him an account of the conduct I had observed, and was still observing in my retirement. Madame de Maintenon was to have supported it by her testimony, but, having had the kindness to communicate it to me, I believed God did not wish me to be justified by that channel, and I required of them that they should leave me to the rigors of his justice, whatever they might be. They consented to defer to my request. The memoir already presented was withdrawn, and they adopted the course of silence, which they have since continued, being no longer able to do anything in my favor, owing to the outburst and prejudice.

CHAPTER XIII

SOME of my friends thought it would be advisable for me to see the Bishop of Meaux, who was reported not to be opposed to spiritual religion. I knew that, eight or ten years before, he had read the "Short Method" and the "Canticles," and that he had thought them very good. This made me consent to it with pleasure; but, O my Lord, how have I experienced in my life that everything which is done through consideration and human views, although good, turns into confusion, shame, and suffering! At that time I flattered myself (and I accused myself of my faithlessness) that he would support me against those who were attacking me. But how far was I from knowing him! And how subject to error is that which one does not see in your light, and which you do not yourself disclose!

One of my friends, of the highest rank, the Duke of Chevreuse, brought the Bishop of Meaux to my house. The conversation soon fell upon that which formed the subject of his visit. They spoke of the "Short Method," and this Prelate told me that he had once read it and also the "Canticles," and that he had thought them very good. The Duke gave him the "Torrents," on which he made some remarks: not of things to be condemned, but which needed elucidation. The Duke had the kindness to remain present. This Prelate said to us such strong things on the interior way and the authority of God over the soul, I was surprised. He gave us even examples of persons he had known, whom he deemed saints, that had killed themselves. I confess I was startled by all this talk of the Bishop of Meaux. I knew that in the primitive Church some virgins had caused their own deaths in order to keep themselves pure; but I did not believe, in this age, where there is neither violence nor tyrants, a man could be approved for such an action. The Duke gave him my history of my life, that he might know me thoroughly; which he thought so good, that he wrote to him, saying, "he found in it an unction he found nowhere else; that he had been three days reading it without losing the presence of God." These are, if I remember rightly, the exact words of one of his letters. What will appear astonishing is, that the Bishop of Meaux, who had had such holy dispositions while reading the history of my life, and who valued it while it remained in his hands, saw in it, a year after it had left them, things he had not seen before; which he even retailed, as if in reality I had written them.

The Bishop of Meaux had requested me to observe secrecy as to his visiting me. As I have always inviolably preserved it for my greatest enemies, I was not likely to fail in it for him. The reason he alleged for the secrecy he wished observed is, that he was not on good terms with the Bishop of Paris; but he himself went and told what he had begged me to be silent on. My silence and his talk have been the source of all the trouble I have since suffered.

The Bishop of Meaux, having then accepted the proposal to examine my writings, I caused them to be placed in his hands; not only those printed, but all the commentaries on Holy Scriptures. I had previously given them to M. Charon the Official, by one of my maids; but the fear they should be lost—as, in fact, they were, the Official having never returned them—led that girl to distribute them among a number of copyists, who made the copy that was afterwards given to the Bishop of Meaux. It was a great labor for him, and he required four or five months to have leisure to go to the bottom of everything, which with much exactitude he did in his country house, where he had gone to escape interruption. To show the more confidence in him, and lay open the inmost recesses of my heart, I made over to him, as I have said, the history of my life, where my most secret dispositions were noted with much simplicity. On that I asked from him the secrecy of the confessional; he promised an inviolable. He read everything with attention, and, at the end of the time stipulated, was in a position to hear my explanations and offer his objections.

It was at the commencement of the year 1694: he wished to

see me at the house of one of his friends, who lived near the Daughters of the Holy Sacrament. He said the Mass in that Community, and gave me there the Communion: afterwards he dined. This conference, that according to him was to be so secret, was known to all the world. Many persons sent to beg him to go to the convent of the Daughters of the Holy Sacrament, that they might speak to him. He went there, and they took care to prejudice him; as he appeared to be so when in the evening he returned and spoke to me. He was not the same man. He had brought all his extracts and a memoir, containing more than twenty articles, to which all his objections were reduced. God assisted me, so that I satisfied him on everything that had relation to the dogma of the Church and the purity of doctrine. But there were some passages on which I could not satisfy him. As he spoke with extreme vivacity, and hardly gave me time to explain my thoughts, it was not possible for me to make him change upon some of those articles, as I had done upon others. We separated very late, and I left that conference with a head so exhausted, and in such a state of prostration, I was ill from it for several days. I wrote to him, however, several letters, in which I explained, the best I could, those difficulties that had arrested him; and I received one from him of more than twenty pages, from which it appeared that he was only arrested by the novelty to him of the subject and the slight acquaintance he had with the interior ways; of which one can hardly judge except by experience.

I explained the nature of the inner life. When a sheet of water is on a different level from another which discharges into it, this takes place with a rapid movement and a perceptible noise; but when the two waters are on a level the inclination is no longer perceived: there is one, however, but it is imperceptible; so that it is true to say, in one sense, that there is none. As long as the soul is not entirely united to her God by a union which I call permanent, to distinguish it from transitory unions, she feels her inclination for God. The impetuosity of this inclination, far from being a perfect thing, as unenlightened persons think it, is a defect and marks the distance between God and the soul. But when God has united the soul to himself, so that he has received her into him, "where he holds her, hidden with Jesus Christ," the soul finds a repose which excludes all sensible inclination, and which is such that experience alone can make it understood. It is not a repose in peace tasted, in the sweetness and mildness of a perceived presence of God; but it is a repose in God himself which participates of his immensity, so much has it of vastness, simplicity, and purity. The light of the sun which should be limited by mirrors would have something more dazzling than the pure light of the air; yet those same mirrors which enhance its brilliance, limit it, and deprive it of its purity. The more things are simple and pure, the more vastness they have. Nothing more simple than water, nothing more pure; but this water has a wonderful extent, owing to its fluidity. It has also a quality, that having no quality of its own, it takes all sorts of impressions. It has no taste; it takes all tastes. It has no color, and it takes all colors. The intellect and the will in this state are so pure and so simple that God gives them such a color and such a taste as pleases him; like the water which is sometimes red, sometimes blue, in short impressed with any color, or any taste, one wishes to give it. It is certain, though one gives to the water the diverse colors one pleases in virtue of its simplicity and purity, it is not, however, correct to say that the water in itself has taste and color, since it is in its nature without taste and without color, and it is this absence of taste and color that renders it susceptible of every taste and every color. It is this I experience in my soul. She has nothing she can distinguish or know in her, or as belonging to her, and it is this which constitutes her purity: but she has everything that is given to her, and as it is given to her, without retaining anything thereof for herself. If you ask the water what is its quality, it would answer you that it is to have none. You would say to it, "But I have seen you red." "Very likely, but I am not, however, red. It is not my nature. I do not even think of what they do to me, of all the tastes and all the colors they give me." It is the same with the form as with the color. As the water is fluid, and without consistence, it takes all the forms of the places where it is put—of a vessel either round or square. If it had a consistence of its own it could not take all forms, all tastes, all odors, and all colors.

Souls are good for but little as long as they preserve their own consistence; all the design of God being to make them lose by the death of themselves all that they have of the "own" in order to act, to move, to change and to impress them, as it pleases him: so that it is true they have none. And this is the reason that, feeling only their simple nature, pure and without specific impression, when they speak or write of themselves, they deny all forms being in them, not speaking according to the variable dispositions in which they are put. They pay no attention to these, but to the root of that which they are, which is their state always subsisting. If one could show the soul like the face I would not, methinks, conceal any of her spots—I submit the whole. I believe, further, what causes the soul to be unable to desire anything is, that God fills her capacity. I shall be told the same is said of heaven. There is this difference, that in heaven not only the capacity of the soul is filled, but, further, that capacity is fixed, and can no longer increase. In this life, when by his goodness God has purified a soul, he fills this capacity: this it is which causes a certain satiety, but, at the same time, he enlarges and augments the capacity; while enlarging it, he purifies it; and it is this causes the suffering and the interior purification. 'n this suffering and purification life is painful: the body is ; burden. In the plenitude nothing is wanting to the soul, she can desire nothing. A second reason why the soul can desire nothing is, that the soul is, as it were, absorbed in God, in a sea of love; so that, forgetting herself, she can only think of her love. All care of herself is a burden to her: an Object which far exceeds her capacity absorbs her and hinders her from turning towards self. We must say of these souls what is said of the children of Wisdom: "It is a nation which is only obedience and love." The soul is incapable of other reason, other view, other thought, than love and obedience. It is not that one condemns the other states, by no means; and thereon I explained myself to the Bishop of Meaux in a manner that ought not, I think, to leave him any doubt thereon.

CHAPTER XIV

I HAVE another defect, which is that I say things as they occur to me, without knowing whether I speak well or ill: while I am saying or writing them, they appear to me clear as day: after that, I see them as things I have never known, far from having written them. Nothing remains in my mind but a void, which is not troublesome. It is a simple void, which is not inconvenienced by the multitude of thoughts or by their dearth. This caused one of my greatest troubles in speaking to the Bishop of Meaux. He ordered me to justify my books. I excused myself as much as I could; because, having submitted them with my whole heart, I did not desire to justify them; but he insisted on it. I first of all protested I only did it through obedience, condemning most sincerely all that was condemned in them. I have always held this language, which was more that of my heart than of my mouth. He still wished me to render a reason for an infinity of things I had put in my writings, which were entirely new and unknown to me. I remember, among others, a passage regarding Eliud—that man who speaks so long to Job, when his friends had ceased speaking to him. I never knew what I had intended to say. The Bishop of Meaux insisted, I said, that all this Eliud says in that long discourse was by the Spirit of God. This did not appear to me that long discourse was by the Spirit of God. This did not appear to me so: on the contrary, one sees an astonishing fulness of himself. I will here say, in passing, that if one will give some attention to the rapidity with which God has made me write of so many things, far above my natural grasp, it is easy to conceive that, having had so small a part in it, it is very difficult, not to say impossible, for me, to render a reason for them in dogmatic style. This it is which has always led me to say, I took no part in them, and, having written only through obedience, I was as content to see everything burned as to see it praised and esteemed. There were also faults of the copyists, which rendered the sense unintelligible, and the Bishop of Meaux wanted to make me responsible for the errors, which he insisted were there: and he overwhelmed me by the vivacity of his arguments, which always reduced themselves to belief in the dogma of the Church, that I did not pretend to dispute with him; whereas he might have discussed quietly the experiences of a person, submissive to the Church, who asked only to be set right, if they were not conformable to the rules she prescribes; which was precisely the thing contemplated when this examination was undertaken.

The objections he made to me sprung, I believe, only from the small knowledge he had of mystic authors, whom he confessed to have never read, and the small experience he had of the interior ways. He had been struck on some occasions by extraordinary things he had seen in certain persons, or that he had read, which made him judge God had special routes by which he made them attain to a great holiness: but this way of simple faith, small, obscure, which produces in souls, according to the designs of God, that variety of special leadings where he leads them in himself, it was a jargon that he regarded as the effect of a crazy imagination, and the terms of which were to him equally unknown and intolerable.

The Bishop of Meaux raised great objections to what I had said, in my Life, of the Apostolic state. What I have meant to say is, that persons, who, by their state and conditions (as, for instance, laics and women) are not called upon to aid souls, ought not to intrude into it of themselves: but when God wished to make use of them by his authority, it was necessary they should be put into the state of which I have written. What had given occasion for it is, that numbers of good souls who feel the firstfruits of the unction of grace—that unction of which St. John speaks, which teaches all truth,—when, I say, they commence to feel this unction, they are so charmed with it, that they would wish to share their grace with all the world. But as they are not yet in the source, and this unction is given them for themselves and not for others, in spreading themselves abroad they gradually lose the sacred oil, as the foolish virgins, while the wise ones preserved their oil for themselves, until they were introduced into the chamber of the Bridegroom; then they may give of their oil, because the Lamb is the lamp who illumines them. That this state is possible, we have only to open the histories of all times to show, that God has made use of laics and women without learning to instruct, edify, conduct, and bring souls to a very high perfection. I believe one of the reasons why God has willed to make use of them in this way, is in order that the glory should not be stolen from him. "He has chosen weak things to confound the strong."

The first time I wrote my Life, it was very short. I had put there in detail my sins, and had only spoken very little of the graces of God. I was made to burn it; and I was commanded absolutely to omit nothing, and to write, regardless of myself, all that should come to me. I did it. If there is anything too much like pride, I am capable only of what is worthless; but I have thought it was more suitable to obey without self-regard than to disobey and conceal the mercies of God through a humility born of the selfhood. God may have had his designs in this. It is ill to publish the secret of one's King, but it is well done to declare the graces of the Lord our God, and to enhance his bounties by the baseness of the subject on whom he exhibits them. If I have failed, the fire will purify all. I can very well believe I may have been mistaken; but I cannot complain, nor be afflicted at it. When I gave myself to our Lord, it was without reserve and without exception; and as I have written only through obedience, I am as content to write extravagances as good things. My consolation is, God is neither less great, nor less perfect, nor less happy for all my errors. When things are once written down, nothing remains in my head. I have no idea of them. When I am able to reflect, it appears to me I am below all creatures, and a veritable nothing.

The Bishop of Meaux insisted on saying I stifled distinct acts, as believing them imperfect. I have never done so; and when I have been interiorly placed in a powerlessness to do them, and my powers were as though bound, I defended myself with all my strength, and only through weakness did I yield to the strong and powerful God. It seems to me that even this powerlessness to do conscious acts did not deprive me of the reality of the act; on the contrary, I found my faith, my confidence, my self-surrender were never more living, nor my love more ardent. This made me understand that there was a kind of act direct and without reflection; and I knew it by a continued exercise of love and faith, which, rendering the soul submissive to all the events of providence, leads her to a veritable hatred of self and a love of only crosses, ignominy, and disgrace. It is true her confidence is full of repose, free from anxiety and inquietude; she can do nothing but love and repose in her love. I am so far from wishing to stifle distinct acts, as being imperfect, that if any one will take the trouble to read my writings, he will remark in many places expressions which are very distinct acts. It would be easy to show that they then flow from the source, and the reason why one, at that time, expresses his love, his faith, his self-surrender, in a very distinct manner; that one does the same in hymns or spiritual songs, and that one cannot do it in prayer unless God impels.

CHAPTER XV

WHEN this conference was finished, I thought only of retirement, following the advice of the Bishop of Meaux; I mean to say, no longer to see any one, as I had already commenced doing for a considerable time. I wrote some letters to the Bishop of Meaux, wherein I tried to explain to him the things he had not allowed me leisure to do in the conference. I addressed them to the Duke, through whom all had passed, and he had the kindness to send me the answers. The vivacity of the Bishop of Meaux, and the harsh terms he sometimes employed, had persuaded me he regarded me as a person deceived and under illusion. From this standpoint I wrote to the Duke, who showed him my letter, in which I thanked him also for all the trouble he had taken. The Bishop of Meaux answered him, that the difficulties, on which he had insisted and some on which he still insisted, neither touched the faith nor the doctrine of the Church. That he thought differently, in truth, from me on those articles, but that he did not believe me the less Catholic; and if, for my consolation and that of my friends, I wished an attestation of his sentiments, he was ready to give me a certificate stating that, after having examined me, he had not found in me anything but what was Catholic, and, in consequence, he had administered to me the sacraments of the Church. The Duke had the kindness to communicate this to me: but I thanked him, and begged him to say that, having wished to see him only for my personal instruction, and for the sake of a small number of friends, who might have been disquieted at all the fracas that had been made, the testimony he had the kindness to render to them and to me also was sufficient for me; that I would do what I could to conform myself to the things he had prescribed for me; but that the sincerity I professed did not allow me to conceal from him that there were some on which I was not able to obey him, however sincerely desirous and whatever effort I made to enter upon that practice. After which I broke all communication with both parties, assuring them nevertheless that, as often as there should be a question of rendering reason for my faith, I would return at the first signal that should be given me through the person who was charged with my temporal concerns.

M. Fouquet was the only person to whom I confided the place of my retirement. He told me, at the end of several months, that the change of Madame de Maintenon towards me having become public, those who already had so much persecuted me kept no longer any measure: there was a horrible outburst, and they retailed stories in which they attacked my morals in a very unworthy manner. This made me take the step of writing to Madame de Maintenon a letter which ought, methinks, to have dissipated her prejudice, or at least, put her as well as the public in a position to know the truth. I wrote her that, as long as they had only accused me of praying, and teaching others to do so, I had contented myself with remaining concealed:—that I had believed, by neither speaking, nor writing to any one, I should satisfy everybody, and I should calm the zeal of certain upright persons; who were troubled only because of the calumny:—that I had hoped thereby to stop the calumny; but, learning I was accused of things which touched honor, and that they spoke of crimes, I thought it due to the Church, to my family, and to myself that truth should be known:—that I requested from her a justice, which had never been refused even to the most criminal,—it was to have my case investigated; to appoint for me commissioners, half ecclesiastic, half laic, all persons of recognized probity and free from prejudice; for probity alone was not sufficient in an affair where calumny had prejudiced numberless people. I added, that, if they would grant me this favor, I would betake myself to any prison it would please her or the King to indicate; that I would go there with a maid, who was serving me for fourteen years. I further told her, if God made known the truth, she would be able to see I was not altogether unworthy of the kindnesses, with which she had formerly honored me; that if God willed me to succumb under the force of calumny, I would adore his justice, and submit to it with all my heart, demanding even the punishment those crimes merited.

I addressed this letter expressly to the Duke de Beauvilliers, in order to be sure it reached her, begging him to give it himself into her own hand, and to say I would send for the answer at the end of seven or eight days. He had the kindness to give my letter; but Madame de Maintenon answered him, that she had never believed any of the rumors that were circulated as to my morals: that she believed them very good; but it was my doctrine which was bad;—that, in justifying my morals, it was to be feared currency might be given to my sentiments, that it might be in some way to authorize them; and it was better, once for all, to search out what related to doctrine, after which the rest would of itself drop.

M. Fouquet, who had fallen into a languishing disease, died at this time. He was a great servant of God, and a faithful friend, whose loss would have been very much felt by me in my then circumstances, if I had not had more regard to the happiness he was going to enjoy than to the help I found myself deprived of, when so universally abandoned. I used to send every day a maid I had to learn news of him; because I did not go out at all. He sent me word that I should have horrible trials: that there would be great persecutions, such that, if they were not shortened in favor of the elect, no one could resist them; but that God would support me in the midst of affliction. As he was full of faith and love of God, he died with very great joy. It happened to me to write to him, that I believed he would die before the Corpus Christi. This was eight days before it. As he had no fever but the languor of which I have spoken, no one believed it; yet he declared it would be as I told him. One of my maids, by whom I had sent my letter, and who read it to him, returned quite startled: "Madame," she said to me, "what have you done to have written that to M. Fouquet? He is sure to live more than two months; and so people say. Madame de ——, who is there, and others will say you are a false prophetess." I began to laugh, and asked her why she had self-love for me. "I have said what occurred to me at the moment: if God wills that I should have spoken only to receive humiliation, what matters it to me? If I have said the truth, there is only a short time to wait." M. Fouquet gave directions for everything and for his interment, which he wished to be with the poor, and as a poor man. Two days before Corpus Christi, that same maid was sent there by me. She found him in his ordinary state. He told her he would come to say adieu to me when dying; but that he would not cause me any fear. She told him he was not likely to die so soon. He answered her with that faith which was usual to him: "I shall die as she has told me." This maid found Madame ——, and said to her, through a self-love, intolerable to me, "Madame perhaps meant to say the little Corpus Christi." She returned, and told me these same reasons: that M. Fouquet was better, and what she had said to Madame —— I blamed her greatly and asked her, who had made her the interpreter of the will of God. As for M. Fouquet, he never hesitated. When I was in bed at midnight, two days before Corpus Christi there came a light into my room, which glistened on the little gilt nails that were in a place near my bed, with a noise as if all the panes of glass in the house had fallen. The maid who was in bed near my room, went up into that of her companion, thinking all the panes of glass had fallen into the garden: yet there was nothing at all. At the moment, I did not make any reflection on it; and, in the morning, I sent as usual to ask news of M. Fouquet. She found he had died, and learned it was at the same hour as that at which what I have related happened. I had only joy at his death, so certain was I of his happiness: and although I lost the best friend I had in the world, who might be useful to me in the tempest with which I was menaced, joy at the happiness he possessed and at the accomplishment of the will of God, left no place with me for grief.

I learned the circumstances of his death, which were these. His nephew the Abbé de Ch—— used never to leave him. When it was half-past eleven at night, he told him to go and rest, and to return in an hour: that he would find him as it would please God. He had received all his Sacraments, even the Extreme Unction. The Abbé de Ch—— did as he was told, and came back three-quarters of an hour later. He found him dead. He had a face so calm, not altered; he did not grow rigid; there was no bad smell: on the contrary, they could not tire of looking at him. Some days afterwards, I dreamed I saw him as when he was in life. I knew, however, he was dead. I asked him how he fared in the other world. He answered me with a contented countenance: "Those who do the will of God, cannot displease him."

I was extremely touched at the refusal of Madame de Maintenon to assign me commissioners. I knew well they desired to deprive me of the last resource by which I might make known my innocence, and this new examination was only meant to impose upon the public and make the condemnation more authentic. They expected thereby to shut the mouths of those of my friends whom a more violent conduct would have wounded; for, although these said nothing to justify me, their silence in the midst of such universal defaming, and their refusal to condemn me, as did the rest, made it clear enough that they thought differently, and that they suffered in peace what they could not prevent. I took the course of letting God order in the matter, whatever might be pleasing to him; for how could I imagine an offer of that nature would not have put an end to prejudice? I was not ignorant of the persons who opposed themselves to it. They feared lest my innocence should be recognized, and the machinations that had been employed to tarnish it. Some even feared being accused; but, thanks to God, I have never had any desire to accuse any of my persecutors: my views are not fixed so low. There is a sovereign hand, which I adore and which I love, that makes use of the malice of the one, and the zeal without knowledge of the others, in order to effect his work by my destruction. I believe, also, God made use thereof to deprive my friends of certain supports, imperfect and too human, which they found in the creature; God wishing they should base all their dependence on him alone.

God has no need of the intervention of any one to effect his work; he builds only upon ruins. We must carefully guard against the temptation of judging the will of God by apparent success; for as we arrange in our heads the probable means by which God desires to be glorified, when he destroys those means, we think he will not be so. God never can be glorified but by his Son, and in that which has most relation to his Son. All other glory is according to man, not according to God.

However, as it was advisable to avoid all intercourse so as not to scandalize anybody,—in order to practise that other verse, "If your eye is a subject of scandal to you tear it out," I determined to withdraw entirely. Before doing so, I communicated to a small number of friends, who remained to me, the resolution I was taking, and that I was bidding them a last farewell. Whether I should die of my then illness (for I had continuous fever for more than forty days, with a severe accession twice a day,) or whether I should recover of it, I was equally dead for them: that I prayed God to finish in them the work he had commenced: that if this wretched nothing had contributed anything good through his grace, he would know how to preserve what was his: that if I had sown error through my ignorance (which I did not believe, since we had never spoken together, except of renouncing ourselves, carrying our cross, following Jesus Christ, loving him without interest or relation to self) they could judge it was for their sake, not for mine, that I deprived myself of all intercourse with them, who had always edified me and been useful; while

I might have injured them without intending it, and been the occasion of scandal. I prayed them, at the same time, to regard me as a thing forgotten.

CHAPTER XVI

I BEGAN to perceive that others were aimed at in the persecution stirred up against me. The object was far too insignificant for so much movement, so much agitation; but, as those they had in view were beyond reach in themselves, they thought to injure them through the esteem they had for a person so decried, and whom they were endeavoring still to render more odious. I had warned the Abbé F [énélon] long before of the change of Madame de Maintenon towards him, and of that of persons who manifested the greatest confidence in him; but he would not believe me. I had known the artifices that were employed for this purpose, and I had endeavored to put him on his guard against persons who had all his confidence; in order that he should not unnecessarily put himself in their power, and to make him perceive they were acting with less upright-ness than he was willing to believe. He persisted still in the idea he entertained, that I was mistaken, and I waited in peace till God should disabuse him by other ways. The event has since justified my conjectures, and we have seen those same persons attack him without disguise, and enjoy exclu-sively a confidence and a favor he might have preserved had he been less devoted to God and more influenced by those kinds of advantages of which the ordinary run of men are so covetous.

I knew Madame de Maintenon would use my letter as an opportunity for speaking against me; that she did it even from a good motive, in the false persuasion she possibly was under, that, as she had some years previously assisted to save me from oppression, she was bound to exert herself to crush me. What caused me the most trouble was that she judged others by the impression she had against me. All this knowledge made me resolve to remain concealed while awaiting the developments of providence. If I could have been sensible to anything, it would have been to the troubles of the others, and to the ills I might cause them, if I could have regarded them otherwise than in the will of God, in which the greatest ills become blessings. But I am too insignificant to attribute to myself either ill or blessing.

Although I took the resolution to withdraw from all intercourse, I nevertheless made it known that, whenever there should be any question of answering for my faith, I would be ready to betake myself wherever it should be desired. A few days after, I learned that Madame de Maintenon, in concert with some persons of the Court, who were already embarked in this business, who had a kindness for me, and who were interesting themselves in good faith, had adopted the course of causing a fresh examination of my writings, and to employ for this purpose persons of knowledge and recognized probity. The Duke undertook to inform me. He wrote me that he, as well as the others in whom I had most confidence, believed it was the surest way to alter public opinion, and to put an end to the prejudice. It would have been so, in fact, if each one had proceeded therein with the same views and the same intention; but it was a condemnation they wished to make sure of, and to render it so authentic that those, who hitherto had remained persuaded of my good faith and the uprightness of my intentions, should be unable to stand out against a testimony, the less open to suspicion, as they seemed to have sought it themselves, and that everything, so to say, had passed through their hands. I did what they wished, and I sent word I was always ready to render reason for my faith; and that I asked nothing better than to be put right, if contrary to my intention, there had escaped from me anything that was not conformable with sound doctrine.

It only remained, then, to choose the persons who should make the examination. The first person on whom they cast their eyes was the Bishop of Meaux. He had already, to the knowledge of Madame de Maintenon, made a private one, some months before. She wished to see him, to ascertain his sentiments, and the point to which she could count upon him in the design she had. It was not difficult for that Prelate to penetrate her intention and to observe the interest she took in the business, or rather her uneasiness for her friends. There is reason to believe he promised her all she wished, and it may be said the event has only too well justified this. On the other hand, those who were interested for me in this business, and I myself, were very well pleased to see him enter upon it. I had had an opportunity of explaining to him an infinity of things on which he had appeared to me satisfied, although on some others he had persisted in a contrary opinion. I did not doubt that, in a quiet discussion in presence of people of consideration and knowledge, who would be all equally conversant with the subject, I should make him at least change his opinion so far as not to condemn in me what he would not dare to condemn in so many saints canonized by the Church, together with their works. He had, moreover, administered the Sacraments to me during his first rigorous examination, and had offered to give me a certificate of it for my consolation. The things on which we did not agree, not having been decided by the Church, did not offend against the faith. All these considerations led me to ask for him. I also asked for the Bishop of Chalons, who had mildness and piety. I thought he would have more knowledge of the things of the spiritual life and of the interior ways than the Bishop of Meaux, and that my language would be to him less barbarous; for, in fact, it was this was in question rather than the dogma of the Church. Two of my most intimate friends wished that M. Tronson should also enter upon it. He had been for a long time Superior of the House of St. Sulpice. They had both a very special confidence in him.

CHAPTER XVII

I SOON perceived the change in the Bishop of Meaux, and how much I had been deceived in the idea I had formed of him. Although he was very reserved in disclosing his sentiments when he spoke to my friends, he was not the same with persons he believed ill disposed to me. I had confided to him, as I have already said, under the seal of confession, the history of my life, wherein were noted my most secret dispositions; yet I have learned he had shown it and turned it into ridicule. He wished to compel me to show it to these other gentlemen, and insisted so strongly thereon (although it had no connection with the examination in progress), I saw myself obliged to submit to what he wished. I caused it to be given them. I communicated to one of his friends and mine—the Duke de Chevreuse—the alteration in my opinion of the Bishop of Meaux, and how I had reason to believe he was only thinking of condemning me. He had said that, without the history of my life, it could not be done, and that in it one would see the pride of the Devil. It was for this reason he wished it should be seen by those gentlemen.

I begged this friend that the subjects, as they were settled by those persons, should be written out, and, in order to have a sure witness of what would take place there, I most urgently begged him to be present at the conferences. I should have much wished they were not decided till the end, and that, until then, they held their judgment in suspense; not doubting that, as they were all assembled after having prayed God, God would at the moment touch their hearts with his truth independently of their intelligence; for otherwise, as the grace promised to those gathered together for truth escapes and departs, the intellect takes the upper hand, and one judges then only according to the intellect. Moreover, being then no longer sustained by this grace of truth, which has only its moment,—and finding themselves carried away by the clamoring crowd who are supported by credit, authority, and favor,—in listening to them the intellect hinders the heart by the continual doubts it forms. My friend proposed it to these gentlemen. The Bishop of Chalons and M. Tronson would willingly have consented, for they were both acting with all the uprightness and good faith imaginable; but the Bishop of Meaux found means to prevent it. He had so assumed control of the business that it was absolutely necessary everything should bend to what he pleased. He was no longer the same he had been six or seven months before, at the first examination. As at that time he had entered upon it only through a spirit of charity and with a view to know the truth, notwithstanding his extreme vivacity, he altered his opinion on many subjects that his prejudice made him at first reject. He appeared even sometimes touched by certain truths, and to respect things which struck him, although he had not the experience of them. But here it was no longer the same thing, he had a fixed point from which he did not swerve, and, as he wished to produce a striking condemnation, he brought to it everything he thought capable of contributing thereto.

I perceived every day that the Bishop of Meaux was going further and further away, and, what was worst for the cause in question, that he was confirming himself in his thoughts; for this confirmation places an almost insurmountable obstacle to the light of truth. What elucidations had I not given at the time of the first conference on the subject of specific requests, desires, and other acts? But nothing found an entrance, because he wanted to condemn. I learned from the Duke that he still repeated over again those same difficulties.

I further learned that one of the great complaints of the Bishop of Meaux was, that I praised myself and had frightful presumption. I would willingly ask, who is the more humble, he who uses of himself words of humility and says nothing to his advantage (though ordinarily such persons, being praised by others in this matter, would find it hard to bear that people should take them at their word), or he, who simply says of himself the good and the ill, quite unconcerned that all the world may think ill of us and decry us in reality? He who humbles himself, or he who is quite content to be humiliated? As for me, I tell what I know of good in me, because it belongs to my Master; but I am not troubled that nothing of it should be believed, that I should be decried at the sermon, that I should be defamed in the gazette. This does not affect me more than when I praise myself; and, as I do not correct my apparent pride because I have no shame of it, so I do not trouble myself at the public decry, because I think more ill of myself than all the others can do.

The Bishop of Chalons, who had returned, after having taken a holiday, to examine as well the books as the commentaries on scripture, consented to the proposal that was made him, that they should meet at the country house of M. Tronson; because he, being weak and much ailing, could not go to the houses of those gentlemen. I had asked as a favor the Duke should be present as a special friend of those two prelates, through whom everything had passed, very well instructed in the matter in hand, as well as in that which had given rise to this examination. I also asked that, after having examined a difficulty, the decision on it should be written, in order to put the facts beyond question. This appeared to me absolutely necessary, not only for the elucidation of the truth, but in order to have a subsisting proof of what I, as well as the others, had to lay down for myself upon the root of things, and on that which had furnished the matter of the examination. But the Bishop of Meaux, who had promised Madame de Maintenon a condemnation, and who wished to make himself master of the business, raised so many difficulties, sometimes under one pretext, sometimes under another, that he found means of evading all I had asked, and letting nothing appear but what seemed good to him. He said then, I might see M. Tronson separately, after I had seen the Bishop of Chalons with him. The meeting was at the house of the Bishop of Meaux, and the Duke was there, expecting to be present at the conference, as I had asked for him. The Bishop of Chalons arrived early. I spoke to him with much ingenuousness, and as he was not yet filled with the impressions which have since been given to him, I had every ground for being satisfied. I had the consolation of seeing him enter with kindness into what I said.

The Bishop of Meaux, after keeping us a long time waiting, arrived towards evening, and, after a moment of general conversation, he opened a portfolio he had brought, and said to the Duke, that, the question being about doctrine and a matter purely ecclesiastical, the discussion of which only concerned the Bishops, he did not think it suitable that he should remain present, and it might be a constraint on them. It was a pure evasion, in order to avoid a witness of that character, on whom, clever as he was, it would not have been possible for him to impose: for he knew him far too well instructed to allow himself to be surprised, and too upright not to testify the truth as to facts which should have taken place under his eyes. The business was not a decision on faith, the judgment of which belongs to the Bishops, but a quiet discussion of my sentiments, which it was desirable to elucidate in order to see wherein I went too far, and whether my expressions on the matters of the interior life were conformable, or not, to those of the approved mystic authors, as I believed I had not departed from them: for I had protested hundreds of times my submission in what these gentlemen should tell me to be of faith and of the dogma of the Church; on which I no ways pretended to dispute with them. But the Bishop of Meaux pursued his course, and would not for anything deviate from it. I felt in the depth of my heart the refusal of that prelate. I at once knew its consequences, and I no longer doubted the engagements he had undertaken for a condemnation. What more natural than the presence of a person of the character of the Duke, who had the merit, the probity, and the depth of knowledge that every one knows, through whom everything had passed, and who was so much interested in the elucidation on hand, in order to undeceive himself and the others, supposing me mistaken, and that I had, contrary to my intentions, inspired sentiments opposed to the purity of the faith? What, I say, more natural than to have a witness of this character, who would have only served to confound me, if I had spoken differently from what he had heard me say at all times; or who might have disabused himself and disabused the others, in a quiet conference where I might have been shown my errors? It was even the end they had in view when they had commenced to speak of this business: but God did not permit it, and the Duke did not deem it proper to insist, seeing the Bishop of Chalons answered nothing: besides this, he only acted through kindness and yielding to my great desire. I remained, then, alone with these two gentlemen.

The Bishop of Meaux spoke a long time to prove all ordinary Christians had the same grace. I endeavored to prove the contrary; but as the business properly was only to justify my expressions on things of more consequence, I did not insist thereon, and only thought of making him see the conformity of my sentiments with those of the approved authors who have written on the interior life. He still reiterated that one gave to that life too perfect a state, and endeavored to obscure and make nonsense of all I said; particularly when he saw the Bishop of Chalons touched, penetrated, and entering into what I was saying to him. There was no use in disputing, but to submit, and to be ready to believe and act conformably to what they should say. It has always been the true disposition of my heart, and I have no trouble in giving up my own judgment.

I had previously written a letter to the Bishop of Meaux with my ordinary simplicity, in which I told him that I would be no way distressed to believe I had been mistaken. He produced it with a malignant turn, as an avowal I had made of having been mistaken in matter of faith; and that, recognizing my errors after he had made me know them, I had declared, as if in scorn, I was no way concerned at it: and it was in the same spirit I had said, in the same letter or in another, that I was as content at writing absurdities as good things; not at all taking into account the obedience in which I wrote, and how I expected my director, who had to judge it, would correct all, and thus my mistakes would serve to make known the unworthiness of the channel which God had pleased to make use of. The Bishop of Meaux made a crime out of a letter so full of littleness and written with so much simplicity. He reproached me numbers of times with my ignorance, that I did not know anything: and, after having made nonsense out of

all my words, he kept incessantly crying out, he was astonished at my ignorance. I answered nothing to these reproaches:
and the ignorance, of which he accused me, ought to make him
see at least that I speak the truth, when I assert it is by an
actual light I write, nothing otherwise remaining in my mind.
He made another crime of what I have said—that to adhere to
God is a commencement of union; and he continually reverted
to his attempt to prove to me, that all Christians with ordinary
faith, without spiritual life, can arrive at deification. But it is
impossible to answer a man who knocks you down, who does
not listen to you, and who incessantly crushes you. As for
me, I lose then the thread of what I wish to say, and remember
nothing.

That conference was of no use for the root of the matters.
It only put the Bishop of Meaux in a position to tell Madame
de Maintenon that he had made the proposed examination,
and that, having convinced me of my errors, he hoped with
time to make me alter my opinion, by engaging me to go and
spend some time in a convent of Meaux, where he would be
able to finish more tranquilly what he had, as it were, sketched
out. As for me, when they spoke to me of being examined by
these gentlemen, I rejoiced at it, because I believed, according to all ordinary usage, they would all three together see
me: and, as a consequence, Jesus Christ would preside there.
I hoped thereby to win my cause: because I did not doubt the
Lord would make them know the truth, my innocence, and the
malice of my accusers. But God, who apparently willed I
should suffer all that has since happened to me, did not permit
it to be thus. He gave power to the Devil to act, to hinder
the union of those three gentlemen, and to introduce disorder
in everything.

As the Bishop of Meaux had come only at night, I had had
previously full opportunity of conversing for a long time with
the Bishop of Chalons, in presence of the Duke. That prelate
appeared very well satisfied with me, and even said to me I
had only to continue my manner of prayer, and he prayed
God to augment more and more his graces to me. In the
outbursts of the Bishop of Meaux he softened the blows as
much as he could, and made me see, on this occasion, that,
when he acted of himself, he did it with all the kindness and

equity possible. All he could do was to write down some answers I made, addressing myself to him, because the Bishop of Meaux, in the heat of his prejudice, abused me without being willing to listen to me.

I wished to see this prelate once again. I saw him alone, and although he had been already prejudiced, he appeared satisfied with the conference, and repeated to me, that he saw nothing to change either in my manner of prayer or the rest: that I should continue: that he would pray God to augment his mercies upon me, and that I should remain concealed in my solitude, as I had been doing for two years. I promised him. It was deemed proper I should go and see M. Tronson. I went to Issi. The Duke had the kindness to be present. M. Tronson examined me with more exactness than the others. The Duke had the kindness himself to write the questions and the answers. I spoke to him with all the freedom possible. The Duke said to him, "You see she is straightforward." He answered, "I feel it indeed." That word was worthy of so great a servant of God as he was, who judged not only by the intellect but by the taste of the heart. I withdrew then, and M. Tronson appeared satisfied, although a false letter against me had been sent to him, which purported to come from a person who denied it.

CHAPTER XVIII

WHO would not have thought, after all these examinations, apparently satisfactory, that I should have been left in peace? Quite the contrary happened; because, the more my innocence appeared, the more those who had undertaken to make me criminal, set in motion springs to reach their end. Things were on this footing when the Bishop of Meaux, to whom I had offered to go and spend some time in a Community of his diocese, that he might know me of himself, proposed to me "The Daughters of St. Mary," of Meaux. This offer had pleased him immensely; for he expected, as I have since learned, to draw from it great temporal advantages. He believed them even still greater; and he said to Mother Picard, Superior of the convent where I entered, that it would be worth the Archbishopric of Paris or a Cardinal's hat to him. I answered the Mother, when she told it to me, that God would not permit him to have either the one or the other. I set out as soon as he told me. It was the month of January, 1695, in the most frightful winter there has been for a long time, either before or since. I was near perishing in the snow, where I remained four hours; the carriage having got into it, and being almost covered in a hollow way. I and my maid were drawn out through the window. We sat upon the snow, awaiting the mercy of God, expecting only death. I have never had more tranquillity, although benumbed and wetted with the snow we melted. These are the occasions that show if one is perfectly abandoned to God. That poor girl and I were without inquietude, in perfect resignation, certain of dying if we passed the night, and seeing no prospect of help. We were there when some carters passed, and they extricated us with difficulty. It was ten at night when we arrived. We were not expected; and when the Bishop of Meaux first learned it, he was astonished, and very pleased that I had thus risked my life to obey him punctually. I had an illness of six weeks, a continued fever.

But that which had at first appeared so good to the Bishop of Meaux, afterwards only seemed "artifice" and "hypocrisy." It is thus they described, and still describe, the little good God makes me do; and far from believing the gospel, which assures us that a tree cannot be bad whose fruits are good, as they will have it that the tree is bad, they attribute the good to a malicious and hypocritical artifice. It is a strange hypocrisy that lasts a whole life, and which, far from bringing us any advantage, causes only crosses, calumnies, troubles and confusions, poverty, discomfort, and all sorts of ills. I think one has never seen the like; for ordinarily one is only a hypocrite to attract the esteem of men, or to make one's fortune. I am assuredly a bad hypocrite, and I have badly learned the trade, since I have so ill succeeded. I take my God to witness, who knows that I do not lie, that if to be Empress of all the earth and to be canonized during my life, which is the ambition of hypocrites, I had to suffer what I have suffered for wishing to be my God's without reserve, I would have rather chosen to beg my bread and die as a criminal. These are my sentiments without disguise. Therefore I bear this testimony to myself in the presence of my God: that I have desired to please but him alone; that I have sought only him for himself; that I abhor my own interest more than death; that this long series of persecutions which is not finished, and which to all appearance will last as long as my life, has never made me change my sentiments, nor repent of having given myself to God and having abandoned all for him. I have found myself at times when nature was fearfully overburdened; but the love of God and his grace have rendered sweet for me, without sweetness, the most bitter bitterness.

I entered the convent in the state I was in. I waited more than an hour in the porter's lodge, benumbed and without fire, because it was necessary to inform the Bishop of Meaux, and to rouse up the nuns. There was in their lodge a good-natured man, who, as I have since learned, was a man of prayer: he said quite aloud, "That lady must indeed belong to God, and be spiritual, to wait in the state she is in with so much tranquillity." By this remark he impressed some sort of esteem for me upon persons who had been strongly set against me. The Bishop of Meaux wished me to change my name, that, as he said, it should not be known I was in his diocese, and that people should not torment him on my account. The project was the finest in the world, if he could have kept a secret; but he told every one he saw, I was in such a convent, under such a name. Immediately, from all sides, anonymous libels against me were sent to the Mother Superior and the nuns. This did not prevent Mother Picard and the nuns from esteeming and loving me. I had come to Meaux in order that the Bishop should examine me, as he told everybody; and yet he set off for Paris the day after my arrival, and did not return till Easter. He ordered I should communicate as often as the nuns, and even oftener if I wished it; but I did not care to do so, conforming as much as possible to the Community.

It happened, meantime, that those who persecuted me circulated a letter that they said was from the Bishop of Grenoble, in which it was stated, he had driven me from his diocese; that I had been convicted, in the presence of Father Richebrac, then Prior of the Benedictines of St. Robert of Grenoble, of horrible things, although I had letters from the Bishop of Grenoble since my return, which proved quite the contrary, and which showed the esteem he had for me.

The Bishop of Grenoble wrote, at the same time to the Civil Lieutenant, that he sent in the letter he did me the honor to write me:—

I could not refuse to the virtue and the piety of Madame de la Mothe Guyon the recommendation she asks to you, Sir, in favor of her family, in a business which is before you. I should have some scruples if I did not know the uprightness of her intentions and your integrity: therefore permit me to solicit you to do her all the justice which is due to her. I ask it with all the cordiality with which I am yours,

CARDINAL CAMUS.

Grenoble, Jan. 25, 1688.

Here is the letter he wrote me:

MADAME,

I should wish to have, more often than I have, opportunities of letting you know how dear to me are your interests, temporal and spiritual. I bless God that you have approved the counsels I have given you for these latter. I omit nothing to engage the Civil Lieutenant to render you the justice which is due to you for the former. Praying you to believe you will always find me disposed to prove to you by everything that I am truly, Madame,

Your Affectionate servant,

CARDINAL CAMUS.

Grenoble, January 28, 1688.

Yet nothing contributed more to the general defaming than

that other pretended letter of the Bishop of Grenoble. For how contradict a testimony such as that of the Curé of St. James, so well known at that time by his connection with a great number of persons of merit, to whom he had given a copy of that letter, so that in fifteen days' time all Paris was full of it! The Bishop of Meaux, who had a copy like the rest, was strangely surprised at the letters of the Bishop of Grenoble, which I let him see. He protested against the blackness of the calumny. He had good moments, which were afterwards destroyed by the persons who urged him against me, and by his self-interest. A Curé of Paris made out another very terrible and very ridiculous story. He went to the house of a person of the highest rank, and, speaking of me, he said I had taken away a woman from her husband, a person of position, and had made her marry her Curé. He was strongly pressed to say how that could be done. He persisted still, that nothing was more true. That gentleman and his wife no longer doubted, and immediately told one of their friends, who went to see them, and who knew me. The thing at first appeared to him incredible; but they maintained so strongly the Curé had assured them of it, that he had the curiosity to clear up the matter, firmly determined never to see me again if the thing was so. He went to see that Curé. He questioned him about me, and pressed him closely. At last the Curé said to him, I was capable of that, and even worse. This gentleman said to him, "But, Sir, I do not ask you what she is capable of. You do not know her. But I ask you if it is true she has done that?" He said no, but I was capable of doing worse. The Curé had never seen me, so this judgment was astonishing. At last it turned out that it was in Auvergne the thing had happened. I believe he even said it was forty years ago. This strangely astonished those to whom he had related the fable, when they had learned its falsehood. I wonder how they could have credited it.

Yet another stratagem was practiced; this was, to send to confession to all the Curés and confessors of Paris a wicked woman, who assumed the name of one of my maids. This woman was La Gautière. She confessed to several in a single day, in order to let none escape. She told them she had served me sixteen or seventeen years, but she had left me, being unable in conscience to live with such a wicked woman; that she had left me owing to my abominations. In less than eight days I was decried through all Paris, and I passed, without contradiction, for the most wicked person in the world. Those who so spoke believed themselves well informed, and that they knew it from a very reliable source. It happened that the maid who served me was at confession to a canon of Notre Dame. She spoke to him of the troubles that were caused to her mistress, who was, she said, very innocent. The Canon begged her to tell him her name. She told it to him. He replied, "You astonish me, for a person who does not in the least resemble you, has come here saying she is you, and has told me horrible things." She disabused him, and showed him the blackness of that procedure. The same thing happened to four or five others. But could she disabuse all the confessors? And I never would suffer her to use confession to make known the truth, leaving everything to God, and not wishing to lose any of the crosses or humiliations he has himself chosen for me. In the midst of so many contradictions, I have not been without illness and very acute pain.

I was, then, all the time from my arrival at Meaux to Easter without seeing the Bishop, who returned from Paris only for that festival. I was still very ill. He came into my room, and the first thing he said to me was, that I had many enemies, and that everything was let loose against me. He brought me the articles composed at Issi. I asked him the explanation of some passages, and I signed them. I was much more ill afterwards. He came back the day of the Annunciation, which had been put back after Easter. I have a very great devotion to the Incarnate Word, and while the nuns were finishing the burning of a triangular candle before an image I had of the Child Jesus, as they were singing a musical motet, the Bishop of Meaux entered. He asked what was the meaning of the music in my closet. They answered, that, as I had a very great devotion to the Incarnate Word, I had given them a treat that day, and they were come to thank me, and sing the motet in honor of the Incarnate Word. They were hardly out of my chamber, when he came to my bed, and said to me that he wished me to sign immediately that I did not believe in the Incarnate Word. Several nuns who were in the antechamber near my door heard him. I was greatly astonished at such a proposition. I told him I could not sign falsehoods. He answered, he would make me do it. I answered him, that I knew how to suffer by the grace of God; I knew how to die; I did not know how to sign falsehoods. He answered, that he begged me, and if I did that, he would re-establish my reputation, which they were endeavoring to tear to pieces; that he would say of me all the good in the world. I replied, that it was for God to take care of my reputation if he approved of it, and for me to sustain my faith at the peril of my life. Seeing he gained nothing, he withdrew.

I am under this obligation to Mother Picard and the Community, that they gave him the most favorable testimony about me. Here is one they gave me in writing:—

We the undersigned, Superior and nuns of the Visitation of St. Mary of Meaux, certify, that Madame Guyon having lived in our House by the order and permission of the Bishop of Meaux, our illustrious Prelate and Superior, for the space of six months, she has not given us any cause for trouble or annoyance, but much of edification; having never spoken to a person within or without except with special permission; having, besides, neither received nor written anything except as the Bishop has permitted her; having observed in all her conduct and all her words a great regularity, simplicity, sincerity, humility, mortification, sweetness, and Christian patience, and a true devotion and esteem of all that is of the faith, especially in the mystery of the Incarnation and Holy Childhood of our Lord Jesus Christ. That if the said lady wished to choose our House to live there the rest of her days in retirement, our Community would deem it a favor and gratification. This protest is simple and sincere, without other view or thought than to bear witness to the truth.

(Signed)

SISTER FRANÇOIS ELIZABETH LE PICARD, Superior.
SISTER MAGDALEN AMY GUETON.
SISTER CLAUDE MARIE AMOURI.
July 7, 1695.

When they spoke to the Bishop of Meaux of me, he answered, "Just as you, I see in her nothing but good; but her enemies torment me, and want to find evil in her." He wrote one day to Mother Picard, that he had examined my writings with great care; that he had not found in them anything except some terms which were not in all the strictness of theology; but that a woman was not bound to be a theologian. Mother Picard showed me that letter to console me, and I swear before God I write nothing but what is perfectly true.

CHAPTER XIX

SOME days afterwards the Bishop of Meaux returned. He brought me a paper written by himself, which was only a profession of faith, that I had always been Catholic, Apostolic, and Roman, and a submission of my books to the Church,—a thing I would have done of myself, had it not been asked of me. And then he read me another, which he said he must give me. It was a certificate such as he gave me long afterwards, and even more favorable. As I was too ill to transcribe that submission in his writing, he told me to have it transcribed by a nun, and to sign it. He took away his certificate to have it copied clean, as he said; and he assured me that, when I gave him the one, he would give me the other; that he wished to treat me as his sister; and that he would be a knave if he did not do so. This straightforward procedure charmed me. I told him I had placed myself in his hands, not only as in the hands of the Bishop, but as in those of a man of honor. Who would not have thought he would have carried it all out?

I was so ill after his departure, from having spoken a little when I was extremely weak, that I had to be brought back with cordial waters. The Prioress, fearing that if he returned the next day it would kill me, begged him by writing to leave me that day quiet; but he would not. On the contrary, he came that very day, and asked me if I had signed the writing he had left me; and, opening a blue portfolio which had a lock, he said to me, "Here is my certificate; where is your submission?" While saying this, he held in his hand a paper. I showed him my submission, which was on my bed, and that I had not the strength to give it to him. He took it. I did not doubt he was about to give me his writing; but nothing of the kind. He shut up the whole in his portfolio, and said he would give me nothing; that I was not at the end; that he was about to torment me more, and that he wanted other signatures—among others this, that I did not believe in the Incarnate Word. I remained without strength and without speech. He ran away. The nuns were shocked at such a trick; for nothing obliged him to promise me a certificate. I had not asked him. It was then I made the protestations, which are initialled by a notary of Meaux; I asked for him, under pretext of making my will.

Some time after, the Prelate again came to see me. He required me to sign his pastoral letter, and to acknowledge I had held the errors therein condemned. I endeavored to make him see, that what I had given him comprehended every kind of submission, and although in that letter he had placed me in the rank of evil-doers, I was endeavoring to honor that state of Jesus Christ without complaining. He said to me, "But you have promised to submit yourself to my condemnation." "I do it with all my heart, Monseigneur," I answered him; "and I take no more interest in those little books than if I had not written them. I will never depart, if it pleases God, from the submission and respect I owe you, however things turn. But Monseigneur, you have promised me a discharge." "I will give it to you when you do what I wish," he said to me. "Monseigneur, you did me the honor to tell me that when I gave you signed that act of submission you had dictated to me, you would give me my discharge." "Those are," said he, "words which escaped before having maturely considered what one can and ought to do." "It is not to make complaint that I say this to you, Monseigneur, but to bring to your memory that you promised it to me; and, to show you my submission, I am willing to write at the foot of your pastoral whatever I can put there." After I had done this, and he had read it, he said that he liked it well enough. Then, after having put it in his pocket, he said to me, "That is not the question. You do not say you are formally a heretic, and I wish you to declare it, and also that the letter is very just, and that you acknowledge to have been in all the errors it condemns." I answered him, "I believe, Monseigneur, it is to try me you say this; for I shall never persuade myself that a Prelate so full of piety and honor would use the good faith with which I have come and placed myself in his diocese, to make me do things I cannot do in conscience. I have thought to find in you a Father. I conjure you that I may not be deceived in my expectation." "I am Father of the Church," he said to me, "but, in short, it is not a question of words. If you do not sign what I wish, I will come with witnesses, and, after having admonished you before them, I will accuse you to the Church, and we will cut you off, as it is said in the gospel." "Monseigneur," I answered, "I have only my God for a witness. I am prepared to suffer everything, and I hope God will give me the grace to do nothing contrary to my conscience, without departing ever from the respect I owe you." He further wished, in the same conversation, to oblige me to declare that I recognized there are errors in the Latin book of Father La Combe, and to declare, at the same time, I had not read it.

The worthy nuns who saw part of the violence and outburst of the Bishop of Meaux could not get over it, and Mother Picard said to me that my too great gentleness emboldened him to ill treat me; because his character was such, that he ordinarily behaved thus to quiet people, and bent to haughty persons. However, I never changed my conduct, and I preferred to accept the rôle of suffering, than to deviate in anything from the respect I owed his character. I am confident that all the persons who have known that I had been to Meaux have believed two things equally false: the one, that I was there by the King's order, while it was of my own accord; the other, that during the six months I was there the Bishop of Meaux had interrogated me at different times, to learn my thought upon the inner life, what was my manner of thought upon the inner life, what was my manner of prayer, or on the love of God. Nothing of the kind. He has never spoken to me on these things. When he came, it was, he said, my enemies who told him to torment me; that he was satisfied with me. At other times he came full of fury, to demand that signature he well knew I would not give him. He threatened me with all that has since been done. He did not intend, he said, to lose his fortune for me; and a thousand other things. After these explosions he returned to Paris, and was some time without again coming.

At last, having been about six months at Meaux, he gave me of himself a certificate, and no longer demanded from me any other signature. What is astonishing is, that, at the time he was most excited against me, he said that if I wished to come and live in his diocese he would be pleased; that he wished to write upon the inner life, and that God had given me upon this very certain lights. He had seen that life of which he has so much spoken. He never told me he found anything to object to therein. All this has happened only since I ceased to see him; or he has seen in that life which he no longer had, what he had not seen when he was reading it. Shortly before I left Meaux, he told the Bishop of Paris and the Archbishop of Sens how satisfied he was, and edified by me. He preached to us on the day of the Visitation of the Virgin, which is one of the principal festivals of this convent. He there said the Mass, and wished me to communicate from his hand. In the middle of the Mass he gave an astonishing sermon on the inner life. He advanced things much stronger than those I have advanced. He said he was not master of himself in the midst of these awful mysteries; he was obliged to speak the truth, and not to dissimulate; that it must be that this avowal of the truth was necessary, since God compelled him to make it in spite of himself. The Prioress went to salute him after his sermon, and asked him how he could torment me, thinking as he did. He answered her it was not he, it was my enemies. A little after, I left Meaux; but my departure has been related with so much malignity, that I must explain all the circumstances.

As I had been six months at Meaux, where I had promised to remain only three, and, besides, my health was very bad, I asked the Bishop of Meaux if he was satisfied, and if he desired anything more of me. He answered, "No." I told him I would go away then, because I had need of visiting Bourbon.

I asked him if he would be pleased that I should come to end my days among those good nuns; for they loved me much, and I loved them, although the air was very bad for me. He was very well pleased at it, and told me he would always receive me gladly; that the nuns were very satisfied and edified by me; that he was returning to Paris. I told him my daughter, or some ladies of my friends, would come to fetch me. He turned to the Prioress, and said to her, "My Mother, I pray you to receive those who come to fetch madame, whether it be her daughter or her friends; to let them sleep and lodge in your house, and keep them there as long as they wish." It is well known how submissive are those nuns of St. Mary to their Bishop, and their exactitude to follow to the letter whatever he orders them, without the least variation. Two ladies then came to fetch me. They arrived for dinner. They dined, supped, and slept, and dined again the next day at the convent; then, about three o'clock, we set out.

Hardly had I arrived when the Bishop of Meaux repented having let me go out of his diocese. What made him change, as we have since known, is that, when he gave an account to Madame de Maintenon of the terms in which this affair was concluded, she let him know she was dissatisfied with the attestation he had given me: that it concluded nothing, and would even have a contrary effect to what was proposed, which was to undeceive the persons who were favorably disposed to me. He believed then, in losing me, he was losing all the hopes with which he had flattered himself. He wrote to me to return to his diocese, and I received at the same time a letter from the Prioress, that he was more resolved than ever to torment me; that, whatever desire she had to have me again, she was obliged to let me know the sentiments of the Bishop of Meaux conformable to what I knew. What I knew is, that he was building a lofty fortune upon persecuting me, and, as he aimed at a person far above me, he thought that, in my escaping him, everything escaped him. Mother Picard, in sending me the letter of which I have just spoken, sent me a new attestation of the Bishop of Meaux, so different from the former which he wished me to return, that I judged henceforth I had no justice to expect from the Prelate. He had written to her to take back the first attestation, and to give me the latter; and, if I had set out from Meaux, she should at once send it to me, in order he might have back the former which he had given me. The Mother, who clearly saw by past treatment what I should be exposed to, if I again fell into the hands of the Bishop of Meaux, let me sufficiently understand it by her letter, to decide me to avoid for the future all discussion with him. However, to observe with him all the rules of politeness from which I have never departed (without complaining of a procedure so peculiar and so full of injustice), I answered the Mother Superior, that I had made over to my family what the Bishop of Meaux asked back; that, after all that had passed, they had such an interest in a document of that nature, which constituted my justification, it was unlikely they would part with it; the more so, as that which she sent me from the Prelate not only served nothing for my justification, but seemed to countenance all that had been said against me, while saying nothing to the contrary.

Here is the copy of the said first attestation:

We, Bishop of Meaux, certify to all whom it may concern, that, by means of the declarations and submission of Madame Guyon which we have before us subscribed with her hand, and the prohibitions accepted by her with submission, of writing, teaching, dogmatizing in the Church, or of spreading her books printed or manuscript, or of conducting souls in the ways of prayer, or otherwise: together with the good testimony that has been furnished us during six months that she is in our diocese and in the convent of St. Mary, we are satisfied with her conduct, and have continued to her the participation of the Holy Sacraments in which we have found her: we declare, besides, we have not found her implicated in any way in the abominations of Molinos or others elsewhere condemned, and we have not intended to comprehend her in the mention which has been made by us of them in our Ordinance of April 6, 1695: given at Meaux, July 1, 1695.

F. BENIGNE, Bishop of Meaux.

Here is the copy of the second:—

We, Biship of Meaux, have received the present submissions and declarations of the said Dame Guyon, as well that of the 16th of April, 1695, as that of the 1st of July of the same year, and we have delivered her a certificate of it to avail her what is proper, declaring we have always received her and receive her without objection in the participation of the Holy Sacraments in which we have found her, as the submission and sincere obedience, both before and since the time she is in our diocese and in the Convent of St. Mary, together with the authentic declaration of her faith and the testimony which has been furnished us and is furnished us of her good conduct for the six months she has been at the said convent, required it. We have enjoined her to make at suitable times the requests and other acts we have marked in the said articles by her subscribed as essential to piety and expressly commanded by God, without any believer being able to dispense with them under pretext of other acts pretended more perfect or eminent, or other pretexts whatever they be, and we have given her repeated prohibitions, both as Diocesan Bishop and in virtue of the obedience she has promised us voluntarily as above, of writing, teaching, or dogmatizing in the Church, or of spreading abroad her books printed or manuscript, or conducting souls in the ways of prayer, or otherwise, to which she has submitted anew, declaring she executed the said deeds. Given at Meaux, at the said convent, the day and year as above.

F. BENIGNE, Bishop of Meaux.

One can judge, from the vivacity of the Bishop of Meaux and the hopes he had conceived, of the effect which such a refusal produced on him. He gave out, I had climbed over the walls of the convent to fly. Besides that I climb very badly, all the nuns were witnesses of the contrary: yet this has had such a currency many people still believe it. A procedure of that kind no longer allowed me to abandon myself to the discretion of the Bishop of Meaux, and, as I was informed they were about to push things to the utmost violence, I believed I should leave to God all that might happen and yet take all prudent steps to avoid the effect of the menaces that reached me from all sides. I had many places of retreat; but I would not accept any, in order not to embarrass any one and not to involve my friends and my family, to whom my escape might be ascribed. I took the resolution of not leaving Paris, of remaining there in some retired place with my women, and withdrawing myself from the sight of all the world. I remained in this way about five or six months. I passed the days alone, in reading, praying God, and working: but, towards the end of the year 1695, I was arrested, ill as I was, and conducted to Vincennes. I was three days in seclusion in the house of M. des Grez, who had arrested me, because the King, full of justice and kindness, would not consent to put me in prison, saying many times, a convent was sufficient. They deceived his justice by the most violent calumnies, and painted me to his eyes with colors so black as even to make him ashamed of his goodness and of his equity. He consented then I should be taken to Vincennes.

CHAPTER XX

I WILL not speak here of that long persecution, which has made so much noise, through a succession of ten years of prisons of all kinds, and of an exile almost as long, which is not yet finished, by trials, calumnies, and all imaginable kinds of sufferings. There are facts too odious on the part of divers persons, which charity makes me cover, and others on the part of those who, having been seduced by ill-intentioned persons, are for me respectable through their piety and other reasons, although they have showed too bitter a zeal for things of which they had no true knowledge. I am silent as to the one, through respect; as to the other, through charity. What I may say is that through so long a series of crosses, with which my

life has been filled, it may be conceived the greatest were
reserved for the end, and that God, who has not cast me off
through his kindness, took care not to leave the end of my life
without a greater conformity with Jesus Christ. He was dragged
before all sorts of tribunals: he has done me the favor to be
the same. He suffered the utmost outrages without complaining: he has shown me the mercy of behaving similarly. How
could I have done otherwise in the view he gave me of his
love and of his goodness? In this resemblance to Jesus Christ I
regarded as favors what the world regarded as strange
persecutions. The inward peace and joy prevented me from
seeing the most violent persecutors other than as instruments
of the justice of my God, who has always been to me so
adorable and so amiable. I was then in prison as in a place of
delight and refreshment; that general privation of all creatures
giving me more opportunity of being alone with God, and the
want of things which appear most necessary making me taste
an exterior poverty I could not have otherwise tasted.

I have borne mortal debility, overwhelming, crushing, and
painful illnesses without treatment. God, not content with
that, abandoned me spiritually to the greatest desolations for
some months, so that I could only say these single words: "My
God, my God, why hast thou forsaken me?" It was at that time
I was led to take the part of God against myself, and to
practice all the austerities I could think of: seeing God and all
creatures against me, I was delighted to be on their side
against myself. How could I complain of what I have suffered
with a love so detached from all *own* interest. Should I now
be interested for myself, after having made such an entire
sacrifice of that *"me,"* and all that concerns it? I prefer, then,
to consecrate all those sufferings by silence. If God permitted,
for his glory, one day something of them to be known, I
would adore his judgments; but as for me, my part is taken in
that which regards me personally.

But, perhaps there will be surprise that, not being willing
to write any detail of the most severe crosses of my life, I have
written of those which are far less. I have had certain reasons
for doing so. I have believed myself bound to touch on some of
the crosses of my youth, to make known the course of crucifixion that God has always led me by. As to those other passages

"... a succession of ten years of prisons of all kinds."

which relate to a more advanced state of my life: since the calumnies did not concern me alone, I have felt obliged in conscience to give details of certain facts to expose not only their falsity, but also the conduct of those through whom they have originated, and who are the true authors of those persecutions, of which I have only been the accidental object; particularly in these latter times, since in reality I have been persecuted in this way only to involve therein persons of great merit, who were out of reach by themselves, and could be attacked personally only by mixing up their affairs with mine. I have thought, then, I should enlarge a little more in detail on what had relation to that class of facts: and the more so, that the question being of my faith, which they wished for that purpose to render suspected, it appeared to me of consequence to make known, at the same time, how far I have always been from the sentiments they wish to impute to me. I have thought it due to religion, to piety, to my friends, to my family, and to myself: but as to personal ill treatments, I have felt bound to sacrifice them, to sanctify them by a profound silence.

I shall only cursorily say something of the dispositions in which I have been at the different times of my imprisonment. During the time I was at Vincennes and M. de la Reinie interrogated me, I continued in great peace, very content to pass my life there, if such was the will of God. I used to compose hymns, which the maid who served me learned by heart as fast as I composed them; and we used to sing your praise, O my God! I regarded myself as a little bird you were keeping in a cage for your pleasure, and who ought to sing to fulfil her condition of life. The stones of my tower seemed to me rubies: that is to say, I esteemed them more than all worldly magnificence. My joy was based on your love, O my God, and on the pleasure of being your captive; although I made these reflections only when composing hymns. The central depth of my heart was full of that joy which you give to those who love you, in the midst of the greatest crosses.

I let others think what they please; for me, I find security only in abandoning myself to the Lord. All scripture is full of testimonies which demand this abandonment. "Make over your trouble to the hand of the Lord: he will act himself. Abandon yourself to his conduct: and he will himself conduct your steps."

Sometimes it seemed God placed himself on the side of men to make me the more suffer. I was then more exercised within than from outside. Everything was against me. I saw all men united to torment me and surprise me—every artifice and every subtility of the intellect of men who have much of it, and who studied to that end; and I alone without help, feeling upon me the heavy hand of God, who seemed to abandon me to myself and my own obscurity; an entire abandonment within, without being able to help myself with my natural intellect, whose entire vivacity was deadened this long time since I had ceased to make use of it, in order to allow myself to be led by a superior intellect; having labored all my life to submit my mind to Jesus Christ and my reason to his guidance. During this time I could not help myself, either with my reason, or any interior support; for I was like those who have never experienced that admirable guidance from the goodness of God, and who have not natural intellect. When I prayed I had only answers of death. At this time that passage of David occurred to me: "When they persecuted me, I afflicted my soul by fasting." I practiced then, as long as my health allowed it, very rigorous fasts and austere penances, but all this seemed to me like burned straw. One moment of God's conducting is a thousand times more helpful.

CHAPTER XXI

As my life has always been consecrated to the cross, no sooner had I left prison, and my mind began to breathe again, after so many trials, than the body was overwhelmed with all sorts of infirmities, and I have had almost continual illnesses, which brought me to death's door.

In these latter times I am able to say little or nothing of my dispositions, because my state has become simple and invariable. The root of that state is a profound annihilation, so that I find nothing in me that can be named. All that I know is, that God is infinitely holy, just, good, happy: that he includes in himself all good, and I, all wretchedness. I see nothing lower than me, nor anything more unworthy than me. I recognize that God has given me graces capable of saving a world, and that perhaps I have paid all with ingratitude. I say, "perhaps," because nothing subsists in me, good or ill. The good is in God. I have for my share only the nothing. What can I say of a state always the same, without forethought or variation; for the dryness, if I have it, is the same to me as a state the most satisfying. All is lost in the immensity, and I can neither will nor think. It is like a little drop of water sunk in the sea; not only is it surrounded by it, but absorbed. In that divine immensity the soul no longer sees herself, but in God she discovers the objects, without discerning them, otherwise than by the taste of the heart. All is darkness and obscurity as regards her; all is light on the part of God, who does not allow her to be ignorant of anything; while she knows not what she knows, nor how she knows it. There is there neither clamor, nor pain, nor trouble, nor pleasure, nor uncertainty; but a perfect peace: not in herself, but in God; no interest for herself, no recollection of or occupation with herself. This is what God is in that creature: as to her, abjectness, weakness, poverty, without her thinking either of her abjectness or her dignity. If one believes any good in me, he is mistaken, and does wrong to God. All good is in him, and for him. If I could have a satisfaction, it is from this, that HE IS WHAT HE IS, and that HE WILL BE IT ALWAYS. If he saves me, it will be gratuitously; for I have neither merit nor dignity.

Nothing greater than God: nothing more little than I. He is rich: I am very poor. I do not want for anything. I do not feel need of anything. Death, life, all is alike. Eternity, time: all is eternity, all is God. God is Love, and Love is God, and all in God, and for God. You would as soon extract light from darkness, as anything from this "nothing." It is a chaos without confusion. All species are outside of the "nothing," and the "nothing" does not admit them: thoughts only pass, nothing stops. I cannot say anything to order. What I have written, or said, is gone: I remember it no more. It is for me as if from another person. I cannot wish either justification or esteem. If God wills either one or the other, he will do what he shall please. It does not concern me. That he may glorify himself by my destruction, or by reestablishing my reputation, the one and the other is alike in the balance.

My children, I do not wish to mislead you, or not to mislead you. It is for God to enlighten you, and to give you distaste or inclination for this "nothing," who does not leave her place. It is an empty beacon: one may in it light a torch. It is perhaps a false light, which may lead to the precipice. I know nothing of it. God knows it. It is not my business. It is for you to discern that. There is nothing but to extinguish the false light. The torch will never light itself if God does not light it. I pray God to enlighten you always to do only his will. As for me, if you should trample me underfoot, you would only do me justice. This is what I can say of a "nothing" that I would wish, if I was able to wish, should be eternally forgotten. If the "Life" was not written, it would run a great chance of never being so; and yet I would rewrite it at the least signal, without knowing why, nor what I wished to say.

Oh, my children, open your eyes to the light of truth! Holy Father, sanctify them in your truth. I have told them your truth, since I have not spoken of myself. Your Divine Word has spoken to them by my mouth. He alone is the truth. He has said to his Apostles, "I sanctify myself for them." Say the same thing to my children. Sanctify yourself in them and for them. But how reconcile your words, O my Divine Word? You say on the one hand, "Sanctify them in your truth. Your word is truth." On the other, "I sanctify myself for them." Oh, how well these two things agree! It is to be sanctified in the truth of all sanctity, to have no other sanctity but that of Jesus Christ. May he alone be holy in us and for us. He will be holy in us when we shall be sanctified in his truth by that experimental knowledge that to him alone belongs all sanctity, all justice, all strength, all greatness, all power, all glory: and to us all poverty, weakness, etc. Let us remain in our "nothing" through homage to the sanctity of God, and we shall be sanctified and instructed by the truth. Jesus Christ will be holy for us, and will be to us everything. We shall find in him all that is deficient in us. If we seek anything for ourselves out of him, if we seek anything in us as *ours*, however holy it may appear to us, we are liars, and the truth is not in us. We seduce ourselves, and we shall never be the saints of the Lord, who, having no other sanctity but his, have renounced all usurpations, and at last their entire SELFHOOD. Holy Father, I have replaced in your hands those whom you have given me. Guard them in your truth, that falsehood may not approach them. It is to be in falsehood to attribute to one's self the least thing. It is to be in falsehood to believe we are able to do anything: to hope anything from one's self or for one's self: to believe we possess anything. Make them know, O my God, that herein is the truth of which you are very jealous. All language which departs from this principle is falsity: he who approaches it, approaches the truth, but he who speaks only the ALL OF GOD and the NOTHING OF THE CREATURE is in the truth, and the truth dwells with him: because, usurpation and the selfhood being banished from him, it is of necessity the truth dwells there. My children, receive this instruction from your mother, and it will procure life for you. Receive it through her, not as from her or hers, but as from God and God's. Amen, Jesus.

Conclusion.

I pray those who shall read this not to be angry against the persons who, through a zeal perhaps too bitter, have pushed things so far against a woman, and a woman so submissive; because, as Tauler says, "When God wishes to purify a soul by suffering, he would for a time cast into darkness and blindness an infinite number of holy persons, in order they might prepare that vessel of election by rash and disparaging judgments, that they would form against her in that state of ignorance. But at last, after having purified that vessel, he would sooner or later lift the bandage from their eyes, not treating with rigor a fault they would have committed through a secret leading of his admirable providence. I say, further, that God would sooner send an angel from heaven to dispose by tribulations that chosen vessel than to leave her without suffering."

December, 1709.